Regulating Non-Existence

Regulating Non-Existence

The Legal Conceptualisation of the Future Child in the Regulation of Reproduction

Lisette ten Haaf

eleven

Published, sold and distributed by Eleven
P.O. Box 85576
2508 CG The Hague
The Netherlands
Tel.: +31 70 33 070 33
Fax: +31 70 33 070 30
e-mail: sales@elevenpub.nl
www.elevenpub.com

Sold and distributed in USA and Canada
Independent Publishers Group
814 N. Franklin Street
Chicago, IL 60610, USA
Order Placement: +1 800 888 4741
Fax: +1 312 337 5985
orders@ipgbook.com
www.ipgbook.com

Eleven is an imprint of Boom uitgevers Den Haag.

ISBN 978-94-6236-582-7
ISBN 978-94-0011-252-0 (E-book)

Table of Contents

1 Introduction

1.1 Preventing Existence: Then and Now

Are we allowed to decide who may come into existence and whose life should be prevented? And if so, how can we justify these choices? These questions have become urgent as the result of advances in reproductive biotechnologies. Due to the rise of birth control, assisted reproductive technologies (hereafter ARTs), and genetic technologies, reproduction has increasingly become a matter of choice. Contraception and fertility treatments allow us to *choose* whether we want to have children or not. And although there is no 100% guarantee that these technologies are always successful, developments in reproductive biotechnology continue to offer possible solutions for overcoming infertility and subfertility; solutions that vary from donor conception and IVF, to outsourcing the pregnancy through surrogacy and, in the future, perhaps even artificial wombs. Moreover, not only can we (to a certain extent) choose whether we want to have a child, reproductive biotechnologies such as prenatal testing, preimplantation genetic testing, and even genetic modification allow us to decide *what type of* child to have or not to have. The possibilities that reproductive technologies bring have instigated various discussions amongst philosophers and bioethicists. Since these technologies are in need of regulation, the question as to whether we may decide who comes into existence also demands a legal answer.

The question of whether certain lives may or should be prevented has surfaced as a result of the introduction of ARTs. Since the birth of Louise Brown in 1978, the first child conceived through IVF, a large number of technologies and modes of reproduction have become a reality. These technologies offer, to a varying extent, the possibility to exercise control over the genetic blueprint of the child that results from the application of these technologies. They include preimplantation genetic testing[1] (PGT), sperm and egg cell donation, and surrogacy, and the possibilities have not been exhausted yet. In the future, human reproduction may take another turn. With the help of mitochondrial replacement therapy (MRT), mitochondrial conditions can be prevented, but as a result of this technology, the child is genetically related to three people. For this reason, MRT is also dubbed *three-parent IVF*. Technologies such as base editing and CRISPR-Cas9 allow for

1 Over the past few years, the medical community has replaced the term PGD (preimplantation genetic diagnosis) with PGT. PGT can be understood as an umbrella term which includes both PGD (screening for monogenetic disorders, also referred to as PGT-M) and PGS (screening for chromosomal disorders, also referred to as PGT-A).

the modification of the future child's genetic profile. And finally, in vitro gametogenesis (IVG) enables the reprogramming of skin cells into gametes and thus has the potential to forfeit all boundaries of natural reproduction: it facilitates the conception of a child by same sex couples, by more than two parents, or even by a single person.

Simultaneous to the advances in reproductive biotechnology, there has been increasing (legal) recognition for the idea of reproductive autonomy. Over the past two decades, reproductive autonomy has gained legal recognition. This is illustrated by the decisions of the European Court of Human Rights. The Court has considered that Article 8, which encompasses the right to private life and is based on the principle of personal autonomy,[2] also includes the right to respect for the decision to become or not to become a genetic parent.[3] Moreover, the Court has ruled that Article 8 also covers the right to have access to ARTs[4] and to select a healthy child.[5] Reproductive biotechnology has become an important aspect of exercising individual freedom,[6] as it offers possible solutions for infertility and subfertility, and for preventing genetic conditions. Rather than serving the interests of the state, these technologies now serve the interests and needs of its individual subjects, such as the desire of prospective parents to have a healthy and/or a genetically related child. Or, as the legal philosopher Pessers summarises: "[I]t is no longer about the destruction of beings considered to be inferior, but about the scientific promise of health, happiness and improvement of life."[7]

Pessers refers here to the eugenic policies of the beginning of the 20th century, which offer an example of reproductive politics taken to its extreme. In those contexts, procreation was not conceived as part of the individual's personal autonomy, but as a matter of public interest. Back then, state programmes to improve the gene pool of the population were not uncommon in some countries. People considered inferior were prevented from having children, for example, by putting them in asylums or through compulsory sterilisation, in order to ensure that their genes were not passed on to future generations. These policies

---

2 ECtHR 29 April 2002 ECLI:CE:ECHR:2002:0429JUD000234602 (Pretty v. the United Kingdom), par. 61.

3 ECtHR 4 December 2007 ECLI:CE:ECHR:2007:1204JUD004436204 (*Dickson v. the United Kingdom*), par. 66; ECtHR 10 April 2007 ECLI:CE:ECHR:2007:0410JUD000633905 (*Evans v. the United Kingdom*), par. 71.

4 ECtHR 3 November 2011 ECLI:CE:ECHR:2011:1103JUD005781300 (*S.H. e.a. v. Austria*), par. 82.

5 ECtHR 28 August 2012, ECLI:CE:ECHR:2012:0828JUD005427010 (*Costa and Pavan v. Italy*), par. 57.

6 See also J.A. Robertson, *Children of choice. Freedom and the new reproductive technologies*, Princeton, Princeton University Press, 1994, p. 24.

7 D. Pessers, *Menselijke waardigheid en het persoonsbegrip in het recht*, Utrecht, Lemma BV, 2005, p. 9-10. In Dutch: "Het gaat nu niet om vernietiging van inferieur geachte wezens, maar om de wetenschappelijke belofte van gezondheid, gelukt en verbetering van de levenscondities." Translation by Lisette ten Haaf (LtH).

aimed to protect the state's interest in improving the population. As a result, individual lives deemed inferior were sacrificed for the greater good. This is illustrated in the famous *Buck v. Bell* case of 1927, in which the US Supreme Court ruled that the compulsory sterilisation of mentally disabled people was justified, for "[t]hree generations of imbeciles are enough."[8] Justice Oliver Wendell Holmes, Jr., who wrote the ruling, argued in this case:

> We have seen more than once that the public welfare may call upon the best citizens for their lives. It would be strange if it could not call upon those who already sap the strength of the State for these lesser sacrifices, often not felt to be such by those concerned, to prevent our being swamped with incompetence. It is better for all the world, if instead of waiting to execute degenerate offspring for crime, or to let them starve for their imbecility, society can prevent those who are manifestly unfit from continuing their kind.[9]

During the Nazi rule, the 'improvement' of the human gene pool was taken a step further; the infamous Aktion T4 facilitated the mass genocide of people considered inferior in order to keep the race pure. The atrocities of the Second World War changed attitudes towards genetics and interfering in procreation substantially. The idea that some lives are worth more than others and that some lives are even unworthy of life itself, so-called 'lebensunwertes Leben', was rejected. Instead, the notion of human dignity and the idea that all lives are worth living was laid down in international treaties, such as Article 1 of the Universal Declaration of Human Rights.[10]

While reproductive technologies are now mostly seen as a means of facilitating reproductive autonomy and promoting individual freedom, the 'right to procreate' or to become a genetic parent is not absolute.[11] Most Western societies have developed different regulatory frameworks that ban certain technologies or restrict their application.[12] For example, human reproductive cloning and human germline genetic modification have been banned, both in national legislation and in international treaties.[13] Other technologies

8 Buck v. Bell, 274 U.S. 200 (1927).

9 Buck v. Bell, 274 U.S. 200 (1927).

10 For a more extensive overview of the discoveries in the field of genetics and their impact on biopolitics and eugenic programs, I recommend S. Mukherjee, *The gene. An intimate history*, London, Penguin Random House, 2016.

11 In fact, in both the *Evans* case and the *S.H. e.a.* case, the Court acknowledged that despite the fact that both cases fell within the scope of Article 8 of the ECHR, there was no breach of this article as the regulation restricting the applicants' freedom was considered to be legitimate.

12 Chapter 2 discusses the regulatory frameworks on reproduction in the Netherlands, Germany, and the United Kingdom.

13 For example, reproductive cloning is banned in Article 11 of the Universal Declaration on the Human Genome and Human Rights (1997) and in Article 1 of the Additional Protocol to the Convention for the

can only be used under certain conditions: PGT is often only allowed if there is a risk of a serious genetic condition[14] and several Western countries only allow non-anonymous sperm and egg cell donation.[15] Access to fertility treatments such as IVF can be refused to prospective parents because of non-medical contraindications, i.e. reasons not to offer a treatment. These regulatory decisions, however, determine what type of child is conceived and consequently born. Or, more precisely, they prevent certain types of children from being conceived, sometimes in favour of another type of child, and sometimes not at all.

In short, as a result of the introduction of reproductive technologies and their regulation, we are still preventing certain lives from coming into existence. The rationale behind these biopolitics has changed. The justification for the regulatory frameworks that ultimately prevent the future child's conception is not sought in the interests of the state, or the improvement of the race or population. On the contrary, the regulatory frameworks are deemed justified because they protect the interests of the individual subjects involved. More precisely, the governance of reproduction mobilises the interests of one entity in particular, namely, the child that could result from the treatment or the application of the technology.

References to this new entity, the future child, can be found in various legal systems. For example, the Dutch professional guidelines on Moral Contraindications for Fertility Treatments[16] prescribes that medical professionals should refrain from providing fertility treatment (thereby preventing the conception of a child), if they believe that the child that would result from the treatment runs the risk of being severely harmed. This harm can be caused by the parents lacking the capability to take care of the child, or an inheritable genetic condition. A similar rule can be found in the UK Human Fertilisation and Embryology (HFE) Act. Section 13(5) holds that "A woman shall not be provided with treatment...unless account has been taken of the welfare of any child who may be born as

---

Protection of Human Rights and Dignity of the Human Being with regard to the Application of Biology and Medicine, on the Prohibition of Cloning Human Beings. Germline modification is banned in Article 13 of the Convention for the Protection of Human Rights and Dignity of the Human Being with regard to the Application of Biology and Medicine: Convention on Human Rights and Biomedicine. The latter convention has not been ratified by several Council of Europe member states, including the Netherlands, Germany and the United Kingdom.

14 See for example, Regeling van de staatssecretaris van Volksgezondheid, Welzijn en Sport van 16 februari 2009, nr. CZ-TSZ-2912089, houdende houdende regels ten aanzien van preïmplantatie genetische diagnostiek (PGD), (*Stcrt.* 2009, 42) (*Ministerial decree PGD*); Art. 3A ESchG; Section 1ZA schedule 2 Human Fertilisation and Embryology (HFE) Act 2008.

15 See for example, Dutch Donor Information Artificial Reproduction Act; German Sperm Donor Registry Act; Section 31ZA of the HFE Act 2008.

16 NVOG Modelprotocol "Mogelijke morele contra-indicaties bij vruchtbaarheidsbehandelingen".

a result of the treatment..."[17] The Human Fertilisation and Embryology Authority (hereafter HFEA) Code of Practice, which fleshes out the Act, states that treatment should be refused if the fertility centre involved concludes that the resulting child (or any existing child of the family) "is likely to be at risk of significant harm or neglect" or if they "cannot obtain enough information to conclude that there is no significant risk."[18] An analogous principle in Australian law[19] resulted in a court case in which the judge ruled that the couple was rightfully denied access to IVF because of the welfare of the future child.[20] Also, in Italian legislation the interests of the future child are introduced to regulate (access to) fertility treatment. In a review on the subject conducted by the Italian Parliamentary Commission for Social Affairs, it was claimed that the ban on heterologous techniques[21] was necessary to prevent a violation of the psycho-social welfare of the child.[22] Similarly, the exclusion of homosexual couples and single women from fertility treatment was justified in order to avoid "psycho-social damage to the child, which can result from parenting models which are not consolidated."[23] Even in rulings of the European Court of Human Rights (ECtHR) the future child appears. In *S.H. et al. v. Austria*, the Court concluded that Austria's ban on heterologous fertility treatments was justified in order to protect several interests, such as the interests of the female donors, but also the interests of the future child. With the help of the current legislation in Austria (including the

17 The full Section entails: "A woman shall not be provided with treatment services unless account has been taken of the welfare of any child who may be born as a result of treatment (including the need of that child for supportive parenting), and of any other child who may be affected by the birth."

18 HFEA Code of Practice 8th Edition 2009 (last revised 2017), Section 8.15 of the HFEA Code of Practice (8th ed, 2009). See also: Human Fertilisation and Embryology Authority, *Tomorrow's Children. Report of the policy review of welfare of the child assessments in licensed assisted conception clinics.*, 2005 p. 8.
Initially, the legislator did not intend this welfare principle to be an eligibility requirement; the principle merely placed a responsibility upon the fertility clinics (Human Fertilisation and Embryology Authority, 2005, p. 4.). In 2005, the Human Fertilisation and Embryology Authority pointed out that there was considerable uncertainty about the interpretation of this principle since the legislation provided no guidance on this point. After a survey, the HFEA concluded that the welfare of the child principle should be understood as the responsibility of the clinics to collect information from patients on possible risk factors to the child's well-being.

19 Section 15(3) of the Assisted Reproductive Treatment Act 2008 (Vic).

20 Victorian Civil and Administrative Tribunal 5 August 2015 - VCAT 1188 (*TRV v. Department of Health and Human Services*).

21 Heterologous artificial reproduction techniques are treatments that besides, for example, IVF or artificial insemination, involve the use of donated gametes, instead of the gametes of the couple involved. The Austrian government argued that the use of donates gametes in combination with ARTs could increase the possibility of 'selecting' a child. Moreover, they argued that it could lead to exploitation of women and undermine traditional forms of motherhood.

22 R.A. Fenton, 'Catholic doctrine versus women's rights: the new Italian law on assisted reproduction', *Medical Law Review*, Vol. 14, No. 1, 2006, 85.

23 Fenton, 2006, 88.

prohibition on heterologous techniques) the government aimed to safeguard the future child's well-being[24] and its interest in knowing its (genetic) descent.[25]

The interests of the future child have become a key factor in the regulation of reproduction, i.e. the body of rules and regulations governing reproductive technologies, such as donor conception, embryo selection and germline modification. Furthermore, the increased attention on this entity has raised the question as to whether the government can also interfere in unassisted reproduction in order to protect the interests of the future child. A recurring question in the Dutch public and political debate is whether the interests of the future child can also require forced contraception. In 2010, a Member of Parliament suggested that in cases of *irresponsible parenthood*, i.e. in cases of extreme child abuse or neglect, the state should have the power to enforce the use of contraception on parents to prevent another child being born to these parents. The MP argued that the child would have no interest in growing up with such parents, since this would constitute too much of a risk that the future child would also become a victim of neglect, abuse, or poor upbringing.[26] Moreover, she maintained that allowing these children to be born imposes both a moral and a financial burden on society.[27] This illustrates that regulation based on the interests of the state and regulation based on the interests of the future child do not necessarily lead to different outcomes, but can co-exist. The proposal instigated an ongoing public debate concerning the question of whether the government should prevent children from being born in order to protect their interests.[28] The tabled motion never resulted in separate legislation, but recently, compulsory contraception has been considered as a valid option in the context of mental health care. The Mandatory Mental Health Care Act, which came into force in 2018, allows for the mandatory treatment of a person in order to prevent severe harm or damage caused by a mental disorder.[29] Since 2020, there have been various cases in which the judge ruled that mandatory treatment could include compulsory

---

24 ECtHR 3 November 2011 ECLI:CE:ECHR:2011:1103JUD005781300 (*S.H. e.a. v. Austria*), par 65.

25 ECtHR 3 November 2011 ECLI:CE:ECHR:2011:1103JUD005781300 (*S.H. e.a. v. Austria*), par 67.

26 *Kamerstukken II* 2009-2010, 32 405, nr. 2 (*Tabled motion on compulsory contraception*).

27 *Kamerstukken II* 2009-2010, 32 405, nr. 2 (*Tabled motion on compulsory contraception*), p. 13.

28 See amongst others: J. Boonekamp, G. de Wert and R, Bergmans, 'Geef een junk geld voor geboortebeperking', *NRC* 9 November 2010; N. Smet, 'Als je haar kind afpakt, neemt ze meteen een nieuwe', *NRC next* 2 September 2011; *Zembla*: 'Vader en moeder: ongeschikt', VARA Nederland 2, 13 April 2012; 'Wij, rechters, willen een wet die verplichte anticonceptie mogelijk maakt', *NRC Handelsblad* 4 March 2015; 'Verplichte anticonceptie bij falende ouders', *Algemeen Dagblad* 17 April 2015; M. Schipper, 'Pleidooi voor gedwongen anticonceptie', *Telegraaf* 22 January 2015; P. de Graaf, 'Verplicht kwetsbare ouder tot tijdelijke anticonceptie', *Volkskrant* 1 October 2016; 'Grondrecht op vrije voortplanting kan wel worden beperkt', NOS.nl 22 January 2017; E. van der Aa, 'Expertgroep: 'geef vrouwen die ongeschikt zijn als moeder anticonceptie'', *Algemeen Dagblad* 27 October 2020; 'Expertgroep; ongeschikte moeders moeten gedwongen anticonceptie krijgen', *Volkskrant* 27 October 2020.

29 Sections 3:3 and 3:4(b) of the Mandatory Mental Health Care Act.

contraception.[30] Compulsory contraception in this context may be deemed necessary if the patient's mental disorder poses a significant risk of severe harm to a potential child. In addition, having the child taken away from the patient by the child protection service could be too traumatising an experience, jeopardising the patient's recovery, and possibly exacerbating her condition.[31] In sum, the measure has been considered necessary both to protect a potential child from harm, and to benefit the mental well-being and recovery of the patient. While the Memorandum to the Mandatory Mental Health Care Act states that a court order for mandatory care includes "all types of care that are necessary to take away the significant risk of severe harm",[32] it does not mention forced contraception explicitly as a possible mandatory health care treatment. In December 2022, the Dutch Supreme Court ruled that the Mandatory Mental Health Care Act did offer the possibility to include contraception as mandatory treatment, but only if the pregnancy or giving birth would endanger the woman's life or physical or mental health.[33] The Court explicitly stated that contraception in order to prevent irresponsible parenthood or to protect the well-being of the future child was not possible under the Mandatory Mental Health Care Act.[34] In other words, compulsory contraception in this situation cannot be justified by the interests of the future child.

The recent emergence of the future child in law can, in several ways, be understood as a result of advances in modern technology. Humankind has always used technology to make life easier, by building cities, ploughing fields, and making weapons. According to the German philosopher Hans Jonas, these traditional or 'old' forms of technology fundamentally differ from modern technology in several ways. Most importantly, as a result of modern technology, the consequences of our actions are no longer confined to the present, but transgress spatial and temporal boundaries, affecting those who live in the future. In addition, humans are no longer solely the subject of technology, they have also become its object. Consequently, mankind can take "his own evolution in hand",[35] which

30 District Court Rotterdam 16 April 2020 ECLI:NL:RBROT:2020:3948; District Court Northern-Netherlands 20 October 2020 ECLI:NL:RBNNE:2020:3684; District Court Amsterdam 2 December 2020 ECLI:NL:RBAMS:2020:6383; District Court the Hague 14 October 2021 ECLI:NL:RBDHA:2021:11864; In one case, the request for compulsory contraception was denied. District Court Zeeland-West-Brabant 12 October 2021 ECLI:NL:RBZWB:2021:5539.

31 District Court Rotterdam 16 April 2020 ECLI:NL:RBROT:2020:3948.

32 Kamerstukken II 2009-2010, 32 399, nr. 3, (*Memorandum Mandatory Mental Health Care Act*), p. 12. In Dutch: "alle vormen van zorg te bevatten die noodzakelijk zijn om het aanzienlijke risico op ernstige schade weg te nemen…" Translation by LtH.

33 Hoge Raad 9 December 2022, ECLI:NL:HR:2022:1850 (*Compulsory Contraception*), R.O. 3.2.3.

34 Hoge Raad 9 December 2022, ECLI:NL:HR:2022:1850 (*Compulsory Contraception*), R.O. 3.2.2.

35 H. Jonas, *The imperative of responsibility. In search of an ethics for the technological age*, Chicago, The University of Chicago Press, 1984, p. 31.

presents new sorts of risks.[36] Taking control over our own evolution implies an acceleration of natural processes, in which potential errors have a greater effect as the time to correct them is shortened. Moreover, the risks are cumulative. Biotechnologies offer a striking example of this point, as they deal with living, evolving material, which may react to the interference in an unforeseen way. For example, alterations made in the germline will be passed on to future generations. Additionally, they can result in unforeseen mutations in the DNA. In the words of Jonas, the endeavours of modern technology are not only "irreversible but also forward-pushing and thus overtake the wishes and plans of the initiators."[37]

Due to its nature, modern technology has confronted us with what Habermas calls "challenges of a new order."[38] Because modern technology, and in particular biotechnology, fundamentally differs from old technology and has the human itself as its object, normative reflection upon it, and consequently regulating it, is a highly complex matter. Reproductive biotechnology has created a number of new possibilities, such as sex selection, designer babies, split motherhood, multiplex parenthood, and even solo procreation. What these examples have in common, is that they transgress biological boundaries. What once was out of our control but 'given by nature', is now, or soon will be, at our disposal. As Habermas points out, the categorical distinction between the grown, which up to now we could not control, and the made, or the subjective and objective, becomes blurred.[39] The blurring of these fundamental categories matters, because our moral vocabulary relies on these categorical distinctions. As Dworkin explains, the overall structure of our moral experience "depends on a fundamental distinction between what we are responsible for doing or deciding, individually or collectively, and what is given to us as a background against which we act or decide, but which we are powerless to change."[40] As reproductive technologies allow us to exercise control over the human being and its genome, what once was considered an unchangeable fact of nature now becomes the object of our control. Or as Buchanan et al. put it, what used to be a matter of chance or nature, has now become a matter of deliberate choice.[41] Because of this increased control, prospective parents and medical professionals can be held responsible for choosing, or failing to choose, certain benefits for our offspring with the help of, for instance, selection or genetic enhancement. In short, modern technology has resulted in a shift in responsibility, or as Sandel puts it,

36 Jonas, 1984, p. 31-32.
37 Jonas, 1984, p. 32.
38 J. Habermas, *The future of human nature*, Cambridge, Polity Press, 2003, p. 28.
39 Habermas 2003, p. 42.
40 R. Dworkin, 'Playing God', *Prospect Magazin*, 1999.
41 A. Buchanan, D.W. Brock, N. Daniels and D. Wikler, *From chance to choice*, Cambridge, Cambridge University press, 2009.

"an explosion of responsibility."[42] Van Beers points out that this expansion of responsibility is multi-faceted; not only can medical professionals and parents be held responsible (or even legally liable) for their actions and choices in the conception of a child, but also society as a whole has become responsible for the future of mankind.[43] Because of this shift in responsibility, modern technology does not just confront us with new moral dilemmas, but questions the very moral assumptions that we use. Some speak of a moral free fall[44] or moral vertigo, "that seizes us when the ground beneath our feet, which we believed to be solid, begins to slip."[45]

From this perspective, the introduction of the future child, or more precisely the awareness of our moral duties towards future people in the regulations on reproduction, becomes understandable. The two aspects of modern technology discussed here – the human as the object of technology and the future-affecting nature of our actions – are, in particular, represented in reproductive biotechnologies. First, reproductive technologies directly aim to affect a child who is not born or even conceived yet. Moreover, with the help of germline modification technologies such as CRISPR-Cas9, the genetic alterations can be passed on to future generations as well. In addition, in using reproductive technologies the future child is not just the object of technology, but it is completely subjected to the control of those who exist now. The child cannot agree or object to technological interference with its own being. Consequently, as reproductive technologies impact the future child's existence in the most intimate ways, making us responsible for the choices we make regarding this entity, we are confronted with two new and complex questions: how can we incorporate future people into our legal and ethical discussions on reproductive technologies? And what do we owe to future people?[46]

'We' in this context refers to those who at the moment exist and whose decisions and actions can affect future people. This does not only pertain to those parties directly involved in the creation of a future child, such as prospective parents, medical professionals, fertility clinics, donors, and surrogates. This question also concerns legal and political actors, such as legislators and judges, who can affect the lives of future people either by direct decisions or through regulation. In addition, what we owe to future people is a question that also pertains to society as a whole. In a liberal democracy, citizens can

42 M.J. Sandel, *The Case against perfection; ethics in the age of genetic engineering*, Cambridge, Massachusetts, the Belknap Press of Harvard University Press, 2007, p. 87.

43 B.C. van Beers, 'Van slaapkamer naar vruchtbaarheidskliniek. Deseksualisering van voortplanting en de 'uitbarsting van verantwoordelijkheid'', *Ars Aequi*, Vol. 2016, No. 4, 2016b, p. 298-306.

44 Dworkin, 1999.

45 Habermas, 2003, p. 39; See also Sandel, 2007, p. 9.

46 The latter question is amongst those raised by Jonathan Glover in J. Glover, *Choosing children. Genes, disability, and design*, Oxford, Oxford University Press, 2006.

indirectly influence regulation, and thus also influence whether and under which circumstances technologies can be used. According to Jasanoff et al., citizens not only have the possibility to decide on how we use technologies such as germline editing, but also a responsibility to participate in this debate. As explained above, advances in biotechnology have not only led to medical-technical questions about the safety and efficiency of newly developed technologies, but also moral questions that the medical experts are not necessarily better equipped to answer.[47] Because the regulation of these technologies require us to think about what we want for future society, Jasanoff, Hurlbut, and Saha argue that this task demands the involvement of citizens alongside experts: "It is our responsibility to decide, as parents and citizens, whether our current genetic preferences should be edited, for all time, into our children and our children's children."[48]

The two questions listed above – what we owe to future people and how we can address future people – are interrelated. To start with the former, the regulatory frameworks on reproduction and reproductive technologies do offer a preliminary answer to the question of what we owe to future people. After all, the legal norms in the regulation can be understood as an expression of, or oriented towards, various ethical values concerning how we should treat people. These values include ideas about, amongst others, preventing the objectification and instrumentalisation of humans, protecting human dignity and personal identity and promoting well-being. Together, these values constitute a normative account of what it means to be human and what the human person is entitled to. In other words, these regulatory frameworks operationalise an implicit, normative account of the human person. Addressing this normative account and its underlying values is indispensable for critical reflection on the existing regulation and its ability to cope with future challenges. Importantly, in order to have a meaningful discussion about these values and the question of what we owe to future people, it is necessary to have a theoretical framework that can conceptualise the future child in such a way that it is able to make sense of these values. Only if we understand how we should approach the future child and what the basis is for our duties towards it,[49] can we start to substantiate those duties. In other words, in order to grasp what we owe to future people, we must first understand how we can address these entities.

---

47 B.C. van Beers, 'De humaniteit van humane biotechnologie. Juridische perspectieven op menselijke waardigheid en medische biotechnologie.' in, *Humane Biotechnologie en Recht (Handelingen Nederlandse Juristen-Vereniging 2009-1)*, Kluwer, Deventer, 2009a, p. 109-110.

48 S. Jasanoff, J.B. Hurlbut and K. Saha (2015) 'Human genetic engineering demands more than a moratorium', *The Guardian*, 2015.

49 For consistency and ease of reference, the pronoun 'it' is chosen for the future child. By doing so I do not intend to discriminate, but this pronoun captures the unknown quality of the future child's characteristics in a simple and neutral manner.

1.2 The Complexity of the Future Child

Despite the important role that the future child plays in the regulation of reproduction, the nature of this entity is highly undertheorised. In various legal systems, the values that underly the regulation of reproduction are currently presented as the interests of the future child. This means, as the examples mentioned earlier demonstrate, that the future child is conceptualised as a 'subject of interests'.[50] One could wonder why this conceptualisation would be problematic. After all, as a subject of interests, the future child is approached in a similar manner as other future entities, such as the unborn child and future generations. However, the future child cannot easily be compared to these other future entities. Both the concept of the unborn child (the child with which the woman is pregnant) and of future generations are discussed below in order to illustrate in which respects the future child as a legal entity fundamentally differs from the two other concepts.

1.2.1 *The Unborn Child*

Within the legal domain, there is not only increasing attention on the protection of the future child, but also on the unborn child. For the purpose of this study, the unborn child is understood as the child that has already been conceived but has not been born yet. In most cases, this is the child with which the woman is pregnant, but in some cases, it can also include the child that develops from the (pre-)embryo in vitro. The unborn child shares an important characteristic with the future child: both are an anticipation of the child that will be born. In most Western legal systems, the embryo in utero or the foetus[51] is not a legal subject. For this reason, reference to the rights and interests of the unborn child actually refer to the rights and interests the child will have after it is born. Due to the fact that these interests can be violated by circumstances that took place before the child's birth, these interests are anticipated in several regulatory frameworks.

Due to recent developments, the legal position of the unborn child has undergone changes which have resulted in a need to rethink the nature of its legal status. One of these developments is the increasing awareness of maternal-foetal conflicts and the growing body of legal measures addressing maternal harm. Maternal harm is harm to the unborn child caused by the behaviour of the woman during the pregnancy, such as alcohol or drug abuse, or refusing necessary medical treatment as a result of a psychological disorder. Because the mother's behaviour during the pregnancy can have severe consequences for

50 For a further elaboration of the subject of interests, see chapter 6.

51 In some cases, the term foetus is used interchangeably with the term embryo in utero, at other times it only refers to the embryo that passed the boundary of viability, i.e. after 24 weeks of pregnancy.

the health of the foetus and the unborn child, various measures have been created that acknowledge the independent status of the unborn child. In some cases, the mother is held criminally liable for causing the death of her unborn or newborn child, or child abuse.[52] Additionally, there are also strategies developed to mitigate or prevent maternal harm. A famous example is Wisconsin's Unborn Child Protection Act, also known as the 'Cocaine Mom Act', which allows the state to hold addicted mothers in custody if they refuse treatment.[53] Another example is Tennessee's Fetal Assault Law of 2014, which allowed women to be prosecuted for drug use during the pregnancy.[54] In the Netherlands, two strategies have been developed in case law.[55] The first is imposing a family supervision order on the unborn child, which basically means that the pregnant woman is kept under supervision by the child protection service. The second strategy is the admission of the pregnant woman into a psychiatric hospital. The latter is of course only possible if the harmful behaviour is the result of a psychiatric condition. Due to the fact that both strategies have been developed in case law, rather than statutory law, they lack a systematic approach to the legal status of the unborn child.[56]

The need to rethink the legal status of the unborn child has also been instigated by various biotechnological developments, such as foetal therapy[57] (including compulsory caesarean-sections), prenatal surgery, and artificial womb technology. These technologies have raised questions concerning the beginning of legal personality. Legal personality for human persons, so-called natural personality, traditionally starts at the moment of birth. The *nasciturus fiction* allows this boundary to be altered. With the help of this fiction, the unborn child can be regarded as being born (and thus as a legal subject) if its interests require this, provided that it will be born alive.[58] In other words, the starting point of the

---

52 B. Steinbock, *Life before birth. The moral and legal status of embryos and fetuses*, 2nd, New York, Oxford University Press, 2011, chapter 4.

53 Section 48.133 and 48.135 Wisconsin Statutes.

54 The Act was given a two-year trial phase and was discontinued after this period because of unwanted effects. Apparently, pregnant women refrained from seeking necessary help out of fear of prosecution.

55 J.H.H.M. Dorscheidt, 'Developments in legal and medical practice regarding the unborn child and the need to expand prenatal legal protection', *European Journal of Health Law*, Vol. 17, No. 5, 2010, p. 433-454.

56 For a more extensive analysis see Dorscheidt, 2010 and L. ten Haaf, 'Unborn and Future Children as New Legal Subjects: An Evaluation of Two Subject-Oriented Approaches—The Subject of Rights and the Subject of Interests', *German Law Journal*, Vol. 18, No. 5, 2017. In 2018, the Dutch Compulsory Admissions in Psychiatric Hospitals Act (Wet BOPZ) was replaced by the Mandatory Mental Health Care Act (in Dutch: Wet verplichte geestelijke gezondheidszorg, or Wvggz). This measure, i.e. the possibility to admit a pregnant woman in order to protect the unborn child, that was developed in case law was explicitly adopted in the new act. See *Kamerstukken II* 2009-2010, 32 399, nr. 3, (*Memorandum Mandatory Mental Health Care Act*), p. 42-43, 56-57.

57 E.J. Oldekamp and M.C. de Vries, 'Nieuwe procreatietechnieken. Achterhaalde juridische kaders?' in, *Nieuwe technieken, nieuwe zorg. (Preadvies Vereniging voor Gezondheidsrecht)*, Sdu, Den Haag, 2018, p. 61-77.

58 Section 5.4.1. offers an elaborate discussion of the nasciturus fiction.

legal person can be artificially changed, but birth remains a requirement for the attribution of legal personality. This nasciturus construction raises several questions that are important for the status of the unborn child. First, in cases of prenatal surgery and artificial womb transfer, the child can exit the womb,[59] but it is unclear whether this qualifies as birth and consequently, what the status of the child is – a legal person or not. Romanis argues that foetal surgery and artificial womb technology challenge the born-alive threshold, which no longer necessarily coincides with 'leaving the womb'.[60] Due to this special status, a third category may be needed, such as 'partially born', in order to give these subjects the necessary legal protection without disrupting other areas of law, such as the regulation of abortion.[61] Moreover, when the nasciturus fiction is invoked to protect the unborn child's health interests, the fiction is applied in a forward-looking manner, that is, before the child's biological birth. This means that there is no certainty that the child will be born alive. In particular, when health interests are at stake, there is a chance that despite treatment, the child dies during the pregnancy. If this indeed happens, then, following the second part of the fiction, the child has legally never existed at all. In cases of a compulsory caesarean-section, the situation becomes even more complex as the fiction is invoked in order to ensure the child is born alive, which is in itself a requirement for invoking the nasciturus fiction in the first place. So, this alternative application of the nasciturus fiction alters the status of the unborn child: being born alive is no longer the requirement for legal personality; the child's assumed future existence is enough for the law to treat it as a person.[62]

Advances in reproductive technologies have resulted in an increased attention on both the future and the unborn child, but it is important to keep in mind that they are different legal entities. Indeed, both are entities that exist as a result of the anticipation of the rights and interests of the person that they will possibly become. However, in contrast to the future child, the unborn child physically exists in the form of an embryo in utero. Due to this physical existence, measures concerning the unborn child differ in two ways. First, the unborn child can be protected with the help of the nasciturus fiction: it is proactively regarded as being born already, which makes the anticipation of its rights and interests easier. Given the fact that the future child whose existence is prevented will never be born

59 See for example, S. Scutti, 'Meet the Baby who was Born Twice' (CNN 20 October 2017) <https://www.cnn.com/2016/10/20/health/baby-born-twice-fetal-surgery/index.html>.

60 E.C. Romanis, 'Challenging the 'Born Alive' Threshold: Fetal Surgery, Artificial Wombs, and the English Approach to Legal Personhood', *Medical Law Review*, Vol. 28, No. 1, 2019.

61 Romanis, 2019, p. 120.

62 For a more extensive analysis of the proactive application of the nasciturus fiction for the protection of the unborn child, see ten Haaf, 2017, p. 1101-1104.

at all, it is impossible to apply a similar construction to the latter entity.[63] Second, protecting the interests of the unborn child occurs by interfering with the circumstances of the pregnancy or birth. For example, measures concerning maternal harm aim to end the harmful conduct of the mother in order to secure the unborn child's health. A compulsory caesarean-section can be ordered if a natural birth is deemed to be too risky and a caesarean-section is deemed necessary to ensure that the child is born alive. In other words, protection measures for the unborn child are geared at safeguarding its health and birth. The measures aim to ensure the child is born (or born healthy). The protection of the interests of the future child, on the contrary, is in various cases achieved by preventing the future child's existence.

1.2.2 Future Generations

Another entity that is closely linked to the future child, but is still a distinct entity, is the future generation. By 'future generations', I refer to the whole population that exists at some point in the future, but whose members have not been born yet. Future generations play, in particular, an important role in normative discussions on environmental issues. Jonas, whose work is discussed more extensively in chapter 7, argues that as a result of the use of modern technology, the consequences of our actions transgress temporal boundaries and can affect those who live in the far future. Since future generations bear the consequences of our actions today, we must take them into consideration.

The legal position of future generations, just like the legal status of the unborn and future child, is unclear. Contrary to the unborn child, a future generation has no physical existence yet, a characteristic it shares with the future child. Because of this lack of existence, the question has been raised as to whether it is possible to speak of the *rights* of future generations.[64] Nonetheless, there remains an important difference between the future child and a future generation. We may perhaps not know which members will be part of it, but we can assume that a future generation will come into existence. Or at least, we aim to ensure that a future generation comes into existence. Preventing the future generation's existence would imply the end of the human race. For this reason, discussions

63 In addition, the nasciturus fiction often refers to the child with whom the woman is pregnant, which is a second reason why this construction cannot be applied to the future child. L. ten Haaf, 'Een slechte toekomst is geen toekomst', *NJB*, Vol. 2012, No. 17, 2012, p. 1178. See also section 5.4.1.

64 J. Feinberg, 'The rights of animals and unborn generations.' in: W.T. Blackstone (ed.), *Philosophy & Environmental Crisis*, The University of Georgia Press, Athens, GA, 1974; S. Fikkers, 'Urgenda, de zorgplicht en toekomstige generaties', *Nederlands Juristenblad*, Vol. 2015, No. 33, 2015, p. 2289-2293.

on future generations and what we owe to them, such as the Dutch *Urgenda* case,[65] are focused on the circumstances under which these generations come into existence, and whether these circumstances should change, rather than their existence itself. Discussions on the future child, on the contrary, focus on whether it should come into existence given those circumstances. In sum, the future child cannot be approached as a member of a future generation.

1.2.3 *The Future Child*

When compared to the other two future entities, the future child's unique nature comes to the fore. Measures concerning the unborn child and future generations pertain to the circumstances under which they come into existence. With regard to the unborn child, the focus primarily lies on safeguarding or improving its health and preventing a stillbirth. With regard to future generations, the debate often centres around the availability of resources. In the case of the future child, what frustrates its interests is often intertwined with its conception. For example, its well-being is compromised by a severe genetic condition or by its parents lacking the ability to properly take care of a child. Or, its dignity is violated because of a certain mode of conception, such as sex selection or reproductive cloning. Therefore, measures that aim to protect the interests of the future child in many cases result in the prevention of the future child's conception. In other words, they are not focused on the circumstances of the child's existence, but its existence itself. For this reason, the regulatory frameworks on reproduction that result in the prevention of the future child's existence call into existence a rather unique entity.

The future child that is introduced in the regulations on reproduction is characterised by its non-existence: it does not physically exist and, as a result of the regulation, it never will. In fact, the future child is a highly fictional entity, which only exists as a legal construction. At the same time, it is partly connected to the entity that may exist in the future. After all, the interests of the future child that regulatory frameworks refer to are not the interests which the non-existent entity has at that moment. It would be impossible to speak of the future child's well-being as if it were the well-being of the non-existent entity itself, since something that does not exist cannot experience well-being or harm. Instead, the interests of the future child refer to the interests the child will have once it has come into existence. Given the fact that actions and decisions made before its birth, and even its conception, can affect the child, these interests need to be anticipated. Consequently, these interests

65 Court of Appeal the Hague 9 October 2018 ECLI:NL:GHDHA:2018:2591 (*Urgenda*); Hoge Raad 20 December 2019 ECLI:NL:HR:2019:2006 (*Urgenda*).

transgress the temporal boundaries of their subject's existence and are attributed to a 'new' entity: the future child. Subsequently, in the regulations on reproduction, the future child seems to be understood as a subject of interests.

Despite its complex nature, and despite the fact that the future child has become a prominent figure in the regulations on reproduction, its status remains generally unaddressed in regulation and in political discussions. Neither the regulatory frameworks nor parliamentary documents (in particular, the Dutch, UK, and German regulations on which this study is focused) discuss the nature of the future child's legal status or address the question as to whether it is capable of having interests and/or rights. Instead, these features of the future child are simply assumed when the regulations on reproduction refers to 'the interests of the future child'.

A closer analysis of this 'interests of the future child' argument reveals that this depiction of the future child is based on four assumptions concerning the future child. The first and second assumption concern the future child's interests themselves. As chapter 2 discusses, when the regulatory frameworks refer to the interests of the future child, they refer to three specific interests: an interest in having its well-being secured and being protected from harm, the possibility to form its identity, and the protection of its human dignity. As explained above, these interests represent the regulatory answer to the question of what we owe to future people. As such, they are based on legal-ethical values that constitute a legal normative account of what it means to be human. The regulatory frameworks do not elaborate on these values, i.e. they do not explain which interpretation of these notions underly the regulation, but they do openly state that these are interests of the future child. This implies that in the regulations on reproduction, these values are presented as interests of an individual entity, namely the future child, that may be born without interference. In other words, the first assumption that underlies the future child's current conceptualisation is that the values the regulation seeks to protect can be understood as interests of an individual entity. The second assumption is barely addressed in the regulation itself and mostly only tacitly implied: namely the assumption of the future child's interest in non-existence. As mentioned earlier, the measures and regulatory frameworks concerning the future child generally result in the prevention of its conception (or, in the case of PGT, implantation) and consequently, in the prevention of the future child's existence. In the Memoranda and in the parliamentary discussions on these regulatory frameworks,[66] the frameworks are justified by invoking the interests of the future child. In plain words, the refusal of fertility treatment, the use of embryo selection, and the bans on donor anonymity, reproductive cloning, and germline modification are deemed to be in the interests of the

66 See chapter 2.

future child. This means that the resulting prevention of the future child's existence is apparently considered to be in the future child's interests. In other words, by claiming that the regulatory frameworks that result in the prevention of the future child's existence serve the future child's interests, it is implicitly assumed that the future child has an interest in its own non-existence.

The third and fourth assumption relate to the future child's nature as a subject. As the regulations on reproduction invokes the interests of the future child, it is implied by the regulation that the future child has legally relevant interests, i.e. interests that need to be taken into account in legal debate. As the future child is the subject of those interests, the future child becomes an actor in the legal debate, or a legal actor. More precisely, as the subject of legally relevant interests that have to be balanced against the interests and rights of other legal actors, it is assumed that the future child is a legal subject or has some form of legal subjectivity.[67] In fact, occasionally the rights of the future child are mentioned. For example, in the discussion on compulsory contraception, proponents of this measure claim that the future child has a 'right not to be born'[68] without further discussing the possibility and extent of its legal personality. Therefore, the third assumption made about the future child is that it has some form of legal subjectivity. Finally, by mobilising the interests of the future child, the regulatory frameworks imply that the future child is capable of having interests. In other words, the regulatory frameworks assume that the future child can be the 'subject of interests', which is the fourth assumption.

In summation, regarding the conceptualisation of the future child in the regulations on reproduction, four assumptions can be distilled from the regulatory frameworks. First, the values the regulation aims to protect can be understood as interests of an individual entity. Second, the future child has an interest in its own non-existence. Third, the future child has some form of legal subjectivity. And fourth, the future child can be the subject of interests. These four assumptions form, so to speak, the four foundational pillars of what I call the 'interests of the future child' construction. This is the construction or theoretical framework currently used in the regulations on reproduction to conceptualise the future child.

67 As I will explain in chapter 5, I consider legal subjectivity to be a broader term than legal personality. For the purpose of this these, legal subjectivity includes both legal personality and other forms of legal subjectivity, such as the subject of legally relevant interests that is discussed in chapter 6.

68 Editorial, 'Hebben sommige kinderen het recht niet geboren te worden? *Telegraaf* (22 January 2015). Editorial, 'Rotterdamse wethouder: verplichte anticonceptie incompetente ouders', *NOS* (1 October 2016) https://nos.nl/artikel/2135331-rotterdamse-wethouder-verplichte-anticonceptie-incompetente-ouders.html.

Here, we come to the core of the concept of the future child, at least the future child that is the central topic of this study. The future child is a non-existent entity, that, if certain basic needs cannot be guaranteed, presumably has an interest in its own non-existence. This allocation of interests makes the future child a somewhat paradoxical entity. On the one hand, the future child is given a voice such that its interests are taken into account. As a result of the attribution of interests, it gains a legal-fictional existence. On the other hand, the future child's voice is silenced, because as a result of taking the interests of the future child into account, its existence is prevented. In other words, the same act that gives the future child a form of existence, prevents its actual existence. However, the paradox is even more complex. Following the regulatory frameworks, the interests of the future child are mobilised to prevent its existence. At the same time, several authors have pointed out that we do not owe anything to those who will never exist, because a non-existent entity cannot be harmed, cannot suffer, or have interests.[69] In other words, the future child's subjectivity is both established and denied.[70] Its paradoxical nature, which so far has been left unaddressed by the regulator and in the academic legal debate in general, reiterates the importance of the question of whether the future child's existence can be prevented by invoking its own interests. In particular, now that the interests of the future child form the paramount factor in the justification of the regulations on reproduction that results in the prevention of the child, it has become necessary to explore the tenability of this construction.

The paradoxical and possibly problematic nature of the 'interests of the future child' construction is not the only reason to further investigate this unique entity. One may also wonder whether the 'interests of the future child' is an adequate framework to articulate what is at stake within the regulation of reproduction. Sandel points out that in liberal societies, challenges caused by biotechnology are usually addressed with concepts that focus on the individual subject, such as autonomy, fairness, and individual rights. One could think of the recently emerged right to procreative autonomy, or Dworkin's proposed approach to these challenges: *ethical individualism*, which includes the *right* of each individual to define what is a successful life to him or her.[71] Also the interests of the future child can be understood as an example of this individual-oriented vocabulary, with the

69 M. Brazier, A. Campbell and S. Golombok, *Surrogacy. Review for health ministers of current arrangements for payments and regulation. (Brazier report)*, 1998, p. 36. D. Beyleveld and R. Brownsword, *Human Dignity in Bioethics and Biolaw*, Oxford, Oxford Scholarship online, 2012, p. 151; Glover, 2006, p. 42.

70 This conflict is also briefly addressed by Den Hartogh. G. den Hartogh, "In het belang van het kind" in: G. den Hartogh and I. de Beaufort (eds.), *Een hoge prijs voor een kind*, Van Gorcum, Assen, 2006, p. 184.

71 R. Dworkin, *Sovereign virtue. The theory and practice of equality*, Cambridge, Harvard University Press, 2000, p. 448-449. Ethical individualism consists, in his view, of two principles. First, "it is objectively important that any human life, once begun, succeed rather than fail" and second, although this objective importance is acknowledged, it "insists nevertheless that one person – the person whose life it is – has a

focus on individual interests instead of individual rights. However, Sandel argues that these concepts are not equipped to fully address what is at stake, in particular with regard to reproductive technologies. Like Dworkin's approach of ethical individualism, they tend to focus on the individual person, while reproduction by its nature is not individual, but intersubjective. It implies making choices for another person who cannot speak for himself, affecting his or her life or preventing it. In addition to that, the fundamental questions that we face transcend the conceptualisation of new rights. They question the very nature of our humanity and personhood. As Habermas emphasises, "[s]hifting the 'line between chance and choice' affects the self-understanding of persons who act on moral grounds and are concerned about their life as a whole."[72] Consequently, Jonas and Sandel, for example, have argued that we are in need of a new normative vocabulary to address (bio)technology.

All in all, the question rises as to whether the 'interests of the future child' construction is an adequate theoretical framework for conceptualising this entity. Speaking of the interests of the future child may seem a logical step. It fits with the liberal or individual-oriented vocabulary that is dominant in Western societies. Moreover, an analogous principle is laid down in Article 3 of the Convention on the Rights of the Child, and plays an important role in family law, prescribing that the best interests of the (existing) child should be paramount.[73] However, a closer look at the future child whose existence is prevented suggests a more problematic side of the 'interests of the future child' construction. Cohen points out, this formula can serve as a smokescreen "that prevents us from excavating the true justification."[74] After all, since the child cannot speak for itself, and third parties determine the contents of its interests, this construction can be interpreted in a way that serves one's argument best, especially when there is no explicit idea of the human person to substantiate these interests. In addition, as Sandel maintains, the liberal vocabulary may not be equipped to provide a satisfactory ethical framework for addressing biotechnology. Because reproduction is intersubjective by definition, an approach focusing on individual interests may not be able to address all stakes. Finally, the future child has a unique nature; its non-existence makes it unlike other (future) entities. This raises the question as to whether it can be represented in a similar way, namely as a subject of interests or even rights.

---

special responsibility for each life, and that in virtue of that special responsibility he or she has a right to make the fundamental decisions that define, for him, what a successful life would be."

72 Habermas, 2003, p. 28.

73 I.G. Cohen, 'Regulating reproduction: the problem with best interests', *Minnesota Law Review*, Vol. 96, 2011, p. 429.

74 Cohen, 2011, p. 426-427.

1.3 Aim and Research Questions

In this study, I aim to assess the tenability of the 'interests of the future child' construction, or the interests-construction for short. That is, whether the future child can adequately be conceptualised as a subject of legally relevant interests so that it can be addressed and included in the legal and ethical debates on reproductive technologies. The question of the conceptualisation of the future child has become particularly urgent because of the important role this construction plays in the regulations on reproduction. Advances in reproductive technologies succeed each other at a rapid pace, raising complex moral and legal challenges. These technologies facilitate control over the most intimate sphere of the lives of future people now that future humans are also the *object* of these technologies. With the help of reproductive technologies, prospective parents can determine from whom the child descends or manipulate its genetic characteristics, matters that used to be beyond control. As a result, these technologies confront us with the question of what do we owe to these future people. What aspects of the human person are at stake and must be protected? In order to be able to answer this question and reflect upon the legal and ethical values that underlie the regulations on reproduction, we first must find a way to address future people and incorporate them into the legal and ethical discussions on reproductive technologies. To be more precise, we must find a way to address the future child whose existence is prevented. In the current regulations on reproduction the future child is conceptualised as a subject of interests. But, if as a result of this attribution of interests, the future child is prevented from coming into existence, we may ask whether this interests-construction is an adequate framework for conceptualising the future child. For this reason, the central questions of this research are: **is the presentation of the future child as a subject of interests an adequate way to conceptualise and understand this entity? And if not, how can the future child whose existence is prevented be conceptualised in a more adequate manner?** In answering these questions, I aim to investigate whether the 'interests of the future child' construction is able do justice to the legal-ethical values that form the foundation of the regulations on reproduction. And, if this construction appears to be untenable, to explore an alternative theoretical framework to help us understand and address the future child.

1.4 Method and Scope

1.4.1 *Method: Constructivism, Fit, and Justification*

In order to investigate whether the theoretical framework for conceptualising the future child is adequate, I need assessment criteria. The approach I take for this assessment, and from which I derive the assessment criteria, is inspired by and building on Dworkin's constructivism. Central to Dworkin's theory of constructivism is the notion of law as integrity, which can be understood as an ideal picture of the law as a coherent body of legal norms and principles. This ideal prescribes that legislators should aim to make "the total set of laws morally coherent"[75] and that judges, so far as possible, should understand law as "a coherent set of principles about justice and fairness and procedural due process."[76] According to this understanding of law, it consists of both legal norms, and ethical values and principles:[77] legal rules or practices do not simply exist but "serve some interest or purpose or enforce some principle."[78] In other words, when a legislator enacts new legal norms, he creates not only those norms but also, indirectly, underlying values. Dworkin developed his theory with particular attention to adjudication as a method for judges to come to a decision. Dworkin maintains that in order to decide a case, a judge must construct the best theory or interpretation of which principles and values can explain and justify legal practice. In order to assess whether that interpretation is indeed the best interpretation, or shows law in "the best light possible",[79] it must be judged against two connected dimensions: the dimension of fit and the dimension of justification.[80] The first dimension entails that an interpretation or a theory of law must be in line with (to some degree) legal practice,[81] or the existing body of law. Dworkin accepts the possibility that multiple theories of law pass this threshold and fit the existing law sufficiently. The dimension of justification then requires that a judge must choose the interpretation that "shows the legal record to be the best it can be from the standpoint of substantive political morality."[82] That is, the judge must choose the interpretation that offers the most coherent explanation or justification of the previous legal decisions and the body of rules.

In order to assess the adequacy of law's conceptualisation of the future child, we could ask ourselves whether conceptualising the future child as a subject of interests is indeed the 'best interpretation' of this entity. To make this assessment, this conceptualisation must be tested against the dimensions of fit and justification. First, testing the construction used to conceptualise the future child on the dimension of fit implies exploring whether the construction is in line with the existing body of legal norms. This does not only involve an assessment of whether the interests-construction is compatible with existing regulation;

75 R. Dworkin, *Law's empire*, Oxford, Hart Publishing, 1998, p. 176.
76 Dworkin, 1998, p. 243 (see also p. 176).
77 Dworkin, 1998, p. 227.
78 Dworkin, 1998, p. 47.
79 Dworkin, 1998, p. 243.
80 R. Dworkin, *Life's dominion. An argument about abortion, euthanasia, and individual freedom*, New York, Alfred A. Knopf, 1993, p. 111; Dworkin, 1998, p. 228.
81 Dworkin, 1993, p. 111; Dworkin, 1998, p. 230.
82 Dworkin, 1998, p. 248.

that would result in a circular reasoning since the construction is often already integrated in those norms. After all, the interests of the future child are used as a justification for various regulatory frameworks, and in some instances, is directly mentioned in legal norms.[83] Moreover, the fact that it is used in those legal frameworks is the reason for scrutinising this conceptualisation of the future child. However, the ideal of approaching law as a *coherent* system of legal norms and principles also requires that the legal construction is coherent with the interpretation of fundamental legal concepts that form the premises of that construction. To be more specific, the 'interests of the future child' construction, for example, rests on the assumption that the future child whose existence is prevented can indeed be a subject of interests. In order to assess whether this construction meets the dimension of fit, we must determine whether the assumption of the future child as a subject of interests is compatible with the legal system's ideas about what the capacity of having interests requires. If it is not compatible with these ideas, the assumption upon which the construction is built is internally contradictory.

Second, testing an interpretation or a reconstruction of the underlying value(s) on the dimension of justification means assessing whether that interpretation can put law in "the best light possible".[84] This means that it is the best explanation or justification of the existing body of law and legal practice. Therefore, for the conceptualisation of the future child as a subject of interests to be the best interpretation of this entity, it must be able to account for the values that the regulations on of reproduction aims to protect. That is, this construction must be able to articulate and to make sense of these values. In other words, the construction must do justice to the values that constitute the normative account of the human person in the regulations on reproduction. If this interpretation of the future child is indeed the best interpretation, understanding these values as interests of an individual future entity must be capable of asserting a coherent justification of the regulations on reproduction and its normative account of the human person. This raises in particular the question of whether the presentation of the values the regulation aims to protect can indeed be understood as individual interests, or whether the normative account of the human person that can be distilled from the regulation also has a collective dimension. I want to emphasise here that it is not the primary concern in this study to explore whether the ethical values represented by the interests of the future child qualify as the best theory of law in the field of the regulations on reproduction. Instead, I aim to scrutinise whether these values can adequately be articulated with the help of the construction or framework

83 For example, Section 13(5) of the HFE Act 2008 states that the welfare of any child who may be born as a result of the treatment must be taken into account in considering whether to offer a woman or couple fertility treatment, referring explicitly to the interests of the future child.

84 Dworkin, 1998, p. 243.

used. In other words, the focus lies on whether the future child's current conceptualisation is an adequate means for articulating the normative account of the person in the regulations on reproduction, and not on whether that account itself forms the best interpretation of this area of law.

In order to explore whether the 'interests of the future child' construction meets these dimensions of fit and justification, I assess the tenability of each of the four assumptions upon which this construction is based. As discussed earlier, these assumptions are: first, that the values underlying the regulations on reproduction can be presented as interests of the individual future child; second, that the future child under some circumstances has an interest in its own non-existence; third, that the future child is a legal subject; and fourth, that the future child is capable of having interests. The tenability of these assumptions is assessed through a legal-philosophical reconstruction of the core values and notions that form, in a way, the premises of these assumptions, such as the interest in non-existence, legal personality, and subjectivity. In some chapters, this legal-philosophical assessment is complemented by philosophical and bioethical literature, such as in chapters 4 and 6. The reason for this interdisciplinary approach is the fact that certain ideas based on legal premises are further thought through in philosophical and bioethical literature. These insights are indispensable for a critical reflection on the current conceptualisation of the future child. Notably, by including philosophical and bioethical literature to supplement the legal-philosophical analysis, I do not aim to prescribe which values or interpretations *should* be adopted in the regulations on reproduction. Nor do I aim to describe and support my own views on fundamental questions regarding personality, existence, or the normative account of the human person. Instead, this exploration serves to further elucidate the premises that can be found in law, and to come to a better understanding of the fundamental legal concepts and premises involved in the regulations on reproduction.

The critical assessment of the four assumptions reveals to what extent the 'interests of the future child' construction meets, or fails to meet, the dimensions of fit and justification. Moreover, this critical assessment helps to understand *why* and under which circumstances the interests-construct fails to articulate the underlying values and offer a justification for the regulations on reproduction, and *why* this construction is inherently contradictory. The identification of the pitfalls of this conceptualisation of the future child helps to understand which problems a theoretical framework for the conceptualisation of the future child must avoid. In the last chapter, I propose an alternative, more adequate theoretical framework for the conceptualisation of the future child. In my opinion, this framework constitutes a better conceptualisation of the future child, because it avoids the pitfalls of the 'interests of the future child' construction. For the construction of this theoretical framework, I combine legal and moral philosophy. I use the work of Hans

Jonas as a starting point. Jonas has developed an ethical theory for conceptualising future people without having to rely upon the attribution of interests or rights, and therefore provides an interesting alternative. In chapter 7, I adapt his theory and apply these ideas to the legal debate. With the help of this alternative framework, it becomes possible to include future people into our normative debates on reproductive technologies and make sense of and critically reflect upon what we owe them in the context of regulating reproduction.

1.4.2 Scope: Reproductive Technologies

This research aims to scrutinise how the future child is conceived[85] in the regulations on reproduction, and in particular the conceptualisation of the future child whose existence is prevented. For this reason, I shall not address every regulatory framework in this field of law extensively. The regulations on reproduction covers a wide variety of reproductive technologies, varying from donor conception, surrogacy, selection, and germline modification. In this study, reproductive technologies or assisted reproductive technologies (ARTs) also include those technologies that strictly speaking do not primarily aim to offer a solution to infertility or subfertility, but are used for the conception of a *healthy* child, such as preimplantation genetic testing (PGT), and genetic intervention, such as mitochondrial replacement therapy (MRT) or CRISPR-Cas9. In other words, reproductive technology includes all technologies that result in the conception (and ultimately the birth) of a child. However, regulatory frameworks that focus on the conception of a child, such as regulatory frameworks concerning surrogacy or egg cell donation, are briefly mentioned and only if they are relevant for the general discussion. The main focus lies on those regulatory frameworks that result in the prevention of the future child's conception and existence, either by banning a technology such as reproductive cloning or germline modification, or restricting its application, such as refusing a fertility treatment to potential parents or banning anonymous donor conception. The regulatory frameworks of the following technologies are extensively analysed and discussed: IVF and access to fertility treatments in general, PGT, donor conception, human germline genetic modification, including mitochondrial replacement therapies, and reproductive cloning. Each of these technologies is further addressed below.

First, I look into the regulation of access to fertility treatments and assisted reproduction, which includes artificial insemination (AI) and in-vitro fertilisation (IVF). In AI, the semen is inserted into the cervix (intracervical insemination or ICI, which can be done at a fertility clinic or at home), or directly into the uterus (intra-uterine insemination or IUI,

85 Pun intended.

which is usually performed in a clinic). In IVF, hormone treatment is used to mature multiple egg cells which are then harvested from the woman's ovaries. The egg cells, also known as ova, are fertilised in a petri dish in a laboratory, and after a couple of days, the embryo is implanted in the woman's uterus with the intention of achieving a successful pregnancy. These technologies can be conducted with the genetic material of the intended parents, or if necessary, with donated gametes. The intended parents can opt for the use of donated egg and sperm cells (or a donated embryo) if one or both of the partners is infertile or subfertile, or if there is a risk of transmitting a genetic illness. In the latter case, the goal of the treatment is not conceiving a child per se, but conceiving a healthy child.

The introduction of IVF has resulted in the development of several other techniques. As an embryo is created outside the female body, IVF facilitates the possibility of egg cell donation and gestational surrogacy. In these cases, the genetic mother, who provides the ovum, and the gestational mother, who carries the child to term, are no longer one and the same person. This phenomenon is called *split motherhood.*

The creation of an embryo outside the female body also makes it possible for the embryo to be screened for anomalies or genetic defects before it is implanted into the uterus. Selective reproduction with the help of preimplantation genetic testing (PGT) encompasses various applications. The first application is preimplantation genetic screening (PGS) or PGT-A. In this, the embryo is screened for chromosomal abnormalities or Aneuploidy, for example, missing chromosomes, or extra chromosomes, such as in the case of trisomy. The latter means that the embryo has three copies of a particular Chromosome, instead of two. Most trisomies result in a miscarriage, but can also result in a live birth, like trisomy 21, which is known as Down's syndrome. Another application of PGT is preimplantation genetic diagnosis (PGD) or PGT-M. In this, the embryo is screened for a monogenetic illness, i.e. a genetic disorder caused by a mutation on a single gene such as cystic fibrosis or the BRCA-gene. If the embryo tests positive for an chromosomal abnormality or a genetic mutation, it will not be implanted. Instead, an embryo without the genetic defect is implanted in order to ensure a successful pregnancy or a healthy child.[86] Most regulatory frameworks on preimplantation testing were drafted before the term PGD was replaced by PGT, and focus therefore primarily on preimplantation genetic diagnosis, i.e. the screening for a monogenetic disorder. Therefore, in this study, the term PGD is still occasionally

86 Since the medical community only recently decided to replace the term PGD with the broader term PGT, various regulatory documents still refer to PGD instead of PGT. For the purpose of this research, the contents of the regulation and the criteria they list for the use of preimplantation genetic testing is still relevant.

used when that specific technology is addressed by the regulatory frameworks and in the political debates.

A genetic mutation can occur in the nuclear DNA, which may result in cystic fibrosis or the BRCA-gene, but also in the mitochondrial DNA (mDNA). The mitochondria are often understood as the cell's batteries, providing the cell with energy to function. The mitochondria contain far less DNA than the cell's nucleus, but a defect in the mDNA may result in a fatal disease. In order to prevent the transmission of a mitochondrial disease, egg cell donation can be used. In that case, the child will not be genetically related to the intended mother. Another possibility is mitochondrial replacement therapy (MRT), also known as mitochondrial donation. Two mitochondrial replacement techniques can be distinguished. First is maternal spindle transfer (MST). For this technique, the nucleus, i.e. the core of the cell containing the chromosomes, is extracted from the ovum of the intended mother (enucleation). Simultaneously, an ovum from a healthy donor is enucleated. The nucleus of the intended mother is transferred to the emptied ovum of the donor, which contains healthy mitochondria. The rest of the intended mother's cell, including the affected mitochondria, is discarded. The newly reconstructed ovum is then fertilised with semen of the intended father (or a donor). In the second technique, pronuclear transfer or PNT, two zygotes are created in vitro. That is, both an egg cell of the intended mother and a healthy donor are fertilised with the semen of the intended father or a sperm donor. After fertilisation, but within 24 hours, the maternal and paternal nuclei are removed from both zygotes and the nuclei with the intended parents' material are transferred to the emptied Zygote that was created with the donor's ovum. In both cases, the reconstructed embryo can then be implanted into the intended mother's uterus or in a surrogate. Both forms of MRT ensure that the resulting child is genetically related to the mother, which is considered a benefit over ordinary egg cell donation. The child receives the nuclear DNA from its intended parents (unless a sperm donor was used), but the mitochondrial DNA from an egg donor. This makes the resulting child genetically related to three people: its intended parents and the egg donor (which is why MRT is sometimes referred to as three-parent IVF). It must be noted though, that only approximately 0,1% of the total DNA consists of mDNA and for this reason, the genetic relationship between the child and the egg donor is not as strong as between the child and the intended parents.

It has been debated whether mitochondrial replacement therapy qualifies as genetic modification or only as germline modification. First, it must be noted that these alternations in the child's genetic constitution can be passed on to next generations, but only via the maternal line (a child inherits mDNA only from its mother, not its father). Alterations in the nuclear DNA are passed on via both lines. Additionally, the UK Government accepted that MRT is a form of germline modification, but maintained that this technology does not constitute *genetic modification*. It argued MRT "only replace[s] rather than alter[s]" the genetic constitution of the child.[87] The US ad hoc committee of the Institute of Medicine, to the contrary, defines genetic modification more broadly, as "changes to the genetic material within a cell" and considers MRT as constituting genetic modification.[88]

A technology that without a doubt is a form of genetic modification (and can also be used for germline modification) is CRISPR-Cas9. Cas9 is a protein that can cut DNA and that can be combined with a DNA-sequence in order to cut the DNA in a specific place. CRISPR-Cas9 is not the only form of genetic modification, but it is considered to be one of the most precise and efficient ways of doing so. It allows us to alter (nuclear) DNA, either through deleting genes or inserting new genes. If this technology is applied to an early-stage embryo, the genetic modification will be present in the child's germ cells and passed on to following generations. This is called germline modification.

A final technology that is extensively discussed in this study is reproductive cloning. In the case of cloning, an exact genetic copy of an existing entity is created. This can be achieved in two ways. The first is via embryo splitting. In its earliest stage of development, the cells of an embryo are totipotent and can develop in any type of cell. If the embryo at this stage is divided into clusters of cells, each cluster can develop into a separate individual. Embryo splitting, or extracting cells from the embryo, is usually done for preimplantation diagnosis, but can also be done for reproductive goals (for example, to create more embryos in order to prevent the intended mother from undergoing extra hormone treatment). In the case of embryo splitting, the embryos are of the same age and develop simultaneously, unless one of them is cryopreserved and used for a pregnancy at a later moment. Embryo splitting can only be used to create a genetic copy of an embryo, but not of an adult entity. The latter is possible with the help of nuclear transplant, or somatic cell nuclear transfer (SCNT). This method is somewhat similar to MRT. However, instead of the nucleus of an ovum or zygote, the nucleus of a somatic cell is transferred into an enucleated ovum (contrary to egg cells, which only contains one chromosome of each pair, a somatic cell contains both chromosomes). The newly reconstructed cell is then stimulated to divide and develop and can be used for a pregnancy. Reproductive cloning could in theory be used for solo-procreation if an intended parent does not have a partner,

87 Department of Health, *Mitochondrial Donation: Government Response to the Consultation on Draft Regulations to Permit the Use of New Treatment Techniques to Prevent the Transmission of a Serious Mitochondrial Disease from Mother to Child*, 2014, p. 15.

88 Department of Health, 2014, p. 88.

or if he or she is infertile. As a result of reproductive cloning, the child has only one genetic parent, namely its prototype.

The regulation of the technologies mentioned above influences which child comes into existence. One of the underlying assumptions of this research is that one's genotype is an important factor for one's numerical identity, in that sense that a different set of genes, for example, caused by the recombination of a different ovum and a different spermatozoon, would result in a different person.[89] With regard to this, it could be argued that not all technologies I discuss here would necessarily result in a different child, and consequently prevent the future child's existence. For example, one could argue that minor genetic modifications or MRT do not result in a different child (and for this reason, banning these technologies should not be understood as preventing a child's existence). This argument is based on the assumption that altering one gene in the genome does not affect a person's identity, which I believe is not self-evident. Without going too much into this, I want to make three remarks regarding this statement. First, perhaps one altered gene does not have much impact on one's identity, personal traits, and life, but where do we draw the line? Second, removing a disease can result in different experiences, and accordingly in a different social identity.[90] Finally, as Scott and Wilkinson point out, the possibility to use these technologies will likely influence not only the decision to have a child, but also the moment of conception and therefore the specific recombination of a sperm and egg cell.[91] Therefore, even genetic technology that focuses on eliminating a monogenetic condition may have a large impact on a child's identity.

A similar point must be made with regard to prohibiting donor anonymity and securing a child's right to identifying information about its genetic parent. Theoretically, it is possible that a person who intends to donate does not change his or her mind when anonymous donation is no longer possible, and that the same recombination of egg and sperm takes place that would have if anonymity were possible. However, although there is no conclusive evidence, research indicates that lifting donor anonymity influences the willingness to

89 D. Parfit, *Reasons and persons*, Oxford, Clarendon Press, 1984, p. 351-352.

90 This point is illustrated by the eloquent young boy named David, who suffers from sickle cell anaemia and who is followed in the documentary 'Human Nature'. When he is asked whether he wishes that he never had the disease, he answers: "I don't wish I never had it, no. I don't think I would be me if I didn't have sickle cell." Human Nature (2019), 1:20:50-1:21:11.

91 R. Scott and S. Wilkinson, 'Germline genetic modification and identity: the mitochondrial and nuclear genomes.', *Oxford Journal of Legal Studies*, Vol. 37, No. 4, 2017, p. 908.

donate[92] and attracts different kinds of donors.[93] This suggests that the ban on donor anonymity may indeed influence one's willingness to donate. If a different donor is involved in the conception of the child, a different recombination of genetic material will occur, resulting in a different child. The ban on anonymous donor conception is thus somewhat of a grey area. Admittingly, the regulation does not necessarily affect which child is born but it may have this effect. Moreover, it remains possible to say that a specific *type* of child is prevented from coming into existence, namely the child of the anonymous donor. In conclusion, because donor anonymity is an important part of the question what we owe to the future child, and has the possibility to affect its existence, this particular regulatory framework is also discussed in this research.

1.5 OUTLINE

This study is structured as follows. Chapter 2 offers a legal analysis of the regulations on reproduction to determine which interests are attributed to the future child and how these interests are interpreted in the regulation. In order to come to a profound understanding of how this entity features in the regulations on reproduction, I conduct an analytical comparison of the regulatory frameworks of the Netherlands, Germany, and the United Kingdom. I do not only analyse the regulation itself, but also Memoranda, explanatory reports, and academic commentaries on the regulation in order to explore which interests are attributed to the future child, and how these interests are interpreted in the different legal systems.

The next four chapters each discuss and problematise one of the four assumptions about the future child. Chapters 3 and 4 deal with the topic of the future child's interests themselves, with the third chapter looking into the first assumption, namely that the various values at stake can be understood as interests of an individual entity. Since the regulatory frameworks, as addressed in chapter 2, do not explicate how these values are defined or interpreted in the regulation, chapter 3 aims to come to a deeper understanding of the core values underlying the regulations on reproduction. Therefore, in chapter 3, I take up where the legal analysis in chapter 2 ends by further elaborating the three core interests of the future child: harm, identity, and dignity. Chapter 2 reveals that the

92 Commissie evaluatie regelgeving, *Bereidheid tot donatie van sperma bij opheffing van de anonimiteitwaarborg van de donor*, Den Haag, 1999, p. 6, 40.

93 K. Daniels, 'Anonymity and openness and the recruitment of gamete donors. Part I: semen donors', *Human Fertility*, Vol. 10, No. 3, 2007b, p. 155; K. Daniels, 'Anonymity and openness and the recruitment of gamete donors. Part 2: Oocyte donors', *Human Fertility*, Vol. 10, No. 4, 2007a, p. 226. See also E. Jackson, *Medial Law. Text, Cases and Materials*, 4, Oxford, Oxford University Press, 2016, p. 832.

regulatory frameworks themselves do not offer a clearly demarcated definition of these core notions. Therefore, chapter 3 supplements the legal analysis by using legal-philosophical literature concerning these three core notions to further reconstruct which interpretation of harm, identity, and dignity underlies the regulations on reproduction. The aim of this analysis is to reveal the stakes involved in reproduction, that is, what it is that existing regulatory frameworks aim to protect.

In chapter 4, I continue my examination of the 'interests of the future child' construction through an assessment of the tenability of the second assumption about the future child. That is, the assumption that the future child has an interest in its own non-existence. By addressing the philosophical discussion of the so-called non-identity problem and so-called wrongful life claims, I intend to answer the question of whether and, if so, under which circumstances an interest in non-existence can be assumed.

In chapters 5 and 6, I shift the focus from the contents of the future child's interests (i.e. the question as to what is in the interest of the future child) to the future child's assumed subjectivity of interests, and problematise the assumptions concerning the future child's subjectivity. Chapter 5 examines the validity of the third assumption which entails that the future child can be understood as a legal subject of some sorts. To this end, it explores the concept of legal personality and discusses three interpretations of this concept which are then applied to the future child.

In chapter 6, I continue the discussion of the third assumption by departing from the traditional legal vocabulary and investigating an alternative form of subjectivity; the subject of legally relevant interests. In this chapter, I intend to answer what it means to be a subject of interests in law and whether the future child, who is characterised by its non-existence, can be understood as such a subject. In other words, in addition to assessing the third assumption, this chapter also addresses the tenability of the fourth assumption of the future child: namely, that the future child can be the subject of interests.

Chapters 2 to 6 answer the first part of the central question: can the future child (whose existence is prevented) be conceptualised adequately as a subject of interests? The analysis in these chapters reveals that conceiving the future child as a subject of interests is a problematic construction. It turns out that the 'interests of the future child' construction fails to justify various aspects of the regulations on reproduction. Moreover, conceiving the future child whose existence is prevented as a legal subject or a subject of interests appears to be inherently contradictory. For these reasons, I argue that the construction fails to meet the dimensions of fit and justification and as a result, is not an adequate construction through which to conceptualise the future child and make sense of what we owe to future people. This raises the question of how the future child should be conceptualised in order to take it into account in the regulations on reproduction. In chapter 7, I construct a new theoretical framework building on Jonas's ethics of responsibility. I argue that this theoretical framework is better equipped to address the future child whose existence is prevented, and the legal-philosophical and ethical values that form the foundation of the regulations on reproduction.

2 The Interests of the Future Child in the Regulations on Reproduction

2.1 Introduction

The regulation of reproductive technologies has resulted in the introduction of a new legal entity: the future child. Various regulatory frameworks refer to the interests of the future child as a justification for the regulatory choices that are made. Of course, the interests of the future child is not the only aspect taken into account to justify the regulatory frameworks. The future child's interests are balanced against other interests and values, including the interests of the prospective parents, infertile couples, and scientific and medical innovation.[1] Nonetheless, the future child's interests are often considered to be the paramount consideration,[2] and thus have become a key factor in the regulations on reproduction.

As explained in the introduction of this research, conceptualising the future child as a subject of interests and referring to the interests of the future child serves as an instrument to articulate and incorporate various ethical values. To determine whether this construction functions as an adequate conceptualisation, it is necessary to first get a better understanding of the interests and values it aims to represent. To this aim, in this chapter I analyse which interests are attributed to the future child and how these interests are interpreted in the

---

1 The UK parliament, for example, mentions "reproductive freedom and responsibility, patient safety, public accountability and professional autonomy" as fundamental notions for the regulation of reproduction in Britain. HL Deb (19 November 2007) vol. 696, col. 664. The Dutch Memorandum speaks of curing the ill or improving their health, and the well-being of infertile couples. *Kamerstukken II* 2000-2001, 27 423, nr. 3 (*Memorandum Embryo Act*), p. 5. In Dutch: "Wij hebben echter ook oog voor andere waarden die in de diverse situaties aan de orde zijn, zoals het welzijn van het toekomstige kind, genezing van zieken of bevordering van hun gezondheid en het welzijn van onvruchtbare paren." BT-Drs. 11/5460, vom 25.10.1989 (*Bill and Memorandum Embryo Protection Act*), p. 6. In Germany: "Zugleich wird er in der Freiheit der Forschung eine der Voraussetzungen jeder freiheitlichen Grundordnung sehen und das Bekenntnis zu dem in Artikel 5 Abs. 3. des Grundgesetzes verankerten Grundrecht deshalb besonders ernst nehmen müssen. Dabei wird er berücksichtigen, daß die Freiheit der Forschung jenen immanenten Schranken unterworfen ist, die sich aus der Verfassung selbst ergeben." Translation by LtH.

2 See for example, (Muster-)Richtlinie zur Durchführung der assistierten Reproduktion, Novelle 2006. Deutsches Ärzteblatt 2006; 103 [20], p. 1392-1393; BT-Drs. 11/5460, vom 25.10.1989 (*Bill and Memorandum Embryo Protection Act*), p. 3; Government Committee on the Reassessment of Parenthood (GCRP), *Child and Parents in the 21st Century*, The Hague, 2016, p. 9; Department of Health and Social Security, *Report of the Committee of Inquiry into Human Fertilisation and Embryology (Warnock Report)*, London, 1984, p. 1; M. Brazier, A. Campbell and S. Golombok, 1998, par 4.44.

regulations on reproduction. More particularly, I explore which interests are attributed to the future child in the regulatory frameworks that result in the future child's non-existence. With the help of this analysis, I aim to reconstruct the underlying values that this construction serves to articulate.

In order to make more general claims about the values underlying the regulations on reproduction, and to demonstrate that the 'interests of the future child' construction is not merely a Dutch phenomenon, I analyse and compare the regulations on reproduction of three different legal systems: the Netherlands, Germany and the United Kingdom. This analysis first demonstrates that the 'interests of the future child' construction is not an incidental phenomenon but appears in various legal systems. More importantly though, analysing three legal systems does not only help to make broader claims about the future child and the normative account of the human person that underlies the regulations on reproduction, but also serves to come to a better understanding of the interpretation of the interests of the future child in each legal system itself.[3] As explained, the regulations on reproduction confronts us with complex questions about our self-understanding as human persons, and involves values that can be of a metaphysical nature and are difficult to put in words. Approaching this hard-to-grasp topic from different angles, that is, from different legal systems, and elucidating the differences and similarities may help to reach a better understanding of what is at stake and why. In addition, a secondary purpose of the discussion of the three legal systems is that they also serve as a sources of examples and illustrations in the latter chapters.

In order to come to a profound understanding of its interests, the interests attributed to the future child in regulation serve as the measure of comparison (*tertium comparationis*) of this comparative research. That is, the three legal systems are compared with respect to which interests are attributed to the future child in the regulations on reproduction and how these interests are interpreted and explained by the regulator. The comparative method adopted in this chapter can best be understood as what Van Hoecke describes as the analytical method: "The analytical method is analysing (complex) legal concepts and rules (e.g., ownership) in different legal systems in such a way that common parts and

3 Various authors have pointed out that comparative legal research can be used, in addition to the harmonisation or evaluation of one's own legal system, to simply gain a better understanding of the legal system or a legal phenomenon. See for example, M. van Hoecke, 'Methodology of Comparative Legal Research', *Law and Method*, Vol. 2015, No. Oc-Dec, 2015, doi: 10.5553/REM/.000010, p. 2; H.P. Glenn, 'The aims of comparative law.' in: J.M. Smits (ed.), *Elgar Encyclopedia of Comparative Law*, Edward Elgard, Cheltenham, 2006, p. 58, 63. Of course, gaining a better understanding of the interests of the child serves its own purpose, namely the reconstruction of the ethical values that underly the regulation of reproduction.

differences are detected ...".[4] The aim of this chapter is to analyse a specific notion, i.e. the interests of the future child, and how this notion is interpreted by the legislator in three legal systems. Van Hoecke summarises the goal of this method as "to get a better understanding, at this deeper level, of the similarities and differences amongst different legal concepts and regulations".[5] By analysing how various regulatory frameworks and accompanying Memoranda or parliamentary debates refer to the future child's interests, explaining how they interpret these interests, and comparing these interpretations, I hope to discern various differences and similarities. The differences and similarities in the interpretations contribute not only to a better understanding of what is deemed to be in the future child's interests, but also at a deeper level to come to a better understanding of the underlying values this construction is supposed to protect.

In the remainder of this introduction, I further elaborate on my choice for selecting the Dutch, German, and UK legal systems for comparison. In doing so, I give a bit more background information on how these legal systems approach the regulation of bioethical issues and reproductive technologies in particular. Moreover, I also explain which sources I use for the analytical comparative research. After that, in the rest of this chapter, I explore which interests are attributed to the future child by the regulators of these three legal systems and how these interests are interpreted in the regulation. A closer look at the regulation reveals that three main interests can be identified. These are: the interest to be free from harm, the interest in forming an identity and the interest in human dignity. I address each of these three main interests of the future child in separate sections. The first part of each section analyses the regulatory frameworks of each legal system that refer to that specific interest of the future child. The second part uncovers the similarities and, if relevant, the differences between the different legal systems and discusses them in order to come to an overall interpretation of the interest that is discussed in that section.

2.1.1 Selection of Legal Systems

In order to gain a better understanding of the interests of the future child, and consequently of the ethical values that underly the regulations on reproduction, I analyse how this concept features in three legal systems: the Netherlands, Germany and the United Kingdom. These three legal systems have been chosen for this analysis for the following reasons. The aim of the comparative analysis is to gain a broader understanding of the interests of the future child and what we owe to future people according to the chosen

4 van Hoecke, 2015, p. 28.
5 van Hoecke, 2015, p. 16.

regulations. Since regulating reproductive technologies touches upon various bioethical questions, analysing interpretations from legal systems with different bioethical orientations helps to gain a broader understanding of the future child's interests. Despite the fact that the Netherlands, Germany, and the United Kingdom are geographically close to each other and that their regulations on reproduction show great similarities, their attitudes towards reproductive issues differs significantly. Germany remains exemplary of a legal system that has adopted a more restrictive attitude toward biotechnologies. Technologies that are more accepted in other countries, such as egg cell donation and surrogacy, remain prohibited, although there are signs that changes are gradually taking place.[6] The United Kingdom, however, has been a world leader in the field of reproductive biotechnology due to its permissive attitude and regulations. For example, it was the first country to explicitly allow and regulate mitochondrial replacement therapy and it seems more open to allow new technologies such as germline modification. The Dutch attitude towards biotechnology can be understood as a combination of the German and UK approach: it is not as restrictive as Germany yet less permissive than the United Kingdom. Because the three legal systems represent different places on the bioethical spectrum, they constitute an interesting case study for understanding how these legal systems interpret the interests of the future child. The analysis shows that despite the different attitudes towards regulating biotechnology, all legal systems attach significant value to the interests of the future child.[7] Moreover, the three main interests of the future child are invoked in all three legal systems and the interpretations of these interests show important similarities. This shows that the interests of the future child has a common core in legal systems with varying bioethical perspectives.

Before addressing the interests of the future child, this chapter first offers some background information on the three legal systems. It addresses the most significant aspects and differences of their regulations on reproduction and discusses which sources are used for this analysis.

6 FDP-politician Katrin Helling-Plahr has proposed to changes the Embryo Protection Act in order to allow egg cell donation and surrogacy. 'FDP-Politikerin für Legalisierung von Leihmutterschaften', Aertzeblatt.de 12 August 2019. Also, the German Ethics Council has stated that germline modification is not "ethically out of the question." Deutscher Ethikrat, press release 03/2019.

7 See for example, the United Kingdom: HL Deb (19 November 2007) vol. 696, col. 664. "How best to safeguard the welfare of children"; for the Netherlands: *Kamerstukken II* 2000-2001, 27 423, nr. 3 (*Memorandum Embryo Act*) p. 3, 5, 14; NVOG Modelprotocol "Mogelijke morele contra-indicaties bij vruchtbaarheidsbehandelingen". For Germany: BT-Drs. 11/5460, vom 25.10.1989 (*Bill and Memorandum Embryo Protection Act*), p. 6; (Muster-)Richtlinie zur Durchführung der assistierten Reproduktion, Novelle 2006. Deutsches Ärzteblatt 2006; 103 [20], p. 1393.

2.1.1.1 Germany

Germany takes a more restrictive approach towards reproductive technologies. Characteristic for the German legal system is the strong legal protection of unborn life and the embryo. Although legal personhood starts at the moment of birth[8] (like in the UK and the Netherlands), some fundamental rights can be applied to the nasciturus (i.e. the embryo after nidation[9]). The nidated embryo has partial legal subjectivity regarding fundamental rights. The German Constitutional Court has ruled that in any case from the moment of nidation, unborn life falls within the scope of Articles 1 I and 2 II of the German Constitution, meaning the human embryo has human dignity and a right to life.[10] The UK legal system, on the contrary, has explicitly denied the latter.[11] It must be noted though, that German constitutional scholars disagree on the question as to whether unborn life before nidation, and in particular the embryo in vitro, is entitled to the same protection.[12] As far as the Embryo Protection Act is concerned, it does not give a definition

8 §1 BGB "Die Rechtsfähigkeit des Menschen beginnt mit der Vollendung der Geburt."

9 Nidation is the process in which a fertilised egg adheres to the wall of the uterus. At this moment, the embryo can no longer divide itself into two individuals, as in the case of identical twins.

10 BVerfGE 25 February 1975 - 39, 1 (*Schwangerschaftsabbruch I*); BVerfGE 28 May 1993 - 88, 203 (*Schwangerschaftsabbruch II*). See also W. Höfling in: M. Sachs, *Grundgesetz Kommentar*, 7nd ed, München, Verlag C.H. Beck 2014 Art. 1, nr. 62 (human dignity) and Art. 2, nr 144 (right to life). In addition, Karnein pointed out that in their decisions on abortion, the constitutional Court also declared that an embryo has human dignity and the right to life. A.J. Karnein, *A theory of unborn life. From abortion to genetic manipulation*, New York, Oxford University Press, 2012, p. 45. According to the German civil code, legal personality, that is the full capacity to be the subject of legal rights, starts at birth. §1 BGB: "Die Rechtsfähigkeit des Menschen beginnt mit der Vollendung der Geburt." See also J.C. Joerden, 'Menschenwürde als juridischer Begriff.' in: J.C. Joerden, E. Hilgendorf and F. Thiele (eds.), *Menschenwürde und Medizin. Ein interdisziplinäres Handbuch*, Duncker & Humblot, Berlin, 2013, p. 236.

11 The Court of Appeal has ruled that an embryo does not have a right to life as protected by Art 2 ECtHR. *Evans v. Amicus Healthcare Ltd* [2004] EWCA Civ 727, CA.

12 Some argue that the embryo after nidation deserves more protection than the embryo in vitro and that the latter is not included in Articles 1 I and 2 II GG. See for example, M. Herdegen in: T. Maunz and G. Dürig, *Grundgesetz-Kommentar. Band 1 Texte Art. 1-5*, 63rd ed, München, Verlag C.H. Beck 2016 GG Art. 1 Abs. 1, nr 60. "Danach reicht der Würdeanspruch des Embryos nach Implantation und Nidation weiter als beim Embryo *in vitro*."; H.D. Jarass in: H.D. Jarass and B. Pieroth, *Grundgesetz für die Bundesrepubliek Deutschland. Kommentar*, 14 ed, München, Verlag C.H. Beck 2016 Art. 1 Abs. 1, nr. 9: "In der Zeit zwischen Befruchtung und Nidation dürfte das Prinzip der Menschenwürde Vorwirkungen entfalten (…) Dieser Schutz ist aber nicht absoluter Natur, sondern dem Prinzipiencharakter Entsprechend ein bloßer Abwägungsschutz. Auch besteht insoweit kein subjektiv-rechtlicher Schutz und damit kein Grundrechtsträger."; Art. 2, Abs. 2, nr. 85: "Extrakorporal erzeugtes Leben dürfte daher vor der Einpflanzung in die Gebärmutter nur begrenzt geschützt sein."
Others argue that the protection of life starts from the moment of conception instead of the nidation, regardless of whether it pertains to the embryo in vitro or the embryo in utero. See for example, P. Kunig in: I. von Münch and P. Kunig, *Grundgesetz Kommentar*, 6th ed, München, Verlag C.H. Beck 2012, Art. 2, nr. 49: "Grundrechtlich geschütztes Leben beginnt mit der Verschmelzung von Ei- und Samenzelle, nicht also erst mit der Nidation, so dass auch extrakorporale Befruchtung Leben zur Entstehung bringt. Im Zeitpunkt der Konzeption setzt die Schutzverantwortlichkeit des Staates ebenso ein wie die eigene Grundrechtspersönlichkeit des Gezeugten." C. Enders in: K. Stern and F. Becker, *Grundrechte-Kommentar. Die Grundrechte des Grundgesetzes mit ihren europäischen Bezügen*, 2nd ed, Köln, Carl Heymanns Verlag

of the beginning of human life and whether human dignity and the right to life is similarly applicable to the embryo in vitro. However, the Act does not prohibit the destruction of the embryo in vitro nor does it entail an obligation to preserve the embryo in vitro.[13]

Germany's restrictive approach comes to the fore in its initial ban on PGT,[14] which was lifted only in 2010, and its precautionary approach towards the possibility of split motherhood.[15] The Memorandum to the Embryo Protection Act deems split motherhood, when the child's genetic and gestational mother are not the same, potentially harmful to the child[16] and therefore undesirable. As a result, the use of reproductive technologies for the purpose of, for example, surrogacy[17] or egg cell donation[18] is not allowed.[19] Due to this restrictive attitude towards reproductive technologies, the German legal system is an interesting case study to explore how the 'interests of the future child' is interpreted.

2016 Artikel 2, nr. 57: "Der Lebensschutz des Art. 2 Abs. 2 S. 1 GG erstreckt sich daher auf alle Entwicklungsphasen des ge- oder erzeugten (Menschen-)Lebens (ob in vivo oder in vitro) vor der Nidation, der Implantation oder der Verbringung in ein funktionales Äquivalent."; Sachs, 2014 Art. 1 I GG, nr 62: "Auch im pränatalen Stadium – ob in vivo oder in vitro – ist der Mensch damit Grundrechtsubjekt und Träger der Menschenwürde."

A third perspective entails that human dignity can only be attributed after birth, implying that the embryo does not have human dignity at all. See for example, H. Dreier in: H. Dreier, *Grundgesetz Kommentar. Band 1, Präambel, Artikel 1-19*, 3rd ed, Tübingen, Mohr Siebeck 2014 Art. 1 I, nr. 66, "Voraussetzung ist allein die Existenz eines geborenen Menschen mit prinzipieller (nicht aktueller) Fähigkeit zur vernünftigen Selbstbestimmung, wie wir sie jedenfalls jedem lebenden menschlichen Wesen konzedieren müssen." Dreier rejects the ruling of the German Constitutional Court, claiming "Diese Auffassung ist indes schon deswegen defizitär, weil essichbei diesen kategorischen Formulierungen in Ermangelung einer normative wertenden Begründung um einen biologistisch-naturalistischen Fahlschluß handelt. Eine solche Biologisierung der Menschenwürde geht grundsätzlich fahl. Daß etwas im biologisch-naturwissenschaftlichen Sinne menschliches Leben darstellt, macht dieses noch nicht zwingend zum Träger der Menschenwürde –einmal ganz abgesehen davon daß in Art. 1 I GG von der Würde *des Menschen* und in Art. 2 II 1 GG von *jeder* die Rede ist, mithin von Individuen und nicht von menschlichem Leben allgemein." Art. 1 I nr. 68.

13 Karnein, 2012, p. 54-55. H.-L. Günther, J. Taupitz and P. Kaiser, *Embryonenschutzgesetz. Juristischer Kommentar mit medizinisch-naturwissenschaftlichen Grundlagen*, 2, Stuttgart, Kohlhammer, 2014, p. 120.

14 Since the amendment of the Embryo Protection Act, preimplantation testing for a 'severe inheritable illness' (Schwerwiegende Erbkrankheit) is allowed. The Memorandum states that this notion includes both monogenetic disorders (monogen bedingte Erkrankungen) and chromosomal defects (Chromosomenstörungen). Therefore, under German law the PGD regulation covers both PGD/PGT-M and PGS/PGT-A. BT-Drs. 11/5460, vom 25.10.1989 (*Bill and Memorandum Embryo Protection Act*), p. 8. See also Günther, Taupitz and Kaiser, 2014, p. 288.

15 In German: "Gespaltenen Mutterschaft". BT-Drs. 11/5460, p. 1, 6.

16 This point was once again emphasised by the German Government in the ECtHR case *S.H. e.a. v. Austria*. ECtHR 3 November 2011 ECLI:CE:ECHR:2011:1103JUD005781300 (*S.H. e.a. v. Austria*), par. 52-55.

17 §1 abs. 1 nr. 7 Embryonenschutzgesetz.

18 §1 abs. 1 nrs 1, 2, 6 Embryonenschutzgesetz.

19 FDP-politician Katrin Helling-Plahr has proposed to change the Embryo Protection Act in order to allow egg cell donation and surrogacy.. 'FDP-Politikerin für Legalisierung von Leihmutterschaften', Aertzeblatt.de 12 August 2019. At the moment of writing, no amendment was proposed yet.

2.1.1.2 United Kingdom

The approach taken in the United Kingdom differs strongly from the approach of the German legal system. The regulation of reproductive biotechnology in the United Kingdom emphasises the importance of innovation, resulting in a permissive approach and allowing the UK to take a leading role in exploring new technologies. The UK was the first country in which IVF was successfully conducted and also the first country that regulated and licensed mitochondrial replacement therapy.[20] In addition, the UK is more liberal than the Netherlands or Germany in the application of other technologies, for instance, allowing HLA-tissue typing for the sole purpose of creating a saviour sibling.[21] This permissive approach might partly be explained by the UK's apparent preference for consequentialist arguments, such as the safety of technologies and the possible dangerous consequences they entail for the future child or society, rather than on deontological arguments, which appeal to an inherent value of human life.[22] Whereas the Netherlands[23] and Germany[24] explicitly mention human dignity and respect for human life as one of the guiding principles for their governance of reproduction, the United Kingdom is clearly more focused on scientific innovation. As the parliamentary discussion shows, one of the key aims of the HFE Act is "to increase the scope of legitimate embryo research activities, subject to controls."[25] During the House of Lords debate, it is stated that the Act intends "to keep regulation abreast of ground-breaking scientific advancements, including embryonic

---

20 The Memorandum to the Dutch Embryo Act explicitly states that mitochondrial replacement therapy or mitochondrial donation is not included in the ban on genetic modification, and consequently, this type of treatment is not necessarily banned. So far, this topic has not been regulated in the Netherlands.

21 In the Netherlands, HLA-typing is only accepted as additional selection and in Germany, HLA- typing is not allowed at all. In the UK, HLA-typing is only allowed to create a suitable donor for a sick sibling and not for another family member. According to Emily Jackson, this is mainly based on practical reasons rather than moral objections, as the success rate to create a suitable donor for a sibling is 1 in 4, while the chances to create suitable donor for another family member are much lower. Jackson, 2016, p. 860.

22 See for example, M.K. Smith, 'The Human Fertilisation and Emrbyology Act 2008: restrictions on the creation of "saviour siblings" and the relevance of the harm principle.', *New Genetics and Society*, Vol. 32, No. 2, 2013, p. 159-160 for how in particular the harm principle forms one of the most important principles in the regulation concerning ARTs. Also Brownsword and Beyleveld have noted that UK law is "... less explicitly committed to the value of human dignity (as constraint)". Beyleveld and Brownsword, 2012, p. 34.

23 *Kamerstukken II* 2000-2001, 27 423, nr. 3 (*Memorandum Embryo Act*), p. 5. In Dutch: "Als algemeen uitgangspunten hebben wij steeds genomen de menselijke waardigheid en het beginsel van respect voor menselijk leven in het algemeen."

24 BT-Drs. 11/5460, vom 25.10.1989 (*Bill and Memorandum Embryo Protection Act*), p. 6. In German: "Bei seiner Abwägung wird der Gesetzgeber vor allem der Wertenentscheidung des Grundgesetzes zugunsten der Menschenwürde und des Lebens Rechnung zu tragen haben."

25 HL Deb (8 November 2007) vol. 696, col. 142. Other aims mentioned were "to ensure that all human embryos outside the body – whatever the process used in their creation – are subject to regulation; to clarify the regulation of 'inter-species' embryos for research; to impose a statutory ban on the sex selection of offspring for non-medical reasons; [and] to recognise same-sex couples as legal parents of children conceived through the use of donated sperm, eggs or embryos" HL Deb (8 November 2007) vol. 696, col. 141, 142.

stem cell research for the treatment of serious diseases"[26] and that the 2008 Bill was needed "to ensure that legitimate medical and scientific uses of human reproductive technology can continue to flourish."[27] Nonetheless, even within the UK approach there remains room for other values. The human embryo, for example, is not a mere thing that is at full disposal of prospective parents and stem cell scientists. On the contrary, the Warnock report concluded that even though the embryo is not similar to a living person, it still "should be afforded some protection in law."[28] Overall, the basic principles in the UK legal frameworks on reproduction differ strongly from the German legal system. This gives rise to the question of how this affects the interpretation of the interests of the future child.

2.1.1.3 The Netherlands

The Dutch legal framework on reproductive technologies as expressed in the regulations on reproduction can be described as a combination of the German and UK perspectives on biotechnology. While the Dutch legal system is clearly more open than the UK to abstract notions such as human dignity, it is also less reluctant than Germany to regulate and allow new technologies. As a result, surrogacy and egg cell donation are not prohibited in the Netherlands, but they are subjected to restrictions. Moreover, the Memorandum of the Dutch Embryo Act explicitly states that mitochondrial donation does not fall under the ban on germline modification.[29] MRT is not explicitly regulated or allowed but as it does not fall within the scope of the ban on germline modification, it may be allowed in the future. At the same time, the Dutch regulatory framework is less permissive than the

26 HL Deb (8 November 2007) vol. 696, col. 231.

27 HL Deb (19 November 2007) vol. 696, col. 665.

28 Department of Health and Social Security, 1984, p. 63. This gradualist approach is supported by the House of Commons Science and Technology Committee: "While this gradualist approach to the status of the embryo may cause difficulties in the drafting of legislation, we believe that it represents the most ethically sound and pragmatic solution and one which permits in vitro fertilisation and embryo research within certain constraints set out in legislation." House of Commons Science and Technology Committee, *Human Reproductive Technologies and the Law. Fifth Report of Session 2004-2005*, 2005p. 16. Also in the parliamentary debates it was emphasised that "human embryos cannot be created and used lightly." HL Deb (19 November 2007) vol. 696, col. 665. What is certain is that the human embryo under UK law is not a legal person, see M. Stauch and K. Wheat, *Text, cases and materials on medical law and ethics*, 5, London, Routledge, 2015, p. 332). The human embryo is also not a mere thing, as the HFE Act imposes several restrictions regarding the use of embryos. Although this approach appears to be similar to the Dutch perspective on the human embryo, the restrictions regarding the use of embryos under UK law are less strict. For example, the creation of human-animal hybrid for research purposes is allowed under certain conditions, and so is creating embryos specifically for research purposes.

29 *Kamerstukken II* 2000-2001, 27 423, nr. 3 (*Memorandum Embryo Act*), p. 46. Unfortunately, the Memorandum does not specify why it differentiates mitochondrial replacement therapy from other forms of germline modification.

UK framework by not allowing the creation of human embryos and human-animal hybrids for research purposes[30] and not allowing non-additional tissue typing.[31]

The Netherlands is of special interest for another reason. The Dutch Supreme Court has acknowledged the possibility of a legal interest in one's own non-existence, in the landmark wrongful life case of *Baby Kelly*.[32] In this and other wrongful life cases, the central question was whether the claimant was entitled to compensation for the fact that she was born into a life severely affected by an genetic illness, whereas if the hospital had not failed to conduct prenatal testing, she would never have been born at all. In the case of Baby Kelly, the Court agreed that the claimant was entitled to compensation for the fact that she was brought into existence as the result of a mistake made by the hospital. Other countries have rejected the legal wrongful life claim, including the UK[33] and Germany.[34] The highest courts of latter two countries argued that non-existence can never be preferred over life. The German Federal Court of Justice categorically rejected the wrongful life claim, arguing that "human life, including unborn life from the moment of nidation, is highly valuable and absolutely worth preserving, and its value cannot be subjected to the judgements of others."[35] Moreover, the Court argued that everyone has to accept his or her life as it is given by nature (including any impairments and disabilities) and that these events caused by fate rather that human actions fall outside the scope of the legal system.[36] As a result, a child cannot have a right to its own non-existence.[37] The UK Court too referred to the

30 In 2016, the State Secretary of Health submitted a proposal to amend the Embryo act on this point. This proposal was withdrawn by her successor. See *Kamerstukken II* 2015/16, 29 323, nr. 101 and *Kamerstukken II* 2016/17, 29 323, nr. 110 for the proposals of the State Secretary, and *Kamerstukken II* 2017-2018, 30 486, nr. 19 for the withdrawal of the proposal.

31 For more information on this, see section 2.4.1.1.

32 Hoge Raad 18 March 2005 ECLI:NL:HR:2005:AR5213 (*Baby Kelly*).

33 (*McKay v. Essex Area Health Authority*) [1982] QB 1166.

34 BGH 18 January 1983 - BGHZ 86, 240 (*Wrongful life*). The wrongful birth claim has been successful, allowing parents to claim damages for the child's upbringing.

35 BGH 18 January 1983 - BGHZ 86, 240 (*Wrongful life*) (40): "Das menschliche Leben, das nach Abschluß der Nidation auch den Nasciturus umfaßt (BVerfG aaO S. 37), ist ein höchstrangiges Rechtsgut und absolut erhaltungswürdig. Das Urteil über seinen Wert steht keinem Dritten zu."

36 BGH 18 January 1983 - BGHZ 86, 240 (*Wrongful life*) (48): "Vielmehr hält der Senat dafür, daß in Fällen wie dem vorliegenden überhaupt die Grenzen erreicht und überschritten sind, innerhalb derer eine rechtliche Anspruchsregelung tragbar ist. Der Mensch hat grundsätzlich sein Leben so hinzunehmen, wie es von der Natur gestaltet ist, und hat keinen Anspruch auf seine Verhütung oder Vernichtung durch andere". See also R. Zuck in: M. Quaas, R. Zuck and T. Clemens, *Medizinrecht*, 3rd ed, München, C.H. Beck 2014, §68 Einzelfelder der Biomedizin, nr 129.

37 BGH 18 January 1983 - BGHZ 86, 240 (*Wrongful life*) (48). According to Riedel, the child also does not have an *interest* in protection against a harmful existence. U. Riedel, *„Kind als Schaden". Die höchstrichterliche Rechtsprechung zur Arzthaftung für den Kindesunterhalt bei unerwünschter Geburt eines gesunden, kranken oder behinderten Kindes*, Frankfurt am Main, Mabuse-Verlag GmbH, 2003, p. 147. As discussed below, such an interest is implicitly assumed in other contexts. The Dutch Supreme Court agreed with the assumption

universal value of life as a reason for not recognising the wrongful life-claim. In *McKay v. Essex Area Health Authority*, it reasoned that life itself cannot be considered to be damage and that doctors do not owe the unborn child a duty to prevent its birth. As one of the judges, Ackner LJ put it: "I cannot accept that the common law duty of care to a person can involve, without specific legislation to achieve this end, the legal obligation to that person, whether or not in utero, to terminate his existence. Such a proposition runs wholly contrary to the concept of the sanctity of human life."[38] However, this rejection of the wrongful life claim is at odds with the regulation of ARTs. Emily Jackson, for example, has pointed out that the claim that life is always better than non-existence does not correspond with the future child's welfare assessment. After all, this assessment serves to withhold fertility treatment and thereby prevent a child's birth if it is expected that the child will suffer severe harm.[39] A similar point has been made by Taupitz, who argues that if one assumes that all life is worth living, the best interests or the well-being of the future child cannot serve as a justification for measures that prevent its existence, such as the ban on egg cell donation. If all life is worth living, one cannot be harmed by being brought into existence.[40] Moreover, both Jackson and Scott have suggested that section 1A of the Congenital Disabilities (Civil Liability) Act 1976, which was added in 1991, does allow for a wrongful life claim now that a child can hold a medical professional liable for selecting an embryo with a genetic defect during a PGT procedure.[41]

---

that the child in question cannot have a right to its own non-existence. As explained in chapter 6, the Court ruled that the child could have an *interest* in its own non-existence.

38 (*McKay v. Essex Area Health Authority*) [1982] QB 1166, [1188].

39 Jackson, 2016, p. 813. The claim that life is always better is also at odds with court rulings stating that sometimes prolonging life is not in the patient's best interests. Moreover, the Congenital Disabilities (Civil Liability) Act 1976, which was enacted before the *McKay* case, does allow a child to claim damages caused by events that occurred before the child's conception. However, during the House of Commons debate it was stressed that the Act did not allow a wrongful life claim, as this Act would only allow a child to claim compensation for its congenital disabilities, but not for its whole life. HC Deb (6 February 1976) vol. 904, col. 1593.

40 Günther, Taupitz and Kaiser, 2014, p. 183-184; See also R. Müller-Terpitz in: A. Spickhoff, *Medizinrecht*, 1st ed, München, Verlag C.H. Beck 2011, ESchG, §1, nr 7.

41 R. Scott, 'Reconsidering 'Wrongful Life' in England after Thirty Years: Legislative Mistakes and Unjustifiable Anomalies', *Cambridge Law Journal*, Vol. 72, No. 1, 2013, p. 16; Jackson, 2016, p. 769. Section 1A(1) of the Congenital Disabilities (Civil Liability) Act reads: In any case where

a. a child carried by a woman as the result of the placing in her of an embryo or of sperm and eggs or her artificial insemination *is born disabled*,

b. the disability results from an act or omission *in the course of the selection*, or the keeping or use outside the body, of the embryo carried by her or of the gametes used to bring about the creation of the embryo, and

c. a person is under this section answerable to the child in respect of the act or omission,

the child's disabilities are to be regarded as damage resulting from the wrongful act of that person and actionable accordingly at the suit of the child. Italics added by LtH.

2.1.2 *Regulations on Reproduction*

In order to gain a proper understanding of which interests are attributed to the future child and how these interests are interpreted, I analyse a wide variety of documents. The discussion of the regulatory frameworks does not only include legislation, but also other regulatory documents such as professional codes and guidelines. Moreover, where possible, also the Memoranda accompanying the legislative proposals are assessed, because they offer important insights into the motivations and choices made concerning the regulatory frameworks. Because the United Kingdom does not have a tradition of Memoranda, parliamentary discussions are analysed instead, in order to gain insight into the way in which the interests of the future child are interpreted. Throughout this chapter case law and commentaries on the regulations are occasionally discussed in order to offer more background information or insight into the reasoning.

In the Netherlands, the Embryo Act from 2002 is one of the most important documents on the regulation of reproduction. This act covers the most important topics regarding the embryo in vitro and the possibilities for (selective) reproduction. It deals with, amongst other things, sex selection, the ban on gamete commodification, and the ban on human cloning and genetic modification. In addition to the Embryo Act, the Donor Information Artificial Fertilisation Act, also from 2002, is also relevant for assessing the interests of the future child. This act covers the ban on anonymous gamete donation. Topics that are not banned but require more detailed regulation, such as PGT and access to fertility treatment, are addressed in additional regulation; the criteria for PGT are listed in a minister's decree[42] and professional guidelines[43] provide rules on when fertility treatment can be refused. All these examples of regulation are accompanied with Memoranda, which explain the motivation behind the regulatory framework and lists arguments to justify these choices. As these Memoranda can be understood as the voice of the regulator, together with the regulation itself they will form the primary source for this analysis of the regulatory framework.

In Germany, embryology and artificial reproduction were addressed by the legislator over a decade earlier in the Embryo Protection Act[44] from 1990. The act offers the embryo protection against misuse[45] and bans several actions with regard to human embryos, such

42 Regeling van de staatssecretaris van Volksgezondheid, Welzijn en Sport van 16 februari 2009, nr. CZ-TSZ-2912089, houdende houdende regels ten aanzien van preïmplantatie genetische diagnostiek (PGD), (*Stcrt.* 2009, 42) (*Ministerial decree PGD*).

43 NVOG Modelprotocol "Mogelijke morele contra-indicaties bij vruchtbaarheidsbehandelingen".

44 "Gesetz zum Schutz von Embryonen" or "Embryonenschutzgesetz".

45 Karnein, 2012, p. 54-55; Günther, Taupitz and Kaiser, 2014, p. 120.

as human cloning, sex selection, gene editing, and the creation of human-animal hybrids. Moreover, § 1 ESchG lists several prohibited actions with regard to IVF treatments and bans egg cell donation and surrogacy. In 2011, the Embryo Protection Act was amended, in order to regulate PGT. This was done after the Federal Court of Justice decided one year earlier that embryo selection under certain circumstances can be in accordance with the ratio of the Act, namely when it aims to achieve a successful pregnancy.[46] Besides the Embryo Protection Act, other pieces of regulation are important as well in the context of regulating reproduction. Specific rules with regard to fertility treatments are regulated in the Code of Conduct on assisted reproduction: the "(Muster-)Richtlinie zur Durchführung der assistierten Reproduktion" issued by the German Medical Association (*Bundesärztekammer*). This Code of Conduct is not a legally binding document but provides further guidelines for the application of fertility treatments. Although this Code already entailed a duty to register the information of the donor in cases of heterologous treatments and sperm donation, new legislation on this topic was enacted in 2017. The new Sperm Donor Registry Act[47] prescribes that the information of sperm donors must be collected in a national databank, so that the information is accessible for donor conceived children. By doing so, this Act aims to secure the future child's right to knowledge and information about its origins which is – on a constitutional basis – protected by the right of personality that follows from Article 2 I GG in conjunction with Article 1 I GG. Like in the Netherlands, the German regulation is accompanied by a Memorandum which explains why the regulation is as it is. These, in combination with scientific commentaries, give a comprehensive insight in which interests German law attributes to the future child.

The UK's regulation of reproduction is mostly codified in the Human Fertilisation and Embryology Act from 1990. Several years before the enactment, a special committee was established to explore developing artificial reproductive technologies such as IVF and to develop principles for the regulation of this topic. The results of this inquiry were published in what came to be known as the Warnock Report,[48] which is considered to be the basis for the later Human Fertilisation and Embryology Act. In 2008, several important amendments were made in order to enable the Act to respond better to the challenges that resulted from scientific developments. The Act establishes a regulatory body, the Human Fertilisations and Embryology Authority (HFEA) which issues additional regulation on fertility treatments and embryo research in the form of the Code of Practice and Directions.[49] The

46 BGH 6 July 2010 - 5 StR386/09 (*PGD*), par. 14, 30.

47 "Der Gesetz zur Regelung des Rechts auf Kenntnis der Abstammung bei heterologer Verwendung von Samen" or "der Samenspenderregistergesetz". This act focuses on sperm donation only; egg cell donation is not allowed in Germany.

48 Department of Health and Social Security, 1984.

49 At least directions are binding: Jackson, 2016, p. 804.

UK does not have Memoranda that explain the motivations and justifications behind the regulation. Therefore, in order to understand why certain regulatory decisions are made and which values and interests the regulation aims to protect, other documents need to be analysed. This chapter scrutinises the hansard on the 2008 amendments. Also, other parliamentary discussions are taken into account when the topic at hand was not addressed during the 2008 amendments.[50] Besides the parliamentary discussions, this analysis also includes reports from governmental committees that were published during the regulatory process and addressed the amended topics. Finally, to gain a more complete understanding of how the regulation invokes and interprets the future child's interest, reports and documents of the HFEA are analysed, as the authority fleshes out the legislation in additional regulation and issues the licences for treatment in concrete cases.

2.2 The Interest to be free from Harm

2.2.1 *The Regulations*

The first interest that the regulations on reproduction attributes to the future child, is the interest to be free from harm. Different regulatory frameworks prescribe that the future child's welfare or well-being must be taken into account.[51] As will be explained below, this duty can be understood as a responsibility to assess whether the future child runs a risk of being harmed and to avoid (severe) harm to the child.[52] A child can be harmed by events that occurred before its birth (prenatal harm), but also by events that took place before its

50 In particular the discussion of reproductive cloning has been addressed in previous parliamentary discussions. The HFE Act 2008 repealed the Human Reproductive Cloning Act, but this topic was not further elaborated on during the 2008 parliamentary debates. Since the essence of the regulation had not changed, the UK government saw no reason to further elaborate on this topic.

51 See for example, *Kamerstukken II* 2000-2001, 27 423, nr. 3 (*Memorandum Embryo Act*) p. 5. In Dutch: "welzijn van het toekomstige kind". NVOG Modelprotocol "Mogelijke morele contra-indicaties bij vruchtbaarheidsbehandelingen" p. 2. In Dutch: "In uitzonderlijke gevallen kan bezorgdheid over het welzijn van het toekomstige kind een reden zijn voor het stellen van een contra-indicatie voor de vruchtbaarheidsbehandeling". Section 13(5) HFE Act 2008: "A woman shall not be provided with treatment services unless account has been taken of the welfare of any child who may be born as a result of the treatment (...)." (Muster-)Richtlinie zur Durchführung der assistierten Reproduktion, Novelle 2006. Deutsches Ärzteblatt 2006; 103 [20], p. 1393. In German: "...trägt die Ärztin/der Arzt für das Wohl des mit ihrer/seiner medizinischen Assistenz erzeugten Kindes eine besondere Verantwortung."

52 The assessment of well-being is often explained in the regulation as a duty to prevent harm. See for example, (Muster-)Richtlinie zur Durchführung der assistierten Reproduktion, Novelle 2006. Deutsches Ärzteblatt 2006; 103 [20], p. 1393. In German: "Die ärztliche Pflicht, zum Wohl der Patienten zu handeln und Schaden zu vermeiden, bezieht sich auf die Mutter und auf die erwünschten Kinder." HFEA Code of Practice 8th Edition 2009 (last revised 2017), Section 8.10; NVOG Modelprotocol "Mogelijke morele contra-indicaties bij vruchtbaarheidsbehandelingen", p. 2. In Dutch: "Artsen moeten afzien van hulp bij voortplanting als naar hun mening sprake is van een groot risico op ernstige schade voor het kind."

conception. Or rather, some forms of harm are intrinsically liked to the child's conception and therefore its existence. An example that comes to mind is a genetic condition that causes severe disabilities. As severe disabilities impact the future child's well-being, it is not surprising that this interest plays a pivotal role in the regulation on preimplantation genetic testing. With the help of this technology an embryo is screened on chromosomal or genetic defects before implantation in the womb in order to ensure the birth of a healthy child. However, the risk of harm can also be constituted by social factors. In recent years, there has been increased attention on so-called *irresponsible parenthood* which exposes the child to the risk of neglect or abuse. Illustrative of this is the regulation on access to fertility treatments, where the lack of capabilities to adequately take care of a child is a contra-indication; or the Dutch discussion on the possibility of compulsory contraception as a (preconceptual) measure of child protection.

2.2.1.1 The Netherlands

In the Dutch legal system, the well-being of the child forms one of the leading principles for the regulation of PGT. While the regulatory frameworks and Memoranda seem to solely focus on PGD,[53] the 2020 annual report of PGT Nederland indicates that PGT is also used to screen for chromosomal disorders,[54] and that the same criteria for PGD are used.[55] As a form of selective reproduction, the regulation of this technique is a sensitive matter. Although it may be used to conceive a healthy child, critics such as Habermas have argued that as a result of this technology the creation of human life becomes conditional or instrumental: only the embryos with the desired genetic characteristics are allowed to further develop.[56] The future child's interest in being free from harm is used as a measuring stick to determine the acceptability of the technology. That is, the use of this technology is restricted and guided by the principle that it must benefit the child who results from the treatment: "PGD is only indicated if this technological intervention (...) in any case benefits the future child itself."[57] As a result, embryo selection is permissible if the future

53 The regulatory frameworks seem solely focused on preimplantation the genetic diagnosis, i.e. screening for a monogenetic disorder. In 2006, the State Secretary briefly commented upon PGS. While some clinics abroad conducted PGS during every IVF treatment in order to increase the success rate of the treatment, the Dutch State Secretary did not deem it reasonable to use PGS as a standard add-on for IVF. *Kamerstukken II* 2005-2006, 30 300 XVI, nr. 136 (*first explanatory letter PGD*), p. 1, 2, 9. Using PGS on request or in specific cases was not discussed. For this reason, the regulation and Memoranda seem to solely focus on PGD as a means to conceive a healthy child.

54 PGT Nederland, *Annual report 2020*, p. 21 (www.pgtnederland.nl).

55 PGT Nederland, *Annual report 2020*, p. 8 (www.pgtnederland.nl).

56 See for example, Habermas, 2003.

57 *Kamerstukken II* 2005-2006, 30 300 XVI, nr. 136 (*first explanatory letter PGD*), p. 3. In Dutch: "PGD is alleen geïndiceerd als deze technische tussenkomst (...) ieder geval ten goede komt aan het toekomstige kind zelf." See also *Kamerstukken II* 2007-2008, 29 323, nr. 46 (*second explanatory letter PGD*), p. 2.

child runs an increased risk of having a severe genetic condition,[58] such as cystic fibrosis, Duchene or the BRCA gene.[59] Without such benefit, de Memorandum reasons, the technology would result in the instrumentalisation of the future child, which would constitute a violation of its human dignity.[60] Sex selection (except for a sex-linked severe condition) or preimplantation tissue typing solely for the purpose of creating a saviour sibling are, for this reason, not allowed in the Netherlands.[61]

The idea that PGT must benefit the resulting child, however, raises the question as to what the supposed benefit is. After all, PGT does not prevent a genetic or chromosomal disorder, but it prevents the nidation and birth of an affected child. Therefore, the explanation must be either that the affected child benefits from not being born, or that the selected child benefits from an increased chance of being implanted. The Memoranda do not address this point. On the contrary, the way PGT is presented obscures the fact that this technology facilitates selection and assumes that under certain circumstances, the future child has an interest in its own non-existence. In her letter to parliament, Bussemaker, the Dutch State Secretary of Health, explicitly refers to the possibility PGD[62] offers to "prevent a child from suffering."[63] This peculiar statement suggests that it prevents a child from being affected by a genetic condition, like a treatment. However, PGD and also PGT, must not be understood as a treatment to cure an affected child. It facilitates the selection of a healthy child. Put differently, contrary to what seems to be suggested by the State Secretary of Health, PGT does not influence the situation the child is born in, but it determines which child is born.[64] The formulation does not do justice to the fact that the technology does not prevent a genetic or chromosomal disorder from manifesting, but rather prevents the birth of a

58 Regeling van de staatssecretaris van Volksgezondheid, Welzijn en Sport van 16 februari 2009, nr. CZ-TSZ-2912089, houdende houdende regels ten aanzien van preïmplantatie genetische diagnostiek (PGD), (*Stcrt.* 2009, 42) (*Ministerial decree PGD*).

59 PGD Nederland, annual report 2015. PGD can also be used in cases of reduced penetrance, such as the BRCA gene. Reduced penetrance means that the disease does not necessarily have to manifest, but the gene in question does increase the risk of developing the condition.

60 See section 2.4.

61 HLA-typing can be used to create a saviour sibling; in that case, the future child would serve as a suitable donor for a sick sibling (or relative). Additional HLA- typing is allowed, because in this case, embryo selection is needed in the first place to prevent the future child from being affected. Since the treatment is already necessary for the future child's sake, the Dutch government deems it acceptable to do additional selection in the form of HLA-typing. For more on this, see section 2.4.1.1.

62 As explained, the Dutch regulation focuses on PGD.

63 *Kamerstukken II* 2007-2008, 29 323, nr. 46 (*second explanatory letter PGD*), p. 4. Translation by LtH. In Dutch: "het voorkómen van het lijden dat het kind dat mogelijk straks wordt geboren te wachten staat." A similar peculiar formulation is used by Bussemaker's predecessor, State Secretary Ross van Dorp. "PGD kan dan een mogelijkheid zijn om zo'n eventuele ernstige ziekte bij het kind uit te sluiten". *Kamerstukken II* 2005-2006, 30 300 XVI, nr. 136 (*first explanatory letter PGD*), p. 12.

64 This conundrum can be understood as a real-life example of Parfit's non-identity problem. See Parfit, 1984, chapter 16, and chapter 4 of this study.

child with such a condition in favour of a healthy child.[65] It obscures the sensitive nature of the matter, and more importantly, it obscures the assumption that the future child has an interest in its own non-existence.

The future child's interest in its own non-existence is also not mentioned in the regulation on access to fertility treatments. Under Dutch law, medical professionals have a general legal obligation to act in accordance with the standard of care of a 'prudent care provider'.[66] According to the medical profession itself, this implies that they also have to consider interests of third parties.[67] The meaning and implications of this standard in the context of assisted reproduction are further fleshed out in the professional guidelines on moral contraindications for fertility treatments. Following these professional guidelines, medical professionals have a double responsibility: a medical professional must consider both the patient's well-being as well as the well-being of the future child. If it is expected that the future child runs a serious risk of being harmed, the physician must refuse the treatment.[68] In this context, 'harm' is a broad concept. Whereas the regulation of PGT focuses on physical harm caused by a genetic condition, the professional guidelines speak of both physical harm and of psychosocial harm. For this reason, treatment can be refused if, for example, one of the partners may pass on a genetic condition, but also if the parents have a history of child abuse or lack the capacity to raise a child.[69] So although the medical professionals have a duty to prevent the future child's existence if the risk of harm is too high, the guidelines do not explicitly state that under those circumstances the child is presumably better off not existing at all.

---

65 A similar argument was used in the 5th Report of the UK's Science and Technology Committee. The Committee found PGD acceptable, if it ensured that the future child "is less likely to face a debilitating disease in the course of [its] life..." House of Commons Science and Technology Committee, 2005, p. 55. Here too, the committee obscures the fact that the technology alters which child is born, rather than the situation a child is born into.

66 Article 7:453 Dutch Civil Code. "In providing the medical treatment, the care provider must observe the standards of a prudent care provider and, in doing so, he has to act in conformity with the responsibilities laid upon him by the professional standard for care providers." Translation by LtH. In Dutch: "De hulpverlener moet bij zijn werkzaamheden de zorg van een goed hulpverlener in acht nemen en handelt daarbij in overeenstemming met de op hem rustende verantwoordelijkheid, voortvloeiende uit de voor hulpverleners geldende professionele standaard."

67 NVOG Modelprotocol "Mogelijke morele contra-indicaties bij vruchtbaarheidsbehandelingen", p. 4.

68 NVOG Modelprotocol "Mogelijke morele contra-indicaties bij vruchtbaarheidsbehandelingen", p. 2. In Dutch: "Artsen moeten afzien van hulp bij voortplanting als naar hun mening sprake is van een groot risico op ernstige schade voor het kind."

69 NVOG Modelprotocol "Mogelijke morele contra-indicaties bij vruchtbaarheidsbehandelingen", p. 2-3.

2.2.1.2 Germany

The double responsibility of physicians is also acknowledged in Germany. The German Code of Conduct for assisted reproduction[70] states that "the professional duty to act in the well-being of the patient and to prevent harm, pertains to both the mother and the child that may result from the treatment."[71] The Memorandum refers to international law for the interpretation of the concept, from which it follows that well-being includes physical, mental and social well-being.[72] The Code of Conduct, though, mostly focuses on physical well-being. Health risks that may thwart the development of the child are listed as a contra-indication for fertility treatments.[73] Moreover, the use of donor semen is allowed in order to prevent the transmission of a severe genetic condition.[74] However, the child's psychological well-being is indirectly addressed in the requirement that fertility treatments are only offered to married couples or to couples in a stable relationship.[75] The Memorandum to the Code of Conduct explains that the aim of this requirement is to ensure that the child will have a stable relationship with both parents.[76]

Concerns for the future child's psychological well-being are presented as a justification for the ban on certain technologies. Under German law, egg cell donation and surrogacy are prohibited.[77] The reason for this is to protect the child against the possible negative

70 (Muster-)Richtlinie zur Durchführung der assistierten Reproduktion, Novelle 2006. Deutsches Ärzteblatt 2006; 103 [20] p. 1392-1403.

71 (Muster-)Richtlinie zur Durchführung der assistierten Reproduktion, Novelle 2006. Deutsches Ärzteblatt 2006; 103 [20], p. 1393. In German: "Die ärztliche Pflicht, zum Wohl der Patienten zu handeln und Schaden zu vermeiden, bezieht sich auf die Mutter und auf die erwünschten Kinder." Translation by LtH.

72 The Code of Conduct refers to international law, such as the Declaration of Ottawa and Article 24 ICRC, which prescribes the child's right to the highest attainable standard of health care. Health, in this context, includes "physical, mental and social well-being". General Comment No. 15 of the UN Committee on the Rights of the Child; http://www.institut-fuer-menschenrechte.de/fileadmin/user_upload/Publikationen/Weitere_Publikationen/Information_Nr_3_Children_have_a_Right_to_Health.pdf. See also S. Schleissing, *Ethik und Recht in der Fortpflanzungsmedizin. Herausforderungen, Diskussionen, Perspektiven* Baden-Baden, Nomos Verlagsgesellschaft, 2014, p. 53.

73 (Muster-)Richtlinie zur Durchführung der assistierten Reproduktion, Novelle 2006. Deutsches Ärzteblatt 2006; 103 [20], p. 1395, par. 2.2. In German; "Eingeschränkte Kontraindikationen: durch eine Schwangerschaft bedingtes, im Einzelfall besonders hohes medizinisches Risiko für (…) die Entwicklung des Kindes…".

74 (Muster-)Richtlinie zur Durchführung der assistierten Reproduktion, Novelle 2006. Deutsches Ärzteblatt 2006; 103 [20], p. 1393-1394, (Sections 2.1.6 and 2.1.7.).

75 (Muster-)Richtlinie zur Durchführung der assistierten Reproduktion, Novelle 2006. Deutsches Ärzteblatt 2006; 103 [20], p. 1395, (Section 3.1.1.). In German: "festgefügten Partnerschaft". Translation by LtH.

76 The Memorandum is not binding, but merely offers an interpretation of the directive. It does suggest that because of this requirement, single women and homosexual couples ought to be excluded from treatment. (Muster-)Richtlinie zur Durchführung der assistierten Reproduktion, Novelle 2006. Deutsches Ärzteblatt 2006; 103 [20], p. 1400.

77 §1 Abs. 1 Nrs. 1, 2, 6 and 7 ESchG.

consequences of *split motherhood*.[78] This means that the genetic mother, who provides the egg cell, is not the gestational mother. The Memorandum points out that at the moment of drafting, there was no information on how children could mentally or psychologically cope with the fact they are born to two mothers.[79] In addition, it assumes that "descending from three parents (the father included) obstructs the future child in forming his or her identity."[80] In a similar vein, because the impact on the future child's well-being was not known at the time,[81] non-consented use of gametes[82] and post-mortem reproduction[83] are banned as well. Presumably, if one or both parents did not consent to the conception of the child, this may affect or frustrate the child's development and will hamper the child-parent relationship.[84] Moreover, with regard to post-mortem donation it is not only uncertain whether the father would have consented with the child's conception, it is also assumed that the knowledge of descending from a deceased parent makes is harder for the child to form an identity.[85]

As the discussion of the regulatory frameworks illustrates, the German legal system adopts a precautionary approach. Due to the lack of information to the contrary, it is assumed that certain situations may be harmful to the child and must thus be avoided. This results in a more extensive interpretation of the interest in well-being of the future child, compared to, for example, the Netherlands. The interest in mental well-being includes both psychosocial harm resulting from abuse or neglect, and psychological harm caused by the child's inability to coupe with non-traditional family circumstances. Or rather the assumed inability, since there is insufficient information on how the future child would be affected. The lack of information is considered a sufficient reason to assume that a ban on these technologies and, consequently, the future child's non-existence, is in the interest of the

78 Günther, Taupitz and Kaiser, 2014, p. 181.

79 BT-Drs. 11/5460, vom 25.10.1989 (*Bill and Memorandum Embryo Protection Act*), p. 7.

80 BT-Drs. 11/5460, vom 25.10.1989 (*Bill and Memorandum Embryo Protection Act*), p. 7. In German: "Unter diesen Umständen liegt die Annahme nahe, daß dem jungen Menschen, der sein Leben gleichsam drei Elternteilen zu verdanken hat, die eigene Identitätsfindung wesentlich erschwert sein wird." Translation by LtH.

81 In addition to this argument, the ban is also supported by the interests of the parents or donor, because the use of their genetic material without their consent violates their right to self-determination.

82 Velte points out that the appeal to the interests of the parents is stronger, as the non-consented use of genetic material will always constitute a violation of the parent's personal right, whilst whether the future child's well-being is endangered may differ per case. G. Velte, *Die postmortale Befruchtung im deutschen und spanischen Recht*, Heidelberg, Springer, 2015, p. 27.

83 §4 Abs. 1 nr. 3 ESchG.

84 BT-Drs. 11/5460, vom 25.10.1989 (*Bill and Memorandum Embryo Protection Act*), p. 10.

85 Günther, Taupitz and Kaiser, 2014, p. 316-317. Velte, 2015, p. 27-28. The Memorandum itself does not offer a justification for §4 abs 3 ESchG in specific but a similar argument is raised with regard to egg cell donation through ovarium transplant of a deceased donor. BT-Drs. 11/5460, vom 25.10.1989 (*Bill and Memorandum Embryo Protection Act*), p. 7-8.

future child. This precautionary approach is one of the reasons for Germany's more restrictive attitude towards reproductive technologies.

A final topic of interest, is the German approach to selective reproduction. Despite the fact that German regulation endorses a more extensive interpretation of the future child's interest in its physical and mental well-being, it does not invoke the future child's interests to justify the regulation of PGT or other selective reproductive technologies. Under rather strict conditions, sperm selection, in case of a sex-linked condition,[86] and preimplantation genetic testing[87] are allowed, to avoid conceiving a child affected by a severe genetic condition such as Duchenne.[88] Selective reproduction is only deemed acceptable if the child runs a "high risk of a severe genetic condition."[89] In addition, PGT, that is the screening for both monogenetic and chromosomal disorders,[90] is also allowed if the embryo has a defect that would result in a stillbirth or miscarriage.[91] Nonetheless, even though the Memorandum mentions that PGT can prevent the manifestation of a serious illness, the justification for deselection is not sought in the future child's interests. In order to justify the prevention of the birth of a child with a severe genetic condition, the interests and rights of the parents, and in particular the prospective mother are invoked.[92] The Memorandum to the PGT regulation argues that the State's responsibility to protect born and unborn life includes protecting women from the physical and psychological impact of

86 §3 ESchG.

87 §3a ESchG.

88 As discussed above, avoiding the transmission of a genetic condition can also be achieved by using donor semen. This technique is only useful if the prospective father is the carrier of the gene in question, as egg donation is not allowed. (Muster-)Richtlinie zur Durchführung der assistierten Reproduktion, Novelle 2006. Deutsches Ärzteblatt 2006; 103 [20], p. 1394-1394 (Sections 2.1.6. and 2.1.7.). Although the Code of Conduct adopts the same criterion (a high risk for a genetic condition) it does not state whose interests are served.

89 In German: "... das hohe Risiko einer schwerwiegenden Erbkrankheit...", or "...hohes Risiko für ein Kind mit Schwerer genetisch bedingter Erkrankung". Translation by LtH.

90 The Memorandum to the German Embryo Act states that a severe genetic illness includes both monogenetic conditions and aneuploidy. BT-Drs. 11/5460, vom 25.10.1989 (*Bill and Memorandum Embryo Protection Act*), p. 8.

91 §3a abs. ESchG, last sentence.

92 BT-Drs. 17/5451 vom 12.04.2011 (*Bill and Memorandum PGD regulation*), p. 2, 7. In German: "Bei der Abwägung zwischen den Ängsten und Nöten der Betroffenen und ethischen Bedenken wegen der Nichtimplantation eines schwer geschädigten Embryos trifft dieser Gesetzentwurf eine Entscheidung zugunsten der betroffenen Frau." Although the German approach differs because of its focus on the interests of the prospective parents, these interests are not completely ignored in the Dutch and UK regulation. The Dutch State Secretary addressed the parents' concerns, yet she prioritised the interests of the future child. *Kamerstukken II* 2005-2006, 30 300 XVI, nr. 136 (*first explanatory letter PGD*), p. 11. Under UK regulation, PGD can also be used to deselect based on genetic conditions that increase the chance of a miscarriage, which is most likely justified by the interests of the parents. After all, if the child does not come into existence as a result of the miscarriage, it cannot have interests. See Schedule 2, Section 1ZA (1)(a) HFE Act 2008.

an (unsuccessful) pregnancy and late-term abortion.[93] In other words, the focus lies on avoiding physical and psychological stress for the prospective parents, and the woman in particular, caused by giving birth to a severely affected child, an abortion, or a miscarriage.[94] This argument was also posed in the parliamentary discussion on sperm selection.[95] Importantly, despite the fact that selective reproduction seems to primarily serve the interests of others, HLA-tissue typing in order to create a suitable donor for an ill sibling or relative is not allowed in Germany.[96] The topic of saviour siblings is barely addressed in the parliamentary discussions on PGT, but selection based on HLA type does not serve the purposes mentioned in §3a (2), i.e. the prevention of a genetic illness or the prevention of a miscarriage.

This alternative focus can be explained by the principles in German law that state that all human life is worth living, and that life starts at the moment of conception. As a result, the interest of the future child, or more precisely the interest of the (pre-)embryo, is that it should not be destroyed or be denied the chance to develop (by being deselected), but that it should be implanted and carried to term. In other words, the German legislation implies that the future child, or rather the embryo in vitro has an interest in its own existence. In addition, Germany allows the prenatal application of certain fundamental rights, including Article 3 III S. 2 GG, (the prohibition of discrimination on basis of disability). This provision implies that life may not be subjected to value judgements, or put simply, that others cannot decide whether the future child's life is worth living. Nonetheless, there is an

---

93 BT-Drs. 11/5460, vom 25.10.1989 (*Bill and Memorandum Embryo Protection Act*), p. 2. In German: "Dies schließt den Schutz von Frauen vor schweren körperlichen und seelischen Belastungen im Hinblick auf die Schwangerschaft sowie die Vermeidung von Spätabbrüchen mit ein."

94 BT-Drs. 11/5460, vom 25.10.1989 (*Bill and Memorandum Embryo Protection Act*), p. 2. In German: "Dadurch können bereits vor Einleitung der Schwangerschaft Fehl- und Totgeburten und die Weitergabe von besonders schweren Erkrankungen an das zukünftige Kind verhindert und schwere Belastungen, insbesondere von den betroffenen Frauen aber auch den Familien insgesamt, abgewendet werden."

95 BT-Drs. 11/8057 vom 08.10.1990 (*Recommendation and notice of the Committee on legal affairs*) p. 15. "Ein völliger Verzicht auf Ausnahmeregelungen erscheine unangemessen, da bei den betroffenen Ehepaaren die Erfüllung des eigenen Kinderwunsches bei Gefahr des Auftretens der erwähnten Erbkrankheiten erschwert oder auch zu vermeidbaren Schwangerschaftsabbrüchen führen würde. (…) Die Koalitionsfraktionen waren demgegenüber jedoch der Ansicht, daß es einem Ehepaar nicht zugemutet werden könne, (…) ein krankes Kind zu erhalten, wen künftig die Möglichkeit bestehen sollte, durch Spermiensektion ein gesundes Kind zur Welt zu bringen." Also Taupitz states that the interests of the parents was the reason to make an exception on sex selection in case of a severe genetic condition. Günther, Taupitz and Kaiser, 2014, p. 272. Finally, in the context of abortion, a similar argument was posed to justify abortion in case of an impaired embryo. In that situation, abortion was acceptable in order to prevent the pregnant woman from suffering extreme stress caused by giving birth to and raising a disabled child. A. Eser in: A. Schönke and H. Schröder, ed, München, C.H. Beck 2014, §218a nr 38.

96 Günther, Taupitz and Kaiser, 2014, p. 292.

ongoing debate on whether this article can also be applied to the embryo in vitro[97] and thus whether embryo selection constitutes a violation of this section.[98]

2.2.1.3 The United Kingdom

Like in the Netherlands and Germany, the regulatory framework in the United Kingdom acknowledges a duty upon physicians to take the interests and well-being of the future child into account when providing fertility treatment. The interests of the future child are explicitly referred to in the Section 13(5) of the HFE Act: "A woman shall not be provided with treatment services unless *account has been taken of the welfare of any child who may be born as a result of the treatment…*"[99] In academic debate, this clause has been criticised for being discriminatory towards infertile people.[100] Still, it appears to be strongly supported by the medical profession.[101] Section 13(5) itself does not prescribe how it should be interpreted or elaborate on the interest of the future child. In 2004, a review was conducted to provide guidance for interpretation. The report of the review, called *Tomorrow's Children*, concluded that "there should be a presumption to provide treatment to all those who request it, unless there is evidence that the child to be born would face a risk of serious medical, physical or psychological harm."[102] In other words, the interests of the future child require that it is protected from significant harm by refusing the treatment where there are such risks. Clinics are required to do a welfare of the child risk assessment to determine "whether there are any specific risk factors which might give cause for

97 See also section 2.1.1.1. Also under discussion is whether Articles 1 and 2 can be applied to the embryo in vitro.

98 According to Starck, embryo selection or PGD would constitute a violation of Art. 3 III 2 GG, just like abortion for 'eugenic' reasons, i.e. because the child will be born disabled. C. Starck in: H. Mangoldt, F. Klein and C. Starck, *Kommentar zum Grundgesetz. Band 1: Präambel, Artikel 1 bis 19*, 6th ed, München, Verlag Franz Vahlen 2010, Art. 3 III 2, nr 421. Importantly, this commentary was written in 2010, the same year in which the Federal Court of Justice ruled that PGD did not violate the Embryo Protection Act, and one year before the Embryo Protection Act was amended to allow the restricted use of PGD. Starck's view implies that this article is applicable to the embryo in vitro, to which Heun disagrees. According to him, because the embryo in vitro is not an addressee of Article 3, PGD does not infringe Article 3 III S. 2 GG. Heun, W. in: Dreier, H. *Grundgesetz Kommentar. Band 1, Präambel, Artikel 1-19*, (Tübingen: Mohr Siebeck 3rd ed. 2014), Art 3 III 2 GG nr. 137.

99 Italics added by LtH.

100 For an overview of arguments see House of Commons Science and Technology Committee, 2005, par. 98-107. The report argues that the welfare clause is discriminatory because it discriminates between prospective parents who need to make use of assisted reproduction and those who can procreate naturally, and also points out that there are questions on how to enforce the provision and whether the provision is effective. E. Jackson, 'Conception and the irrelevance of the welfare principle', *Modern Law Review*, Vol. 65, No. 2, 2002 J. Harris, 'The welfare of the child', *Health Care Analysis*, Vol. 8, 2000, p. 32; S.E.P. Walker, 'Potential persons and the welfare of the (potential) child test', *Medical Law International*, Vol. 14, No. 3, 2014, p. 158.

101 S. Sheldon, E. Lee and J. Macvarish, "Supportive Parenting', Responsibility and Regulation: The Welfare Assessment under the Reformed Human Fertilisation and Embryology Act (1990)', *Modern Law Review*, Vol. 78, No. 3, 2015, p. 468-470.

102 Human Fertilisation and Embryology Authority, 2005, p. 3, 6, 8.

concern about a future child's well-being."[103] Possible risk factors mentioned in the report and later adopted by the Code of Practice include a history of child abuse, mental conditions, and drug or alcohol abuse. Clinics can also take other circumstances into account if they deem them "likely to cause serious harm to [a future or existing] child."[104] In short, also in the UK legal system, the possible risk of both physical and psychosocial harm can require the prevention of the future child's existence.

The regulation on PGT[105] is rather similar to the regulatory frameworks of the Netherlands and Germany. The HFE Act 2008 allows preimplantation testing only for specific purposes, namely in order to establish whether the embryo has a genetic or chromosomal abnormality that "may affect the capacity to result in a live birth"[106] or when there is "a significant risk that a person with the abnormality will have or develop a serious physical or mental disability, a serious illness or any other serious medical condition."[107] In addition, PGT can also be used to deselect a serious sex linked condition, thereby allowing sex selection for medical purposes.[108] However, whereas the Dutch and German legal system are very clear about whose interests are served by this regulatory framework, the motivation of the UK regulator is less explicit. It seems that the UK regulation intends to protect the interests of both the parents and the future child itself. For example, embryo testing to prevent a miscarriage seems primarily beneficial to the prospective parents. Nonetheless, during the parliamentary debate in the House of Commons, MP Lansley was very explicit over the fact that the interest of the future child must be paramount but can also require its non-existence: "[T]he testing of embryos to prevent the implantation of an embryo with an inherited or genetic condition will, in many cases, be in the best interests of that child if the condition is life-threatening or would severely impair their quality of life."[109] This is

103 Jackson, 2016, p. 814.

104 HFEA Code of Practice 8th ed. Section 8.10. Full text: The centre should consider factors that are likely to cause a risk of significant harm or neglect to any child who may be born or to any existing child of the family. These factors include any aspects of the patient's or (if they have one) their partner's: (a) past or current circumstances that may lead to any child mentioned above experiencing serious physical or psychological harm or neglect, for example: (i) previous convictions relating to harming children; (ii) child protection measures taken regarding existing children, or (iii) violence or serious discord in the family environment; (b) past or current circumstances that are likely to lead to an inability to care throughout childhood for any child who may be born, or that are already seriously impairing the care of any existing child of the family, for example: (i) mental or physical conditions; (ii) drug or alcohol abuse; (iii) medical history, where the medical history indicates that any child who may be born is likely to suffer from a serious medical condition, or (iv) circumstances that the centre considers likely to cause serious harm to any child mentioned above.

105 The HFEA Act allows testing for genetic and chromosomal abnormalities (and mitochondrial abnormalities). Schedule 2, 1ZA (1) HFE Act 2008.

106 Schedule 2, 1ZA (1)(a) HFE Act 2008.

107 Schedule 2, 1ZA (2) HFE Act 2008.

108 Schedule 2, 1ZA (1)(d) HFE Act 2008.

109 HC Deb (12 May 2008) vol. 475, col. 1078.

one of the rare instances where the assumption of the future child's interests in its own non-existence is made explicit.

In 2018, the Nuffield Council published a report addressing the question of whether human germline modification is permissible. Up until then, human germline modification had been banned in national and international regulation for years. The introduction of the technology CRISPR-Cas9 had made gene editing a real-life possibility, which in various countries resulted in a reassessment of this technology.[110] The Council deemed human germline gene editing morally permissible, provided that (amongst others) it was in line with the welfare of the child-principle:

> Gametes or embryos that have been subject to genome editing procedures (or that are derived from cells that have been subject to such procedures) should be used only where the procedure is carried out in a manner and for a purpose that is intended to secure the welfare of and is consistent with the welfare of a person who may be born as a consequence of treatment using those cells.[111]

Welfare is considered to be a broader term than well-being, which is seen as a synonym for 'healthy'. The avoidance of genetic illnesses is considered to be a component, but the report explains that welfare also encompasses psychosocial welfare.[112] The Council concludes that in the future, when the technology is deemed safe enough for clinical use, germline modification may be permitted. Notably, the Nuffield Council believes a strict distinction between therapeutic germline editing and human enhancement is not feasible, since germline intervention differs from the traditional medical model where a patient is treated.[113] Consequently, as van Beers points out, it seems that the Council is open to the possibility of using germline modification for human enhancement.[114] The Council itself does not offer any principled argument against enhancement. Instead, it only states that it

110 In addition to the Nuffield Report, also the Dutch Health Council and the German Ethics Council each published a report addressing the permissibility of genome editing in the wake of the development of CRISPR-Cas9. Nuffield Council on Bioethics, *Genome Editing and Human Reproduction: social and ethical issues*, London, 2018; Commissie Genetische Modificatie (COGEM) & Gezondheidsraad, *Ingrijpen in het DNA van de mens. Morele en maatschappelijke implicaties van kiembaanmodificatie*, Bilthoven, 2017; Deutscher Ethikrat, *Intervening in the Human Germline. Opinion. Executive summary and recommendations.*, Berlin, 2019.

111 Nuffield Council on Bioethics, 2018, p. 75.

112 Nuffield Council on Bioethics, 2018, p. 76.

113 Nuffield Council on Bioethics, 2018, p. 71.

114 B.C. van Beers, 'Rewriting the human genome, rewriting human rights law? Human rights, human dignity, and human germline modification in the CRISPR era', *Journal of Law and the Biosciences*, Vol. 7, No. 1, 2020, p. 23-24.

expects extreme forms of human enhancement to be impossible: "there are few complex characteristics that could be reliably secured by heritable genome editing interventions."[115]

2.2.2 *Discussion*

As shown in the previous sections, all three legal systems refer to the future child's well-being, or its interest to be free from harm. The double responsibility of medical professionals is acknowledged in the Netherlands as well as the UK and Germany. Moreover, all three assume that the protection of the future child's well-being can be a contra-indication for fertility treatment. In cases where there is a significant risk of severe harm, the treatment can be refused, thus preventing the child's existence. Nonetheless, apart from MP Lansley's comment, it is never explicitly stated that in the face of too much harm the child would be better off not existing at all. Hereafter, I will examine the regulations more closely in order to further reconstruct the future child's interest to be free from harm. I elaborate the three aspects of this interest that come to the fore in the regulatory frameworks. These are the type of harm, the severity of harm, and the likelihood of its manifestation. These aspects are relevant for determining whether non-existence is indeed in the interest of the future child.

2.2.2.1 Type of Harm

Not every occurrence that is experienced as negative qualifies as harm. Legally relevant harm is restricted to mainly two categories within the three examined regulatory frameworks. These are physical or medical harm, and mental, psychological, or psychosocial harm. These types are, for instance, explicitly mentioned in the report, *Tomorrow's Children*. The report states that fertility clinics should determine whether the future child is at risk of "serious medical, physical or psychological harm".[116] The Nuffield Report on *Genome Editing and Human Reproduction* also argues that the concept 'welfare' encompasses both "psychosocial welfare, and not just good health."[117] The German Code of Conduct does not explicitly mention these categories but refers to the future child's right to health care ex Article 24 CRC. Health in this context pertains to both physical or medical health and mental or psychosocial health. Therefore, the duty to prevent harm

115 Nuffield Council on Bioethics, 2018, p. 96.

116 Human Fertilisation and Embryology Authority, 2005, p. 8.

117 Nuffield Council on Bioethics, 2018, p. 76. The report argues that in their framing of welfare and well-being, these concepts are not to be used interchangeably, as welfare (doing well) is a broader concept that well-being, which implies being well or healthy.

and protect the future child's health can be understood as a duty to protect the child from both psychosocial and physical harm.[118]

Medical or physical harm[119] pertains to those health risks that affect the body, for example caused by a genetic condition.[120] The avoidance of physical harm can be a reason to allow a specific treatment, such as PGT, which creates the possibility to deselect embryo's with a genetic or chromosomal abnormality. In addition to that, the German Code of Conduct lists the risk of an inheritable condition as a valid reason to use donor semen, i.e. in order to prevent the condition being passed on from father to child. In addition, the risk of physical harm can also be a contra-indication. The Dutch professional guidelines on access to fertility treatments and the UK's HFEA Code of Practice also mention physical or medical harm caused by a genetic defect as a reason to withhold fertility treatment.

In addition to preventing physical harm, several regulatory frameworks aim to avoid psychological harm as well. Importantly, instead of defining what is understood by mental or psychological harm, the relevant Memoranda only list possible risk factors. The Dutch professional guidelines, for example, state the following: "there is a significant risk of severe harm if existing children are removed from parental custody because of abuse or neglect, or if a mental retardation or psychological problems provide reasons to doubt the parents' capacities to raise a child."[121] Similar risk factors are listed in the UK HFEA Code of Practice and include: mental or physical conditions, drug or alcohol abuse, violence in the family environment etc.[122] The guidelines do not further elaborate on what sort of harm these risk factors may cause, but it is likely that they aim to prevent a severe developmental deficit to the child. In short, both protocols can be understood as an assessment of the parents' capability to raise a child. The German regulatory frameworks

---

118 Although he splits psychosocial harm into psychological and social harm, Schleissing also limits the discussion of the future child's well-being in the German regulation of reproduction to these aspects: on the one hand physical harm and on the other hand psychosocial harm. Schleissing, 2014, p. 44-46.

119 It seems that there is no significant distinction between 'physical harm' and 'medical harm'. The Dutch guidelines do not seem to distinguish between them. Also, the *Tomorrow's Children* report sometimes mentions medical harm separately besides physical and psychological harm (on p. 3 and p. 8) and sometimes mentions only physical and psychological harm (p. 6.). For the purpose of this paper, they are used interchangeably.

120 NVOG Modelprotocol "Mogelijke morele contra-indicaties bij vruchtbaarheidsbehandelingen", p. 3.

121 NVOG Modelprotocol "Mogelijke morele contra-indicaties bij vruchtbaarheidsbehandelingen", p. 2. In Dutch: "Van een groot risico op ernstige schade kan sprake zijn als eerdere kinderen wegens mishandeling of verwaarlozing uit huis zijn geplaatst of als er vanwege zwakbegaafdheid of psychische problematiek gegronde redenen zijn om ernstig te twijfelen aan de ouderschapscompetenties van het paar." Translation by LtH.

122 HFEA Code of Practice 8th Edition 2009 (last revised 2017), Section 8.10.

adopt a wider interpretation of mental well-being. Psychological harm[123] may not only lead to developmental deficits, but also frustrates the future child's self-understanding and development as a human person. Illustrative of this is the argument given in the context of posthumous reproduction: "knowing to descend from someone who already passed away before the child's conception might be harmful to the child's psychosocial development".[124] With regard to split motherhood, resulting from egg cell donation, surrogacy, or fallopian tube transplant, the Memorandum even assumes that this may affect the future child's identity formation, which consequently would affect its psychological well-being. Due to the lack of information indicating the opposite, "...it is reasonable to assume that for the young adult, who owes his life to three parents, finding his own identity will be much more difficult."[125] The relation between identity formation and psychological well-being in the context of split motherhood was once repeated in the third party submission of the German government in the ECtHR case *S.H. e.a. v. Austria*:

> In addition, the relationship with the mother was assumed to be important for the child's discovery of identity. As a result, the child would have extreme difficulties in coping with the fact that in biological terms two women had a part in his or her existence. Split motherhood and the resulting ambiguousness of the mother's identity might jeopardise the development of the child's personality and lead to considerable problems in his or her discovery of identity. It was therefore contrary to the child's welfare.[126]

This precautionary approach has been met with criticism.[127] Moreover, the regulatory framework on donor anonymity, in which the interest in identity formation plays a central

---

123 The Memorandum speaks of 'seelisch', while Müller-Terpitz speaks in this context of 'sozio-psychologischen Folgen'. Spickhoff, 2011 ESchG §1, nr 19.

124 Spickhoff, 2011 ESchG §4, nr 1. In German: "... [die] Vorstellung, dass die Kenntnis, von einem zur Zeit der Zeugung bereits Verstorbenen abzustammen, für die geistig-seelische Entwicklung des Kindes abträglich sein könnte." Translation by LtH. See also Velte, 2015, p. 28. In a similar vein, the Memorandum mentions as one of the arguments against the non-consented use of gametes, that there was no information on how the fact that one of the parents did not consent would affect the development of the child. In German: "Daneben will die Vorschrift aber auch Gefahren für die Entwicklung des Kindes entgegenwirken, die zumindest dann nicht ausgeschlossen werden können, wenn seine Erzeugung in einer dem Willen der Beteiligten nicht entsprechenden Weise erfolgt ist." BT-Drs 11/5460 vom 25.10.1989, p. 10.

125 BT-Drs. 11/5460, vom 25.10.1989 (*Bill and Memorandum Embryo Protection Act*), p. 7. In German: "[Unter diesen Umständen] liegt die Annahme nahe, daß dem jungen Menschen, der sein Leben gleichsam drei Elternteilen zu verdanken hat, die eigene Identitätsfindung wesentlich erschwert sein wird." Translation by LtH.

126 ECtHR 1 April 2010 ECLI:CE:ECHR:2010:0401JUD005781300 (*S.H. e.a. v. Austria)*, par. 53.

127 See for example, R. Ratze and B. Luxenburger, *Handbuch Medizinrecht*, 3, Heidelberg, C.F. Müller, 2015, p. 1380; Günther, Taupitz and Kaiser, 2014, p. 181-182; F.C. Schroeder, 'Die Rechtsgüter des Embryonenschutzgesetzes.' in: H.-H. Kühne (ed.), *Festschrift für Koichi Miyazawa. Dem Wegbereiter des japanisch-deutschen Strafrechtsdiskurses*, Nomos Verlagsgesellschaft, Baden-Baden, 1995, p. 534-535, 544.

role, has departed from the idea that an obstructed identity formation necessarily qualifies as harm. This is further addressed in section 2.3.1.2.

Both types of harm cover many aspects, partly due to the fact that they are not further defined.[128] However, it is important to note that 'harm' does not cover the violation of interests of a more metaphysical nature, such as human dignity or narrative identity, two aspects that will be discussed later. Instead, because harm is connected to well-being and the impact it has on well-being, and because the regulations explicitly speak of *medical* and *psychosocial* harm, it seems that they only refer to types of harm that are somehow measurable or which could be tested with the help of empirical evidence, in the form of physical malfunctioning, adjustment problems or socio-emotional functioning. In other words, harm is somehow tangible or concrete. In chapter 3, I will go deeper into this aspect of the notion of harm.

2.2.2.2 Degree of Harm

In addition to type, severity of harm is also relevant for the future child's interest in being free from harm. Only if the degree of harm meets a certain degree, interference is acceptable. Put differently, the harm in question must be severe enough. According to the Dutch regulation, embryo selection is only acceptable if there is "a high risk of a *severe* genetic condition or illness"[129] and fertility treatment can only be refused if the future child runs a "significant risk of *severe* harm."[130] Also the German Embryo Protection Act allows embryo selection only if there is a risk of a severe condition.[131] According the Memorandum, this includes "in particular those conditions that distinguish themselves

---

128 For example, a survey conducted by the Netherlands Institute of Human Rights revealed that all of the Dutch fertility clinics appealed to the interests of the future child to justify their refusal to work with donor semen, but that this 'best interest of the future child' notion was interpreted in many different ways. For example, some clinics argued that it is in the best interests of the child to grow up with its biological mother and father, or that the involvement of a donor might cause distress if he would want to be involved in the child's life, or that single women would like a child out of loneliness, which was not in the best interests of the child. CGB-oordeel 2000-4. Also van Beers points out that 'the interest of the future child', even when it is narrowed down to an interest in well-being, remains a broad and extendable concept, susceptible to multiple interpretations. Moreover, there is no hard evidence that all of these assumed risk factors indeed cause significant harm. B.C. van Beers, 'Leeftijdsgrenzen en het grenzeloze verlangen naar een kind. De discussie over de oudste moeder van Nederland vanuit rechtsfilosofisch perspectief', *Ars Aequi*, Vol. 2011, No. 7-8, 2011, p. 578.

129 Regeling van de staatssecretaris van Volksgezondheid, Welzijn en Sport van 16 februari 2009, nr. CZ-TSZ-2912089, houdende houdende regels ten aanzien van preïmplantatie genetische diagnostiek (PGD), (*Stcrt.* 2009, 42) (*Ministerial decree PGD*), p. 5; *Kamerstukken II* 2007-2008, 29 323, nr. 46 (*second explanatory letter PGD*), p. 7. Italics added by LtH. It is important to notice that the nature of the condition is one criterion, and other criteria, such as possible treatments, are also taken into account.

130 NVOG Modelprotocol "Mogelijke morele contra-indicaties bij vruchtbaarheidsbehandelingen", p. 2. In Dutch: "Een groot risico op *ernstige* schade voor het kind." Italics added by LtH.

131 §3a ESchG. In German: "schwerwiegend".

from other genetic conditions by their low life expectancy or the severity of the symptoms and limited treatment."[132] The UK Code of Practice prescribes that treatment can be refused when the future child is at risk of *significant* harm.[133] This is the case when risk factors may cause *serious* harm or neglect.[134] Moreover, PGT is allowed only if there is a risk of a *serious* medical condition or illness.[135] In short, although every future child has an interest in protection against harm, not every harmful factor is considered a violation of this interest. Because the harm in question can only be prevented by preventing the child's whole existence, the actual harm needs to be balanced against this non-existence in order to determine whether the prevention of harm can justify the interference. Only when the expected harm meets this specific threshold is interference deemed acceptable and justified.

It is not always clear when this threshold is met or what qualifies as 'serious' or 'severe' harm. It may be that the legislators deliberately chose to use an open norm in order to prevent the adoption of a strict list of conditions that qualify, preferring a case-by-case approach in which cases are individually assessed.[136] The Dutch professional guidelines offer a little more insight into the applied standard. The threshold used in Dutch regulation is the standard of 'reasonable well-being', which means that "physicians should refrain from treatment if the resulting child runs a high risk of severe harm".[137] By choosing this standard, the Dutch regulation aims to find a balance between the two extremes of the spectrum, namely the standards of 'maximum well-being' and 'minimum well-being'. The regulation explicitly rejects the standard of maximum well-being, in which case any degree of harm would allow interference. The guidelines argue that if any degree of harm was sufficient reason to refuse a prospective parent fertility treatment, only a few prospective parents would be eligible for treatment,[138] which is deemed undesirable. More controversial is the fact that the regulation also rejects the standard of minimum well-being. According to this standard, interference is only allowed if the degree of harm has such a severe impact on the child's well-being, that its life is considered not worth living.

---

132 BT-Drs. 11/5460, vom 25.10.1989 (*Bill and Memorandum Embryo Protection Act*), p. 8. In German: "["Schwerwiegend" sind diese] insbesondere, wenn sie sich durch eine gerichte Lebenserwartung oder Schwere des Krankheitsbildes und schlechte Behandelbarkeit von anderen Erbkrankheiten wesentlich unterscheiden." Translation by LtH.

133 Section 8.15. Code of Practice, 8th ed.

134 Section 8.10 (a) Code of Practice, 8th ed.

135 Schedule 2, Section 1ZA (1)(c) HFE Act 2008.

136 Taupitz adds that regarding PGD, creating a list of the conditions that are eligible for PGD may lead to stigmatisation of existing people born with those conditions. Günther, Taupitz and Kaiser, 2014, p. 290.

137 NVOG Modelprotocol "Mogelijke morele contra-indicaties bij vruchtbaarheidsbehandelingen", p. 2. In Dutch: "artsen moeten afzien van hulp bij voortplanting als naar hun mening sprake is van een groot risico op ernstige schade voor het kind." Translation by LtH.

138 NVOG Modelprotocol "Mogelijke morele contra-indicaties bij vruchtbaarheidsbehandelingen", p. 2.

As I will explain in chapter 4, it follows from the philosophical debate that only then can it be assumed that the future child is indeed better off not existing at all and thus has an interest in its own non-existence. This raises the question as to whether the regulation on access to fertility treatments and PGT actually serves the interests of the future child. Nonetheless, the professional guidelines do not address this so-called *wrongful life* debate and simply point out that the standard of minimum well-being demands too little of both parental and medical professional responsibility.[139]

A final note of interest here is a recent development in the Netherlands. In 2016, Minister of Health, Edith Schippers, issued a proposal for amending the Embryo Act on three points, including allowing sex selection in order to prevent a carrier child.[140] The Embryo Act only allows for sex selection in cases where there is a risk of a severe, sex-linked condition. The proposal would extend selection to those cases in which the resulting child is a healthy carrier. The child itself would in that case be healthy, but still possess the defective gene. For this reason, it would be at risk of passing the condition on to the following generation and thus it would be confronted with "difficult reproductive choices" of its own.[141] After assessing the proposal, the Dutch Council of State gave a negative advice. It argued that in light of the protection of embryos it is a bridge too far to deliberately destroy embryos with the potential to develop into a healthy human being. Moreover, it stressed that the fact that the resulting child may be confronted with a difficult reproductive choice does not mean that the child should not be born at all.[142] In other words, the Council of State concluded that simply carrying a recessive gene does not in itself qualify as harm. Eventually, the full proposal was withdrawn by Schippers's successor.[143]

2.2.2.3 Risk of Harm

The third aspect of the future child's interest to be free from harm pertains to the chance the harm will actually manifest. The regulations do not require the harm to necessarily manifest itself. Instead, it deems interference justified if there is a certain risk that the child will face severe harm. For example, the regulation of fertility treatments lists the risk of severe harm as a contra-indication. The UK HFEA Code of Practice states that fertility centres should conduct a welfare assessment in order to determine whether there are "factors that are likely to cause *a risk* of significant harm or neglect to any child who may be born", including factors that "*may* lead to any child mentioned above experiencing

139 NVOG Modelprotocol "Mogelijke morele contra-indicaties bij vruchtbaarheidsbehandelingen", p. 2.

140 A carrier child is a child who carries one version of the mutated gene. The child is capable of passing on the gene, but will not experience symptoms itself.

141 Council of State advise, 30 July 2018 (*Stcrt.* 2018, 42606), p. 19.

142 Council of State advise, 30 July 2018 (*Stcrt.* 2018, 42606), p. 9-10.

143 *Kamerstukken II* 2017-2018, 30486, nr. 19.

serious physical or psychological harm or neglect" or "*are likely* to lead to an inability [of the parents] to care [for the child]."[144] The Dutch professional guidelines state that the guiding criterion for interference is "a *high risk* of severe harm."[145] Also regulatory frameworks that focus on physical harm caused by a genetic condition deem a risk of harm as sufficient reason for interference. For instance, both the German and Dutch regulations allow PGT and medical sex selection in cases where there is of a "high risk" of harm caused by a genetic defect.[146] Another example is the German Code of Conduct which allows heterologous treatments where there is a "high risk of a child with a severe genetic condition."[147]

The reason why interference is allowed if the future child is at risk of being harmed, is because at the moment of deciding upon refusing a fertility treatment or conducting PGT, the harm has not manifested itself yet and there is no 100% certainty that the child indeed will suffer harm. Moreover, there is no absolute certainty the child will be harmed, either psychosocially and/or physically. Psychosocial harm caused by irresponsible parenting is by its nature contingent; the possible risk factors, such as alcohol abuse or an unstable relationship, may result in harm, but this does not necessarily have to be the case. After all, it is possible that the prospective parents turn out to be (sufficiently) able to take care of the child. Also, physical harm caused by a genetic defect cannot be predicted with absolute certainty. That is, a genetic defect will not necessarily result in an illness. In cases of so-called incomplete penetrance, only some of the carriers of the affected gene show symptoms of the condition. For example, in the case of a penetrance of 80%, only eight out of ten carriers will become ill. Even though the genetic defect will be the most important cause of the condition, other factors play a substantial role in whether and how the condition will manifest itself as well. In her commentary on the PGD regulation, the Dutch State Secretary stated that it is more suitable to speak of high penetrance instead of complete penetrance,[148] suggesting that there is never absolute certainty on how and if a genetic defect will manifest and cause harm.

---

144 HFEA Code of Practice 8th Edition 2009 (last revised 2017), Section 8.10. Italics added by LtH.

145 NVOG Modelprotocol "Mogelijke morele contra-indicaties bij vruchtbaarheidsbehandelingen", p. 2. In Dutch: "een groot risico op ernstige schade". Italics added by LtH.

146 §3 and §3a ESchG. In German: "Ein hohes genetisches Risiko". What this exactly entails, is left open. See Kommentar 2014, p. 291. Regeling van de staatssecretaris van Volksgezondheid, Welzijn en Sport van 16 februari 2009, nr. CZ-TSZ-2912089, houdende houdende regels ten aanzien van preïmplantatie genetische diagnostiek (PGD), (*Stcrt.* 2009, 42) (*Ministerial decree PGD*).

147 (Muster-)Richtlinie zur Durchführung der assistierten Reproduktion, Novelle 2006. Deutsches Ärzteblatt 2006; 103 [20], par. 2.1.6. and 2.1.7.

148 *Kamerstukken II* 2007-2008, 29 323, nr. 46 (*second explanatory letter PGD*), p. 6.

Although the possibility of harm can be enough to prevent the future child's life, *any* possible risk is not sufficient to justify interference. The risk (just like the degree of harm) has to be significant. Most examples of regulation speak of a *high* risk[149] or a *significant* risk, with the only exception being the UK Code of Practice on the welfare-assessment, which only speaks of "a risk."[150] According to Taupitz, a high risk implies that there must be "a certain probability that the child will inherit the disease."[151] However, there is no specific boundary, such as a 50% or 75% chance, that must be met in order to speak of a high risk.[152] Moreover, the Dutch State Secretary notes that the degree of penetrance and severity of the condition must be balanced against each other in order to determine whether a case is eligible for PGD: "On the one hand, there are conditions with complete penetrance that are usually not considered eligible for PGD by the medical profession, because, for example, the illness is treatable or bearable. On the other hand, there are conditions with incomplete penetrance that, all individual circumstances considered, are with regard to risk and symptoms equal to illnesses with complete penetrance."[153] In sum, if there is a significant chance that the child will face severe physical or psychosocial harm, then interference is justified, which will result in the prevention of the child's existence.

2.3 The Interest in forming an Identity

2.3.1 The Regulations

A second interest of the future child that can be distilled from the regulations on reproduction pertains to the necessary conditions for the development of a personal identity. This interest plays an important role in the bans on donor anonymity, where the information about one's genetic origins is seen as an important factor for one's identity.

---

149 In fact, in 2008, the Dutch State Secretary decided a stricter criterion for the application of PGD was more appropriate, and changed the criterion from an 'increased risk to a high risk'. See also E. Aarden, I. van Hoyweghen, R. Vos and K. Horstman, 'Providing preimplantation genetic diagnosis in the United Kingdom, The Netherlands and Germany: a comparative in-depth analysis of health-care acces', *Human Reproduction*, Vol. 24, No. 7, 2009, p. 1544.

150 With regard to refusing fertility treatments, the Code of Practice mostly speaks of a risk of significant harm. Section 8.15 (b) allows the clinics to also refuse treatments if it "cannot obtain enough information to conclude that there is no *significant* risk." Italics added by LtH.

151 In German: "... eine gewisse Wahrscheinlichkeit für die Übertragung..." Translation by LtH.

152 Günther, Taupitz and Kaiser, 2014, p. 275, 291.

153 *Kamerstukken* II, 2007-2008, 29323, 46, p. 6. Translation by LtH. In Dutch: "Enerzijds zijn er namelijk ziekten met volledige penetrantie die ook nu meestal niet door de beroepsgroep voor PGD worden geaccepteerd, omdat bijvoorbeeld de ziekte in voldoende mate behandelbaar danwel [sic] dragelijk is. Anderzijds zijn er ziekten met onvolledige penetrantie die zich door een optelsom van factoren in individuele gevallen qua risico en ernst laten vergelijken met de ziekten met volledige penetrantie."

Nonetheless, as already briefly touched upon in the previous section, the future child's identity formation is in the German legal system also linked to psychosocial harm. The lack of knowledge on how a certain situation affects the child's identity formation is used as an argument for the German ban on egg cell donation and posthumous reproduction.

2.3.1.1 The Netherlands

In the Dutch regulation, the interest in identity formation is not mentioned as such.[154] More commonly, reference is made to the future child's *self-understanding* as an important interest for the justification of regulation. This notion is most prominently mentioned in the regulation prohibiting anonymous sperm and egg cell donation, the Dutch Donor Information Artificial Fertilisation Act. In 2002, after ten years of political debate,[155] legislation was enacted that banned anonymous gamete donation. Both identifying and other information, such as general characteristics or medical data, needs to be registered in a database so that when the donor conceived child reaches the age of 16, it can ask for the donor's identifying information.[156] Identifying information will only be provided after the donor has consented.[157] At the same time, the donor's refusal can only prevent disclosure if "important interests of the donor require not disclosing the information."[158] Otherwise, the information will be provided to the donor conceived child.

The justification for the Donor Information Artificial Fertilisation Act is based in the interests of the child that would result from donor conception: the Memorandum acknowledges that the child has an interest in having access to information on its genetic parent(s). This information, it is argued, is pivotal for the child's self-understanding. More precisely, the Memorandum describes knowledge of one's origins as a foundation that offers people a "deeper insight into themselves"[159] and is necessary for understanding "the child's youth and development into an adult."[160] Having this information is considered to

154 Except for in the context of reproductive cloning. *Kamerstukken II* 2000-2001, 27 423, nr. 3 (*Memorandum Embryo Act*), p. 41. One of the arguments, but not the most important argument, against reproductive human cloning was the expectation that the clone would face serious problems with its identity. In Dutch: "... het gevaar dat een kloonmens te zware problemen omtrent zijn of haar identiteit zal krijgen..." The appeal to identity was only a secondary argument and not further developed.

155 The first bill was issued in 1992. *Kamerstukken II* 1992-1993, 23 207, nr. 1-2 (*Donor Information Artificial Fertilisation Bill*).

156 Non-identifying information can be requested from the age of 12.

157 Art. 3(2) WDKB (Donor Information Artificial Fertilisation Act).

158 In Dutch: "Verstrekking blijft, indien de donor daar niet mee instemt, uitsluitend achterwege indien (...) zwaarwegende belangen van de donor meebrengen dat verstrekking niet behoort plaats te vinden."

159 *Kamerstukken II*, 1992-1993, 23 207, nr. 3 (*Memorandum Donor Information Artificial Fertilisation Act*), p. 1. Translation by LtH. In Dutch: "Kennis omtrent de afstamming biedt mensen een basis. Ontbreekt die basis dan missen mensen een bouwsteen die hen een dieper inzicht in zichzelf zou kunnen geven."

160 *Kamerstukken II*, 1992-1993, 23 207, nr. 3 (*Memorandum Donor Information Artificial Fertilisation Act*), p. 16. Translation by LtH. In Dutch: "... gaat het om zeer persoonlijke informatie die omtrent de afstamming

be significant, but not because it would avoid psychosocial harm. Occasionally, the Memorandum seems open to the possibility that an (individual) child may "suffer" psychologically from not knowing its genetic origins.[161] In those cases, the child's interest is attributed more weight and can overrule the donor's interest in not revealing the information.[162] However, the Memorandum does not elaborate on what qualifies as suffering. Moreover, even if the lack of knowledge does not have a negative impact on the child, it apparently still has an interest in knowing its donor parent(s). This suggests that the interest in identity, and the corresponding interest in the disclosure of donor information, is not primarily understood as a component of the future child's (mental) well-being, but has an independent value.[163] It touches upon another aspect of the child's person, which I will further elaborate on in section 2.3.2 and in chapter 3.

The importance of knowledge of one's origins was several years earlier already emphasised in the Dutch *Valkenhorst* case.[164] The claimant, born out of wedlock, wanted the Valkenhorst institution to grant her access to her files, which contained information on the identity of her biological father. The institution refused out of respect for her mother's right to privacy. The Dutch Supreme Court ruled that this knowledge is not merely an important interest, but that the claimant even had a *right* to know the identity of her biological father,[165] and that this right to knowledge of one's origins is part of a *general personality right*.[166] The Court reasoned that the general personality right forms the foundation of our fundamental rights, including the right to private life and freedom of expression and religion. These fundamental rights allow us to shape different aspects of our personal lives without governmental interference, and thereby allow us to develop

---

van het kind die voor het kind noodzakelijk kan zijn om de jeugd en ontwikkeling tot volwassene beter te begrijpen."

161 *Kamerstukken II*, 1992-1993, 23 207, nr. 3 (*Memorandum Donor Information Artificial Fertilisation Act*), p. 11, 22.

162 Put differently, the interests of the child are balanced against the interests of the donor. If the lack of knowledge has a negative impact on the child, its interest in access to the information becomes more important.

163 Bosch comes to a similar conclusion in her analysis of the way this interest is addressed in the GCRP report *Child and parents in the 21st century*. L. Bosch, 'Welk beleid kan het belang van het kind dragen? Het nieuwe wetsvoorstel draagmoederschap nader bekeken.', *Podium voor Bio-ethiek*, Vol. 27, No. 2, 2020, p. 10.

164 Hoge Raad 15 April 1994 ECLI:NL:HR:1994:ZC1337 (*Valkenhorst*). The institution Valkenhorst took care of unmarried, pregnant women, including the claimant's mother, in a time in which being born out of wedlock was considered a disgrace. The claimant asked the institution to grant her access to her files, which may contain information on the identity of her biological father. The institution refused this request, because the claimant's mother, who was still alive, did not consent to disclosure. The Supreme Court ruled in favour of the claimant.

165 Hoge Raad 15 April 1994 ECLI:NL:HR:1994:ZC1337 (*Valkenhorst*), R.O. 3.2. "...het recht om te weten van welke ouders men afstamt".

166 Hoge Raad 15 April 1994 ECLI:NL:HR:1994:ZC1337 (*Valkenhorst*), R.O. 3.2. "Het algemene persoonlijkheidsrecht".

those aspects of our personal identity. In other words, from the fundamental rights that are codified in the Dutch constitution, the Court distilled the general personality right,[167] and from that it deduced a right to know one's biological parents. The Court added that the right to know one's parents is included in Article 7 of the Convention on the Rights of the Child (hereafter CRC), which was not yet ratified by the Netherlands at the time. For this reason, an alternative route was needed in order to construct the right to knowledge of one's origins. The Court does acknowledge that this right is not absolute[168] and can be overruled by important interests of other parties, including the parents.[169] Nonetheless, by stating that the right to access information about one's origins is part of a general personality right, the Court reveals that what is at stake here transcends one's well-being and touches upon the more fundamental level of one's personal identity. In 2022, the Dutch Supreme Court confirmed the importance of the child's right to know compared to the biological parent's right to privacy. In a recent case, the claimant sued a man whom he suspected was his biological father, in order to make him undergo a paternity test to confirm his suspicions. The Court ruled that given a DNA test was a minor interference with the defendant's bodily integrity and that a biological parent is partly responsible for the child's existence, the right of the child to know its biological origins should prevail over the suspected father's right to privacy.[170]

The importance of accessing donor information was recently once again emphasised in a case started by donor conceived children who were conceived before 2004, when the Dutch Donor Information Artificial Fertilisation Act was entered into force. The Act states that the ban on donor anonymity cannot be applied retrospectively. In the case of children conceived before 2004, the donor must always consent to disclosure of identifying information, according to Article 12(3).[171] If the donor does not consent, identifying information will not be provided to the child. The problem of this section is that it did not take into account the two-track approach that existed at the time in the Netherlands. Before 2004, treatment seeking couples could choose between anonymous donors

167 The general personality right was acknowledged in this case for the first time in Dutch case law. Attorney General Koopmans commented that the construction used by the Dutch Supreme Court appeared to have been inspired by the German Constitutional Court, who distilled a "allgemeine Persönlichkeitsrecht" from Articles 21(1) and 1(1) of the German Constitution. Hoge Raad 15 April 1994 ECLI:NL:HR:1994:ZC1337 (*Valkenhorst*), Conclusion A-G paragraph 18-19. See also B.C. van Beers, *Persoon en lichaam in het recht. Menselijke waardigheid en zelfbeschikking in het tijdperk van de medische biotechnologie*, Hoofddorp, Boom Juridische Uitgevers, 2009b, p. 129.

168 Hoge Raad 15 April 1994 ECLI:NL:HR:1994:ZC1337 (*Valkenhorst*), R.O. 3.3.

169 This restriction is also adopted by the Donor Information Artificial Fertilisation Act, in Article 3(2).

170 Hoge Raad 11 March 2022, ECLI:NL:HR:2022:349, R.O. 3.1.4.

171 Article 12(2) of the same Act maintains that donors have the possibility to state in writing that they withhold their consent in any case a request for information is filed. If they do not use this option, they are asked for their consent every time a donor conceived child requests identifying information.

(A-donors) and non-anonymous donors (B-donors). The latter had, at the moment of donation, explicitly agreed that their identifying information would be provided to the child once the latter reached a certain age and requested the information. The crux was that Article 12 required donors who donated before 2004 to always be asked for their consent before disclosing information when a request was filed, not distinguishing between A- and B-donors. This Article allowed for B-donors to switch to anonymity and withhold their consent when the child filed the request for identifying information years later. In response to this situation, two independent lawsuits were started by donor conceived children who sued the clinics where they were conceived for information about their donor. In the first case, the District Court Gelderland concluded that it was impossible to judge whether the interests of the donor conceived child should prevail over the donor's interests, since the latter was not a party to the case due to his anonymity, and therefore, the Court could not overrule the donor's withdrawal of consent.[172] The Court simply reasoned that it had reached its limits and it was up to the legislator to amend the law.[173] Only a few months later, the District Court of the Hague took a bolder approach. The Court argued that Article 12(3) of the Act, which made an exception for donors pre-2004 and allowed B-donors to switch to anonymity, constituted a violation of the donor conceived children's right to information about their origins, as acknowledged under Article 7 CRC and Article 8 ECHR. It declared Article 12(3)for this reason inapplicable.[174] As a result, the Court ruled that the request for identifying information should be judged in light of the rules that are applicable to donor conception from 2004 onwards, meaning that the information must be disclosed unless the donor has pivotal reasons to remain anonymous.[175] In short, due to the importance attributed to the children's right to know their genetic origins, the Court declared the existing legislation inapplicable.

2.3.1.2 Germany

In the German regulation, the child's interest in identity formation was initially linked to its interests in (psychological) well-being. According to the Memorandum to the Embryo Protection Act, split motherhood, resulting from egg cell donation or surrogacy, may "seriously thwart the formation of the child's own identity" and consequently have a negative impact on the child's psychological development.[176] This point was reiterated by

---

172 District Court Gelderland 24 March 2021 ECLI:NL:RBGEL:2021:1388 (*Switching Donor K34*), R.O. 4.15-4.16.

173 District Court Gelderland 24 March 2021 ECLI:NL:RBGEL:2021:1388 (*Switching Donor K34*), R.O. 4.16.

174 District Court the Hague 2 June 2021 ECLI:NL:RBDHA:2021:5461 (*Switching Donor 605*), R.O. 5.18-5.19. Under Dutch law, international law prevails over national law, based on Article 94 of the Dutch Constitution.

175 District Court the Hague 2 June 2021 ECLI:NL:RBDHA:2021:5461 (*Switching Donor 605*), R.O. 5.27.

176 BT-Drs. 11/5460, vom 25.10.1989 (*Bill and Memorandum Embryo Protection Act*), p. 7. In German: "So wird das Kind entscheidend sowohl durch die von der genetischen Mutter stammenden Erbanlagen als auch durch die enge während der Schwangerschaft bestehende Bindung zwischen ihm und der austragenden

the German Government in the aforementioned case of *S.H. v. Austria*.[177] In this context, the obstructed identity formation is seen as not only problematic in itself, but also as potentially causing psychological harm, since there is no evidence indicating that it does not affect the child.[178] Because of this assumed connection between identity formation and psychological well-being, Taupitz concludes in his commentary on the Embryo Protection Act, that regarding the bans on egg cell donation and post-mortem reproduction, the Memorandum essentially invokes the well-being of the future child as a justification.[179] This assumption has been questioned.[180]

In the context of disclosure of donor information, the connection between thwarted identity formation and psychological harm is no longer mentioned; the future child's interest in its identity is presented as an independent interest or value. The child's right to information on its origins is laid down in the Code of Conduct of 2006,[181] but it is further fleshed out in the German Sperm Donor Registry Act of 2017.[182] This act bans anonymous sperm donation and aims to make it possible for donor conceived children to have access to the donor's identifying information from the age of 16.[183] The foundations for this

---

Mutter geprägt. Unter diesen Umständen liegt die Annahme nahe, daß dem jungen Menschen, der sein Leben gleichsam drei Elternteilen zu verdanken hat, die eigene Identitätsfindung wesentlich erschwert sein wird. Indes lassen nicht nur die besonderen Schwierigkeiten bei der Selbstfindung des Kindes in Fällen der gespaltenen Mutterschaft negative Auswirkungen auf dessen seelische Entwicklung befürchten." The Memorandum also refers to the possibility that the donor dies before the child is conceived and points out that there is no information on how this information may affect the child's well-being and self-understanding. BT-Drs. 11/5460, vom 25.10.1989 (*Bill and Memorandum Embryo Protection Act*), p. 7-8. Also Taupitz addresses this point in relation to post-mortem use of gametes. Günther, Taupitz and Kaiser, 2014, 316-317.

177 ECtHR 3 November 2011 ECLI:CE:ECHR:2011:1103JUD005781300 (*S.H. e.a. v. Austria*), par. 53.

178 BT-Drs. 11/5460, vom 25.10.1989 (*Bill and Memorandum Embryo Protection Act*), p. 7. In German: "... so liegen andererseits doch keine Erkenntnisse darüber vor, wie junge Menschen – etwa in der Pubertätszeit – seelisch den Umstand zu verarbeiten vermögen..."

179 Günther, Taupitz and Kaiser, 2014, p. 181, 317. The Memorandum does not offer an explanation for the ban on post-mortem donation itself, but the same argument against egg cell donation and ovarium transplantation (§1 Abs. 1 nr 1 ESchG) can be applied to post-mortem donation.

180 Ratze and Luxenburger, 2015, p. 1380; Günther, Taupitz and Kaiser, 2014, p. 181-182, 317; Schroeder, 1995, p. 534-535, 544.

181 (Muster-)Richtlinie zur Durchführung der assistierten Reproduktion, Novelle 2006. Deutsches Ärzteblatt 2006; 103 [20], p. 1393.

182 Gesetz zur Regelung des Rechts auf Kenntnis der Abstammung bei heterologer Verwendung von Samen, abbreviated to "Samenspenderregistergesetz". Before the Sperm Donor Registry Act, a duty to register the donor's information was codified in the Code of Conduct. (Muster-)Richtlinie zur Durchführung der assistierten Reproduktion, Novelle 2006. Deutsches Ärzteblatt 2006; 103 [20], p. 1398. §13 abs. 3 of the Sperm Donor Registry Act retrospectively prescribes that all information gathered and stored before 2018 must be kept for a period of 110 years, in order to prevent this information from being destroyed and depriving previous donor conceived children of the right to know their origins. BT-Drs. 18/11291 vom 22.02.2017 (*Bill and Memorandum Sperm Donor Registry Act*), p. 22.

183 If the child is younger than 16, its parents may claim the donor's information on the child's behalf. §10 abs. 3 Samenspenderregistergesetz.

legislation were laid down by the German Federal Court of Justice in a case two years earlier, in which the Court ruled that donor conceived children have a *right* to information about their genetic origins. The full title of the Sperm Donor Registry Act also refers to this right: *Gesetz zur Regelung des Rechts auf Kenntnis der Abstammung bei heterologer Verwendung von Samen* (which translates to: the Act regulating the right to information about descent in cases of heterologous use of semen). Moreover, both the Court and the legislator maintain that this right is part of a general personality right or a "allgemeine Persönlichkeitsrecht".[184] This general personality right is not enacted as such, but it is distilled out of Art. 2 Abs. 1 in combination with Art. 1 Abs. 1 of the German Constitution. In other words, disclosure of donor information is not simply an interest, but a constitutionally protected right. The Federal Court and the Memorandum state that information about one's descent is not a necessary element for one's identity, but *may* be of particular importance for the child to form its identity.[185] Finally, neither the Federal Court nor the Memorandum connect the possible obstruction of one's identity formation (as result of not knowing one's origins) to the child's psychological well-being. The Federal Court does mention that the lack of knowledge may be perceived as a burden, yet it is nowhere stated that it may result in psychological harm. This indicates a different perception on identity formation than that what was previously assumed in the Memorandum to the Embryo Protection Act.

2.3.1.3 The United Kingdom

In the German and Dutch legal systems, the right to access to donor information is understood as part of a general personality right, which is a legal principle that forms the foundation of fundamental rights. Whether, according to the UK perspective, this right is also embedded in a fundamental rights context is unknown. In *Rose v. Secretary of State*,[186] the Court was faced with the question as to whether the child's right to information about

184 BGH 28 January 2015 - XII ZR 201/13 (*Disclosure of donor information*), paragraph 7. In German: "Das Recht eines Kindes auf Kenntnis der eigenen Abstammung wird von dem in Art. 2 Abs. 1 i.V.m. Art. 1 Abs. 1 GG verbürgten allgemeinen Persönlichkeitsrecht umfasst und genieβt daher verfassungsrechtlichen Schutz." BT-Drs. 18/11291 vom 22.02.2017 (*Bill and Memorandum Sperm Donor Registry Act*), p. 1, 16.

185 BGH 28 January 2015 - XII ZR 201/13 (*Disclosure of donor information*), paragraph 41. "Die Kenntnis der Herkunft kann wichtige Anknüpfungspunkte für das Verständnis des familiären Zusammenhangs und für die Entwicklung der eigenen Persönlichkeit geben." BT-Drs. 18/11291 vom 22.02.2017 (*Bill and Memorandum Sperm Donor Registry Act*), p. 17. In German: "dass es für die Identitätsfindung des Kindes von großer Bedeutung sein kann, von den besonderen Umständen seiner Entstehung und familiären Einbindung zu erfahren." According to Starck, knowledge of one's biological origins is of such importance, that the use of an anonymous sperm donor would even violate the future child's human dignity. Mangoldt/Klein/Starck, 2010, Art. 1, Abs. 1, nr. 96.

186 R (on the application of Rose) v. Secretary of State for Health, [2002] EWHC 1593.

her genetic parentage is protected by Article 8 of the Human Rights Act 1998.[187] The judge ruled that Article 8 was engaged. However, before the Court could consider the question of whether Article 8 was actually violated by the failure to disclose donor information, and whether this article constituted a duty to ban donor anonymity, the government amended the law. Now, based on Section 31ZA of the HFE Act 2008, a donor conceived child can request identifying information about its donor parent(s) once it has reached the age of 18.[188] What makes the UK system unique, though, it the fact that a donor conceived child can also request information on donor conceived half-siblings.[189]

The topic of donor anonymity was addressed in the Warnock report, before the HFE Act was enacted. The report recommended openness about the child's (medically assisted) conception. At the same time it concluded that anonymity was in the interest of all parties involved, as it would prevent legal complications and emotional difficulties:[190] "Anonymity would give legal protection to the donor but it would also have the effect of minimising the invasion of the third party into the family."[191] Moreover, it expressed the concern that without guaranteeing anonymity, potential donors would be less likely to donate, which may result in shortages in donor eggs and semen. The report does not explain in what way donor anonymity is in the interest of the future child; it seems more focused on the interests of the donor and the prospective parents. Over the years, the idea that donor conceived children have an interest in identifying information of the donor, and that this interest should take priority over the interests of the parents and the donor has gained more support. In the House of Commons debate, the importance of openness to the child was not questioned.[192] During the House of Lords debate, the necessity of knowing one's origins for the child's identity was stressed, and like in the Netherlands and German this interest was presented as a right. Baroness Andrews, for example, argued that future children have "the right to access information about their origins which will help them, if they so choose, to complete their life history."[193] Also Lord Clement-Jones emphasised the

187 The human rights Act 1998 gives effect in the UK to the European Convention of Human Rights. Article 8 of the Human Rights Act corresponds with Article 8 ECHR. In the case of *Pretty v. UK*, the European Court of Human Rights did acknowledge "that the notion of personal autonomy is an important principle underlying the interpretation of its guarantees." See ECtHR 29 April 2002 ECLI:CE:ECHR:2002:0429JUD000234602 (*Pretty v. the United Kingdom*).

188 The child can request non-identifying information once it is 16.

189 Section 31ZA (2)(b) HFE Act 2008. In addition to finding out about half-siblings, a donor conceived child may also inquire about whether its partner is conceived by the same donor. Section 31ZB HFE Act 2008.

190 Department of Health and Social Security, 1984, p. 15.

191 Department of Health and Social Security, 1984, p. 25.

192 The debate in the House of Commons focused on possible negative consequences of the ban on donor anonymity, such as a shortage of donors, and not on whether the child had an interest in the disclosure of donor information.

193 HL Deb (9 June 2004) vol. 662, col. 345.

importance of disclosure, by claiming that "[k]nowing who one's biological parents are is part of one's identity, and it is important to have that information, if it is available".[194] Moreover, also in the UK debate, the interest in access to information on one's origins is often framed in terms of rights rather than interests. Several MPs spoke about the child's right to access to donor information.[195] Lord Patel even maintained that disclosure of donor information is not an ethical issue, but a rights issue: "It is about the right of children to know their biological identity."[196] Notably, Earl Howe noted that this right to access information is not an absolute right, since it does not include a right to be told the truth about one's conception.[197]

The right to donor information has gained renewed importance in the contact of mitochondrial replacement therapy (MRT). The United Kingdom has been first to regulate this technology,[198] and to allow its use to prevent the transmission of a mitochondrial disease.[199] With the help of MRT, the nuclear DNA of the intended mother is placed in a donated ovum from which the (donor's) nuclear DNA is removed, but which contains healthy mitochondrial DNA. Since only the mother's nuclear DNA is transferred into the donor egg, and not the mother's affected mitochondrial DNA, the transmission of a mitochondrial disease is prevented. However, the child is, as a result of this technique, not only related to its prospective parents, but through the mitochondrial DNA also related to the egg donor, which is why this technology is also referred to as three-parent IVF. The genetic contribution of the egg donor is relatively small, though, and is much less than in the case of regular sperm or egg cell donation, since approximately only 0,1% of our DNA is mitochondrial DNA. Consequently, the question arises as to whether the child's right to information about its origins applies to the mitochondrial donor as well. The UK government expressed that they do not regard the donor as a "second mother" to the child. Moreover, it rejected the idea that "mitochondrial donation results in uncertainty about

194 HL Deb (9 June 2004) vol. 662, col. 352.

195 See for example, HL Deb (9 June 2004) vol. 662, col. 345, 349 (Baroness Andrews); col. 351 (Earl Howe); col. 352 (Lord Clement-Jones) and col. 356 (Baroness Warnock).

196 HL Deb (9 June 2004) vol. 662, col. 363.

197 HL Deb (9 June 2004) vol. 662, col. 351.

198 The Human Fertilisation and Embryology (Mitochondrial Donation) Regulations 2015 expands the definition of 'permitted egg and embryo' in order to facilitate MRT.

199 Apart from preventing the transmission of a mitochondrial disease, MRT can also be used for other purposes. Cavaliere and Palacios-Gonzáles have proposed to allow lesbian couples to use MRT, in order to make both partners genetically related to the resulting child. G. Cavaliere and C. Palacios-González, 'Lesbian motherhood and mitochondrial replacement techniques: reproductive freedom and genetic kinship', *Journal of Medical Ethics*, Vol. 44, 2018, p. 835-842. Dr. John Zhang, who was the first to successfully use this technique to create a child, has expressed the intention to use MRT to 'rejuvenate' egg cells, in order to improve the fertility of older women. See his company website: https://www.darwinlife.com/nuclear-transfer-applications.php.

identity."[200] Because of the small genetic contribution, the government argued that MRT should not be considered similar to ordinary gamete donation, but rather as "a new and distinct form of donation that falls somewhere between gamete donation and organ/tissue donation."[201] Therefore, contrary to children conceived through egg or sperm donation, a child resulting from MRT will not be able to apply for identifying information.[202] In other words, the mitochondrial donor remains anonymous.[203]

2.3.2 *Discussion*

The future child's interest in identity formation is addressed in all three legal systems in the context of the disclosure of donor information. In this section I will draw several parallels between the legal systems in order to provide more insight into the way this interest is interpreted in the regulations on reproduction. First, in the regulatory frameworks that ban donor anonymity, the interest in identity is presented as an independent value. Of course, the German regulation on posthumous conception and split motherhood connects this interest to protecting the future child's psychological well-being. As explained above, this connection has received criticism by scholars who pointed out that there is no empirical evidence for this relation.[204] In addition, the German government seems to have abandoned the assumption, since the possible relation between an obstructed identity formation and psychological well-being has not been addressed in the German legislation on anonymous donor conception. In the Dutch, German, and UK legislation on donor anonymity, identity is perceived as a value in itself, and not merely instrumental in protecting one's mental well-being.

Second, the child's genetic origins are deemed of great importance to its identity, which has led to the ban on anonymous gamete donation. More precisely, all three legal frameworks maintain that this information *may* be crucial, leaving it up to the donor conceived child to decide whether it considers the information to be relevant. Despite this, great weight is attributed to this interest, as access to identifying information about the

---

200 Department of Health, 2014, p. 16.

201 Department of Health, 2014, p. 29.

202 Section 11 (c) the Human Fertilisation and Embryology (mitochondrial donation) regulations 2015.

203 Elsewhere, I criticised the idea that due to a limited genetic relationship between the child and the donor, the child has no right to information about one's origins. Instead, what matters is the fact that the donor contributed to the child's conception and without the donor, it is likely that the child would not exist at all. Therefore, I believe that a right to know one's genetic origins should include a right to receive information about the mitochondrial donor as well. L. ten Haaf, 'Het recht op donorgegevens bij Mitochondrial Replacement Therapy', *Podium voor Bio-ethiek*, Vol. 27, No. 2, 2020, p. 12-14.

204 See for example, Ratze and Luxenburger, 2015, p. 1380; Günther, Taupitz and Kaiser, 2014, p. 181-182; Schroeder, 1995, p. 534-535, 544.

donor is presented as a right.[205] The German regulatory framework and the Dutch *Valkenhorst* case even derived this right to knowledge from a general personality right, which underlies constitutionally protected fundamental rights. Also in UK law, there are clues that the right to access to information may be embedded in a fundamental rights context.[206] However, this rights-vocabulary has not been adopted in the Memorandum of the Dutch Donor Information Artificial Fertilisation Act. Instead, it refers to the *interest* of the future child in having access to identifying information.[207] The Memorandum does emphasise the importance of this interest for the child's identity but does not present it as a (fundamental) right. This difference in vocabulary may account for another difference between the Dutch legal system on the one hand, and the German and UK regulations on the other. The Dutch regulation offers the possibility to the donor to object the disclosure of identifying information. This refusal to disclose information, nonetheless, will only be respected if the donor's interest outweighs that of the child.[208] The German Sperm Donor Registry Act does not allow for the donor to object the registration of its information in the national database once his semen has been used to conceive a child.[209] Also the UK legal system does not seem to leave room for the donor to refuse the disclosure of identifying information.[210]

The assumption that our genetic backstory is relevant for our identity raises the question as to which genetic relationships are part of our identity: only our ancestors who contributed to our existence, or also other genetic relatives? The UK Donor Disclosure regulations seem to include the latter, creating the possibility for donor conceived children to request non-identifying information about donor conceived half-siblings.[211] In addition,

205 The German Federal Court spoke of a right to knowledge about one's origins (in German "Recht auf Kenntnis ihrer Abstammung"), and the rights vocabulary was later adopted in the Memorandum of the Sperm Donor Registry Act, see BT-Drs. 18/11291 vom 22.02.2017 (*Bill and Memorandum Sperm Donor Registry Act*), p. 1. Also the Dutch *Valkenhorst* case spoke of a right to know from which parent(s) one descends. Hoge Raad 15 April 1994 ECLI:NL:HR:1994:ZC1337 (*Valkenhorst*), R.O. 3.2. "Het recht om te weten van welke ouders men afstamt."

206 R (on the application of Rose) v. Secretary of State for Health, [2002] EWHC 1593 (Admin).

207 One of the parties who advised the government on this topic spoke of a "fundamental right of every individual to be able to find out from whom he descends." Unfortunately, it was not further explained why this was a fundamental right. *Kamerstukken II*, 1992-1993, 23 207, nr. 3 (*Memorandum Donor Information Artificial Fertilisation Act*), p. 4.

208 The donor's position was even stronger in the original proposal. In case of the donor's refusal to disclose the information, the child had to prove that its interests outweighed the donor's interests, and were so significant that it justified the disclosure of the information against the donor's will. In the act itself, the burden of proof now lies with the donor. *Kamerstukken II*, 1992-1993, 23 207, nr. 3 (*Memorandum Donor Information Artificial Fertilisation Act*), p. 8.

209 BT-Drs. 18/11291 vom 22.02.2017 (*Bill and Memorandum Sperm Donor Registry Act*) p. 24.

210 S.D. Pattinson, *Medical Law and Ethics*, 4, London, Sweet & Maxwell, 2014, p. 286.

211 Section 31ZA (2)(b) HFE Act 2008. This information can be refused if it is likely that the child applying for the information would be able to identify its half-sibling(s) with it.

if both donor conceived half-siblings consent, they can also receive identifying information about each other.[212] Research has confirmed that donor conceived children take interest in their half-siblings as well. A survey has shown that a large portion of donor conceived children are not only interested in finding their donor-parent, but also in identifying their half-siblings.[213] Reasons given for wanting to know their half-siblings included "to know and understand a 'missing' part of me", "to have a better understanding of why I am who I am", and a "desire for secure sense of identity." Under Dutch and German law, the donor conceived child can only request information on the donor. The Dutch Minister of Health, however, has expressed the intention to assist donor conceived children to find donor conceived half-siblings.[214]

The three legal systems show strong similarities regarding the interpretation of the future child's interest in identity. In all the Dutch, German, and UK regulations on donor anonymity, identity is deemed a value in itself and access to information about one's genetic origins is part of a general personality right. The three regulatory frameworks have also in common the fact that they leave several questions unanswered. None of them explain which concept of *identity* underlies these proposals and why one's genetic origins is of such importance to a child's self-understanding. Chapter 3 goes further into this matter, aiming to reconstruct the notion of identity underlying the donor anonymity bans.

2.4 The Interest in Respect for Human Dignity

2.4.1 The Regulations

The third interest attributed to the future child is the interest in safeguarding its human dignity. In addition to human dignity, the regulatory frameworks operationalise various other concepts to refer to the inherent value of the human person or the human embryo. For example, the Dutch regulation uses human dignity, but also respect for humanity[215], respect for the dignity of the human person[216] and the need to protect the value of human

212 Jackson, 2016, p. 835.

213 V. Jadva, T. Freeman, W. Kramer and S. Golombok, 'Experiences of offspring searching for and contacting their donor siblings and donor', *Reproductive Biomedicine Online*, Vol. 20, No. 4, 2010.

214 *Kamerstukken II* 2016-2017, 30 486, nr. 16, p. 3.

215 *Kamerstukken II* 2000-2001, 27 423, nr. 3 (*Memorandum Embryo Act*), p. 48. In Dutch: "Respect [en piëteit] jegens mens [en dier]."

216 *Kamerstukken II* 2000-2001, 27 423, nr. 3 (*Memorandum Embryo Act*), p. 45. In Dutch: "respect voor de waardigheid van de menselijke person."

life.[217] In the UK debate on reproductive cloning, concepts such as sanctity of human life[218] or the special and sacred nature of human life[219] were mentioned. These abstract concepts have in common that they demand a certain piety for and even protection of human life because it is *human* life. Consequently, they demand a certain restraint in, amongst other things, the application of biotechnology. Importantly, various of these concepts also aim to articulate the special status of the human embryo. According to German constitutional law, the human embryo (at least the embryo in utero) possesses human dignity,[220] while under Dutch law, the human embryo is not considered to possess human dignity; instead, the special status of the human embryo is articulated through the term "respect for human life."[221] Nonetheless, the regulatory frameworks also use the mentioned terms to address how various reproductive technologies affect the person that results from them, i.e. the future child.

Human dignity and related concepts are particularly mobilised in the regulation of technologies that offer the possibility to exercise control over the genetic constitution of the future child. In the Memoranda and parliamentary discussions, the argument was raised that this control may result in the objectification of the child, which would be a violation of its dignity. In general, there are two types of technologies that enable such control over the future child's genetic makeup. The first group are those technologies that facilitate the *selection* of a child based on its genetic characteristics, such as PGT or reproductive human cloning. The second group includes those technologies that entail *altering* the genome, both on an individual level, in the case of, for example, germline cell therapy, or on a species level the creation of human-animal hybrids and chimaera's.

2.4.1.1 The Netherlands

In the Netherlands, the notion of human dignity is invoked in order to prohibit several technologies that affect the human genome, such as human reproductive cloning,[222] germline genetic modification[223] and the creation of human-animal hybrids.[224] These technologies are assumed to "violate what is permitted out of respect for human life."[225]

217 *Kamerstukken II* 2000-2001, 27 423, nr. 3 (*Memorandum Embryo Act*), p. 64. In Dutch: "de beschermwaardigheid van het menselijk leven."
218 HL Deb (26 November 2001) vol. 629, col. 21.
219 HL Deb (26 November 2001) vol. 629, col. 27.
220 See section 2.1.1.1.
221 See for example, *Kamerstukken II* 2000-2001, 27 423, nr. 3 (*Memorandum Embryo Act*), p. 3, 5, 6, 22. In Dutch: "respect voor menselijk leven". See also van Beers, 2009b, p. 235.
222 Article 24(f) Embryo Act.
223 Article 24(g) Embryo Act.
224 Article 25 Embryo Act.
225 *Kamerstukken II* 2000-2001, 27 423, nr. 3 (*Memorandum Embryo Act*), p. 9. Translation by LtH. In Dutch: "... de (in acht te nemen) grenzen van eerbied voor het menselijk leven zouden overschrijden". With regard

Why these technologies are an affront to human dignity is most clearly elaborated in the Memorandum's discussion on prohibiting reproductive cloning. Reproductive human cloning facilitates the creation of genetically identical persons, which according to the Memorandum qualifies as the "instrumentalisation" of humans.[226] Moreover, this technology entails "the possibility to clone a person because of a specific trait instead of the person himself",[227] in which case, the person would be valued for one or a few characteristics, instead of being valued as a (whole) person. Both these aspects, the instrumentalisation and basing a person's value on a few of its traits, are considered to be a violation of the child's human dignity.

With regard to germline genetic modification, the Memorandum does not take a clear stance on whether germline therapy violates the child's dignity. Instead, it raises questions as to whether human dignity entails acknowledgement for a right to inherit "A genome that is not intentionally modified by other people", or whether germline therapy is in accordance with respect for human dignity, without offering an answer.[228] The Memorandum concludes by stating that genetic engineering has to be banned for now since the technology is not yet safe enough for clinical application. Nonetheless, it leaves open the possibility that it might be allowed in the future.[229] The initial bill of the Embryo Act contained a provision that offered the possibility to lift the ban on germline engineering by royal decree, that is, without parliamentary vote,[230] but this provision did not make it into the final Act. Due to this, lifting the ban on germline modification requires the approval of parliament. In 2016, Minister of Health Schipper tried to create more possibilities for research into germline modification with a proposal to lift the ban on creating embryo's for research purposes. In addition to IVG and MRT, human germline

to reproductive cloning, the Memorandum explicitly states this is a violation of human dignity. With regard to human-animal chimaera's, it says that the actions prohibited in Article 25 of the Embryo act are not compatible with the notion of respect and piety from human and animal. *Kamerstukken II* 2000-2001, 27 423, nr. 3 (*Memorandum Embryo Act*), p. 48.

226 *Kamerstukken II* 2000-2001, 27 423, nr. 3 (*Memorandum Embryo Act*), p. 41. This is in line with international treaties such as the Protocol to the Convention on Human Rights and Biomedicine on the Prohibition of Cloning Human Beings, which the Netherlands has signed.

227 *Kamerstukken II* 2000-2001, 27 423, nr. 3 (*Memorandum Embryo Act*), p. 42.

228 *Kamerstukken II* 2000-2001, 27 423, nr. 3 (*Memorandum Embryo Act*), p. 45. In Dutch: "Het gaat immers om principiële vragen als de vraag of respect voor de waardigheid van de menselijke persoon de erkenning moet inhouden van het recht om een niet door gericht menselijk ingrijpen veranderd genetisch patroon te erven of dat therapie op het niveau van de kiembaan juist aan dat beginsel tegemoet komt." Translation by LtH.

229 *Kamerstukken II* 2000-2001, 27 423, nr. 3 (*Memorandum Embryo Act*), p. 46.

230 *Kamerstukken II* 2000-2001, 27 423, nr. 2 (*Bill Embryo Act*). See Section 32(3). See also B.C. van Beers, C. de Kluiver and R. Maas, 'The regulation of human germline genome modification in the Netherlands.' in: A. Boggio, C. Romano and J. Almqvist (eds.), *Human Germline Genome Modification and the Right to Science: A Comparative Study of National Laws and Policies*, Cambridge University Press, Cambridge, 2020, p. 325.

editing was listed as one of the reasons for the necessity of research embryo's. Schippers deemed the only possible objection to these technologies was that they were not safe yet for clinical use.[231] After the Chinese scientist Jiankui He announced that he had used CRISPR-Cas9 to genetically modify two human babies, the Dutch Health Council and the Dutch Committee Genetic Modification wrote a report in which they indirectly addressed the question raised in the Memorandum. In their report, they stated that germline modification can be in line with respect for human dignity, provided it aims to prevent suffering by removing the causes of illness.[232] Therefore, if the technology is deemed safe and effective, it serves the interest of future children if the technology is used to replace affected genes with healthy genes.[233] Despite Schippers's efforts and the report of the Health Council and the Committee on Genetic Modification, the new Minister of Health withdrew Schippers proposal, not continuing her policy on creating embryo's for research and germline modification.[234] As van Beers et al. pointed out, it remains to be seen how the Dutch political and legal debate concerning germline modification will turn out in the future. Nonetheless, van Beers et al. emphasise that the notion of human dignity should not only be understood as "respect for autonomy but also as protection against dehumanization."[235]

The future child's interest in human dignity is also mobilised in the context of non-medical selection. Selective reproduction entails the risk that the future child is instrumentalised, and that the creation of human life becomes conditional.[236] This would be an affront to human dignity. Here, a tension between various interests of the future child come to the fore. As I already pointed out in section 2.2.1.1., in various regulatory frameworks selective reproduction when used to prevent a genetic disorder is considered to be in the interest of the future child, and in those cases selection is justified. As follows from the regulatory framework on PGT, embryo selection is deemed acceptable if the future child runs a high risk of severe harm. The interplay between the future child's interests in well-being and dignity can be illustrated with the regulation of sex selection.[237] Sex selection for medical

231 van Beers, de Kluiver and Maas, 2020, p. 332.
232 Commissie Genetische Modificatie (COGEM) & Gezondheidsraad, 2017, p. 55-56.
233 Commissie Genetische Modificatie (COGEM) & Gezondheidsraad, 2017, p. 73.
234 Letter Minister of Public Health, Well-being and Sports of 9 July 2017 (*Stcrt.* 2018, 42606). See also van Beers, de Kluiver and Maas, 2020, p. 331.
235 van Beers, de Kluiver and Maas, 2020, p. 334.
236 Habermas, 2003, p. 30.
237 *Kamerstukken II* 2007-2008, 29 323, nr. 46 (*second explanatory letter PGD*), p. 4. In this letter to parliament, the State Secretary says that subject of PGD requires a balance between protecting the worthiness of life on the one hand, and the prevention of suffering of a future child on the other. The latter would advocate a more extensive use of selection, and for this reason, the former concept can be understood as containing a demand for restraint and cautiousness with regard to controlling human life before conception.

reasons is allowed under Dutch law.[238] That is, if there is a risk the future child will be afflicted with a severe, sex-linked condition. In this case, the future child's interest to be free from harm justifies the selection. At the same time, non-medical sex selection is prohibited as it does not serve the interests of the future child.[239] On the contrary, it would constitute a violation of the future child's interest and dignity. According to the Memorandum to the Embryo Act, selection for non-medical traits reduces the child "to nothing more than the object of its parents' wishes and desires."[240]

Characterising instrumentalisation and being born to serve the wishes or needs for others as a violation of human dignity is also mentioned in the regulation of HLA-tissue typing. With the help of tissue typing, a suitable donor for a sick sibling, a so-called saviour sibling, can be selected. Under Dutch law, tissue typing is only allowed for *additional* selection. That is, if PGT is in the first case necessary to prevent a future child from being affected by the same inheritable condition, further selection based on HLA-tissue type is allowed. According to the ministerial decree, only in these situations does PGT serve, in the first place, the interests of the future child. However, if the selection does not (primarily) benefit the child, PGT is not acceptable, because "the 'new' child would be brought into existence only to serve the needs of another child."[241]

2.4.1.2 Germany

In German law, similar actions are prohibited. The Embryo Protection Act bans non-medical sex selection,[242] germline modification,[243] reproductive cloning,[244] and the creation of chimaera's and hybrids.[245] Similar to the Dutch regulation, the concept of human dignity

238 Article 26(2) Embryo Act.

239 Article 26(1) Embryo Act; Regeling van de staatssecretaris van Volksgezondheid, Welzijn en Sport van 16 februari 2009, nr. CZ-TSZ-2912089, houdende houdende regels ten aanzien van preïmplantatie genetische diagnostiek (PGD), (*Stcrt.* 2009, 42) (*Ministerial decree PGD*).

240 *Kamerstukken II* 2000-2001, 27 423, nr. 3 (*Memorandum Embryo Act*), p. 48. In Dutch "...tot louter voorwerp van de wensen en verlangens van hun ouders." Translation by LtH. This argument is echoed in Regeling van de staatssecretaris van Volksgezondheid, Welzijn en Sport van 16 februari 2009, nr. CZ-TSZ-2912089, houdende houdende regels ten aanzien van preïmplantatie genetische diagnostiek (PGD), (*Stcrt.* 2009, 42) (*Ministerial decree PGD*), p. 12.

241 Regeling van de staatssecretaris van Volksgezondheid, Welzijn en Sport van 16 februari 2009, nr. CZ-TSZ-2912089, houdende houdende regels ten aanzien van preïmplantatie genetische diagnostiek (PGD), (*Stcrt.* 2009, 42) (*Ministerial decree PGD*), p. 8.

242 §3 ESchG.

243 §5 ESchG.

244 §6 ESchG.

245 §7 ESchG. On the creation of chimaera's, it merely states that the creation of a chimaera's using one human embryo or a human-animal hybrid disregards human dignity. BT-Drs. 11/5460, vom 25.10.1989 (*Bill and Memorandum Embryo Protection Act*), p. 12. In German: "Ebenfalls in besonders krasser Weise verstößt es gegen die Menschenwürde, Chimären unter Verwendung mindestens eines menschlichen Embryos oder auch Hybridwesen aus Mensch und Tier zu erzeugen."

plays an important role in the justification of these prohibitions. In the German regulation, a slightly different interpretation of the nature of the possible violation can be found. Whereas the Dutch Memorandum primarily maintained that these technologies facilitated the instrumentalisation of the human child, which would constitute a violation of its dignity, the German Memorandum presumes that the violation of human dignity lies in the possibility of designing and breeding humans. The ban on reproductive cloning, for example, is supported by the claim that a person's dignity is violated if his genetic constitution is decided for him by another person.[246] With regard to germline modification, the Memorandum warns for the dangers of misuse, in particular if the technique would be used for "human breeding" by designing another person's genetic constitution.[247] The Memorandum does not directly state that altering the genetic constitution of future persons violates human dignity because it leads to designing humans. After all, it only warns for the possibility of this type of misuse. In the wake of the introduction of CRISPR-Cas9 and the news of the genetically modified Chinese babies, the German Ethics Council published a report on genome editing. In this report, it showed some openness to the possibilities of genetic modification. The Council unanimously agreed that the human germline was not inviolable.[248] yet it was divided on the question as to whether this implied that genetic modification is ethically acceptable.[249] It recommended that:

> The assessment of the permissibility of germline interventions should not be reduced to a mere risk and opportunity analysis. Rather, it should be based on the ethical concepts of human dignity, protection of life and integrity, freedom, non-maleficence and beneficence, naturalness, justice, solidarity and responsibility.[250]

Human dignity remained one of the paramount considerations, but the Ethics Council also pointed out that there are different views as to what human dignity entails in the context of germline modification. Similar to the Memorandum of the Dutch Embryo Act, the Council stated that the introduction of this technology has raised the question as to whether germline modification must be understood as a form of instrumentalisation and

246 BT-Drs. 11/5460, vom 25.10.1989 (*Bill and Memorandum Embryo Protection Act*), p. 11. In German: "In besonders krasser Weise würde es gegen die Menschenwürde verstoßen, gezielt einem künftigen Menschen seine Erbanlagen zuzuweisen."

247 BT-Drs. 11/5460, vom 25.10.1989 (*Bill and Memorandum Embryo Protection Act*), p. 11. In German: "Menschenzüchtung." Translation by LtH.

248 Deutscher Ethikrat, 2019, p. 36, 39.

249 Deutscher Ethikrat, 2019, p. 40-41.

250 Deutscher Ethikrat, 2019, p. 36.

thus would be a violation of human dignity, or whether the prevention of suffering caused by a genetic defect could also be understood as respect for human dignity.[251]

In the context of sex selection, the German regulation distinguishes between medically indicated, which is allowed, and non-medical selection.[252] The Memorandum is surprisingly short and, in the words of Taupitz, "vague"[253] in its motivation. It only states that non-medical sex selection is banned because it encourages designing humans.[254] On this point, the Memorandum does not directly connect the possibility of designing humans to the violation of human dignity, as it does with regard to reproductive cloning and genome editing. This connection is made in academic literature. For example, in his commentary on the Embryo Protection Act, German scholar Müller-Terpitz argues that the ban on sex selection also aims to protect human dignity, by preventing the resulting child from understanding itself as a human being.[255] but solely as a design object. Taupitz has criticised the idea that sex selection is a violation to human dignity. Although he admits that the creation of designer babies would be a violation, simple sex selection does not qualify as design, in his opinion.[256]

2.4.1.3 The United Kingdom

As discussed in the introduction of this chapter, the UK is characterised by a more permissive attitude towards biotechnology than the Netherlands and Germany. This difference in attitude becomes particularly visible in the regulation of genetic technologies. Illustrative of this is the fact that mitochondrial replacement therapy[257] and non-additional HLA-typing[258] are permitted in the UK. Still, technologies that allow extensive control over the future child's genome, such as germline modification and reproductive cloning,

---

251 Deutscher Ethikrat, 2019, p. 17.

252 §3 ESchG.

253 Günther, Taupitz and Kaiser, 2014, p. 267.

254 BT-Drs. 11/5460, vom 25.10.1989 (*Bill and Memorandum Embryo Protection Act*), p. 10. In German: "Einer derartigen, nicht zuletzt auch Züchtungstendenzen Vorschub leistenden Manipulation ist entgegenzutreten."

255 Spickhoff, 2011, ESchG § 3, nr 1. In German: "Zudem wird auf eine Schutzfunktion zugunsten des objektivrechtlichen Gehalts des Menschenwürdesatzes (Art. 1 I GG) verwiesen: Dieser garantiere, dass der Staat Versuchen begegne, die es einem entstehenden Individuum unmöglich machten, sich als unfestgestelltes, offenes Wesen "Mensch" zu verstehen."

256 Günther, Taupitz and Kaiser, 2014, p. 269.

257 Section 3(2) and Section 3ZA(5) HFE Act 2008. MRT is only allowed if it aims to prevent a serious mitochondrial condition. Although in the Netherlands MRT technically does not fall within the scope of the ban on germline modification ex article 24(g) of the Embryo Act, it is not officially regulation. *Kamerstukken II* 2000-2001, 27 423, nr. 3 (*Memorandum Embryo Act*), p. 45.

258 Section 1ZA (1)(d) HFE Act 2008; Quintavalle v. Human Fertilisation and Embryology Authority. 2005. UKHL 28.

are not allowed.[259] Importantly, the UK is characterised not only by different regulatory choices, but also by a different doctrine altogether. In general, the justification for its regulations on reproduction is based on consequentialist arguments, focusing on the prevention of harm,[260] instead of the concept of human dignity.

The preference for consequentialist thinking is visible in the ban on sex selection. In the Dutch and German regulations, non-medical sex selection was prohibited because it is seen as a violation of human dignity. The UK government took a different route in their motivation, banning sex selection because of "the possible effects (…) on cultures where there is a clear preference for male children."[261] In addition, it referred to the public opinion: before deciding on the permissibility of sex selection, the HFEA first conducted a public consultation which showed that most of the respondents were against sex selection for non-medical reasons. By invoking these arguments, the UK government focuses on the possible consequences of the technology, rather than discussing whether sex selection is objectionable in itself. Nonetheless, indirectly, the idea of an inherent value of the human came to the fore in the survey. The reasons the respondents had for being against sex selection varied widely, but the HFEA pointed out that some of these arguments were based on "a recognition that in having a child parents are bringing into existence a human being whom they should seek to nurture, but not to design or control."[262] Notably, the HFEA merely repeated arguments that were mentioned in the consultation, rather than offering moral arguments of its own. Consequently, we can merely conclude that the appeal to human dignity only contributed indirectly to the regulation on sex selection and that it was just one of the many arguments against social sex selection.

With regard to the permissibility of germline modification, the UK government also strongly relies on consequentialist arguments instead of protecting human dignity. The most important argument used against germline modification is that the consequences of

259 Section 3ZA (4) HFE Act 2008 defines a permitted embryo as an embryo whose nuclear or mitochondrial DNA has not been altered and which has no cells added to it. Not only can the embryo itself not be modified, but also the gametes that were used for the creation of the embryo may not be genetically altered. This provision does prohibit genetically modified embryos (and future children) and reproductive cloning. The cloning process would require that the nuclear DNA of an unfertilised egg cell is replaced by the nuclear DNA of the original (the technique that was also used to create the cloned sheep Dolly), and therefore, it does not fall under the definition of a permitted embryo. HFE Act 2008 Explanatory notes, no. 29.

260 A. Smajdor, 'How useful is the concept of the 'harm threshold' in reproductive ethics and law?', *Theoretical Medicine and Bioethics*, Vol. 35, 2014, p. 322-324.

261 Department of Health, *Review of the Human Fertilisation and Embryology Act. Proposals for revised legislation (including establishment of the Regulatory Authority for Tissue and Embryos)*, 2006, p. 15.

262 Human Fertilisation and Embryology Authority, *Sex Selection: choice and responsibility in human reproduction*, 2003p. 25.

genome editing are at the moment unknown and would most likely harm the future child that would result from it.[263] Because this is not an absolute objection to genetic modification, it is not surprising that the advisory bodies are open to permitting genome editing technologies once they are proven safe. In 2006, the government argued that genome editing should be prohibited "for the foreseeable future"[264] and the House of Commons Science and Technology Committee recommended "to relax this ban under tightly controlled circumstances if and when the technology is further advanced."[265] In 2018, the Nuffield Council came to a similar conclusion, considering genome editing "ethically acceptable in some circumstances", provided that the technology was safe for use and intended to secure the welfare of the future child resulting from the procedure.[266] In addition to the strong focus on harm prevention and the future child's well-being, these discussions on the permissibility of germline modification barely address the concept of human dignity and what the future child's dignity entails in this context.[267] Moreover, the Nuffield Council explicitly dismissed this notion as a relevant concept. Because the concept is hard to pin down and it is assumed not to be of added value to the functioning of the human rights discourse.[268] the Council concluded that the concept was not helpful in this context.[269]

The explicit dismissal of the concept of human dignity by the Nuffield Council does not imply that this concept is completely absent in the UK debate. It has played a particular prominent role in the regulation and discussion of reproductive cloning, alongside consequentialist arguments.[270] One of the main reasons for the ban on reproductive cloning was motivated by welfare-arguments, pointing out that the technology was unsafe and dangerous.[271] The technology would likely cause health damage to the clone, as it had

263 See for example, Department of Health, 2006, p. 16: "However, the Government is persuaded that for the foreseeable future, and until such time as safety and efficacy are assured, genetic alterations of gametes and embryos should not be permitted for reproductive purposes." Also the Science and Tech Committee appeals mostly to safety reasons to object genome editing for now. House of Commons Science and Technology Committee, 2005, p. 39-40.

264 Department of Health, 2006, p. 16.

265 House of Commons Science and Technology Committee, 2005, p. 40.

266 Nuffield Council on Bioethics, 2018, p. 75, 157. See also section 2.2.1.3.

267 See also van Beers, 2020, p. 26-27.

268 Nuffield Council on Bioethics, 2018, p. 93-94.

269 Nuffield Council on Bioethics, 2018, p. 158.

270 Human Reproductive Cloning Act was repealed by the HFE Act 2008 amendments. Yet, the parliamentary debates prior to these amendments did not focus on issues that were 'already accepted'. Department of Health, 2006, p. 3. In order to understand the justification for the prohibition of reproductive cloning, it is worth looking at the previous Act.

271 See for example, HL Deb (26 November 2001) vol. 629, col. 10; HL Deb (26 November 2001) vol. 629, col. 27; HC Deb (29 November 2001) vol. 375, col. 1180-1181.

done to Dolly, the cloned sheep, and should accordingly be banned.[272] Nonetheless, the Science and Technology report commented that an absolute ban on reproductive cloning could not be supported by safety concerns alone, as it is imaginable that in the future, the technology will be safe and effective. Instead, it should be supported by "principled arguments" as well.[273] Such arguments were raised during the parliamentary debate on the Human Reproductive Cloning Act, in which there were several mentions of the "sanctity of human life"[274] or the "special and sacred nature of human life"[275]. Moreover, Earl Howe argued that:

> Reproductive cloning has no claim whatever to any moral equivalence with in vitro fertilisation. That is not simply because of the scientific risks associated with the technique – significant as those are – but because reproductive cloning, if successful, would result in the creation of an individual deprived of two fundamental rights that, I dare say, each of us has up to now taken for granted. Those are the right to have a genetic father and mother and the right to a genetic identity of one's own, separate from that of any adult already living. Those rights are – or should be – as inalienable as any in our constitution. They go to the heart of what we mean by human dignity and what it is to be an individual.[276]

Other arguments concerning the violation of human dignity mirrored both the Dutch and the German interpretations. For example, it was argued that reproductive cloning violated the future child's dignity, because the child would be treated as a commodity.[277] which expresses a similar fear of instrumentalisation as seen in the Dutch Memorandum. Additionally, Lord Brennan pointed out that reproductive cloning would lead to the "manufacture of human beings",[278] which is in line with the German focus on designing humans as a violation of human dignity.

2.4.2 Discussion

With regard to the mobilisation of human dignity, the differences in attitude towards regulating biotechnology between the three legal systems becomes clear. First, some

272 HL Deb (26 November 2001) vol. 629, col. 19, 27.
273 House of Commons Science and Technology Committee, 2005.
274 HL Deb (26 November 2001) vol. 629, col. 21.
275 HL Deb (26 November 2001) vol. 629, col. 27.
276 HL Deb (26 November 2001) vol. 629, col. 52.
277 HL Deb (26 November 2001) vol. 629, col. 23, 51; HC Deb (29 November 2001) vol. 375, col. 1196.
278 HL Deb (26 November 2001) vol. 629, col. 20.

differences in the regulation itself can be noted. For example, HLA-typing is completely banned in Germany, partly prohibited in the Netherlands, and allowed in the UK. In addition, the UK allows a specific form of genetic intervention, MRT. Despite these differences, there are also important similarities. All three countries explicitly prohibit non-medical sex selection, reproductive cloning, and (nuclear) germline modification. Moreover, advisory bodies in all three legal systems have shown some willingness to remove the ban on the latter. Yet, even in the regulatory frameworks that are rather similar, different motivations are used. The Netherlands and Germany point out that these technologies violate the future child's human dignity. The UK justifies the ban on these technologies primarily by referring to the fact that they are unsafe and could therefore jeopardise the future child's well-being. The difference in attitude is best seen in the regulation of technologies that on the one hand could be understood as a violation of human dignity, but on the other hand could contribute to the health and well-being of the future child, or in the case of HLA-typing, a third party. Here, the UK's preference for arguments based on rights or the harm or welfare principle is shown. At the same time, despite this preference for consequentialist reasoning, the concept of human dignity is touched upon in the UK legislation on reproductive cloning.

Given that it is such a fundamental notion in national and international legislation, it is remarkable that the concept of human dignity is nowhere clearly defined.[279] Stix-Hackl even argued that hardly any legal concept is harder to define than human dignity.[280] Its lack of a coherent definition was, for the Nuffield Council, a reason to consider this notion problematic and useless. The Memoranda and parliamentary discussions on the regulations on reproduction also do not offer a demarcated meaning of this concept. Some definitions are offered in the reports of the advisory bodies. According to the German Ethics Council, in its reflection upon germline modification: "In modern use, "human dignity" stands for that value which is resistant to any trade-offs and which is due to man as such and independently of all social provisions: man is regarded as an "end in himself". This results in the ethical-philosophical and common jurisprudential prohibition of the "complete instrumentalisation" of any human being."[281] The Dutch Health Council and Committee on Genetic Modification state that the notion is connected with "respect for human life, individual autonomy and the duty to prevent suffering."[282] Still, a closer analysis of the regulations on reproduction allows us to distil several aspects of the future child's interest in human dignity. In the following sections, I will address three aspects of this interest that

279 van Beers states that despite the fact that the concept of human dignity is a fundamental concept in the Dutch legal system, its meaning is nowhere clarified. van Beers, 2009b, p. 15.

280 Conclusion Stix-Hackl EU CoJ 18 March 2004 ECLI:EU:C:2004:162 (*Omega*), par. 74.

281 Deutscher Ethikrat, 2019, p. 17.

282 Commissie Genetische Modificatie (COGEM) & Gezondheidsraad, 2017, p. 53, 54.

are implied by the regulatory frameworks: the prohibition of instrumentalisation, the right to a unique identity, and finally the subject of human dignity.

2.4.2.1 Instrumentalisation and Design

Perhaps the most prominent aspect of the future child's interest in the protection of its human dignity is the prohibition of instrumentalisation or commodification.[283] This aspect is, amongst others, pointed out by the German Ethics Council. Also in the Dutch and UK regulatory frameworks, instrumentalisation is seen as a violation of the future child's dignity.[284] In particular, in the context of reproduction, "[t]he dignity of life demands that a life should not be created simply to serve the interests of another."[285] This concern was expressed with regard to non-medical sex selection. The Dutch regulator maintained that non-medical sex selection reduces the child to an object of its parents' desires, in which case reproduction would have an instrumental character. For this reason, it should be prohibited.[286] While both legal systems agree upon the prohibition of instrumentalisation, there is a difference in the interpretation of what qualifies as being born to solely serve the needs of others. This comes to the fore in the regulation of HLA-typing. In Germany, HLA-typing is prohibited, because, according to the Ethics Council, "such a selection of embryos would carry too great a danger that a person would be instrumentalised for the purposes of another."[287] The Dutch regulator deems that non-additional selection (i.e. when PGT is solely used for the purpose of finding a suitable donor) qualifies as instrumentalisation. In that case, the selection would be focused on selecting a donor, and the child would only be born for the needs of its sibling.[288] A similar regulatory approach was initially adopted by the UK HFEA, only allowing non-additional

283 These concepts are closely related. Wilkinson, for example, sees instrumentalisation, or treating a person as a mere means, as a component of commodification, alongside fungibility. S. Wilkinson, *Choosing tomorrow's children. The ethics of selective reproduction*, Oxford, Oxford University Press, 2010, p. 131-133.

284 *Kamerstukken II* 2000-2001, 27 423, nr. 3 (*Memorandum Embryo Act*), p. 41 48; *Kamerstukken II* 2005-2006, 30 300 XVI, nr. 136 (*first explanatory letter PGD*), p. 7, 9; HL Deb (26 November 2001) vol. 629, col. 23, 51; HC Deb (29 November 2001) vol. 375, col. 1196.

285 HC Deb (12 May 2008) vol. 475, col. 1078.

286 *Kamerstukken II* 2005-2006, 30 300 XVI, nr. 136 (*first explanatory letter PGD*), p. 9; *Kamerstukken II* 2000-2001, 27 423, nr. 3 (*Memorandum Embryo Act*), p. 48.

287 Deutscher Ethikrat, *Preimplanation genetic diagnosis. Opinion*, Berlin, 2011, p. 87.

288 *Kamerstukken II* 2005-2006, 30 300 XVI, nr. 136 (*first explanatory letter PGD*), p. 11; Regeling van de staatssecretaris van Volksgezondheid, Welzijn en Sport van 16 februari 2009, nr. CZ-TSZ-2912089, houdende houdende regels ten aanzien van preïmplantatie genetische diagnostiek (PGD), (*Stcrt.* 2009, 42) (*Ministerial decree PGD*).

HLA-typing,[289] until it changed its policy in 2004.[290] Since then, HLA-typing has been allowed even if the resulting child was not at risk of inheriting the same genetic condition as its sibling. Various scholars have supported the idea that non-additional HLA-tissue typing does not result in the instrumentalisation of the child; they argue that the child is not conceived *solely* for the purpose of donating. After all, the parents in most cases wanted another child, and therefore, the child is also an end in itself.[291]

The German regulation frames the possible violation of human dignity differently, focusing on the problematic potential for designing humans. For example, the ban on human cloning stresses that the violation lies in the fact that the clone's genetic constitution is determined for him,[292] making it a "creation of technocrats", rather than a product of chance.[293] Also with regard to the bans on genome editing and sex selection, the Memorandum states that human dignity is or may be endangered because of the possibility to design humans.[294] A similar argument was raised in the UK parliamentary debate on reproductive cloning, where Lord Brennan argued it results in the "manufacture of human beings."[295] Even though the German regulation does not make this connection explicit (and nor does Lord Brennan), the appeal to human dignity can be connected to a prohibition of the objectification or instrumentalisation of humans. Under German law, human dignity is protected in Article 1 of the German Constitution. In explaining its content, commentaries on this article often refer to the so-called *Objektformel,*[296] which entails that human dignity is violated when a person is treated as a mere object.[297] As a

---

289 The report of the Science and Technology Committee refers to the Whittaker case, in which permission for conducting tissue typing was refused, because the illness of the affected sibling was a result of a spontaneous mutation and not inherited. House of Commons Science and Technology Committee, 2005, p. 59.

290 The permissibility of this new possibility was confirmed by the House of Lords in the Quintavalle case. Quintavalle v. Human Fertilisation and Embryology Authority. 2005. UKHL 28.

291 House of Commons Science and Technology Committee, 2005, p. 59-60; S. Sheldon and S. Wilkinson, 'Should selecting saviour siblings be banned?', *Journal of Medical Ethics*, Vol. 30, 2004, p. 533-534; N.R. Ram, 'Britain's new preimplantation tissue typing policy: an ethical defence', *Journal of Medical Ethics*, Vol. 32, 2006, p. 279-280.

292 BT-Drs. 11/5460 vom 25.10.1989 (Bill and Memorandum Embryo Protection Act), p. 11.

293 Günther, Taupitz and Kaiser, 2014, p. 331.

294 In German: "Züchtung". BT-Drs. 11/5460, vom 25.10.1989 (*Bill and Memorandum Embryo Protection Act*), p. 10 and 11.

295 HL Deb (26 November 2001) vol. 629, col. 20.

296 See for example, Maunz/Dürig, 2016, Art. 1 abs. 1 para 36, "Die Menschenwürde ist getroffen, wenn der konkrete Mensch zum Objekt, zu einem bloßen Mittel, zur vertretbaren Größe herabgewürdigt wird." Stern/Becker, 2016, Art. 1, p. 107-108; Sachs, 2014, Art. I, p. 83f; Münch/Kunig, 2012, Art. 1, p.73f.

297 Persons are often also the object of state actions, but that does not mean that they are treated as a *mere* objects. This is the case when the treatment lacks any respect for the person's own value, for example, in case of human trafficking or torture. Sachs, 2014, Art. 1, p. 83. Also van Beers concludes that the instrumentalisation of humans implies that they are treated as a means, or an object, and that this is a violation of a core aspect of human dignity, namely the distinction between persons and things. van Beers,

result, respecting human dignity under Article 1 of the German Constitution requires the prohibition of instrumentalisation, something that is also mentioned in the interpretation by the German Ethics Council.[298] Moreover, the connection between design and instrumentalisation is strengthened with the realisation that exercising control over one's genetic constitution happens with a specific goal in mind. This point is raised with regard to reproductive cloning, for example by Rosenau: "No one is allowed to dispose over another person, by making him into an object of his desire. However, a clone is such an object. After all, his characteristics and qualities are not caused by coincidence; his personality is the result of another person's intention."[299]

The Dutch regulatory framework on sex selection offers additional insight into why being born for the sake of others is a violation of human dignity. The Memorandum states that selecting a child for a specific purpose *reduces* the child to the object of the parents' desires and goes against the commonly accepted notion that children are *more* than a way to satisfy needs.[300] Following this reasoning, the instrumentalisation of children implies that children are treated as something less than what they are. The child is no longer appreciated as a full, autonomous person with a mind of its own and with characteristics its parents may or may not like. Instead, the selected future child is only appreciated for some of its traits because these are the traits that serve a purpose. The Memorandum to the Dutch Embryo Act raises a similar point regarding reproductive cloning. It warns of the possibility that this technology will be used to create children with specific characteristics, only for the sake of these characteristics.[301] Consequently, the value of these children would be determined by and dependent on these characteristics, and the child would no longer be

---

2009b, p. 570. Pessers even calls the distinction between persons and things "the first commandment" of human dignity. Pessers, 2005, p. 8.

298 Deutscher Ethikrat, 2019, p. 17.

299 H. Rosenau, 'Reproduktives und therapeutisches Klonen.' in: K. Amelung, W. Beulke, H. Lilie, H. Rosenau, H. Rüping and G. Wolfslast (eds.), *Strafrecht, Biorecht, Rechtsphilosophie. Festschrift für Hans-Ludwig Schreiber zum 70. Geburtstag am 10. Mai 2003*, C.F. Müller Verlag, Heidelberg, 2003, p. 766. Translation by LtH. "[Das eigentliche Menschenunwürdige, also die Missachtung der Subjektqualität des Klons, wird mit einer weiteren Überlegung treffender bezeichnet.] Niemand darf über eine andere Person verfügen, sie zum Objekt seiner Wünsche machen. Der Klon aber ist ein solches Objekt. Denn hinter seinen Eigenschaften und Anlagen steht nicht der Zufall; das was er in seiner Person vorfindet, ist das Ergebnis fremder Absicht." A similar point is raised by Michael Sandel: "The desire to control the genetic characteristics of one's offspring points to the heart of the ethical issue. The moral problem with reproductive cloning lies not in its asexual character, but in its assault on the understanding of children as gifts rather than possessions, or projects of our will, or vehicles for our happiness." M.J. Sandel, 'The ethical implications of human cloning', *Perspectives in Biology and Medicine*, Vol. 48, 2005, p. 242.

300 *Kamerstukken II* 2000-2001, 27 423, nr. 3 (*Memorandum Embryo Act*), p. 9, 48; Regeling van de staatssecretaris van Volksgezondheid, Welzijn en Sport van 16 februari 2009, nr. CZ-TSZ-2912089, houdende houdende regels ten aanzien van preïmplantatie genetische diagnostiek (PGD), (*Stcrt.* 2009, 42) (*Ministerial decree PGD*), p. 12.

301 *Kamerstukken II* 2000-2001, 27 423, nr. 3 (*Memorandum Embryo Act*), p. 42.

valued as a whole person. By using this specific argument, the Dutch Memorandum assumes that the interest in human dignity also includes an interest in being appreciated and valued as a whole and not only for a single trait.

All in all, it follows from the different regulatory frameworks that instrumentalising the future child is considered a violation of human dignity. Selective and genetic reproductive technologies bear the risk of instrumentalisation because they facilitate the conception of a child with specific genetic traits. Various regulatory frameworks warn of the possibility of the child no longer being valued in its entirety, but only appreciated for those specific traits. The question remains open as to what exactly qualifies as (problematic) instrumentalisation. This is illustrated by the different ways each legal system approaches HLA-tissue typing. The Dutch and German frameworks deem the use of PGT only for the creation of a suitable donor a form of instrumentalisation, while the UK regulator reasons that the saviour sibling is not solely wanted for donation purposes, since the child is not discarded or given up for adoption after the donation has taken place. Consequently, the child is not only valued for being a suitable donor, but also as a unique person and a welcome addition to the family. In other words, all three legal systems acknowledge that instrumentalisation of the human person qualifies as a violation of human dignity but differ somewhat in considering which actions qualify as instrumentalisation.

2.4.2.2 Unicity

In addition to the prohibition of instrumentalisation, the regulatory frameworks also assume that the concept of human dignity encompasses a right to a unique identity.[302] This element is featured in the Dutch and UK debates on reproductive cloning. In addition to the safety concerns and the possibly instrumental nature of this technology, the Dutch Memorandum states that cloning violates the future child's right to "develop into a unique being."[303] A similar argument was mentioned by Earl Howe in the UK debate, maintaining that deliberately creating a genetically identical human being violates that person's right to have "a genetic identity of one's own."[304] In other words, both examples assume that respect for human dignity requires that the subject is a unique individual rather than a copy of its predecessor. In this interpretation of human dignity, the concept does not only demand respect for the human as a person rather than a thing or commodity, but also perceives the

302 Both aspects are mentioned in the Universal Declaration of the Human Genome and Human Rights. Article 2(b) states: "That dignity makes it imperative not to reduce individuals to their genetic characteristics and to respect their uniqueness and diversity." See also van Beers, 2009b, p. 571-573.

303 *Kamerstukken II* 2000-2001, 27 423, nr. 3 (*Memorandum Embryo Act*), p. 42. In Dutch: "Verder wordt gesteld dat het mensen het recht ontneemt om langs natuurlijke weg verwekt te worden evenals het recht om zich tot een uniek wezen te ontwikkelen."

304 HL Deb (26 November 2001) vol. 629, col. 52.

human as a genetically unique being. In my opinion, this argument could explain the differences between the approaches to genetic modification and reproductive cloning.[305] Like genetic modification, reproductive cloning is deemed too risky for clinical application. In addition, both technologies imply control over one's genetic blueprint and, once proven safe, bear the potential to create a healthy child. In the wake of the introduction of CRISPR-Cas9 and the announcement of the birth of genetically modified twins in China, the Dutch, German, and UK advisory bodies wrote reports on the permissibility of genetic modification.[306] All three seemed open to the possibility of genome editing, provided that the technology is safe for clinical use and contributes to the welfare of the child. A possible lift on the ban on reproductive cloning, however, is not considered in any of the three legal systems. Apparently, in addition to the risk of designing and instrumentalising humans, reproductive cloning is an affront to the right to have a unique genetic identity. For this reason, it implies a graver violation of human dignity.

A right to a unique genetic identity cannot fully account for the objections against reproductive cloning. After all, identical twins are not considered to be a violation of human dignity. Moreover, we may wonder whether this technology violates the dignity of the clone and of the original in the same way, and to the same extent. I believe the core of the problem is that the duplication is done deliberately.[307] This aspect is addressed in the explanatory report of the Cloning Protocol: "As naturally occurring genetic recombination is likely to create more freedom for the human being than a predetermined genetic make-up, it is in the interest of all persons to keep the essentially random nature of the composition of their own genes."[308] In short, reproductive cloning constitutes a violation of human dignity, not only because of the potential for designing humans, but also because it deliberately takes away a person's right to a unique genetic identity.

2.4.2.3 The Subject of Human Dignity

A final aspect of this interest reveals that the interest in human dignity is even more complex than the other two interests. Even though the regulatory frameworks often refer

---

305 For example, the Dutch legislator does not answer the question of whether germline modification is a violation of human dignity, but it does take a stand on reproductive cloning being a violation of human dignity. See also van Beers, 2009b, p. 572-573.

306 Commissie Genetische Modificatie (COGEM) & Gezondheidsraad, 2017; Deutscher Ethikrat, 2019; Nuffield Council on Bioethics, 2018.

307 See also H. Jonas, 'Biological engineering - a preview.' in: H. Jonas (ed.), *Philosophical essays. From ancient creed to technological man*, Prentice-Hall, Inc., Englewood Cliffs, New Jersey, 1974, p. 159. The impact of intentional interference in the future child's genome is further addressed in chapter 7.

308 Council of Europe, Explanatory Report to the Additional Protocol to the Convention for the Protection of Human Rights and Dignity of the Human Being with regard to the Application of Biology and Medicine, on the Prohibition of Cloning Human Beings ETS No.168 (*Cloning Protocol*), p. 2. See also van Beers, 2009b, p. 571-572.

to human dignity or a related concept, they are not always explicit on *whose* dignity is at stake. Or more precisely, the same technologies that endanger the future child's dignity also pose a risk to the dignity of other subjects.

On various occasions, the regulatory frameworks refer to the interests and the dignity of the future child. For example, the Dutch ban on non-medical sex selection is motivated with the argument that the resulting child should not be reduced to "the object of its parents' wishes and desires."[309] Müller-Terpitz commented on the German ban on sex selection that with the ban the state aims to prevent situations that make it impossible for the child to understand itself as a human being.[310] With regard to reproductive cloning, the Dutch and UK regulations also refer to the future child's dignity, by pointing out that this technology violates the right to "develop into a unique being"[311] or "the right to have a genetic father and mother and the right to a genetic identity of one's own."[312] Also the German Ethics Council mentions the dignity of the individual future child. In its discussion on the admissibility of germline modification, it addresses the question as to whether this technology affects future persons' human dignity. Germline modification may "completely instrumentalise future persons, assign them a legally devalued status and thereby violate their dignity." On the other hand, "the question also arises as to whether the renunciation of germline intervention, which could spare the people concerned severe suffering, would not violate their human dignity, too."[313] The presentation of human dignity as an *interest* of the individual future child comes most clearly to the fore in the advisory reports of the Dutch Health Council on MRT and germline modification. The Council reasoned that these forms of genetic intervention should be understood as an expression of respect for human dignity, referring to the technologies that are used to prevent the transmission of an inheritable genetic illness. Therefore, the Council concluded that both MRT and germline modification, provided that they are safe for clinical use, "do

309 *Kamerstukken II* 2000-2001, 27 423, nr. 3 (*Memorandum Embryo Act*), p. 48. In Dutch "...tot louter voorwerp van de wensen en verlangens van hun ouders." Translation by LtH. This argument is echoed in Regeling van de staatssecretaris van Volksgezondheid, Welzijn en Sport van 16 februari 2009, nr. CZ-TSZ-2912089, houdende houdende regels ten aanzien van preïmplantatie genetische diagnostiek (PGD), (*Stcrt.* 2009, 42) (*Ministerial decree PGD*), p. 12.

310 Spickhoff, 2011, ESchG § 3, nr 1. In German: "Zudem wird auf eine Schutzfunktion zugunsten des objektivrechtlichen Gehalts des Menschenwürdesatzes (Art. 1 I GG) verwiesen: Dieser garantiere, dass der Staat Versuchen begegne, die es einem entstehenden Individuum unmöglich machten, sich als unfestgestelltes, offenes Wesen "Mensch" zu verstehen."

311 *Kamerstukken II* 2000-2001, 27 423, nr. 3 (*Memorandum Embryo Act*), p. 42. In Dutch: "Verder wordt gesteld dat het mensen het recht ontneemt om langs natuurlijke weg verwekt te worden evenals het recht om zich tot een uniek wezen te ontwikkelen."

312 HL Deb (26 November 2001) vol. 629, col. 52.

313 Deutscher Ethikrat, 2019, par. 53.

not violate the interests of future persons (...) but serve their interests."[314] In these examples, the primary concern seems to be the possible violation of the human dignity of the future child.

In other cases, it appears that it is not only the future child's dignity that is at stake. The Memorandum to the German Embryo Protection Act, for example, does not refer to the subject of human dignity at all. According to Günther, this is because reproductive technologies that are banned in name of human dignity do not only violate the dignity of the resulting child; they also are an affront to the dignity of the other parties involved. Reproductive cloning does not only violate the dignity of the clone, i.e. the future child, but also the dignity of the prototype whose genome is copied, and even of the surrogate who carries the clone to term.[315] More importantly, it follows from the Dutch and the German regulatory frameworks that technologies such as reproductive cloning and the creation of human-animal hybrids are an affront to the dignity of individual parties involved, and also violate the dignity of humanity itself. Günther states that the bans on these technologies also aim to protect the dignity of the human species as a whole (*der Menschheit ingesamt als Gattung*).[316] This claim is criticised by the health law scholar Spickhoff. The latter rejects the idea that Article 1 GG also protects the dignity of the species, because the human species cannot be the subject of fundamental rights in his opinion.[317] The Dutch Memorandum also occasionally suggests that the dignity of humanity as a whole is at stake. This is illustrated in the motivation for the ban on chimaeras. The Memorandum states that creating human-animal hybrids deliberately crosses natural boundaries which is an affront to the respect and piety of both humans and animals.[318] Finally, during the parliamentary debate on the UK Human Reproductive Cloning Act, several MP's referred to this collective dimension of human dignity, claiming that reproductive cloning endangers the "sanctity of human life"[319] and fails "to value the uniqueness and equality of *each of its members*."[320]

Based on this, it appears that legislators and regulators acknowledge two dimensions of human dignity. First, there is the individual dimension, focusing on the dignity of the individual human. In various instances, as discussed above, the regulatory frameworks do

314 Gezondheidsraad, *Celkerntransplantatie bij mutaties in het mitochondriale DNA*, 2001, p. 35-36; Commissie Genetische Modificatie (COGEM) & Gezondheidsraad, 2017, p. 55, 56.

315 Günther, Taupitz and Kaiser, 2014, p. 331.

316 Günther, Taupitz and Kaiser, 2014, p. 331, 340.

317 Spickhoff, 2011, §1 BGB nr 13.

318 *Kamerstukken II* 2000-2001, 27 423, nr. 3 (*Memorandum Embryo Act*), p. 48.

319 HL Deb (26 November 2001) vol. 629, col. 21, 27.

320 HL Deb (26 November 2001) vol. 629, col. 52.

indeed refer to the dignity of the individual future child.[321] In addition, the individual dimension is also involved if reproductive technologies violate the dignity of other individual subjects. In particular, the German debate raised the argument that technologies such as reproductive cloning and creating chimaeras not only violate the dignity of the resulting child, but also the dignity of the prototype, donors, and the surrogate. On a few occasions, this individual dimension is connected to prevention of suffering and empowerment of the individual, such as in the advisory reports of the Dutch Health Council and the German Ethics Council. In other contexts, the future child's human dignity is invoked in order to prevent the objectification and dehumanisation of the child, such as in the context of sex selection. It is with regard to this aspect of human dignity, the prevention of objectification and dehumanisation, that, particularly in the German debate, a connection is made to the second dimension of human dignity: the collective dimension or the dignity of the human species.[322] In this dimension, human dignity is an objective notion that transcends the individual.[323] As pointed out in various regulatory frameworks, individual cases of reproductive technologies, such as a single case of reproductive cloning, sex selection, or germline modification, has larger affects surpassing the human subjects directly involved, and can even be said to affect humankind as a whole.[324] This implies that the individual dimension of human dignity and the collective dimension are intertwined since the violation of dignity on an individual level also implies a violation of dignity on a collective level. First of all, the consequences of reproductive technologies such as germline modification are not restricted to the individual child, but also affect other parties, such as future generations, donors, surrogates, and prototypes. But the individual and collective dimensions are also related in another way. The individuals who result from reproductive technologies (or are involved as donors, prototypes, or surrogates) are members of the human species and what we allow to happen to certain human individuals says something about the way we see and think of human persons in general. Allowing humans to be treated as commodities, selected, or genetically manipulated to fulfil their parents' desires does not only say something about how the individual future child is treated, but also about human beings in general. Therefore, the appeal to human dignity does not only pertain to the individual, but also to the whole of humankind.

321 See for example, HL Deb (26 November 2001) vol. 629, col. 42; *Kamerstukken II* 2005-2006, 30 300 XVI, nr. 136 (*first explanatory letter PGD*), p. 7.

322 van Beers, 2009a, p. 136.

323 Pessers, 2005, p. 7.

324 This point is further elaborated on in chapter 7.

2.5 Conclusion

In this chapter, I aimed to demonstrate how the future child is conceived of in the regulations on reproduction and what legal interests are attributed to it. For this purpose, I analysed the Dutch, German, and UK regulatory frameworks on reproduction, more specifically those that result in the prevention of the future child's existence. These three legal systems are compared with respect to which interests are attributed to the future child and how are these interests interpreted. The analysis demonstrated that in all three legal systems, the future child is included in the legal debate with the help of the 'interests of the future child' construction, as a subject of interests.

In addition to using the interests-construction, all three legal systems refer to the same three legal interests of the future child. First, several regulatory frameworks aim to protect the future child's well-being. This interest is invoked both to restrict the use of certain technologies, such as access to fertility treatments, and to justify technologies, such as PGT. In both cases, the regulatory frameworks allow interference if there is a high or significant risk of severe harm, which is understood as physical or psychosocial harm. The second interest that is attributed to the future child is its interest in forming an identity. This interest appears in the regulation on disclosure of donor information. According to Dutch, German, and UK law, the child has a right to identifying information about the donor, because knowledge about one's genetic descent is deemed important for the child's identity formation. Interestingly, this interest is often presented as a right. The third and final interest is the future child's human dignity. Compared to the Netherlands and Germany, this interest plays a less prominent role in the UK regulations on reproduction, as the UK leans more towards consequentialist reasoning, where the acceptability of a technology depends on whether it results in harm or not. Nonetheless, also in the UK parliamentary debate, dignity and similar concepts such as the sanctity of human life were mentioned. In addition, important similarities can be found in the way this concept in interpreted in the three legal systems. Within the regulatory frameworks investigated, respect for human dignity implies a prohibition on the instrumentalisation or breeding of humans. This means that the child would be born solely to meet the needs and desires of others. Moreover, respect for human dignity also encompasses a right to a unique genetic identity.

Another interesting similarity between the regulatory frameworks is that the nature of these interests, and correspondingly, the nature of the future child's subjectivity is left unaddressed in all three legal systems. The Netherlands, Germany and the United Kingdom operationalise the 'interests of the future child' construction, without questioning – or sometimes even without explicit addressing – four underlying assumptions.

First, the regulation's core values of well-being, identity, and to a large extent dignity, are all connected to the future child. Memoranda and parliamentary debates claim that the regulations serve the future child's interests because the future child's well-being, identity, or dignity is at stake. The notion of human dignity is an exception since in various cases the regulation also refers to the dignity of other parties, and even the dignity of humanity as a whole. Still, in various cases the regulations speak explicitly of the human dignity of the future child as a reason to justify, for example, the ban on reproductive cloning and non-medical sex selection. In other words, by operationalising the interests of the child, the regulations seems to be based on the assumption that the values it aims to protect can be, in these cases, understood as interests of an individual entity.

Second, by banning reproductive technologies, refusing to treat certain prospective parents, and deselecting embryos in the process of PGT the future child does not come into existence. As the regulations leading to this result is considered to be in the interest of the future child, so must the outcome be. This aspect is, however, barely addressed. A striking example is the Dutch debate on PGT. The Dutch State Secretary for Health focused on the prevention of suffering,[325] obscuring the fact that PGT does not cure or prevent an illness, but prevents the carrier of that illness from being born. In contrast, during the UK debate on PGT, MP Lansley stated that preventing the implantation of a severely genetically affected embryo (and consequently, the birth of a severely genetically affected child) is in the best interests of the child.[326] What Lansley makes explicit, but what in most regulatory frameworks in only tacitly assumed, is the suggestion that the future child has an interest in its own non-existence. Nonetheless, whether and under which circumstances such an interest in non-existence can actually be assumed has been left unaddressed.

Third, all three legal systems take the interests of the future child seriously. In various cases, it is even considered as the paramount interest. For example, the Dutch regulation on PGD states that the interests of the future child ought to be the point of departure for drafting or amending the regulation.[327] Also during the UK parliamentary discussions, it was several times emphasised that the interests of the child should be considered paramount.[328] In the case of access to information about one's genetic origins, as discussed above, the vocabulary of rights is even endorsed. All this indicates that the future child has

325 *Kamerstukken II* 2007-2008, 29 323, nr. 46 (*second explanatory letter PGD*), p. 4. Also the State Secretary's predecessor focused on prevention of illnesses. *Kamerstukken II* 2005-2006, 30 300 XVI, nr. 136 (*first explanatory letter PGD*), p. 12.

326 HC Deb (12 May 2008), vol. 475, col. 1078.

327 *Kamerstukken II* 2005-2006, 30 300 XVI, nr. 136 (*first explanatory letter PGD*), p. 3.

328 See also, for example, HC Deb (12 May 2008) vol. 475, col. 1078, 1097; HL Deb (10 december 2007), vol. 697, col. 30, 37.

become an important actor on the legal stage. It is no longer an object third parties have a right to,[329] but a subject with its own interests or even rights. Put differently, the regulations rest upon the assumption that the future child has some form of subjectivity. Or more specifically, legal subjectivity.

Fourth and finally, the various legal frameworks refer to the interests of the child, albeit sometimes in different terms. For example, the Memoranda to the Dutch regulation of PGD and to the Dutch Embryo Act refer multiple times to "the interest of the future child."[330] While Section 13(5) of the UK HFE Act 2008 speaks of the "welfare of the child", the parliamentary discussions do often mention the (best) interests of the (future) child.[331] Also the German Bill of the Embryo Protection Act refers to the interests of the child.[332] This indicates that in these discussions, it is assumed by the regulator that the future child can be a subject of interests.

In conclusion, the Dutch, German, and UK regulations on reproduction address the future child with the help of 'the interests of the future child' construction. This construction rests on four pillars, consisting of four assumptions that are implied in the regulations, but not explicitly addressed or discussed. In order to assess whether this 'interests of the future child' construction is tenable, I explore these assumptions in the following four chapters. In chapter 3 I start with the first assumption, which is that the core values of well-being, identity, and dignity can all be represented as interests of an individual entity, namely the future child. Then, in chapter 4 I assess the tenability of the second assumption, i.e. that the future child has an interest in its own non-existence. Chapters 5 and 6 continue the analysis of interests-construction by discussing the future child's subjectivity and legal status. First, in chapter 5 I focus on the (third) assumption that the future child is a legal subject, by investigating whether the future child's subjectivity can be understood with the help of law's traditional concept of the legal subject. Second, in chapter 6, I assess the fourth assumption and discuss whether the future child can be a subject of (legal) interests.

329 It is also telling that the European Court of Human Rights does not speak of a right to a child, but a right to respect for the decision to become a parent in the genetic sense. ECtHR 10 April 2007 ECLI:CE:ECHR:2007:0410JUD000633905 (*Evans v. the United Kingdom*), par. 72.

330 *Kamerstukken II* 2005-2006, 30 300 XVI, nr. 136 (*first explanatory letter PGD*), p. 3, 5, 10, 11; *Kamerstukken II* 2007-2008, 29 323, nr. 46 (*second explanatory letter PGD*), p. 2; *Kamerstukken II* 2000-2001, 27 423, nr. 3 (*Memorandum Embryo Act*), p. 3, 14, 18, 19, 37, 38.

331 HC Deb (12 May 2008) vol. 475, col. 1078, 1079, 1097, 1131, 1134; HL Deb (10 december 2007), vol. 697, col. 30, 52.

332 BT-Drs. 11/5460, vom 25.10.1989 (*Bill and Memorandum Embryo Protection Act*), p. 9, 11.

3 Harm, Identity and Dignity

3.1 Introduction

In the legal analysis in chapter 2, I demonstrated that the regulations on reproduction attributes three core interests to the future child. First, the future child's interest in well-being and in being protected against harm is invoked to, for example, justify the refusal of fertility treatment or to justify the use of PGT. In order words, this interest is mobilised both to prevent certain modes of reproduction that are potentially harmful and to facilitate technologies that can prevent the transmission of a harmful genetic condition. Second is the future child's interest in forming an identity. This interest encompasses a right to information about one's genetic origins and forms the foundation of the regulations on disclosure of donor information. The final interest that emerges in the regulatory frameworks is the future child's dignity. As this interest includes a ban on instrumentalisation and a right to genetic unicity, it is operationalised in regulatory frameworks addressing, for example, non-medical selective reproduction and reproductive cloning.

In this chapter, I start with a critical discussion of the 'interests of the future child' construction, by scrutinising the first of the four assumptions made about the future child. This assumption entails that certain core values, namely well-being, identity, and dignity, can be understood as interests of the future child, that is, as interests of an individual entity. In order to assess this assumption, these core values need to be elaborated further. The legal analysis conducted in chapter 2 revealed various aspects of these notions, but not clearly demarcated definitions. Therefore, in order to assess whether these core values can be articulated with the help of the interests-construction, we need to come to a better understanding of these notions. In this chapter, I aim to further reconstruct the values that underly the regulations on reproduction by expanding the scope of the analysis. Through analysing the academic literature that addresses and reflects upon these notions, and the corresponding regulations, from a legal-philosophical angle, I hope to answer those questions that remain implied and unaddressed in the regulations on reproduction itself. Therefore, in this chapter I discuss the academic literature that offers a definition or interpretation of one of the core notions, in order to elucidate which interpretation of harm, identity, and dignity underlies the different regulations. Notably, I do not aim to come to a new definition of these concepts to replace the interpretation that surfaces in the regulations on reproduction, but to further elaborate the three core values as they are operationalised in the regulatory frameworks. In other words, this discussion serves to come to a better understanding of these legal notions.

3.2 THE CONCEPT OF HARM

In the previous chapter, I demonstrated that different regulatory frameworks deemed the prevention of the future child's existence as justified if the future child ran a significant risk of suffering severe harm. This justification can be explained as rooted in Mill's harm principle.[1] According to Mill, individual freedom ends when another person is harmed by it, and for this reason the government can rightfully interfere and restrict the freedom of individual members of society to prevent harm to others.[2] The question here is whether a non-existent, unconceived child can qualify as 'another'. The regulatory frameworks seem to assume it can. Exemplary of this are the regulations on access to fertility treatments: the refusal of a treatment, which infringes upon the prospective parents personal life and, more specifically, reproductive freedom, is considered acceptable if it prevents harm to the future child. Notably, the concept of harm itself is not elaborated. That is, the regulatory frameworks do not go into the question of what harm is and simply refer to harm (in Dutch "schade"[3] and in German "Schaden"[4]) or suffering (in Dutch "lijden"[5]) without any further explanation. So, in order to understand the scope of this interest, which helps elucidate this part of the notion of the human person, the concept of harm, as presupposed within current legislation, needs to be further elaborated.

To start with, the notion of harm surfacing in these regulatory contexts is strongly connected to notions of well-being and development. The Dutch professional guidelines explicitly mention this relationship: if the child's well-being cannot be sufficiently guaranteed, that is, if it faces a risk of being harmed, the physician can refuse to perform the fertility treatment.[6] The German Code of Conduct also connects well-being and harm. It refers to the physician's double responsibility to "take care of the patient's well-being and to prevent harm."[7] Moreover, the Memorandum to the Embryo Protection Act states that special attention needs to be paid to safeguarding the future child's well-being,[8] which according to Taupitz addresses those actions that endanger the child's development.[9] This

1 J.S. Mill, *On Liberty*, 1859. Reprint: Mineola, New York, Dover Publications, Inc., 2002, p. 8, 46.
2 Mill, (1859) 2002, p. 8.
3 NVOG Modelprotocol "Mogelijke morele contra-indicaties bij vruchtbaarheidsbehandelingen", p. 2.
4 (Muster-)Richtlinie zur Durchführung der assistierten Reproduktion, Novelle 2006. Deutsches Ärzteblatt 2006; 103 [20], p. 1393, 1401.
5 *Kamerstukken II* 2007-2008, 29 323, nr. 46 (*second explanatory letter PGD*), p. 4.
6 NVOG Modelprotocol "Mogelijke morele contra-indicaties bij vruchtbaarheidsbehandelingen", p. 2.
7 (Muster-)Richtlinie zur Durchführung der assistierten Reproduktion, Novelle 2006. Deutsches Ärzteblatt 2006; 103 [20], p. 1393. In German: "Die ärztliche Pflicht, zum Wohl der Patienten zu handeln und Schaden zu vermeiden..." Translation by LtH.
8 BT-Drs. 11/5460, vom 25.10.1989 (*Bill and Memorandum Embryo Protection Act*), p. 6.
9 Günther, Taupitz and Kaiser, 2014, p. 181. In German: "Einzelne Handlungen, die von Besonderer Gefährlichkeit für die Entwicklung des Kindes sind..." Translation by LtH.

connection between harm and well-being is generally also acknowledged in academic literature, in particular by Raz and Feinberg. According to Joseph Raz, "one harms another when one's action makes the other person worse off than he was, or is entitled to be, in a way which affects his future well-being."[10] His account of harm implies a comparison between the situation resulting from the alleged harmful act, and the counterfactual situation if such act had not taken place.[11] Importantly, a person is only harmed if his *well-being* is impacted in a negative way. Raz mentions injury and severe pain as examples of harm.[12] Also Feinberg's definition of harm depends on a relationship between harm and well-being. Feinberg defines harm as the "setback of an interest."[13] An interest is defined as a "distinguishable component of a person's well-being."[14] In brief, according to Raz's and Feinberg's interpretations, harm can be understood as the decrease of one's well-being, that is, as being worse off than one would have been otherwise.

If we follow the interpretation of harm that surfaces in the regulatory frameworks, and in Raz's and Feinberg's discussions of the notion, harm is interpreted as a decrease of or negative impact on someone's well-being. This raises the following question: what qualifies as well-being and, more particularly, how does this notion relate to identity and human dignity? As demonstrated in chapter 2, the regulatory frameworks also aim to protect the future child's possibility to form an identity, to access information about its origins, and its human dignity. Yet it appears that these values are generally understood as independent values in the context of the regulations on reproduction, and that the violation of these interests does not necessarily impact the future child's well-being. The regulatory frameworks do not offer a complete definition of well-being, but they seem to primarily refer to physical and psychosocial well-being.[15] One's physical well-being can be affected by poor health, (severe) pain, or a genetic illness, which all compromise the physical functioning of one's body. It is difficult to see how objectifying a child, or denying it an

---

10 J. Raz, *The morality of freedom*, Oxford, Clarendon Press, 1988, p. 514.

11 Whether such a comparison can be made if the counterfactual situation is non-existence is discussed in chapter 4.

12 Raz, 1988, p. 513.

13 J. Feinberg, *The Moral Limits of the Criminal Law Volume 1: Harm to Others*, Oxford, Oxford University Press, 1987, p. 33. Feinberg distinguishes harm in a descriptive sense (a setback of interests) from harm in a normative sense, in which case harming equals wronging. For the purpose of this text, it is sufficient to focus on harm in the descriptive sense, since the normative component follows from the regulation itself: if the harm is seen as sufficient reason to intervene, it is apparently also a wrong.

14 J. Feinberg, *Harm to others. The moral limits of the criminal law*, Oxford, Oxford University Press, 1984, p. 34.

15 The Nuffield report sees well-being as relating only to one's physical or medical health, whereas welfare encompasses both one's physical state and one's mental or psychological state. For the purpose of this study, following the discussion in chapter 2, well-being covers both the child's physical well-being and mental well-being.

origin story results in physical harm. In some instances, it is assumed that violating the future child's interest in identity formation may result in psychosocial harm, which is often understood as a developmental deficit or a negative state of mind. For example, the German Memorandum to the Embryo Protection Act considers the possibility that split motherhood might obstruct the child's identity formation and might therefore have a negative impact on the child's well-being.[16] Also the Memorandum to the Dutch Donor Information Artificial Fertilisation Act states that is it conceivable that the child suffers psychologically from not knowing its genetic parent.[17] This indicates that a frustrated identity formation is by itself not understood as harm, but may give rise to mental or psychological problems that are qualified as psychosocial harm. Nonetheless, it is not proven that a thwarted identity formation leads to psychosocial harm. With regard to split motherhood, the German Memorandum merely states that it might result in psychological harm, since there is no evidence indicating otherwise. Several authors have pointed out that up until today, no proof exists that split motherhood harms the child.[18] It is also telling that the Sperm Donor Registry Act, which was drafted almost 30 years later, does not mention the possibility that the child might suffer or even be harmed by not having access to the donor's information, even though this is considered to be important for the formation of the child's identity. From this it follows that the regulatory frameworks consider identity formation as an independent interest and not merely instrumental to avoiding harm.[19] With regard to human dignity, the connection is not made to harm in the regulatory frameworks.

So, in the context of the regulations on reproduction, harm is mostly understood as physical or psychological harm.[20] This suggests that harm is seen as something quantifiable or measurable. That is, it is possible to determine and clearly describe the consequences of what is causing harm, in terms of pain, physical or mental malfunctioning, or traumas. As discussed in chapter 2, the regulatory frameworks deem interference and preventing the future child's existence acceptable if the degree of harm is severe enough. This also suggests that in the frameworks, harm is understood as something that can be measured. The idea that harm is something that can be quantified and expressed in measurable results is also visible in Raz's and Feinberg's notions of harm. They conceive harm as being 'worse off' or a 'setback', implying that in order to establish the harm done, different situations can be

16 BT-Drs. 11/5460, vom 25.10.1989 (*Bill and Memorandum Embryo Protection Act*), p. 7.

17 *Kamerstukken II*, 1992-1993, 23 207, nr. 3 (*Memorandum Donor Information Artificial Fertilisation Act*), p. 11, 22.

18 See for example, Ratze and Luxenburger, 2015, p. 1380; Günther, Taupitz and Kaiser, 2014, p. 181-182; Schroeder, 1995, p. 534-535, 544.

19 Bosch, 2020, p. 10.

20 Also in the literature, relevant harm is often limited to physical or psychosocial/psychological harm. See for example, Wilkinson, 2010, p. 110.

compared, and the difference can be measured. Moreover, Feinberg defines as "harmless" something that does not set back interests of a "tangible and material kind."[21] The idea that harm is something measurable is also expressed in other studies. A clear example is Pennings's paper on the disclosure of donor conception. Considering whether telling donor conceived children about their conception is in their best interest, he concludes that non-disclosure does not harm the child, since there are no "measurable, stable differences in psychological well-being of donor offspring who are informed of the mode of their conception compared to those who are not."[22] Put differently, in order to establish whether non-disclosure causes harm, Pennings argues that harm can only be established by measurable evidence.

In sum, the analysis of the regulatory frameworks reveals the contours of the notions of harm and well-being, but it remains difficult to exactly pinpoint how the regulatory frameworks interpret these notions, as they do not give an explicit, demarcated definition. Still, several regulatory frameworks connect harm to well-being, and interpret a negative impact on the child's well-being as harm. This connection is also made by Feinberg and Raz. Moreover, in the regulations on reproduction, according to Feinberg, harm is seen as something that is tangible or measurable to a certain extent. Consequently, harm does not pertain to interests of a metaphysical nature, consequences of which are much harder to grasp and articulate.[23] In the context of the regulatory frameworks examined, harm and well-being do not seem to include the violation of the child's interests in identity formation or human dignity. These appear to be understood as independent values, justifying the regulation in their own right. The relation between the future child's interest in preventing harm and its interests in identity and dignity is further discussed in the following sections.

3.3 The Concept of Identity

3.3.1 Identity and Harm

The regulatory frameworks on donor anonymity acknowledge the future child's interest in identity, and correspondingly its interest in information about its genetic origins. As

21 Feinberg, 1987, p. 35.

22 G. Pennings, 'Disclosure of donor conception, age of disclosure and the well-being of donor offspring', *Human Reproduction*, Vol. 32, No. 5, 2017, p. 972.

23 B.C. van Beers, 'Imagining future people in biomedical law: From technological utopias to legal dystopias within the regulation of human genetic modification technologies ' in: M. Ambrus, R. Rayfuse and W. Werner (eds.), *Risk and the regulation of uncertainty in international law*, Oxford University Press, Oxford, 2017b, p. 125-126.

explained above, it follows from the regulatory frameworks that these interests are understood as values in themselves, and that the violation of these interests does not necessarily qualify as (psychological) harm. Critics of this *right to know* have pointed out that the child is not harmed if it has no information about its genetic parent. However, this has led them to question the importance of donor identifying information. They have pointed out that the case for the right to know and access to identifying information often is built by referring to stories of donor conceived or adopted children who seek contact with their biological parents, wanting to understand their roots.[24] Critics have pointed out that this 'evidence' is only anecdotal and that no empirical studies prove that not knowing who one's biological parents are actually harms the child.[25] For example, De Melo-Martín and Vonk suggests that donor conceived children develop in an equal manner compared to children who are raised by their biological parents.[26] In addition, Vonk argues that the lack of knowledge can be experienced as a "frustration" rather than harm.[27] In other words, while knowledge of one's biological roots may be of some importance for the constitution of an identity, there is no empirical evidence that it is a *necessary* factor. The donor conceived child may miss an aspect of its identity, but provided it has a "healthy identity" and does not suffer psychosocial harm, this gap does not provide a sufficient argument for disclosure, according to De Melo-Martín.[28] In other words, critics doubt whether donor conceived children must have access to identifying information of the donor, since apparently there is no scientific evidence proving that the lack of knowledge indeed has a significant impact on the child's physical or psychosocial well-being. The core of this argument lies in the assumption that in order for the child to have a valid interest, the violation of this interest must be understood as a measurable harm.

This idea is clearly not adopted in the regulations on reproduction. The regulatory frameworks state that the future child has an interest in donor information, regardless of whether it suffers psychological harm. In the UK Parliamentary debate, Lord Clement-Jones commented on the notion of identity and not knowing one's genetic roots, saying that "[i]t is not necessarily a scientific thing to know where you came from, it is partly

24 M. Somerville, 'Donor conception and children's rights: 'First, do no harm'', *Canadian Medical Association Journal*, Vol. 183, 2011, p. 280; N. Cahn, 'Necessary subjecs: the need for a mandatory national donor gamete databank', *DePaul Journal of Health Care Law*, Vol. 12, No. 1, 2009, p. 203-223; J. Glover, *Fertility & the family. The Glover report on reproductive technologies to the European commission*, London, Fourth Estate 1989, p. 36, 37.

25 I. de Melo-Martín, 'The ethics of anonymous gamete donation: is there a right to know one's genetic origins?', *Hastings Center Report*, Vol. 44, No. 2, 2014, p. 32; V. Ravitsky, 'Conceived and deceived: the medical interests of donor-conceived children', *Hastings Center Report*, Vol. 42, No. 1, 2012, p. 18, 19.

26 de Melo-Martín, 2014, p. 32; M. Vonk, 'Een huis voor alle kinderen: de juridische verankering van meeroudergezinnen in het afstammingsrecht', *Nederlands Juristenblad*, Vol. 2013, No. 33, 2013, p. 2247.

27 Vonk, 2013, p. 2247.

28 de Melo-Martín, 2014, p. 32.

emotional."[29] That is, it touches upon a very fundamental and intimate aspect of the person's identity. The idea that identity and one's genetic origins are an independent value, regardless of whether it can be understood in terms of harm, is emphasised in the regulatory frameworks, which not only speak of an interest in donor information, but also a *right* to access this information. As discussed, the Dutch and German legal systems even consider this right to be derived from a general personality right, which forms the foundation for fundamental rights.[30]

The assumption that genetic origins are of such importance to the child's identity that they fall within the scope of a general personality right is not further elaborated in the regulatory frameworks themselves. Still, this assumed connection is a central component of how the human person is perceived in these three legal systems, and more specifically in the regulations on reproduction. By assuming that knowledge of one's origins and genetic bonds is pivotal for identity and self-understanding, the regulatory frameworks build upon the idea that identity is not something that the individual can create all by himself; it is also influenced by relations with other people. Because of this interdependent nature of the concept of identity that follows from the regulations on reproduction, not having information about one's descent or biological parents may perhaps not count as harm, but it still has an effect. Glover offers an explanation of what this effect is: "Our sense of who we are is bound up with the story we tell about ourselves. A life where the biological parents are unknown is like a novel with the first chapter missing."[31] Identity here is seen as a narrative in which others, such as a child's biological parents, play a role. Information about these others is necessary in order to complete the story of one's self-understanding. This idea – expressed in Glover's metaphor and which is also implied by the regulations' interdependent understanding of identity – is articulated through the notion of *narrative identity*. In order to gain a deeper insight into the value underlying the future child's right to access to donor information, it is worthwhile further exploring the notion of narrative identity.

3.3.2 Narrative Identity

The idea of narrative identity assumes that personal identity is explained through the stories we tell about our lives. For example, Ricoeur claims that we equate life with the

29 HL Deb (9 June 2004) vol. 662, col. 353.

30 See for example, the German regulation and the Dutch *Valkenhorst* case. Also in UK case law, a link is made between the right to access to donor information and the personality principle. See section 2.3.

31 Glover, 1989, p. 37.

story or stories we tell about it[32] and also MacIntyre – tapping from different philosophical sources – understands people as, in essence, story-telling animals.[33] So if one tries to understand who one is and to make sense of one's life, it is not sufficient to refer to official names[34] or social security numbers, which only help to determine one's civil identity. The narrative identity is, as Dutch legal philosopher Pessers calls it, more personal: it pertains to the person's self-understanding and the stories one tells about oneself.[35]

According to Ricoeur, narrative identity is the best way to understand personal identity, or to answer the question 'who am I?' The pronoun 'who' can only refer to persons, whereas the pronoun 'what' refers to things. This is because, according to Ricoeur, the identity of a person consists of two modalities: the 'same' or the *idem*, which represents a certain stability and unchangeability over time,[36] and the 'self' or the *ipse*, which represents the capable and autonomous actor, who can be held and holds himself responsible for his actions. These modalities can overlap but can also be completely separated.[37] What is important, is that because the identity of persons consists of these two poles, personal identity changes over time yet also remains unchanged. Over the course of a life, a person changes. For example, I can say that I am not the same person anymore as I was when I started my PhD research in the sense that I have grown, learned a lot, and that my ideas have evolved. Nonetheless, the texts I wrote years ago are still mine.

This tension between changing and not changing raises the following question. We can identify a person by ascribing a (proper) name to him, but how do we know this name will still be applicable over time? How do we know that this person at moment t1 is the same person he was at moment t2?[38] Or as Ricoeur puts it: "What is the basis for the permanence of this proper name?"[39] The answer according to Ricoeur must be narrative identity, because only the notion of narrative identity creates the certain coherency that is necessary to be able to speak of the same person but also account for the changes someone undergoes over the course of a lifetime.[40] A narrative does not only put events or actions in

32 P. Ricoeur, 'Narrative Identity', *Philosophy Today*, Vol. 35, No. 1, 1991, p. 77.

33 A. MacIntyre, *After Virtue*, 2, Notre Dame, Indiana, University of Notre Dame Press, 1984, p. 216.

34 D. Teichert, 'Narrative, Identity and Self', *Journal of Conscious Studies*, Vol. 11, No. 10-11, 2004, p. 185.

35 D. Pessers, 'De terugkeer van de bastaard: een beschouwing over het wetsvoorstel Lesbisch ouderschap van rechtswege.', *Nederlands Juristenblad*, Vol. 88, No. 37, 2013, p. 2591.

36 Please understand this is only a simplified view of Ricoeur's work. Ricoeur distinguishes different interpretations of sameness. P. Ricoeur, *Oneself as Another*, Chicago, The University of Chicago Press, 1992, p. 116, 117.

37 See Ricoeur elaboration on character and keeping one's word. Ricoeur, 1992, p. 119-124.

38 Teichert, 2004, p. 178.

39 P. Ricoeur, *Time and Narrative volume 3*, Chicago, The University of Chicago Press, 1985, p. 246.

40 See also P. Ricoeur, *The Just*, Chicago, The University of Chicago Press, 2000, p. 3.

chronological order the way a chronicle does, but by telling a story it also reveals the relationships between these events and by doing so, it creates coherence.[41]

This coherence is strongly connected to self-understanding. By telling a story of one's life, a narrative is created that gives an explanation or a motivation for certain events and actions. Due to this, such a narrative both is a summary of past events and includes the values of the individual and his relations to other people that are necessary to make sense of these past events. Notably, this explanatory function does not merely work retrospectively. Because the story of one's life also includes ideas of what this person deems important, such narratives are also used to identify goals, plan actions, and develop expectations about the future.[42] In other words, a narrative identity helps to make sense of past as well as future events; it helps to make sense of the goals one pursues, of the hopes and dreams one has, and thus, it helps to make sense of one's own identity. This explanatory function is also recognised by others. For example, Sandel points out that knowing 'what to do' is only possible if one knows who one is and has constructed a narrative identity.[43] He argues a narrative conception of identity can explain why we feel loyalty and responsibility to those whose lives are connected to ours and can therefore explain why we act differently towards them.[44] Also DeGrazia maintains that asking the question 'who am I?' is about self-definition and finding out what is important to someone, "which can guide [a person] satisfyingly through major life decisions".[45] In short, following this interpretation, a narrative identity does not just provide an answer to the question 'who am I?'; by giving the person a coherent story of his life it offers an explanation of who this person is, which values he holds high and what motivates him, and to give meaning to it.

This explanatory or meaning-giving function of narrative identity does not explain fully why knowledge of genetic descent is considered so important for forming an identity. Why are the other people in one's life, and in particular genetic parents, crucial for one's self-understanding? This aspect of narrative identity is explained by MacIntyre, who points out that forming an identity depends to a large extent on our social relations.[46] It is above all important, MacIntyre stresses, to understand that identity is not something we

41 Teichert, 2004, p. 181-182.

42 Teichert, 2004, p. 183.

43 M.J. Sandel, *Justice. What's the right thing to do?*, London, Penguin Books, 2009, p. 221.

44 Sandel, 2009, p. 224.

45 D. DeGrazia, 'Enhancement technologies and human dignity', *Journal of Medicine and Philosophy*, Vol. 30, 2005, p. 266.

46 MacIntyre and Ricoeur both refer to the importance of storytelling in forming an identity and claim that the narrative account of identity gives unity or coherence to a person's life, yet their accounts do differ at several points, see for example, Ricoeur, 1991, p. 77, and Ricoeur, 1992, p. 157-163. Because those difference do not matter for the purpose of this chapter, they are there for not further elaborated.

can simply construct by ourselves. The story we tell about our lives is deeply influenced by the lives of others. We are not the sole, autonomous authors of the stories of our lives; we cannot simply construct our life and give meaning to it all by ourselves. According to MacIntyre, we are rather co-authors, because our lives are affected by factors that lie beyond our choice: "We enter upon a stage which we did not design and we find ourselves part of an action that was not of our making."[47] In other words, the story of our life is also determined by external factors, such as our social environment. Ricoeur also acknowledges that narratives of different people are connected and intertwined, and that a person does not have full control over the story of his life.[48] The people around us influence our life story and who we are, first by restricting us in the choices we can make and second because we play a role in their life stories. As Mela puts it: "… we are protagonists of our own story, but at the same time, part of the stories of others. We are characters of a parallel series of intermerging narrations, some of which are often integrated in others …".[49] Our identity includes the 'roles' we play in the lives or narratives of others. For example, I am someone's daughter, someone's sister, and someone's aunt.[50] I am an employee at a university and an inhabitant of the country I live in. Because of the interconnectedness of my life with those of many others, my identity does not stand on its own, as my own construct. I rather inherit from the past of my family and my country "a variety of debts, inheritances, rightful expectations and obligations."[51] In other words, we are all part of a specific history.[52] For this reason, MacIntyre considers understanding this specific history to be an important factor for understanding ourselves and to making sense of our lives.

In this idea of interconnectedness and being part of a history, one's family is of particular importance.[53] According to Pessers, the story one tells about his or her life as an answer to

---

47 MacIntyre, 1984, p. 213.

48 Although Ricoeur does refer to the interconnectedness of narratives, this aspect does not play such a large role in his account of narrative identity as it does in MacIntyre's. See for example, "Life stories are so intertwined with one another that the narrative anyone tells or hears of his own life becomes a segment of those other stories that are the narratives of others' lives". Ricoeur, 2000, p. 7. "When I interpret myself in terms of a life story, am I [author, narrator and character] at once, as in the autobiographical narrative? Narrator and character, perhaps, but of a life of which, unlike the creatures of fiction, I am not the author but at most (…) the coauthor…" Ricoeur, 1992, p, 160.

49 L. Mela, 'MacIntyre on Personal Identity', *Public Reason*, Vol. 3, No. 1, 2011, p. 106.

50 I am still grateful that Meike and Stef did not remain merely future children.

51 MacIntyre, 1984, p. 220.

52 MacIntyre, 1984, p. 221.

53 The idea that one's biological parents are important to one's identity, has also been expressed in popular culture, most prominently in George Lukas' Star Wars series. The reveal that Darth Vader was Luke Skywalker's father is considered to be one of the biggest revelations in movie history. The theme of descent was also addressed in the latest trilogy, in which main character Rey's origins was considered one of the most urgent questions that the final instalment of the trilogy had to answer.

the question 'who am I?' is most of all a story about family.[54] After all, in most cases, it is within the context of a family that these connections between our own life and the lives of others are the strongest, because of both the social and biological bonds. Moreover, not only is the child's identity dependent on who its parents, grandparents, and ancestors are, the child's *existence* is dependent on it, too. Hence, the relation between the child and its genetics parents is perhaps one of the most important factors in its self-understanding. This is why Glover maintains that not knowing your biological parent(s) is like missing the first chapter or the beginning of your life story.[55] Pessers also stresses the importance of these relations for the child's identity, because it is through these familial relations that the child is incorporated in the genealogical lineage of its ancestors and given a place in society.[56] This interconnectedness makes clear why the concept of narrative identity plays a crucial part in debates on reproduction. Of course, with the help of legal fictions, such as adoption or distinguishing between genetic and legal parenthood in case of donor conception, the child can be incorporated in the lineage of someone other than its genetic parents. Nevertheless, that does not alter the fact that there is a genetic bond between the donor and the child and, more importantly, an existential relationship. Based on the idea of narrative identity, it is the fact that the child's existence (co-)depends on the donor that generates their connection and that makes the donor part of the life story of the child, and accordingly its identity. Consequently, from this perspective, disclosure of donor information can be considered essential for donor conceived children to complete their life histories.[57]

As per the regulatory frameworks, access to donor information seems to be sufficient to do justice to the future child's interest in identity formation. Although the identifying information enables the child to contact the donor, this possibility is rather unaddressed in the parliamentary debates. The UK debate only briefly pondered upon the possibility that donor conceived children also have an interest in contacting the donor (which for possible donors could be a reason to refrain from donating).[58] The Dutch Memorandum addresses the question of whether it would be possible for the child or the donor to request a legally binding contact arrangement, the question was answered negatively, because the

54 Pessers, 2013, p. 2591.

55 Glover, 1989, p. 37.

56 Pessers, 2013, p. 2591.

57 The conceptualisation of one's identity as a life story is also done by Baroness Andrews in the House of Lords debate on the disclosure of donor information regulations. HL Deb (9 June 2004) vol. 662, col. 344.

58 HL Deb (9 June 2004) vol. 662, col. 347, 350, 355. Also the second complaint in the *Valkenhorst* case pointed out that without identifying information the child would not be able to contact her biological father. Yet, contact was not presented as a pivotal aspect of the case. Hoge Raad 15 April 1994 ECLI:NL:HR:1994:ZC1337 (*Valkenhorst*).

relation between the donor and the child does not qualify as family life.[59] It does not discuss the possibility of the child being interested in meeting or getting to know the donor. It only briefly points out that identifying information and in particular information about the donor's physical traits and appearance enable the child to form an image of the donor,[60] which seems to suggest that the legislator considers this to be sufficient to satisfy the child's right to know. In sum, the regulatory frameworks seem to assume that having actual contact with a genetic parent is not necessary to develop one's narrative identity. Instead, they seem to consider that information on its origins is sufficient for the child's identity and self-understanding. This point of view is likely to be influenced by practical reasons since establishing contact with the donor depends on the willingness of the donor to do so.

3.3.3 Genetic Resemblance or Origin Story

The introduction of MRT has put the child's interest in information on its genetic origins and forming an identity in a new light. A child conceived through MRT receives (usually) the nuclear DNA of its intended mother and father, and the mitochondrial DNA (mDNA) of an egg cell donor. Since three genetic parents are involved, this technology is sometimes called three-parent IVF.[61] This popular name has been criticised for not being accurate.[62] Critics argue that since mitochondrial DNA contains less than 0,1% of the total DNA, there is only a weak genetic bond between the child and the egg cell donor. This has raised the question of whether a child conceived through MRT also is entitled to identifying information about the ovum donor. Of the three legal systems, MRT is only regulated in the United Kingdom. The UK legislator decided that, contrary to regular gamete donation, the MRT conceived child does not have a right to identifying donor information.[63] One of the key arguments is that mDNA does not affect the child's characteristics, and therefore, it supposedly does not contribute to the child's identity.[64] As a result, there is apparently no reason to assume that the child resemblances the egg cell donor, and consequently, there

59 *Kamerstukken II*, 1992-1993, 23 207, nr. 3 (*Memorandum Donor Information Artificial Fertilisation Act*), p. 17.

60 *Kamerstukken II*, 1992-1993, 23 207, nr. 3 (*Memorandum Donor Information Artificial Fertilisation Act*), p. 11.

61 The UK legislator deems this term inappropriate. Department of Health, 2014, p. 29.

62 Staatscommissie Herijking Ouderschap, *Kind en ouders in de 21ste eeuw*, Den Haag, 2016, p. 102; Human Fertilisation and Embryology Authority, *Mitochondria replacement consultation: Advice to Government*, 2013, p. 21.

63 Section 11 (c) the Human Fertilisation and Embryology (mitochondrial donation) regulations 2015.

64 Department of Health, 2014, p. 29-30; Nuffield Council on Bioethics, *Novel techniques for the prevention of mitochondrial DNA disorders: an ethical review*, London, 2012, p. 77; Human Fertilisation and Embryology Authority, 2013p. 25-26.

is no ground for a right to disclosure of donor information.[65] The assumption that mDNA does not affect characteristics or the child's identity has been questioned in academic debate.[66] I, however, want to focus on a more fundamental question. Is our genetic descent important for our identity because we want to be able to *identify* ourselves by our (genetic) parents and ancestors, that is, we look for similarities that result from the genetic relationship? Or is our descent important because it forms our origin story and for this reason, the contribution of genetic parents and donors does not (solely) matter because we are genetically related to them, but because they contributed to our existence?

In my opinion, the latter is the case: the mitochondrial donor may not contribute much DNA, but her role is important for the conception of the child. As Scott and Wilkinson correctly argue, the use of MRT could have a significant impact on the child's identity. After all, if the parents would have opted for natural procreation instead of MRT, it is likely that a different combination of a spermatozoon and ovum would take place, resulting in a different child.[67] Or perhaps the parents would have chosen not to conceive at all, in order to prevent the birth of a child affected by a mitochondrial disease. From this perspective, the contribution of the mitochondrial donor is crucial for the child's existence. Moreover, as one of the respondents to the UK consultation points out, for donor conceived children resemblance is not the only reason for wanting to know their genetic roots:

> ...for donor-conceived children the importance of finding out identifying information about their donor lies not only in the contribution the donor has made to their identity but also in other factors such as the desire to thank the donor, to understand something missing, to find out the donor's motivations etc.[68]

Children born via MRT could have the same desires. For these reasons, I would argue that the information about one's genetic origins is not merely important so the child can find someone it resembles with and identifies with. From the idea of a narrative identity, this information is important because it tells a part of how and why the child has come into existence. It tells the child's origin story, which in the age of assisted reproduction, involves more actors than only the child's biological parents. The idea that the way in which the

65 As Brandt points out, not all documents refer to resemblance as the key factor, but it does play an important role in the argument of the Nuffield Council. R. Brandt, 'Mitochondrial donation and 'the right to know'', *Journal of Medical Ethics*, Vol. 42, 2016, p. 679.

66 Brandt, 2016; Scott and Wilkinson, 2017; A.L. Bredenoord, W. Dondorp, G. Pennings and G. de Wert, 'Ethics of modifying the mitochondrial genome', *Journal of Medical Ethics*, Vol. 37, No. 2, 2011, p. 97-100.

67 Scott and Wilkinson, 2017, p. 907-908.

68 Department of Health, 2014, p. 28.

child is brought into existence is of the utmost importance for its narrative identity is also emphasised by the Dutch Government Committee on the Reassessment of Parenthood.[69] The committee even proposes to speak of *a right to information about one's origin story*[70] instead of a right to donor information. This right to information about one's origin story should be interpreted extensively, and covers information about gamete or embryo donors, but also the other parties involved in the child's conception. This includes the surrogate (even when the surrogate is not the egg cell donor), the organisations that mediated between the different parties, and the clinics that facilitated the fertility treatment.[71] Although the committee does not address the role of the mitochondrial donor in this context, given their interpretation of the interest of the future child, it follows from it that the child should also have access to identifying information about the mitochondrial donor.

In sum, the regulatory frameworks on donor disclosure operationalise an intersubjective notion of identity. The future child's identity is seen as a narrative or an origin story in which others play a part. Those to whom the child is genetically related and who contributed to its existence are considered to be of such importance, that according to the legal systems, the child not only has an interest in information about its descent, but this right to know is understood to be a part of a general personality right. From the way the future child's interest in identity and in information about its descent is addressed in the regulations, it follows that the regulatory frameworks understand identity as something that the child can construct by itself or something that others can construct for the child. Nonetheless, some subjective influence on one's identity is still acknowledged: all three legal systems are leaving it up to the child to decide whether it wants to request the information, thereby allowing for the possibility that the child does not believe the information is relevant for who it is.

3.4 The Concept of Human Dignity

3.4.1 *Dignity and Harm*

Like the future child's interest in identity and access to information about its origins, reference to the notion of human dignity in debates on reproductive technologies has been criticised. A frequently heard point of critique, which amongst others, can be found

69 Staatscommissie Herijking Ouderschap, 2016, p. 45.

70 In Dutch: een recht op informatie over de ontstaansgeschiedenis. Translation by LtH.

71 Staatscommissie Herijking Ouderschap, 2016, p. 383.

in the Nuffield Report on genome editing and human reproduction,[72] is that the concept is not helpful as a normative guideline. Also in academic debates, the importance of the notion of human dignity has been criticised. Pinker is a firm critic of the concept; in his essay, 'The stupidity of dignity', he writes that the problem is "that 'dignity' is a squishy, subjective notion, hardly up to the heavyweight moral demands assigned to it."[73] Pinker's critique that human dignity is a subjective concept is because of the fact that this notion is undefined and ambiguous. According to Bagaric and Allan, although the notion is prominently featured in international rights documents, national constitutions, and even in case law, nowhere is it clearly defined. They maintain that dignity is a boundless and vacuous concept.[74] Because it is not clearly defined, or as Macklin puts it, "hopelessly vague",[75] critics of the concept argue that it cannot be the foundation of a fundamental rights discourse[76] or that invoking it without defining it is nothing more than a "mere slogan."[77] Furthermore, because of its lack of clear content human dignity can be used to support both sides of an argument. For example, on the topic of euthanasia, it can on the one hand be argued, along the lines of Kant's argument, that self-killing is a violation of dignity because the human person is treated as a means to avoid suffering.[78] On the other hand, it can also be argued that euthanasia allows people to die with dignity, respecting their autonomous choice. Because of its vague nature, some authors suggest abandoning this concept all together and to replacing it with more clearly defined notions. According to Macklin, dignity implies nothing more than respect for the person's autonomy and can thus be replaced by notions such as autonomy and informed consent.[79] Also, Pinker argues that notions such as autonomy and informed consent would suffice. If the violation of dignity results in "identifiable harm" he reasons that it is because it involved coercion, which can be condemned on basis of autonomy and respect for persons.[80] In addition to that, it is difficult to make a convincing argument that the violation of future child's dignity in the context of reproduction qualifies as harm.[81] Instrumentalisation through, for

---

72 Nuffield Council on Bioethics, 2018, p. 94.

73 S. Pinker, 'The Stupidity of Dignity', *The New Republic*, 2008.

74 M. Bagaric and J. Allan, 'The vacuous concept of dignity', *Journal of Human Rights*, Vol. 5, No. 2, 2006, p. 257-270.

75 R. Macklin, 'Dignity is a useless concept. It means no more than respect for persons or their autonomy', *BMJ*, Vol. 327, 2003, p. 1420.

76 Bagaric and Allan, 2006, p. 269.

77 Macklin, 2003, p. 1420.

78 I. Kant, *Grundlegung Zur Metaphysik Der Sitten*, 1785, Reprint: T. Mertens *Fundering voor de metafysica van de zeden*, Amsterdam, Boom, 2008, p. 106.

79 Macklin, 2003.

80 Pinker, 2008.

81 T.M. Spranger, *Recht und Bioethik. Verweisungszusammenhänge bei der Normierung der Lebenswissenschaften*, Tübingen, Mohr Siebeck, 2010, p. 103. See also chapter 4.

example, sex selection does not by itself necessarily set back the child's physical or mental health interests.

However, this negative view of the notion of human dignity is not accepted by everyone. For example, Khaitan argues that the added value of human dignity lies precisely in the fact that it is able to address something beyond harm and measurable consequences. According to Khaitan,[82] human dignity can perform "a task that other fundamental values cannot perform."[83] That is, with the help of the notion of human dignity we can articulate that disrespecting or humiliating a person (without this resulting in "material harm",[84] "economic loss",[85] or another form of measurable harm) is objectionable. Khaitan points out that only focusing on the consequences of an act would render the concept of dignity superfluous: "if we are interested in the consequences of an act, we don't need dignity as a tool to target them. There are other values, like the harm principle...which will do the work."[86] He sees dignity as an expressive norm that can address "the expression of disrespect/insult/humiliation etc to a cherished person."[87]

By referring to human dignity as an expressive norm, Khaitan touches upon the symbolic functions of the concept of dignity and of law in general. In academic debate on the symbolic functions of law, the idea has been adopted that law is more than a tool to influence human behaviour in the form of commands backed up with sanctions – it also offers a platform for debate and interaction.[88] In addition, law is said to act as a mediator to helps us understand and attribute meaning and value to biological and natural facts.[89] One of these symbolic functions is the expressive function, in which law makes statements through mentioning and explicating fundamental values.[90] According to Khaitan, human dignity is such an "expressive norm", and thus, the violation of human dignity is not wrong because it results in harm, but it expresses a wrong, namely degrading a human being.[91]

---

82 Khaitan focuses on antidiscrimination law but some of his ideas are also applicable on the use of human dignity in biolaw and the regulation of reproduction.

83 T. Khaitan, 'Dignity as an expressive norm: neither vacuous nor a panacea', *Oxford Journal of Legal Studies*, Vol. 32, No. 1, 2012, p. 5.

84 Khaitan, 2012, p. 6.

85 Khaitan, 2012, p. 7.

86 Khaitan, 2012, p. 11.

87 Khaitan, 2012, p. 4.

88 L. Poort, B.C. van Beers and B. van Klink, 'Introduction: symbolic dimensions of biolaw.' in: B. van Klink, B.C. van Beers and L. Poort (eds.), *Symbolic legislation theory and developments in biolaw*, Springer Verlag, Switzerland, 2016, p. 2.

89 B.C. van Beers, 'Is Europe "giving in to baby markets"? Reproductive tourism in Europe and the gradual erosion of existing legal limits to reproductive markets', *Medical Law Review*, Vol. 23, No. 1, 2014, p. 128.

90 van Beers, 2014, p. 128.

91 Khaitan, 2012, p. 4, 8.

Other scholars have argued that the concept of human dignity is in particular connected to what they see as law's anthropological function.[92] Van Beers explains this function as law's contribution to "the symbolic mediation of the bare, biological facts of life into the meaningful events of the lives that we lead."[93] An example of such mediation is the transformation of the biological human being into the legal subject, which according to Pessers is "the symbolic core activity of the law."[94] Being subjected to the legal system enables the human to become the bearer of legal rights and duties, and to live in an ordered society where the legal subject's freedom and equality to others are protected. It is telling that Pessers states that law does not only try to influence people's behaviour, but also their identity.[95] This is not their personal identity, as discussed in the previous section, but their identity as human persons. According to her, the human person in law is not an animalistic being who is in a war of all against all, but a social and rational being, who has subjected himself to a legal order and thereby bound himself to other subjects and to a mutual respect of each other's equality, rights and freedoms.[96] Pessers, van Beers, and also the French legal scholar Alain Supiot, whose work *Homo Juridicus*[97] centres around the anthropological function of law, argue that this legal transformation starts at the moment of birth. Through law, they claim, the birth of a new born is not merely the existence of a new biological entity, but the child is inserted in the genealogical order of the family and through the attribution of legal subjectivity, it becomes part of the legal order.[98] And as part of this legal order, the child is endowed with fundamental freedoms and the protection of its autonomy.[99] In other words, through the anthropological function of the law, the biological human being can become a human person and a legal subject.[100]

92 van Beers, 2009b, p. 646-652; van Beers, 2014, p. 129; B.C. van Beers, 'From winged lions to frozen embryos: the functions of law in the symbolic mediation of biomedical hybrids.' in: B. van Klink, B.C. van Beers and L. Poort (eds.), *Symbolic legislation theory and developments in biolaw*, Springer Verlag, Switzerland, 2016a, p. 195; J.C. Byk, 'Is human dignity a useless concept? Legal perspective.' in: M. Düwell, J. Braarvig, R. Brownsword and D. Mieth (eds.), *The Cambridge handbook of human dignity: interdisciplinary perspectives*, Cambridge University Press, Cambridge, 2014, p. 364; A. Supiot, *Homo juridicus. On the anthropological function of the law*, London, Verso, 2007.

93 van Beers, 2016a, p. 195.

94 D. Pessers, 'The symbolic meaning of legal subjectivity.' in: B. van Klink, B. van Beers and L. Poort (eds.), *Symbolic legislation theory and developments in biolaw*, Springer, Switzerland, 2016, p. 202-203.

95 Pessers, 2016, p. 202.

96 See also D. Pessers, *Verdwaalde seksen. Over sperminators, metroseksuelen en autocopieën*, Nijmegen, Uitgeverij Valkhof Pers, 2003b, p. 21; D. Pessers, *Big Mother. Over de personalisering van de publieke sfeer*, Den Haag, Boom Juridische Uitgevers, 2003a, p. 33-34; Pessers, 2016, p. 207.

97 Supiot, 2007.

98 Pessers, 2016, p. 202; van Beers, 2009b, p. 652-661; Supiot, 2007, p. viii, 37.

99 Pessers, 2005, p. 26-29.

100 See also van Beers, 2009b, p. 646, who speaks of law's *humanising* function.

The notion of human dignity is considered to play an important role in this legal transformation. As van Beers explains, through legislation and regulation, special meaning is attached to biological aspects of a human's life, such as the body, birth, and death.[101] Put differently, the legal system attributes a symbolic value to these entities based on the idea of human dignity. For example, the corpse is not merely a legal object, but still deserves some form of respect. The human body is also not something a person can fully dispose over, as this power of disposal is restricted by legal norms that prevent for example, the instrumentalisation and commercialisation of the body. Most importantly, the human's membership to the human species is symbolically converted into legal subjectivity and the endowment with inalienable rights.[102] This is elucidated in the Universal Declaration of Human Rights, the preamble of which states: ".... Recognition of the inherent dignity and of the equal and inalienable rights of all members of the human family..." Its first article reads, "All human beings are born free and equal in dignity and rights. They are endowed with reason and conscience and should act towards one another in a spirit of brotherhood." Article 1 of the Universal Declaration of Human Rights also illustrates that this transformation of the biological human into a legal subject does not render it void of content. The legal subject is not only entitled to inalienable rights, but also endowed with reason. From this, it follows that the legal order offers its own perspective on what the human person is, which is expressed in the notion of human dignity. According to van Beers, human dignity can be seen as "a legal-symbolic representation of what it means to be human."[103] Similar ideas have been expressed by Byk, who argues that human dignity helps us "define what humanity is",[104] and by Calo who maintains that dignity entails a symbolic claim, namely "an anthropological claim about the nature of human identity and personhood."[105] Following these interpretations of law's anthropological function, it is through the operationalisation of the concept of human dignity that law aims to influence the identity of people as persons.

In sum, in the interpretation by these scholars, human dignity fulfils an important role in protecting the human person in law, even if the violation of his dignity cannot be understood in terms of harm. In fact, the violation of human dignity touches upon a deeper level than harm, as according to van Beers it serves to protect the legal subject's *humanity*.[106] In order to do so, human dignity must adopt an idea of what this humanity

101 van Beers, 2009b, p. 648; van Beers, 2014, p. 130; van Beers, 2016a, p. 195-196.

102 van Beers, 2009b, p. 650.

103 van Beers, 2016a, p. 192.

104 Byk, 2014, p. 364.

105 Z.R. Calo, 'Human dignity and health law: personhood in recent bioethical debates', *Notre Dame Journal of Law Ethics & Public Policy*, Vol. 26, 2012, p. 474.

106 van Beers, 2009a, p. 125.

entails and this idea is fundamental to the legal order and to the legal concept of a person. However, it is hard to exactly determine what this perspective on humanity entails. Fundamental Rights treaties that explicitly refer to human dignity, such as the Universal Declaration of Human Rights and the European Convention on Human Rights and Biomedicine, stress that all human beings are born equal, free, and with inalienable fundamental rights. As such, human dignity is considered to be the foundation for recognising our liberties and fundamental rights.[107] Within this perspective, the individual is characterised by its autonomy and equality to other persons, which is, amongst others, expressed through notions such as informed consent and freedom of contract. As such, the autonomous, free, and equal person is not a realistic representation of the human being, but an ideal, a legal construct.[108] However, human dignity does not conceive humans as solely characterised by autonomy and equality, as shown in the regulations on reproduction. Instrumentalising, breeding, and designing humans are considered to be an affront to human dignity, but not because the resulting child does not consent to such treatment. After all, since the future child does not exist yet, it cannot give or withhold its consent. Moreover, since the child will not come into existence at all, it is also not possible to anticipate its consent. Apparently, human dignity means something more. In the literature, scholars have identified two main interpretations of human dignity[109] which can conflict with each other and are the reason for the critique of human dignity being a "two-edged sword."[110]

3.4.2 *Two Interpretations of Dignity*

In chapter 2 I demonstrated that the regulations on reproduction acknowledges two dimensions of human dignity. Besides the dignity of the individual child, the frameworks also refer to the dignity of humankind as a whole.[111] These two dimensions, the individual

---

107 Beyleveld and Brownsword, 2012, p. 12-13.; van Beers, 2009a, p. 123. H. Somsen, *Regulering van humane genetica in het neo-eugenetische tijdperk*, Nijmegen, Wolf Legal Publishers, 2006, p. 31-32. Also the ECtHR has acknowledged that human dignity, along with human freedom, form the foundation of the European Convention on Human Rights. ECtHR 29 April 2002 ECLI:CE:ECHR:2002:0429JUD000234602 (*Pretty v. the United Kingdom*), par. 65: "The very essence of the Convention is respect for human dignity and human freedom." This view is contested by den Hartogh. G. Den Hartogh, 'Is human dignity the ground of human rights?' in: M. Düwell, J. Braarvig, R. Brownsword and D. Mieth (eds.), *The Cambridge Handbook of Human Dignity: Interdisciplinary Perspectives*, Cambridge University Press, Cambridge, 2014, p. 200-207.

108 van Beers, 2009b, p. 578; Pessers, 2005, p. 14.

109 Beyleveld and Brownsword, 2012, p. 11; van Beers, 2009a, p. 135-139; van Beers, 2009b, p. 167; Somsen, 2006, 31-33. Pessers, 2005, p. 7.

110 Beyleveld and Brownsword, 2012, p. 25.

111 See section 2.4.2.3.

and the collective dimension of human dignity, roughly correspond with the two interpretations of this concept.

The first interpretation, which is often connected to human dignity in the individual dimension, is closely related to Macklin's and Pinker's accounts in which individual autonomy is prioritised. Respecting human dignity in this perspective entails recognising humans as autonomous beings, capable of making their own decisions, designing their own lives, and planning their own futures.[112] This interpretation is dubbed by Beyleveld and Brownsword as *human dignity as empowerment*.[113] According to Pessers, human dignity in this interpretation can be understood as a subjective notion; it is up to the subject himself to determine how to shape his life and to determine what a dignified life is.[114] Respecting the individual's human dignity according to this perspective requires respecting the individual's autonomous choice. Or as Beyleveld and Brownsword put it, the individual's dignity entitles it to protection against unconsented interventions and to the conditions necessary to exercise their autonomy and to flourish.[115]

In the context of reproduction, this interpretation can be found in several contexts. First, acknowledging the prospective parents' reproductive autonomy is in line with this account of dignity.[116] As having children is considered to be an important part of one's life, people should be free to use reproductive biotechnology to help shape that aspect of their lives. The EctHR has acknowledged that reproductive freedom falls within the scope of Article 8, which is an expression of the principle of personal autonomy. According to the Court, Article 8 protects the right to respect for the decision to become a genetic parent or not,[117] the right to make use of medically assisted procreation,[118] and even the right to select a healthy child.[119] The reproductive interests of prospective parents are also considered to be an important factor in the regulation of reproduction.[120]

---

112 J. Raz, *The Authority of law: essays on law and morality*, New York, Oxford University Press, 1979, p. 221; Beyleveld and Brownsword, 2012, p. 14, 28.

113 Beyleveld and Brownsword, 2012, p. 11.

114 Pessers, 2005, p. 7.

115 Beyleveld and Brownsword, 2012, p. 15.

116 Beyleveld and Brownsword, 2012, p. 146.

117 ECtHR 4 December 2007 ECLI:CE:ECHR:2007:1204JUD004436204 (*Dickson v. the United Kingdom*), par. 66; ECtHR 10 April 2007 ECLI:CE:ECHR:2007:0410JUD000633905 (*Evans v. the United Kingdom*), par. 71-72.

118 ECtHR 3 November 2011 ECLI:CE:ECHR:2011:1103JUD005781300 (*S.H. e.a. v. Austria*), par. 82.

119 ECtHR 28 August 2012, ECLI:CE:ECHR:2012:0828JUD005427010 (*Costa and Pavan v. Italy*), par. 57.

120 *Kamerstukken II* 2000-2001, 27 423, nr. 3 (*Memorandum Embryo Act*), p. 3; BT-Drs. 17/5451 vom 12.04.2011 (*Bill and Memorandum PGD regulation*).

Human dignity as empowerment can also be applied to the future child. Using reproductive technologies to ensure the child is born healthy is considered to be in line with human dignity.[121] A striking example is the argument of the Dutch Health Council and Committee for Genetic Modification. In their report, human dignity is interpreted as empowerment: it states that human dignity is understood as an intrinsic quality of the human person and as such it is interpreted as respect for human life, individual autonomy, and the duty to prevent human suffering.[122] The report continues by pointing out the interests of the future child include the right to an open future: "… every child is entitled to the conditions that are necessary to become an autonomous person."[123] A genetic illness could compromise the child's capacity to exercise its autonomy. Therefore, MRT and genetic modification are not an affront to human dignity, according to the report. On the contrary, provided that these technologies aim to prevent a severe genetic condition, they are a form of respect for the child's dignity, as they contribute to the child's capacity to exercise its autonomy.[124]

Whereas the Dutch Health Council and Committee for Genetic Modification argue that editing the child's genome should be understood as a way of respecting human dignity, the regulatory frameworks seem reluctant to follow this line of reasoning. As discussed in chapter 2, within the regulations on reproduction, the selection of a child's genetic characteristics (in particular for non-medical reasons) is mostly seen as a violation of human dignity, as it is understood as an instrumentalisation of a human person. Beyleveld and Brownsword consider the instrumentalisation of the human person to be a violation of human dignity as empowerment. This would be the case if a person is treated "as a mere thing, as an object, as having no intrinsic value, or as lacking the distinctive human capacities."[125] Slavery, for example, qualifies as an instrumentalising practice because slaves are regarded as property. In most cases they would have limited to no opportunity for autonomous action, and thus, the authors maintain, they are not treated as humans.[126]

---

121 Beyleveld and Brownsword, 2012, p. 146.

122 Commissie Genetische Modificatie (COGEM) & Gezondheidsraad, 2017, p. 54.

123 Commissie Genetische Modificatie (COGEM) & Gezondheidsraad, 2017, p. 55. In Dutch: "[Het principe van een open toekomst houdt in dat] elk kind het recht heeft op condities die nodig zijn om later een autonoom persoon te worden." Translation by LtH. See also B.C. van Beers, 'Welkom in de CRISPR-dierentuin. Juridische grenzen aan genetische modificatie van het nageslacht in het CRISPR-tijdperk', *Nederlands Juristenblad*, Vol. 2019, No. 24, 2019, p. 1728-1729.

124 Commissie Genetische Modificatie (COGEM) & Gezondheidsraad, 2017, p. 55-56; A similar argument was made with regard to MRT. See Gezondheidsraad, 2001p. 35-36.

125 Beyleveld and Brownsword, 2012, p. 17; A similar argument is posed by Jan Joerden with regard to reproductive cloning, arguing that if conception as a clone would be against the future will of the clone, the creation of the clone could then be understood as using the clone as a means. In German: "Gefragt werden muss allerdings, ob die Erzeugung eines Klons gegen dessen mutmaßlichen künftigen Willen verstoßen könnte, da dann seine Erzeugung eine Verwendung des Klons als bloßes Mittel darstellen könnte." Joerden, 2013, p. 233.

126 Beyleveld and Brownsword, 2012, p. 16-19.

However, Beyleveld and Brownsword's interpretation does not provide an answer to the question of self-instrumentalisation. How should we understand the situation in which someone willingly sells himself as a slave, agrees to commodify her body as a commercial surrogate, or is willing to clone himself? Are these examples an expression of human dignity because they involve autonomous action, or a violation because they violate the objective value of the human person? As the possibilities to mould and shape our own life and body increase, the question arises, why should the freedom to use these possibilities be restricted?[127] More particularly, for reproduction, Beyleveld and Brownsword's interpretation of instrumentalisation cannot adequately address the instrumentalisation of the future child. After all, the child does not exist at the moment the decision is made, so it cannot express its consent or objection.[128] Moreover, the existence of the child as an autonomous being depends on the act that possibly qualifies as instrumentalisation. As van Beers explains, the legal boundaries to germline modification, reproductive cloning, and sex selection cannot be understood from the interpretation of human dignity that puts the focus on autonomy and self-determination.[129] After all, these actions remain prohibited despite the possible consent of the involved parties. Instead, they are based on the second interpretation of human dignity.

In a second interpretation, i.e. the collective dimension of human dignity, this notion is understood as what Pessers calls a "supra-individual, or at least a more or less objectifiable principle."[130] This implies that it is not up to the individual to determine what to him dignity entails. Instead, human dignity is understood as a value that resides in every human because they are a member of the human species. Hence it represents a collective idea of what humanity is and is invoked to protect the human person against instrumentalisation, commodification, or dehumanisation. For this reason, as van Beers points out, in this interpretation it is not the individual but humankind that is the subject of human dignity.[131] This collective dimension is also addressed in international conventions. For example, the Preamble of the Council of Europe's Convention on Human Rights and Biomedicine emphasises "the need to respect the human being both as an individual and as a member of the human species."[132] In this collective dimension of human dignity, the notion can also be invoked to curb free choice and physical self-

127 Pessers, 2005, p. 7-8; Pessers, 2016, p. 208-209.

128 See also van Beers, 2009b, p. 566.

129 van Beers, 2009a, p 120-122, 136. See also R. Andorno, 'Human dignity and human rights as a common ground for a global bioethics', *Journal of Medicine and Philosophy*, Vol. 34, 2009, p. 228.

130 Pessers, 2005, p. 7.

131 van Beers, 2009a, p. 136. See also Pessers, 2005, p. 7; Andorno, 2009, p. 233.

132 Council of Europe, Convention for the protection of Human Rights and Dignity of the Human Being with regard to the Application of Biology and Medicine: Convention on Human Rights and Biomedicine, ETS No.164 (*Oviedo Convention*).

determination. For this reason, this interpretation is dubbed *human dignity as constraint* by Beyleveld and Brownsword.[133] Similar to the interpretation of human dignity as empowerment, dignity requires that the human is treated as a person and that his humanity is respected. However, in human dignity as constraint, this humanity is not equated with the person's autonomy and capacity to design his own life. In this interpretation, human dignity is a collective value that transcends individual choice and subjective interpretation.[134]

The interpretation of human dignity as constraint, or rather as an objective value, is prominently represented in the regulations on reproduction. In chapter 2, I discussed several regulatory frameworks that invoke human dignity to justify the ban on certain technologies. The bans on reproductive cloning and non-medical sex selection, for example, restrict prospective parents in their reproductive choices, illustrating that human dignity can be invoked to curb individual freedom. Nonetheless, the regulatory frameworks occasionally appeared to refer to the dignity of an individual subject, namely the dignity of the future child. For example, in the context of sex selection, some Memoranda expressed the fear that the future child would be reduced to an object of its parents' desires[135] and that reproductive cloning would violate the future child's right to unicity.[136] As explained, the regulatory frameworks that refer to the future child's dignity aim to protect the future child from being treated as a commodity or a design object. In other words, the future child is protected from instrumentalisation, commodification, or dehumanisation. In particular, in the frameworks on sex selection, HLA-typing and reproductive cloning, human dignity plays an important role and is possibly violated because in these contexts the future child could be used as a means. That is, the child is conceived to meet the desires of its parents, or the needs of an ill sibling. Importantly, within the regulatory frameworks, the instrumentalisation is not deemed problematic because it restricts the child's possibility to autonomous action or because the child did not consent to this treatment. Given the fact that the future child has not even been conceived yet, it cannot express its autonomy. This is reflected in the fact that the regulatory frameworks do not refer to the future child's consent, or more appropriately, *anticipated* consent. The latter would also be impossible if the future child does not come into existence at all: in that case, there is no person whose autonomy or consent can be anticipated. Instead, as came to the fore in the chosen formulation of the Dutch regulatory frameworks,

133 Beyleveld and Brownsword, 2012, p. 11.

134 van Beers, 2009a, p. 137; Beyleveld and Brownsword, 2012, p. 34.

135 *Kamerstukken II* 2000-2001, 27 423, nr. 3 (*Memorandum Embryo Act*), p. 48; Regeling van de staatssecretaris van Volksgezondheid, Welzijn en Sport van 16 februari 2009, nr. CZ-TSZ-2912089, houdende houdende regels ten aanzien van preïmplantatie genetische diagnostiek (PGD), (*Stcrt.* 2009, 42) (*Ministerial decree PGD*), p. 12.

136 *Kamerstukken II* 2000-2001, 27 423, nr. 3 (*Memorandum Embryo Act*), p. 42.

the possible violation of the child's dignity lies in the fact that the child is *reduced* to something less, implying a collective idea of what the human person is, and what must be protected. This implies that human dignity in this context is presented as an objective value, that is not subjected to the subjective interpretation of the individual. Moreover, it is precisely in these contexts that not only is the human dignity of individual subjects is at stake, but also the dignity of humankind as a whole, as expressed in various regulatory frameworks.

It is the restrictive interpretation of human dignity in particular that has received criticism from liberal scholars, because in this interpretation, human dignity can be invoked to constrain autonomous choice. For example, Somsen has argued that this version of human dignity is not only restricting, but also repressive.[137] Also Beyleveld and Brownsword see a threat in this interpretation, as it "is precisely to close down rather than to open up the freedom to take advantage of the technology now being developed in the biosciences."[138] Moreover, Pinker has even argued that the concept of human dignity has stagnated scientific development.[139] Most of them favour the interpretation of human dignity as empowerment, putting the focus on individual autonomy.

However, even though certain tensions may rise between the two interpretations, Andorno argues that the interpretations are not rival notions, but complement each other: "Indeed, the same principle stating that human beings have intrinsic worth results in two consequences. First, that each individual is entitled to fundamental rights and freedoms. Second, that people deserve to be protected from serious threats to their dignity, even if they might appear to be consenting to such acts."[140] In a similar vein, van Beers maintains that the dimension of human dignity that focuses on individual autonomy and freedom is "inextricably and fundamentally connected"[141] to the dimension that approaches human dignity as an objective value and is invoked to constrain certain choices. She explains that the idea that the individual human person is entitled to the freedoms protected by fundamental rights, i.e. the subjective dimension, depends on a collective notion of humanity, which is protected by the objective interpretation of human dignity.[142] After all, those fundamental freedoms and rights are attributed to the individual once it has subjected itself to the legal order.[143] Only then does it becomes a legal subject, whose image

137 Somsen, 2006, p. 33.
138 Beyleveld and Brownsword, 2012, p. 28.
139 S. Pinker, 'The moral imperative for bioethics', *The Boston Globe*, 2015.
140 Andorno, 2009, p. 232.
141 van Beers, 2020, p. 26.
142 van Beers, 2009b, p. 585.
143 Pessers, 2005, p. 26-29.

is based on law's collective notion of the human person. Therefore, in this perspective where both interpretations of human dignity are combined, human dignity is not something that is completely subjected to the subject's interpretation, despite the fact that this notion forms the foundation of our liberty. As van Beers argues, it is precisely because of this fundamental character that human dignity cannot be the object of the same freedom and liberties it constitutes.[144] If the concept of human dignity becomes completely subjected to subjective interpretation, it indeed becomes an empty shell at the cost of law's protective function.[145] Importantly though, the subjective dimension prevents the human person from being subordinated to collective interests, such as "the sole interest of society or science."[146] As van Beers points out:

> The underlying thought which unites both dimensions is that fundamental freedoms cannot be exercised to the detriment of the collective foundations of these freedoms, which is the humanity of humankind. (…) The other way around, collective dignity should always serve the long-term goal of protecting individual dignity, just as human dignity as empowerment and human dignity as constraint both serve to protect the individual. Without this caveat, there is a danger that individual freedoms are sacrificed to preserve 'the dignity of the whole'.[147]

This fundamental connection between both interpretations of human dignity elucidates one of the blind spots of a sole focus on the individual dimension or equating human dignity to respect for individual autonomy. Autonomy in this sense seems to be limited to being able to choose and having options available to choose from. It does not address the question of why we understand ourselves as autonomous and what the continuation of this self-understanding requires. Habermas, for example, has explored how biotechnologies such as gene editing and reproductive cloning (technologies that allow others to determine the genetic blueprint of the future child) affect our self-understanding as autonomous and equal beings.[148] In chapter 7, I explore these ideas more extensively. In brief, the idea of the human person being autonomous, which is the focus of the subjective interpretation of human dignity, rests on a collective notion of humanity. In order to protect this collective notion, there are boundaries in place that restrict individual choice. Such a boundary was also noted by Mill, who argued that freedom does not include the liberty to alienate one's

144 van Beers, 2009a, p. 137.

145 Pessers, 2005, p. 12, 55-56; Pessers, 2016, p. 209-210.

146 Article 2 of the European Convention on Human Rights and Biomedicine and Article 3(2) of the Universal Declaration on Bioethics and Human Rights.

147 van Beers, 2020, p. 26.

148 Habermas, 2003, p. 40-41.

freedom.[149] Freedom of autonomous choice finds its boundary when it undermines the view of humanity that underlies this freedom.[150] As reproductive technologies contain the possibility of dismantling the ideal of humanity that is the foundation of freedom and fundamental rights, their application can be restricted on grounds of human dignity. However, only in these extreme cases, where the normative self-image of the human person as free and autonomous is jeopardised, can individual autonomy be restricted.[151]

In sum, various authors have rebutted the idea that human dignity is a vacuous concept that could mean just anything. Human dignity can be understood as law's understanding of the human person, which encompasses two dimensions: the human person as an individual being, and the human person as a member of humanity. Each dimension has its own interpretation of the concept and in extreme cases, these interpretations may even conflict with each other. In particular, due to advances in biotechnology which facilitate self-instrumentalisation and instrumentalisation of future people, the tension between both interpretations becomes clear. Nonetheless, as I already discussed in chapter 2, both dimensions are intrinsically linked to each other. Because law's understanding of the human person includes both the individual and the collective dimension, it adopts an interpretation of the human person that is intersubjective. Characteristics that are deemed essential to the individual such as autonomy and equality, are derived from a collective image of humanity. Put differently, each individual is connected to humanity as a whole. Consequently, as van Beers puts it, the sort of 'harm' involved in the violation of human dignity "goes beyond the harm principle and the violation of rights."[152] Individual cases that affront human dignity may affect the collective perspective of humankind. As international treaties such as the Convention of Human Rights and Biomedicine and the Cloning Protocol point out the violation of human dignity does not only affect the individual involved, but also the human species[153] and the possibilities to understand ourselves as free beings.[154] In other words, with regard to protecting human dignity, it is not just the interest of the future child that is at stake.

---

149 Mill, (1859) 2002, p. 86-87.

150 van Beers, 2009a, p.137, 141.

151 van Beers, 2009a, p. 143. See also article 2 of the Convention on Human Rights and Biomedicine, that states that: "The interests and welfare of the human being shall prevail over the sole interest of society or science."

152 van Beers, 2017b, p. 128.

153 Council of Europe, Convention for the protection of Human Rights and Dignity of the Human Being with regard to the Application of Biology and Medicine: Convention on Human Rights and Biomedicine, ETS No.164 (*Oviedo Convention*), par. 89.

154 Council of Europe, Explanatory Report to the Additional Protocol to the Convention for the Protection of Human Rights and Dignity of the Human Being with regard to the Application of Biology and Medicine, on the Prohibition of Cloning Human Beings ETS No.168 (*Cloning Protocol*), par 3. A similar point is made by Habermas who poses the question as to "... whether the instrumentalisation of human nature changes

3.5 Conclusion: the Individual and Collective Dimensions of the Human Person

In this chapter, I scrutinised the first assumption regarding the future child, namely that the core values the regulatory frameworks aim to protect, i.e. well-being, identity, and dignity, can be understood as interests of the individual future child. To this end, a profound understanding of these core values is needed. As discussed in the previous chapter, the regulatory frameworks themselves refrain from explaining which interpretations of the notions of harm, identity, and dignity underly the regulatory frameworks. In order to gain a deeper understanding of these values (compared to what could be distilled from the legal analysis) that are presented as interests of the future child, I elaborated on the underlying interpretations of harm, identity, and dignity with the help of academic literature. This discussion complements chapter 2 and serves to come to a better understanding of these notions as they are promoted in the regulations on reproduction. Put differently, this philosophical discussion aims to offer further insight into what the regulations on reproduction intends to protect. The core values, which are presented as interests of the future child, are derived from an idea of what, according to the regulator, we owe to future people. As such, they represent a normative idea of what the human person is according to the regulations on reproduction. The discussion in this chapter allows for a further reconstruction of the idea of the human person that underlies the regulation.

As the reconstruction of the three core notions reveals, the interpretation of the human person in the regulations on reproduction is a multi-facetted one, incorporating both subjective and intersubjective elements. The interest to be free from harm and to secure the future child's well-being illustrates the subjective nature of the person, as it focuses on the child's physical and mental well-being as needs that must be allowed to flourish. The notions of identity and dignity can be understood as examples of the human person's intersubjective nature. In the interpretation of these notions, as operationalised in the regulations on reproduction, every individual human is considered to be a part of something more, as connected to other members of the human family. Both someone's individual identity and his identity as a human person is understood as (co-)dependent on their relation to others. With regard to personal identity, which features in the regulation on donor anonymity, the regulatory frameworks appear to adopt a narrative account of identity and consider our personal identity to be co-dependent on our (genetic) family and social bonds. These genetic and biological relations play an important role, as they are

---

the ethical self-understanding of the species in such a way that we no longer see ourselves as ethically free and morally equal beings guided by norms and reasons." Habermas, 2003, p. 40-41.

part of the child's origin story. In the case of human dignity, the human person's intersubjective nature pertains to his connection to mankind as a whole. Human dignity, as it is operationalised in the regulations on reproduction, encompasses an individual and a collective dimension. Both dimensions are intertwined. In chapter 2, I already addressed the idea that even when the regulatory frameworks refer to the dignity of the future child in the context of possible instrumentalisation or commodification, the dignity of humankind as a whole is also at stake. This chapter elaborated on that connection, arguing that the idea of the individual being autonomous and free is derived from a collective notion of what the human person is in law, or in this case, the regulations on reproduction. Some technologies may not only affect the future child on an individual level, by inflicting harm, but also on a transcendental level, by violating the dignity of humanity itself and thus eroding the collective image of the person in law. In other words, it is not necessarily merely the future child's dignity that is as stake, but also the dignity of humanity. Consequently, in addition to the future child's individual interests, collective interests too, i.e. the self-understanding of humanity, play a role in the regulatory frameworks that invoke human dignity.

An interesting parallel can be drawn between these three interests and the three 'births' of the child. As Pessers explains, at the moment of birth the future child becomes a legal subject, it is inscribed into a genealogical line of a family and attributed legal rights and freedoms. As such, the human person is born three times.[155] First, the child is born in a biological sense, in possession of a biological body that can experience well-being, but also pain and suffering. Second, it is born in a social sense, "as a member of a family and social environment." The human person is thus not born completely devoid of other persons, but as part of a family line with its own origin story. Third and finally, the child is born in a legal sense, as a legal subject and a member of a legal community. According to Pessers, this last birth "is a miraculous one", because it pertains to an ideal image of the human being: "free, equal, dignified and in the possession of human rights." In other words, it is the human person in the image of human dignity. As, for example, family law and human rights law contribute to these different births of the human person, its intersubjective nature is not only acknowledged by the regulations on reproduction.

The question arises of whether the 'interests of the future child' construction is the adequate framework to capture all the interests and values that are at stake in the regulations on reproduction. This construction operationalises a vocabulary that puts focus on the individual entity and its interests. As the regulatory frameworks articulate the stakes as the 'interests of the future child', they seem to suggest that only the future child is

155 Pessers, 2016, p. 202.

affected by the reproductive technologies. Nonetheless, the consequences of using reproductive technologies transcend the individual child. First, they affect future generations, as genetic traits can be passed on. Second, and more importantly, these technologies affect the collective self-image of humanity. Technologies such as sex selection or reproductive cloning do not only affect the dignity of the future child, but also the dignity of humanity. For these reasons, collective interests play a role in the regulations on reproduction as well. This collective dimension that transcends the individual is not always made explicit in the regulations on reproduction. For example, in its discussion on the ban on reproductive cloning, the Memorandum to the Dutch Embryo Act seems mostly focused on the dignity of the child, as it refers to the violation of the cloned person's right to develop into a unique being.[156] In a similar vein, the Dutch regulator considers the possible instrumentalisation of the future child in the context of non-medical sex selection,[157] but it neglects to address how the conditional creation of human life may erode the collective self-image of humanity. By adopting the interests-construction and focusing on the interests of an individual entity, the collective interests or the individual transcending consequences of reproductive technologies are overlooked. This calls the adequacy of the 'interests of the future child' construction into question, at least in so far as collective interests are at stake. The 'interests of the future child' construction appears unable to articulate the collective values that are at stake. In terms of the assessment criteria for the four pillars of this construction: the interests of the future child does not meet the criterion of justification. Not because this multi-facetted image of the human person, and the ethical principles it represents fails to offer the best justification of legal practice, but because the individual-oriented vocabulary cannot articulate the collective interests that transcend the individual future child.

Of course, the account of the human person that can be distilled from the regulations on reproduction does not only encompass the collective dimension. The notions of harm, identity, and the individual dimension of human dignity represent the subjective or individual dimension of the human person. I believe that the 'interests of the future child' construction could be capable of articulating these individual values. In other words, based on the assessment of the first assumption, the interests-construction appears to be only partially untenable, in so far as it cannot adequately make sense of collective interests. Still, the 'interests of the future child' construction may be confronted with another challenge. As I discussed in this chapter, it follows from the regulatory frameworks analysed and the academic debate that the violation of dignity and identity does not qualify as harm. This point will, in the following chapter, prove to be important for the

156 *Kamerstukken II* 2000-2001, 27 423, nr. 3 (*Memorandum Embryo Act*), p. 42.
157 *Kamerstukken II* 2005-2006, 30 300 XVI, nr. 136 (*first explanatory letter PGD*), p. 9.

assessment of the second assumption regarding the future child: the implicit assumption that the future child under certain circumstances has an interest in its own non-existence. Several scholars have argued that such an interest can only be assumed if the child's life is of such poor quality that it is *harmed* by being brought into existence. So, if the violation of the child's interest in identity and dignity do not qualify as harm, the question arises of whether in these cases it can be concluded that the prevention of its existence is in the interest of the future child. This question, and more generally, the possibility of an interest in non-existence is discussed in the following chapter.

4 An Interest in Non-Existence

4.1 Introduction

In chapter 2, I demonstrated that the regulations on reproduction attribute three different interests to the future child, namely the interests in well-being, identity, and dignity. In chapter 3, I argued that these interests also include collective interests that cannot be adequately articulated with the help of the 'interests of the future child' construction. In this chapter, I continue the assessment of this construction by scrutinising the second assumption on which this construction is built. According to the regulatory frameworks, legal interference in reproduction is acceptable in order to protect one of the three interests mentioned above. As explained in the introduction, this interference results in the prevention of the child's conception and existence. This has resulted in the second assumption of the future child: as the regulatory frameworks that prevent the future child's existence claim that they serve the interests of the future child, they imply that the future child has an interest in its own non-existence.

This interest, however, is barely openly mentioned in the regulatory frameworks and parliamentary debates. An exception is MP Lansley, who stated during the UK parliamentary debates that in case of a life-threatening or severe genetic condition, using PGT to prevent the implantation of a genetically affected embryo is in the best interests of that child.[1] The possibility of an interest in non-existence has been addressed in so-called wrongful life lawsuits. In these cases, a claim on behalf of the child is filed stating that the child is born into a life of such poor quality that it has been harmed by being born, thus implying that the child has an interest in its own non-existence. Although some legal systems have acknowledged this interest in non-existence, the possibility of assuming such an interest remains highly contested.[2] In the UK[3] and German[4] wrongful life cases, the possibility of such an interest was rejected because "a disabled life is better than no life"[5] and the idea that life itself could be considered as damage would be an affront to the

1 HC Deb (12 May 2008) vol. 475, col. 1078.

2 The Netherlands has acknowledged the wrongful life claim but the claim has been rejected in the UK and in Germany. Hoge Raad 18 March 2005 ECLI:NL:HR:2005:AR5213 (*Baby Kelly*); BGH 18 January 1983 - BGHZ 86, 240 (*Wrongful life*); (*McKay v. Essex Area Health Authority*) [1982] QB 1166. The French court initially accepted the wrongful life claim, but this was made undone by the legislator. van Beers, 2009b, p. 289-290.

3 (*McKay v. Essex Area Health Authority*) [1982] QB 1166.

4 BGH 18 January 1983 - BGHZ 86, 240 (*Wrongful life*).

5 (*McKay v. Essex Area Health Authority*) [1982] QB 1166, 1169.

sanctity of life and public policy. As addressed in previous chapters, various authors have pointed out that the rejection of the interest in non-existence is inconsistent with the regulations on reproduction.[6] In the Dutch wrongful life case,[7] the possibility of an interest in non-existence was assumed, albeit indirectly. The Dutch Supreme Court did not go into the nature of this interest, nor did they give any insight into the circumstances under which they believe that the assumption of this interest would be possible. Either way, the courts do not offer a systematic analysis of the possibility of an interest in non-existence.

In order to assess whether the 'interests of the future child' construction is an adequate way of representing the future child, the tenability of this assumed interest must be explored. That is, is the assumption of an interest in one's own non-existence not at odds with its own premises, namely the legal interpretation of the notions of 'harm' and 'interest'? Neither the wrongful life lawsuits nor the regulations on reproduction offer a systematic analysis of the possibility of an interest in one's own non-existence. For this reason, I rely in this chapter on academic literature that has explored this topic from a (legal-)philosophical angle. These discussions start from basic assumptions that are also acknowledged in the legal debate, namely ideas about the definition of harm and interest. Overall, being harmed is understood as being made worse off or having experienced some significant disadvantage,[8] while having an interest in something is often understood as that something creates a benefit or makes that person better off.[9] With this understanding of harm and interest in mind in mind, various authors have explored the possibility of having an interest in non-existence or being harmed by being brought into existence with different outcomes. Benatar, for example, supports an anti-natalist view and has argued

---

6 In case of the UK, some authors have argued that the rejection of the wrongful life claim is at odds with the 1990 amendment of the Congenital Disabilities (Civil Liability) Act, which does allow a child to hold a medical profession liable if it is born disabled as a result of selecting a genetically afflicted embryo during a PGT procedure. Scott, 2013, p. 16; Jackson, 2016, p. 769.

7 Hoge Raad 18 March 2005 ECLI:NL:HR:2005:AR5213 (*Baby Kelly*).

8 Various authors point out that establishing legal damages requires a comparison between the situation and the counterfactual situation that would have been if the fault in question would not have been made. See for example, S.C.J.J. Kortmann, *Geld voor leven: schadevergoeding voor 'niet beoogd' leven.* Address on the occasion of the 80th foundation day of the University of Nijmegen 2003, p. 13; B. Steinbock, 'The logical case for "wrongful life"', *Hastings Center Report*, Vol. 16, No. 2, 1986, p. 17; J. Feinberg, 'Wrongful life and the counterfactual element in harming.' in: J. Feinberg (ed.), *Freedom and Fulfillment: Philosophical Essays*, Princeton University Press, Princeton, 1994, p. 3, 7. A similar point is made in various wrongful life cases, such as Hoge Raad 18 March 2005 ECLI:NL:HR:2005:AR5213 (*Baby Kelly*), par 4.14; (*McKay v. Essex Area Health Authority*) [1982] QB 1166, par. 1181. As discussed in chapter 3, in philosophical debate a similar notion of harm is proposed. For example, Raz defines harm as being made worse off than he was." Raz, 1988, p. 514. See also D. Fox, *Birth right and wrongs. How medicine and technology are remaking reproduction and the law*, New York, Oxford University Press, 2019, p. 59.

9 Feinberg, 1994, p. 4; L.F. Wiggers-Rust, *Belang, belanghebbende en relativiteit in bestuursrecht en privaatrecht*, Den Haag, Boom juridische uitgevers, 2011, p. 17-19; P. Cane, *Tort law and economic interests*, 2nd, Oxford, Clarendon Press, 1996, p. 4; Fox, 2019, p. 59.

that being brought into existence is always harmful to the child and therefore having children is morally wrong.[10] Heyd, on the other hand, argues that a child can never be harmed nor benefitted by being brought into existence because as the child is the consequence of reproductive action; it cannot be affected by it, which is a necessary condition for being harmed.[11] In this chapter, I focus on the line of thought that is more commonly accepted,[12] and can be found in the regulations on reproduction that are discussed in chapter 2. Overall, the regulators of the three legal systems do not consider procreation to be morally wrong or problematic. Instead, choosing to reproduce (or not) is seen as an expression of procreative autonomy,[13] which has been acknowledged by, amongst others, the European Court of Human Rights.[14] The regulatory frameworks also accept that prospective parents have a legally relevant interest or a right to conceive a genetically related child.[15] At the same time, it also follows from the regulations on reproduction that this procreative autonomy is not absolute. Reproductive rights can be legitimately restricted to protect other interests and in some cases it is claimed they should be restricted in order to protect, for example, the future child from being harmed. While overall reproductive autonomy is supported, some forms of procreation are actively prevented, such as reproductive cloning. In other words, underlying the regulatory frameworks is the idea that there is a distinction between non-wrongful procreation and so-called *wrongful procreation*.

Proponents of procreative freedom acknowledge that state interference restricting this freedom can be justified in order to prevent harm to another person.[16] The regulatory frameworks are mostly geared towards preventing harm to the future child. For example, fertility treatment can be refused to a couple when, because of irresponsible parenting, the child runs a risk of significant harm. In the Netherlands, several politicians have even argued that in order to prevent a child from being born into severely harmful conditions that compromise its well-being, imposing compulsory contraception on the prospective

10 D. Benatar, *Better never to have been. The harm of coming into existence*, Oxford, Clarendon Press, 2006; D. Benatar, 'Kids? Just say no', *Aeon*, 2017.

11 D. Heyd, *Genethics. Moral issues in the creation of people*, Berkeley, University of California Press, 1992. See also Walker, 2014, p. 158-159.

12 B. Steinbock, 'Wrongful life and procreative decisions.' in: M.A. Roberts and D.T. Wasserman (eds.), *Harming future people. Ethics, genetics and the nonidentity problem*, Springer, Dordrecht, 2009, p. 155.

13 Robertson, 1994, p. 22-23.

14 ECtHR 4 December 2007 ECLI:CE:ECHR:2007:1204JUD004436204 (*Dickson v. the United Kingdom*); ECtHR 10 April 2007 ECLI:CE:ECHR:2007:0410JUD000633905 (*Evans v. the United Kingdom*); ECtHR 3 November 2011 ECLI:CE:ECHR:2011:1103JUD005781300 (*S.H. e.a. v. Austria*); ECtHR 28 August 2012, ECLI:CE:ECHR:2012:0828JUD005427010 (*Costa and Pavan v. Italy*).

15 See section 2.1.

16 E. Wicks, *The state and the body. Legal regulation of bodily autonomy*, Portland, Hart Publishing, 2016, p. 46-47; Robertson, 1994, p. 24.

parents can be justified.[17] However, the assumption that the future child is harmed by being born into a disadvantageous situation is considered problematic by, amongst others, Derek Parfit. He argues that in most cases the future child is not harmed by being brought into existence. Following his reasoning, several authors have pointed out that regulation preventing the future child's existence cannot be in the best interests of the future child.[18]

In this chapter, I explore the possibility of an interest in one's own non-existence which constitutes the second pillar of the 'interests of the future child' construction. As explained above, the regulations on reproduction and the wrongful life lawsuits do not offer a critical examination of the possibility of an interest in one's own non-existence. In order to fill in this gap, I discuss the philosophical debate where interpretations of harm and interest, similar to the legal debate, are used as a starting point and applied to the case of reproduction with the aim of determining whether and under which circumstances an interest in non-existence can be assumed. I start this exploration by elaborating the inspiration for many important critiques on the 'interests of the future child' construction: the non-identity problem. This problem, first coined by Derek Parfit, is introduced in section 4.2. It pertains to situations in which, according to Parfit, there exists a widely shared intuition (which is also visible in the regulations on reproduction) that tells us that certain modes of reproduction are against the future child's best interests, or harmful to it. In line with Mill's harm principle, if the child would indeed be harmed by its parents' procreative decisions there would be a reason to restrict the parents' procreative freedom. Assuming that being harmed indeed implies being made worse off, Parfit shows that we cannot conclude that the child is harmed by being brought into existence one way rather than another. Consequently, our moral objection to wrongful procreation cannot be based on the interests of the child. According to Parfit, a non-person affecting principle is able to explain the intuition that some issues regarding reproduction are morally wrong. In section 4.3, I discuss two important shortcomings of this principle. Because of these shortcomings, the non-person affecting principle is not able to explain the moral wrong in most reproductive cases, and thus it cannot offer an alternative justification for the regulatory frameworks that result in the prevention of the future child. Notably, there is an exception to the claim that the future child cannot be harmed by being brought into

---

17 *Kamerstukken II* 2009-2010, 32 405, nr. 2 (*Tabled motion on compulsory contraception*); Gemeente Rotterdam (2017), Zorg bij kwetsbaar ouderschap. https://www.rotterdam.nl/nieuws/anticonceptie/Informatieblad-Zorgbijkwetsbaarouderschap.pdf, p. 3. With regard to the compulsory contraception measure based on the Act mandatory mental health care, courts have ruled that such contraception was necessary in order to avoid severe harm (in Dutch "ernstig nadeel") to the patient herself and the unborn child. See for example, District Court Amsterdam 2 December 2020 ECLI:NL:RBAMS:2020:6383; District Court the Hague 14 October 2021 ECLI:NL:RBDHA:2021:11864.

18 Cohen, 2011, p. 423-519; Harris, 2000; M. Parker, 'The welfare of the child', *Human Fertility*, Vol. 8, 2005, p. 13-17; Wilkinson, 2010, p. 82-85.

existence. Following the non-identity problem, Parfit argues that the child can only be harmed if it has *a life not worth living*. Only in those cases, the child would have had an interest not to come into existence. Section 4.4 elaborates on the question of whether such an interest can be assumed and, if so, under which circumstances. From this, the wrongful life-criterion is derived: only in case of a life not worth living is non-existence in the interests of the future child. In the final section, I apply this wrongful life-criterion to the regulations on reproduction, in order to assess whether it can indeed be in the interest of the future child to have its existence prevented, as the regulatory frameworks assume.

4.2 The Non-Identity Problem

The question of when it is justified to prevent a child's existence, i.e. when it is actually in the best interests of the child, has been extensively addressed in academic literature that takes a moral or philosophical approach instead of a legal perspective.[19] The complexity of invoking the interests of the child is best illustrated by the following real-life case. A Canadian lesbian couple, Sharon Duchesneau and Candy McCullough, both deaf, wished to conceive a child. Because they regarded their deafness as part of their identity and culture, they thought it important that their child should be able to share this identity. To this aim, they chose a sperm donor with an inheritable hearing impairment in order to ensure that their child would be deaf as well. The couple was criticised in the media for harming their child by making it deliberately worse off than it would have been if they had not chosen a hearing-impaired donor.[20]

Several scholars, including bioethicist Wilkinson, have contradicted the media's criticism and argued that the couple did nothing wrong, because they did not harm the child.[21] Wilkinson's statement may seem counterintuitive. Why is it not harmful to the child to be born deaf rather than hearing? This situation, in which our intuition may tell us that the

---

19 See for example, D. Archard, 'Wrongful life', *Philosophy*, Vol. 79, 2004, p. 403-420; M.D. Bayles, 'Harm to the unconceived', *Philosophy and public affairs*, Vol. 5, No. 3, 1976, p. 292-304; Buchanan, et al., 2009; Cohen, 2011; Feinberg, 1984, chapter 2, section 8; Feinberg, 1994; M. Freeman, 'Do children have a right not to be born?' in: M. Freeman (ed.), *The moral status of children: essays on the rights of the child*, Martinus Nijhoff Publishers, Den Haag, 1997; R. Bennett and J. Harris, 'Are there lives not worth living? When is it morally wrong to reproduce.' in: D. Dickenson (ed.), *Ethical issues in maternal-fetal medicine*, Cambridge University Press, Cambridge, 2002; Steinbock, 1986, p. 15-20; B. Steinbock and R. McClamrock, 'When is birth unfair to the child? ', *Hastings Center Report*, Vol. 24, No. 6, 1994, p. 15-21.

20 See for example, Jeanette Winterson, "How would we feel if blind women claimed the right to a blind baby?", *The Gaurdian*, 9 April 2002; John F. Kilner, "The ends don't justify the genes", *Center for Bioethics and Human Dignity* <http://cbhd.org/content/ends-dont-justify-genes>; David Teather, "Lesbian couple have deaf baby by choice", *The Guardian*, 8 April 2002.

21 Wilkinson, 2010, p. 68-77. This assumption is supported by Glover, 2006, p. 52, and Feinberg, 1994, p. 27.

child is harmed by being brought into existence in one state rather than another can be addressed as an example of Parfit's non-identity problem..[22] Parfit's theory is based on the assumption that if people procreate at another time or with another partner, a different recombination of gametes occurs and accordingly, a different person will be born.[23] As a result, the decisions prospective parents make now, such as choosing a certain sperm donor, affect the identity of the child who will be born in the future. So, in order to establish whether the child is harmed by these decisions, Parfit maintains that we must determine whether it is made worse off in the resulting situation compared to the counterfactual situation. And the counterfactual situation in reproduction is rather unique: if the circumstances of the child's conception were different, that is, if a different donor were used, a different child would have been born and not the child in question. This has led Parfit to argue that in order to establish whether, for example, Duchesnau and McCullough's child has been harmed by being born deaf, we must not compare his impaired existence to an existence in which he would have been born without a hearing impairment, since this was never an option for the child. Instead, we must compare the child's impaired existence to not existing at all. So, if the child has a so-called *life worth living*,[24] that is, if its life is of sufficient quality that it is preferable over not existing at all, the child has not been harmed, because it is not made worse off. As Harman puts it:

> But this woman's act of conceiving [under the given circumstances] does not make her child worse off that he would otherwise have been. Had she not performed this action, he would not exist. Furthermore, he has a life worth living. Either he is better off than he would otherwise have been (because existence can be compared to non-existence, and it is better to have a life worth living than not to exist) or he is not worse off because he is neither worse off nor better off (because existence cannot be compared to non-existence). Either

22 Parfit, 1984, p. 359. The non-identity problem is not only applicable to individual cases, such as the future child, but also to future generations (p. 361-363). For example, we could now choose to deplete our resources giving us a higher quality of life than if we choose conservation. Over a certain period of time, all resources will be used, causing the people of future generations to have a lower quality of life than if we would have chosen conservation. Nevertheless, Parfit argues that the people who will come into existence in case of the depletion policy will not be the same people who will come into existence if the conservation policy was chosen. Provided that they will have a life worth living, those people have not been harmed, even though we know their quality of life will be lower by choosing to use up resources, because those people would otherwise not have existed at all. In other words, lowering the quality of life might be worse for no one.

23 Parfit, 1984, p. 351-352.

24 The concept of a life worth living is further discussed in section 4.4.

way he is not worse off than he would have been had she not performed this action.[25]

Because of the non-identity problem, mobilising the interests of the future child as a justification of the regulations on reproduction becomes problematic. Given that the child's only alternative is non-existence, it would be in its interest to come into existence, even under disadvantageous circumstances. Notably, the fact that the alternative is non-existence is barely explicitly mentioned in the regulations on reproduction. A striking example is the poorly chosen formulation by the Dutch State Secretary on PGD.[26] In a letter to parliament, she maintained that one of the important benefits of the technology is that "PGD can be a possibility to exclude a serious illness in the child."[27] This statement gives the impression that the child can be born into two situations. On the one hand, if natural conception is used, the child will likely be born with a severe genetic condition. On the other hand, if PGD (or PGT) is used, this condition can be prevented and the child is born healthy. Put like this, the use of embryo selection seems justified without further question. However, through PGD the affected child is prevented from coming into existence. And if the child's existence with the genetic defect is not considered to be worse than not existing at all, then it cannot be concluded that PGD (or other regulatory frameworks) serve the interests of the future child.

In some cases, it may be possible to assume that the child's existence is worse than not existing at all. Several authors have suggested that only then, it would be in the interest of the future child to have had its existence prevented. I address this interest in non-existence in section 4.4. Still, if we accept Parfit's line of reasoning, we cannot conclude that in most cases, like the case of the deaf sperm donor, the child born would have been better off not existing at all. If we are willing to accept that in those cases the child has a life worth living, it apparently has not been made worse off, and therefore it has not been harmed by being brought into existence. Nor does it follow from this line of reasoning that preventing its existence is in the child's interest. So, Parfit reasons, if we claim that it is objectionable to conceive a child whose life will be of reduced quality, then it must be objectionable for another reason than that of the interests of the future child.

---

25 E. Harman, 'Harming as causing harm.' in: M.A. Roberts and D.T. Wasserman (eds.), *Harming future fersons. Ethics, genethics and the nonidentity problem*, Springer, Dordrecht, 2009, p. 138.

26 As explained in chapter 2, the Dutch regulation only focused on PGD, and not on PGS. For that reason, I deem using 'PGD' more appropriate in this context.

27 *Kamerstukken II* 2005-2006, 30 300 XVI, nr. 136 (*first explanatory letter PGD*), p. 12. In Dutch: "PGD kan dan een mogelijkheid zijn om zo'n eventuele ernstige ziekte bij het kind uit te sluiten." Translation by LtH.

4.3 Abandoning the Harm Principle

4.3.1 A Non-person Affecting Principle

As explained above, Parfit claims that the interests of the future child and the harm principle cannot explain why in some situations procreation is considered wrong. Nonetheless, he and others maintain that most people would still believe it to be wrong to deliberately choose to bring an impaired child into existence if conceiving a healthy child is a reasonable option,[28] for example, by using PGT. Buchanan et al. too believe it is a "common intuition" that we consider it wrong to choose to conceive a child who is impaired, if one could have chosen to conceive a healthy child.[29] A similar statement is made by Harman, who also suggests the distinction between wrongful procreation and non-wrongful procreation – or in her words, the non-identity cases and ordinary procreation – lies in the fact that the latter does not appear to many people as intuitively wrong.[30]

Generally speaking, two approaches can be identified that attempt to explain the harm done in cases of the non-identity problem.[31] The first approach is re-interpreting the concept of harm. Parfit's account of harm is a comparative account: in order to establish harm, one must be worse off compared to the counterfactual situation. In the case of reproduction, the counterfactual situation is non-existence, which gives rise to the non-identity problem. Some authors have tried to solve the non-identity problem by proposing an alternative account of harm. Following the reformulated concept of harm, the child is allegedly harmed by being brought into existence, despite having a live worth living.[32] The problem with these proposed alternative accounts of harm is that they tend to be

28 Parfit, 1984, p. 359.

29 Buchanan, et al., 2009, p. 251. The works of Savulescu and the critical responses to the Duchesneau-McCullough case provide a foundation for such an assumption. For example, Savulescu states that choosing the best outcome, in his opinion the healthy child, would be the rational choice: J. Savulescu, 'Procreative Beneficence: why we should select the best children', *Bioethics*, Vol. 15, No. 5/6, 2001, p. 414.

30 Harman, 2009, p. 143.

31 Feinberg, 1994, p. 31.

32 Hanser, for example, defines harm as "being harmed more". M. Hanser, 'Harming future people', *Philosophy and public affairs*, Vol. 19, 1990, p. 55. Importantly, Hanser does not believe that being 'harmed more' is the correct account of harm, p. 57. Nevertheless, he does suggest that this reformulation of harm is a more appropriate concept than Parfit's 'worse off' account, and therefore preferable. Harman and Shiffrin offer a non-comparative account of harm. Shiffrin argues that "[t]o be harmed primarily involves the imposition of conditions from which the person undergoing them is reasonably alienated or which are strongly at odds with the conditions she would rationally will." S.V. Shiffrin, 'Wrongful life, procreative responsibility and the significance of harm', *Legal Theory*, Vol. 5, 1999, p. 123-124. Harman defines harming as "causing harm", that is, putting a person in a bad state. Harman, 2009, p. 139.

overinclusive. If harming someone is understood as simply causing someone to be in pain or to suffer from an illness (instead of making someone worse off than he otherwise would have been), then everyone is harmed by being brought into existence. After all, life itself comes with certain burdens, and even healthy children will be confronted with pain, distress, disappointment, illness etc. Consequently, even healthy children are harmed by being brought into existence.[33] In short, it seems that these alternative accounts of harm cannot distinguish between the cases in which we believe conceiving a child is problematic, and those cases in which conception is not deemed morally wrong.[34]

The second strategy abandons the idea that a moral wrong occurs only when the harm principle is satisfied, and does not try to find a justification for preventing procreation in the interests of the future child. Parfit takes this approach and invokes a non-person affecting principle, which he calls the *same number quality claim*. He explains that it is wrong to bring a child into existence who is worse off than a reasonably possible alternative child.[35] The reason why selecting a child with a low quality of life instead of another child is wrong is not because it harms the first child, but because it brings more suffering into the world. In other words, Parfit takes a utilitarian approach, in which the right course of action is determined by the degree of well-being introduced into the world.[36] A similar utilitarian approach is endorsed by other authors as well. Feinberg, for example, also maintains that the wrong is not caused by harming the child, or by violating its rights, but by "wantonly introducing a certain evil into the world."[37] Buchanan et al. claim that if parents choose to bring an ill child into the world instead of an healthy one, they cause "(…) suffering and limited opportunity to exist that would be prevented and not exist if [they had chosen] (…) to conceive a different normal child."[38] Preventing the former child to exist does not serve that child's interests, but is justified "for the sake of less overall suffering and limited opportunity."[39] Savulescu has coined the term 'principle of procreative

33 Both Shiffrin and Harman admit that even in the case of non-wrongful procreation, the child is harmed while at the same time has benefitted. Shiffrin, 1999, p. 137-139; Harman, 2009, p. 144. The conclusion that a child is always harmed by being brought into existence has led Benatar to believe that procreation is always wrong. Harman attempts to distinguish between wrongful and non-wrongful procreation by claiming that the harms a healthy child faces can be justified by the benefits of life. "My view is thus that whether harming is justified is a matter of threshold crossing", p. 143. Her view is therefore not much different than the zero-line view which is discussed in section 4.4. Harman seems to put the threshold higher but does not explain convincingly why such a higher threshold is justified.

34 I.G. Cohen, 'Beyond best interests ', *Minnesota Law Review*, Vol. 96, 2012, p. 1249-1250.

35 Parfit, 1984, p. 360.

36 D.W. Brock, 'The non-identity problem and genetic harms - the case of wrongful handicaps', *Bioethics*, Vol. 9, 1995, p. 273; J.A. Robertson, 'Procreative liberty and harm to offspring in assisted reproduction', *American Journal of Law & Medicine*, Vol. 30, 2004, p. 16.

37 Feinberg, 1994, p. 27.

38 Buchanan, et al., 2009, p. 249.

39 Buchanan, et al., 2009, p. 251.

beneficence', which entails that parents should always aim to select the embryo out of the available possible embryos, "who is expected to have the best life, or at least as good a life as the others, based on the relevant, available information."[40] This principle is not based on the interests of the future child, which Savulescu deems irrelevant since it is not the same child who is affected by the decision. Instead, the principle of procreative beneficence seeks to promote overall well-being.[41]

Of particular interest is Glover's proposition; he attempts to address the issue from within the framework of the harm principle. He argues that a ban or restriction on reproductive technologies can only be justified if it prevents harm.[42] For this reason, Glover proposes to re-interpret Mill's harm principle in order to avoid the conundrum of the non-identity problem, so that harm includes also *transpersonal harms*. This refers to harms caused when "one course of action brings about a world where those who exist are worse off than would have been the different people who would have existed on the alternative course".[43] Transpersonal harm thus occurs when person A is worse off than person B, who could have existed if the decision leading to person A's existence was different. In other words, transpersonal harm does not refer to a comparison between two situations that one and the same person could experience, but between two situations in which two different persons are born. In that sense, regardless of his attempt to frame his approach in terms of harm, which may make it seem that Glover takes the first strategy towards solving the non-identity problem, his proposal does not significantly differ from Parfit's same number quality claim.[44]

This non-person affecting principle can offer a justification for PGT and other modes of selective reproduction. By choosing a healthy embryo over an affected embryo, less suffering is brought into the world. Of course, this means that PGT does not benefit or serve the interest of the future child. Consequently, this alternative principle cannot

40 Savulescu, 2001, p. 415. Savulescu does not take a stand on why selecting the child with the most well-being is important. He mentions different utilitarian principles that can provide a further motivation. He claims that it can be because the child in question has better prospects than the alternative child would have had (wide person-affecting version) or because the overall outcome is better, even if it is not better for the child created (impersonal versions). According to Savulescu and Kahane, the principle of procreative beneficence is compatible with both views. J. Savulescu and G. Kahane, 'The moral obligation to create children with the best chance of the best life', *Bioethics*, Vol. 23, No. 5, 2009, p. 277.

41 Savulescu, 2001, p. 419.

42 Glover, 2006, p. 75. Glover adds that harm, though a necessary requirement, may not always be a sufficient reason to regulate technology.

43 Glover, 2006, p. 75.

44 Glover adds that with regard to his idea of transpersonal harm, he assumes that the number of people in both alternative situations are the same in order to avoid further difficulties. The problems that arise when there are a different number of cases are discussed in the following section.

replace the interests of the future child-framework as a justification for the regulations on reproduction for several reasons. First, it fails to offer a justification for regulatory frameworks such as the ban on cloning and regulating access to fertility treatments. The reason for this shortcoming is the fact that Parfit's non-person affecting principle is only applicable to *same number choices.*[45] That is, those cases in which there is a 'better' substitute for the impaired child, so that in both alternatives, the same number of children will live. In addition to that, this utilitarian principle is faced with a second challenge: it may prove too much. The principle cannot distinguish between the cases in which PGT or other modes of selective reproduction would be allowed because the child is at risk of a severe genetic condition, and cases in which PGT is not allowed because of minor genetic defects or a non-affected carrier. Instead, it would urge to maximise utility by always striving for selecting the best child possible, even if there is no risk of harm. I elaborate on both objections in the following sections.

4.3.2 *Limited to Same Number Choices*

The examples given above – the case of the deaf, lesbian couple and embryo selection – focus on a choice between a child with a lower quality of life and a child with a higher quality of life. In this case, the decision of the parents may alter the identity of the child, but the number of children born in both alternatives is the same. In other cases, such as compulsory contraception and denying a couple access to fertility treatment, the situation is different. In those cases, the harm is caused by irresponsible parenthood. The only way to prevent the child's interests from being violated is to prevent any child from being born to these parents. In other words, in these regulatory frameworks, any child would be at risk of having its interests violated, and there is no alternative child born in the prevented child's place. These cases are also known as *different number choices*: the interference alters the number of children born. In such cases, Parfit's utilitarian principle cannot offer a justification, for it is only applicable to *same number choices,*[46] that is, choices that result in the same number of people, such as selective reproduction.

Parfit's non-person affecting principle states that we should strive to achieve the most welfare. However, in different number choices, aiming to achieve the maximum possible welfare results in an unwanted outcome.[47] If we want to achieve a maximum total utility,

---

45 Parfit, 1984, p. 360. Parfit explicitly mention this requirement in his 'same number quality claim': "If in either of two *outcomes the same number of people would ever live*, it would be bad if those who live are worse off, or have a lower quality of life, than those who would have lived." Italics added by LtH.

46 Parfit, 1984, p. 360, 370.

47 Parfit, 1984, p. See also: Robertson, 2004, p. 17; Cohen, 2011, p. 485-493.

we need to pursue a society in which the sum total of welfare is the highest. It is possible that this total sum of welfare is higher in a very large population with a low quality of life, perhaps even if they have lives barely worth living, than in a small population of people with high welfare lives. In a society of 1000 people who would grade their quality of life 2/10 (0 being a life not worth living), the total utility is higher than that of a society of 100 people whose quality of life is graded 9/10. Total utilitarianism prescribes us to choose for the former society, which consists of people whose lives are barely worth living. In the context of reproduction, if we want to achieve the highest overall welfare or utility, we should allow parents with a history of child abuse access to a fertility treatment. Provided that the resulting child's quality of life is above the bare minimum despite the abuse, it contributes to a higher utility. Parfit calls this the "repugnant conclusion."[48] It tells us to select the lives that are barely worth living, instead of preventing them. This conclusion is also at odds with, for example, the Dutch professional guidelines on moral contraindications for fertility treatment. The guidelines explicitly state that medical professionals should only continue with treatment if the resulting child will likely experience reasonable well-being. Aiming for minimum well-being simply sets the bar too low for medical professionals and prospective parents.[49]

A possible response is to choose average utilitarianism over total utilitarianism; instead of trying to achieve the highest total welfare possible, average utilitarianism would aim to achieve the highest average welfare per person. A child whose life is barely worth living would increase the total welfare but decrease the average welfare. Consequently, bringing such a child into existence would be morally wrong since it diminishes the average welfare per person. Still, average utilitarianism also leads to unwanted results as it sets the bar too high. It prefers a world in which only a few people all with very high utility would live, to a world in which, apart from these people, other people would live with a slightly lower utility.[50] In fact, average utilitarianism even prefers a world in which only one person would live who has the highest utility of all, since the existence of other people would only lower the average utility. This outcome seems also undesirable and not in line with the current regulations on reproduction in the jurisdictions examined, because in that case the existence of everyone but one person would be morally wrong. In other words, it fails to make a distinction between wrongful procreation and reproductive acts that do not constitute a moral wrong. Cohen raises another objection to focusing on average welfare. This objection focuses on the fact that in average utilitarianism, the moral wrongness of

48 Parfit, 1984, p. 387. See also: Robertson, 2004, p. 17; Cohen, 2011, p. 486; Wilkinson, 2010, p. 93-95.

49 NVOG Modelprotocol "Mogelijke morele contra-indicaties bij vruchtbaarheidsbehandelingen", p. 2.

50 Cohen, 2011, p. 489; P.G. Peters, 'Protecting the unconceived: nonexistence, avoidability, and reproductive technology', *Arizona Law Review*, Vol. 31, 1989, p. 523.

an act depends on the utility or welfare of all other individuals. "Because we are in a *different*-number case it is not an argument that I could have done better by substitution but instead an acknowledgement that, although I could not have done better, because others *did* do better, my act is wrong."[51] In other words, following this line of reasoning, prospective parents should be refused fertility treatment, not because they pose a significant risk to the child, but simply because other parents are better at parenting, or because their children experience more well-being. Cohen maintains that this interpretation is not the correct explanation of *why* we believe certain modes of reproduction are wrong: "... it errs in identifying what it is we think is wrong in reproduction when we think it is wrong."[52]

Parfit's non-person affecting principle may be able to justify some regulatory frameworks, such as PGT and other forms of selective reproduction. Most regulatory frameworks, though, do not only affect which child is born, but also whether a child is born. Regulation on access to fertility treatments, for example, which prevents certain parents from having a child, results in a different number-choice: they affect the number of children that are born using reproductive technologies. In these cases, the non-person affecting principle apparently fails to explain why wrongful procreation is wrong and why the regulation thereof is justified. Parfit admits that the only way to solve the non-identity problem for all cases (including different number choices) would involve a theory that contains person-affecting and non-person-affecting principles, provided that it would be possible to solve the problem. So far, Parfit himself has not succeeded in developing this so-called theory X.[53] Consequently, we must for now conclude that it seems that neither the liberal approach of harm and interests, nor the utilitarian approach of maximising welfare, are capable of offering an adequate justification for the majority of regulatory frameworks that result in the future child's non-existence.

4.3.3 *Choosing the Best Child*

In addition to the first objection to Parfit's same number quality claim – its limitation to same number choices – his solution faces a second obstacle. Its core idea, that one must strive to bring the better child into the world, has been criticised as well. First, it has been questioned whether health necessarily amounts to more welfare. Bennet, for example, has argued that it cannot be established which child would enjoy a higher welfare. She has pointed out that it is not self-evident that a disabled child would suffer more, since there

51 Cohen, 2011, p. 493.
52 Cohen, 2011, p. 492.
53 Parfit, 1984, p. 442.

may be other relevant factors that are important to the quality of life.[54] Furthermore, the same number quality claim cannot distinguish those cases of reproduction that the regulations aim to prevent, from those cases that are not considered wrongful procreation according to the regulatory frameworks. As discussed in chapter 2, the regulatory frameworks on fertility treatments and selective reproduction allow interference if the future child is at risk of suffering severe harm. Only then can, for example, PGT be used to prevent an affected embryo and select a healthy embryo. According to Parfit's non-person affecting principle, however, we would be morally obliged to prevent the future child's existence, even if that future child is not at risk of being severely harmed and will likely lead a happy life, if there is a better, alternative child whose existence is reasonably possible.[55] The principle entails the moral obligation to choose the 'best' child, because it is morally wrong to bring suffering or less welfare into the world if there is a better substitute. Put differently, the moral obligation to choose the 'best child' does not only prescribe choosing a healthy child over a disabled child, such as in the case of PGT. This obligation also prescribes that we should choose an above average child over a normal child (assuming that an above average child experiences more welfare). Especially with modern reproductive technologies and the expected developments in genetics, it is imaginable that there is always a better child, whose quality of life and well-being will be better because of its enhanced characteristics. For this reason, I believe Parfit's non-person affecting principle is overinclusive and cannot by itself give a full justification for the regulations on reproduction. It cannot explain why the regulators deem PGT acceptable if the child is at risk of severe harm, but not in case of minor illnesses or if the child is an unaffected carrier. Following Parfit's principle, we would have a moral obligation to also use the technology to select a healthy child in the latter cases. Moreover, Parfit's principle to choose the child with a higher level of well-being may even entail a duty to enhance.[56] Therefore, it cannot justify the common intuition that underlies the regulations on reproduction.

---

54 Bennett and Harris, 2002, p. 329.

55 Kamm appeals to Parfit's claim in order to explain that a woman who conceives a healthy child with an IQ of 120 would be acting morally wrongly if she could have conceived a child with an IQ of 140. F.M. Kamm, *Creation and Abortion. A study in moral and legal philosophy*, Oxford, Oxford University Press, 1992, p. 126-127.

56 Cohen, 2011, p. 497. Savulescu's principle of procreative beneficence which is similar to the same number quality claim entails that deselection should not be restricted to disabilities and disease traits. Savulescu, 2001, p. 414. Of particular interest here is the Nuffield report on germline modification, which suggests abandoning the treatment/enhancement distinction and use the child's well-being as the criterion instead, which, as explained in section 2.2.1.3, may lead the way to human enhancement. See also van Beers, 2020, p. 23-24.

Not only do the regulatory frameworks distinguish between preventing a severe illness and enhancing the child's traits, several scholars also maintain that there is a significant difference between treatment and enhancement. Wilkinson deems the implication of a duty to enhance is problematic, because according to him, choosing a disabled child over a healthy child is different from choosing a normal child over an enhanced child; he claims that most people would believe selecting a disability is worse than not choosing for enhancement.[57] Also Habermas and Sandel believe there to be a significant difference between disease prevention and enhancement. Habermas suggests that if interference in prepersonal life aims to prevent a disease, one can assume that the child will later consent to the interference, but this consent cannot be assumed when the interference has a non-therapeutic goal.[58] Sandel maintains that curing a disease does not defile nature, whereas enhancement does. On the contrary, preventing and curing disabilities honours nature, since it does not "override a child's natural capacities."[59] Cohen argues as well that there is a relevant difference between the two by pointing out the undesirable consequences if there would be a duty to enhance:

> Notice, though, what adopting a duty to enhance would mean: it is not enough to avoid an incestuous reproductive partner, one would have failed in one's duty if one did not choose as good a reproductive partner for one's child as possible. It is not enough to abstain from reproductive sex during one's adolescent years, instead a woman might fail in her duty to her child unless she waits until her career, wealth, etc. are in the ideal position for child-rearing. And, if genetic enhancements improving the lives of the children who result are possible, one who fails to use them would have failed in this duty.[60]

In other words, wrongful procreation would no longer only cover those reproductive acts that would result in a child whose life is barely worth living but would also include children who are healthy and have an average quality of life, provided a better child could have been born.

Not everyone is convinced of this point of critique. Savulescu maintains that decisions to select the 'best child' should not only focus on preventing (severe) genetic disorders. He rejects the idea that curing or preventing an illness and enhancing are fundamentally

---

57 Wilkinson, 2010, p. 92. See also chapter 7.

58 Of course, with regard to the measures that are discussed here, the child's life will be prevented and therefore it cannot express its consent at a later moment. The main point though is that there is a distinction between preventing a disease and enhancing non-medical qualities. Habermas, 2003, p. 43, 51-52, 62.

59 M.J. Sandel, 'The case against perfection', *The Atlantic*, 2004; Sandel, 2007, p. 46.

60 Cohen, 2011, p. 497-498.

different, since according to him health itself is not intrinsically valuable. The value of health is instrumental, namely a means to maximise well-being.[61] Yet, other non-medical qualities, like intelligence, can also contribute to well-being.[62] So, if we attempt to achieve the highest level of well-being, we should take medical and non-medical traits equally into account. A fortiori, Savulescu argues that in order to promote well-being "human enhancement can become a moral obligation."[63]

In line with Savulescu's argument, the idea that health is an important contributing factor to a child's well-being can be distilled from the regulations on reproduction. Regulatory frameworks that aim to prevent the transmission of a genetic illness refer to the future child's interest in well-being. However, the regulatory frameworks still maintain that there is a fundamental difference between treatment and enhancement. As the discussion of the regulatory frameworks demonstrates, well-being is not the only thing we owe to the future child. The PGT regulation, for example, explicitly prohibits non-medical selection and even the use of embryo selection to prevent the birth of a child with a genetic illness that is not deemed "severe" or who is a non-affected carrier. These restrictions to the use of PGT (which indeed could contribute to the child's physical or mental well-being) are put in place by the regulator to protect the future child's dignity. Selecting children because of non-medical traits and the attempt to enhance their natural traits is considered to be a form of instrumentalisation in the regulations, which affects the child on another level. In short, a sole focus on well-being offers a too superficial a representation of what we owe the future child.

In conclusion, Parfit's same number quality claim can explain the intuition that preventing one child's life in favour of another, who is born into better circumstances, is justified, based on the idea that this choice prevents suffering and generates a better level of well-being. However, this alternative principle only offers a partial solution to the non-identity problem and does not seem equipped to support all cases in which the child's life is prevented. First of all, in a significant number of cases covered by the regulations, one child's life is not prevented in favour of another; rather, no child will be born at all. This happens, for example, when prospective parents are excluded from fertility treatment. Additionally, this utilitarian approach fails to differentiate between curing and enhancing, or preventing severely, life-affecting diseases and minor diseases that according to the regulatory frameworks do not provide a ground for, for example, embryo selection. Put

61 J. Savulescu, 'New breeds of human: the moral obligation to enhance', *Reproductive BioMedicine Online*, Vol. 10, 2005, p. 37-38; Savulescu and Kahane, 2009, p. 277.

62 Savulescu, 2001, p. 420.

63 Savulescu, 2005, p. 37.

differently, it fails to make an adequate distinction between cases of wrongful procreation that the regulations on reproduction aim to prevent, and non-wrongful procreation. More importantly, Parfit's principle abandons the idea that certain modes of reproduction ought to be banned because they are an affront to the interests of the future child. As Savulescu points out, the interests of the child are in fact irrelevant in this utilitarian reasoning.[64] It follows from Parfit's non-identity problem that invoking the interests of the future child is problematic, because the child is not harmed by being brought into existence. So, in most cases in which the regulatory frameworks on reproduction invoke 'the interests of the future child' in order to justify a regulatory choice that results in the child's non-existence, it appears that from the perspective of Parfit's non-identity problem, it is logically incorrect to claim that the regulation serves the future child's interests.

4.4 Better Off Not Existing

Notably, the non-identity problem only arises when the child has a life worth living.[65] If the child has a life worth living, that is, if the benefits of life outweigh the burdens, then it is not harmed by being brought into existence, since it would not have been better off not existing at all. In the opposite case, if the quality of life is so low that the burdens of life outweigh the benefits, the child is supposedly made worse off by being brought into existence and as a result, the child has been harmed by existing. In this case, generally called a life not worth living or a wrongful life, the child is made worse off by existing and therefore it is in its interest not to exist at all.[66] If it can be concluded that under the circumstances, the future child has an interest in its own non-existence, then bringing the future child into existence would be a violation of its interests and the regulatory frameworks that aim to prevent such a wrongful life do indeed serve the interests of the future child.

In the legal debate, the assumption of an interest in non-existence is not uncontested. In fact, the same idea has been at the crux of so-called wrongful life lawsuits.[67] In these law

---

64 Savulescu, 2001, p. 419. Savulescu defends his utilitarian principle of procreative beneficence, which says: "couples (or single reproducers) should select the child, of the possible children they could have, who is expected to have the best life, or at least as good a life as the others, based on the relevant, available information." Savulescu, 2001, p. 415.

65 Parfit, 1984, p. 358-359; M.A. Roberts, *Child versus childmaker. Future persons and present duties in ethics and the law*, Lanham, Rowman & Littlefield Publishers, Inc., 1998, p. 23.

66 See also Robertson, 1994, p. 75; Buchanan, et al., 2009, p. 239; Wilkinson, 2010, p. 70-71, 97; Cohen, 2011, p. 439; Peters, 1989, p. 487.

67 The wrongful life claim, or the possibility to claim damages for the fact someone has been brought into existence, is acknowledged in only a limited number of countries. For example, in the Netherlands, the

cases, a child already born claims (or rather, the claim is usually filed on behalf of the child) that it has been wronged, because it has been brought into existence under harmful conditions. Often in these cases, the parents are not informed about the unborn child's genetic defect before or during the pregnancy.[68] As a result of this defect, the child is born severely disabled. If the child's parents had known beforehand that their child would have a severe genetic illness, they would have opted for abortion. Or in case of preconception counselling, they would have postponed the pregnancy. As a result of this 'mistake', the child has wrongly been brought into existence and now claims that its own life is 'damage' for which it asks compensation.[69] Importantly, wrongful life cases are not about the responsibility for causing a disability or the harmful situation, implying that the child could have been born healthy. These cases are about the responsibility for the birth of the child and the harm caused by the mere fact the child exists.[70] Due to the wrongful life lawsuits, the question of whether a child can have an interest in its own non-existence is no longer a thought experiment but has become a real question for lawyers. Wrongful life suits have been filed in several legal systems, including the Netherlands, Germany, and the United Kingdom. In the Netherlands, the child's claim has been accepted, acknowledging the possibility that under severe circumstances the child can have an interest in its own non-existence.[71] The Netherlands forms an exception, though, as in other legal systems, the claim is rejected. Both the German and the UK courts argued that the child cannot have a right to be aborted and considered the idea that preferring to not exist at all to be a violation of human dignity.[72]

Rejecting the wrongful life claim seems at odds with the regulations.[73] After all, one of the arguments raised by the courts to reject the claim was that life itself, however disabled, is

---

claim was acknowledged in the *Baby Kelly* case. Hoge Raad 18 March 2005 ECLI:NL:HR:2005:AR5213 (*Baby Kelly*).

68 Jackson also mentions two other possibilities, namely if the wrong embryo is placed back in the uterus during a PGD treatment, or if the genetic defect is not detected during prenatal testing. Jackson, 2016, p. 762. Although in most cases disabilities or genetic illnesses are considered to be harmful conditions that make life an unbearable burden, there is one case in which the claimant argued he was harmed by being brought into existence because he was born out of wedlock, which in that time still carried a social stigma. *Williams v. State of New York*, 46 Misc. 2d 824, 260 N.Y.S. 2d 953 (Ct. Claims, 1965); *reversed*, 25 A.D. 2d 906, 264 N.Y.S. 2d 786 (App. Div. 1966); *reversal affirmed*, 18 N.Y. 2d 481, 233 N.E. 2d 343 (1966). This case is discussed in Feinberg, 1984, p. 100-101.

69 Feinberg, 1994, p. 14; Shiffrin, 1999, p. 117; Bennett and Harris, 2002, p. 321.

70 Bennett and Harris, 2002, p. 321-322.

71 The Supreme Court ruled that the child does not have a right to its own abortion, but it implied that it does have an interest in its own non-existence. Hoge Raad 18 March 2005 ECLI:NL:HR:2005:AR5213 (*Baby Kelly*), R.O. 4.13. See also van Beers, 2009b, p. 317, and section 6.2.

72 (*McKay v. Essex Area Health Authority*) [1982] QB 1166, BGH 18 January 1983 - BGHZ 86, 240 (*Wrongful life*).

73 See also Jackson, 2016, p. 813; Günther, Taupitz and Kaiser, 2014, p. 183-184; Spickhoff, 2011, ESchG, §1, nr 7.

always better than not existing at all, or that life is always a benefit. The regulatory frameworks that prevent the future child's existence claim that they serve the child's interests. This implies that in those cases addressed by the regulatory frameworks, life is not considered an absolute benefit, but that it is sometimes in the interests of the child not to be born at all. The following sections discuss in further length the philosophical discussion of wrongful life and explore whether such an interest in non-existence can be assumed and, if so, under what circumstances.

4.4.1 Comparison with Non-existence

One of the central points of discussion in the wrongful life debate, is whether life itself can constitute harm. In order to establish harm, a comparison must be made with the counterfactual situation that would have been if the harm-causing act had not taken place. In case of the wrongful life lawsuits, had the 'mistake' not been made, the parents would have chosen to abort or postpone the pregnancy, in which case the child would not exist. Therefore, in order to determine whether the child is harmed, the child's life must be compared with non-existence, which, allegedly, is impossible.[74] Bonnie Steinbock maintains that this comparison is impossible, because it is impossible to be better off (or for that matter worse off) not existing at all:

> The claim is that it is impossible for a person to be better off never having been born. For if I had never been born, then I never was; if I never was, then I cannot be said to have been better off. The problem can be put another way. To be harmed is to be made worse off; but no individual is made worse off by coming to exist, for that suggests that we can compare the person before he existed with the person after he existed, which is absurd. Therefore, it is logically impossible that anyone is harmed by coming to exist and wrongful life suits are both illogical and unfair in that they require the defendant to compensate someone he has not harmed.[75]

74 See for example, S.C.J.J. Kortmann, 'Schadevergoeding voor leven?', *Themis*, Vol. 4, 2004, p. 206-207. For more information on this objection, see also van Beers, 2009b, p. 319-322. In the Dutch wrongful life case, the Court admitted that it is impossible to establish the exact degree of the damage suffered by the child, because it is not possible to compare life to non-existence. The Court also stated that if it is not possible to exactly determine the damage, it must be estimated in accordance with its nature. Hoge Raad 18 March 2005 ECLI:NL:HR:2005:AR5213 (*Baby Kelly*). R.O. 4.15.

75 Steinbock, 1986, p. 17. Even though Steinbock rejects the possibility of being worse off or harmed by coming into existence, she does believe that one can be wronged by birth. Steinbock, 1986, p. 19.

This argument was also one of the reasons why the UK court rejected the wrongful life claim.[76]

This argument is not very convincing in my opinion since comparisons between life and non-existence are made in the context of end of life-decisions. Feinberg, for example, points out that it is possible to *prefer* to be dead, that is, not to exist at all.[77] Not only Feinberg, but also others have pointed out that this claim is acknowledged with regard to euthanasia: if the quality of life has decreased significantly, the patient may prefer death over continued suffering and may therefore have a reasonable claim to request the ending of his life.[78] Buchanan et al., for example, argue that there are different situations in which a person compares his life to non-existence; for instance, in decisions regarding the use or termination of life-sustaining treatment or euthanasia. In these cases, patients "ask themselves whether the best quality of life that they can expect in the future with life-sustaining treatment would be sufficiently poor that that life would be worse than no further life at all."[79] In other words, it follows from this line of reasoning that a patient can believe he or she is better off not existing at all.

In addition to these real-life examples, Feinberg further supports his claim with the following hypothetical case. Imagine a person recently died and now stands before God. The latter offers him the possibility to be reincarnated and live again. There is a catch though: the only possibility is to be reincarnated with Tay-Sachs.[80] If the person does not choose this life, the only other option is immediate and permanent extinction. According to Feinberg, most people would choose extinction, thus preferring non-existence over a life with Tay-Sachs.[81] Even though not everybody would deem non-existence the better choice, Feinberg thinks most people would opt for extinction if given the choice. Because most people would prefer non-existence over a life with Tay-Sachs, preferring non-

76 In *McKay*, this point was raised by all three judges (*McKay v. Essex Area Health Authority*) [1982] QB 1166, [1181], [1188], [1192-1193]. Also, the German Court of Appeal pointed out that it was impossible to establish harm. "Auch lasse sich die Alternative zwischen Existenz und Nicht-Existenz nicht mit juristischen Schadenskategorien erfassen." BGH 18 January 1983 - BGHZ 86, 240 (*Wrongful life*), par. A1.

77 Feinberg, 1994, p. 16. Also Jackson points out that in the case of withholding or withdrawing life support, courts have decided that continuing the patient's life is not in the patient's best interests. Jackson, 2016, p. 763.

78 See also Buchanan, et al., 2009, p. 234; Bennett and Harris, 2002, p. 323: Wilkinson, 2010, p. 70-71.

79 Buchanan, et al., 2009, p. 234.

80 Tay-Sachs, or more specifically infantile Tay-Sachs, is a disease that usually develops after a few months after the child is born. Symptoms include degradation of mental and physical abilities, for example, blindness, deafness, the inability to swallow, muscle atrophy, paralysis, dementia, and seizures. Death occurs around the age of four. Currently, there is no treatment for this illness.

81 Feinberg, 1994, p. 22.

existence is consistent with reason, he argues.[82] Therefore, if preferring non-existence over a severely impaired life is possible, he continues, this must be because non-existence makes someone better off. In conclusion, given end-of-life decisions and Feinberg's thought experiment, I believe it is imaginable (at least for a majority of people) that under severe circumstances death or not existing may be preferable. It follows from this that not only is it possible to compare life with non-existence but it is also possible that someone can be or believes to be better off not existing at all.

I do want to point out a fundamental difference between the examples above and the future child. Since the future child does not physically exist, it cannot have or express a preference for non-existence itself. However, preferring one situation over another is not a necessary requirement for being better off in one state rather than another. Feinberg's appeal to preferences merely shows that we sometimes believe that not existing at all makes us better off, thereby rejecting Steinbock's claim that a comparison with non-existence is impossible.[83] In individual situations, the valuation of the child's life could occur by means of a fiction. Scott argues that in extreme cases where the burdens of life outweigh the benefits, we may assume that "*if the child were able to reflect rationally on this* s/he would consider that her or his life is 'not worth living'."[84] In addition, as Archard points out, the decision can also be made by a "fully informed and rational proxy adult", who decides on behalf of the child.[85]

4.4.2 *Harmed by Existence: the Zero Line*

Following Feinberg's line of reasoning, I would argue that it is possible to compare existence to non-existence, and that it is also possible to prefer non-existence over life itself. For this reason, it is in theory possible to assume an interest in non-existence. Such an interest in non-existence can of course only be assumed if the burdens of life outweigh the benefits. Only in this case, when the quality of the child's life falls below the "zero

82 Feinberg, 1994, p. 23.

83 Importantly, Steinbock does believe that the wrongful life claim is feasible but argues that the correct interpretation should avoid a comparison with non-existence, which she deems impossible. Instead, she follows Feinberg's argument of birthrights, maintain that if a child is born under conditions that dooms its interests or birthrights to total defeat, the child is *wronged* by being born. Steinbock, 1986, p. 18-19. In this line of reasoning, the question no longer is whether the child is *harmed*, but whether it is *wronged*. This may prove to be problematic in a legal context, since harm is often one of the requirements for claiming damages based on a tort.

84 Scott, 2013, p. 130. Italics added by LtH.

85 Archard, 2004, p. 407.

line",[86] it can be argued that the child has been harmed by being brought into existence.[87] Interestingly, neither in case law nor in literature, are exact criteria mentioned for what constitutes such a wrongful life. The reason for this might be similar to the reasoning on the PGT criteria: listing the conditions that result in a wrongful life may have a stigmatising effect on those born with the listed conditions. Feinberg gives the start of a definition, although it remains rather abstract. According to Feinberg, this is the case when the future child's *birthrights* are violated. Birthrights are the most basic interests of which the satisfaction is necessary for a "decent life."[88] In other words, the child has an interest in "the possession of those unimpaired faculties that are essential to the existence and advancement of any ulterior interests."[89] Consequently, a child allegedly is harmed by being brought into the world if it is deprived of that to which it has a birthright.[90]

Despite the fact that the exact point of the zero line cannot be established, many authors seem to agree on one point. Because only in the most extreme cases can it be claimed that one is harmed by being brought into existence, only a small number of cases would actually qualify as a wrongful life.[91] For example, Buchanan et al. state that "only a very small proportion" of conditions or diseases likely leads to harm by existence.[92] In a similar vein, Wilkinson states that the cases in which life itself constitutes harm are "extremely rare" and that most genetic conditions and disabilities are not so extreme that they result in a wrongful life.[93] Also Feinberg believes that only in the "most extreme cases"[94] would it be rational to prefer non-existence over existence. Such extreme cases would, for example, include:

> ...some of the more severely victimized sufferers from brain malformation, spina bifida, Tay Sachs disease, polycystic kidney disease, Lesch-Nyhan syndrome, and those who, from whatever cause, are born blind and deaf, permanently incontinent, severely retarded, and in chronic pain or near-total paralysis, with life expectancies of only a few years.[95]

---

86 Glover, 2006, p. 52.
87 See for example, Robertson, 1994, p. 75; Buchanan, et al., 2009, p. 239; Wilkinson, 2010, p. 77.
88 Feinberg does not elaborate what a decent life entails.
89 Feinberg, 1984, p. 99.
90 Feinberg, 1984, p. 99.
91 See for example, Cohen, 2011, p. 472-473. J. Savulescu, 'Is there a right not to be born? Reproductive decision making, options and the right to information', *Journal of Medical Ethics*, Vol. 28, 2002, p. 65; Scott, 2013, p. 118; Robertson, 1994, p. 75.
92 Buchanan, et al., 2009, p. 239.
93 Wilkinson, 2010, p. 71.
94 Feinberg, 1994, p. 17.
95 Feinberg, 1994, p. 17. Tay-Sachs disease is also mentioned as a syndrome that makes life not worth living by Buchanan, et al., 2009, p. 233.

4.4.3 Reasonable Well-being

Since a wrongful life only rarely occurs, it appears that in most cases the child's life is worth living, even if it is at risk of significant harm or has a poor quality of life. As long as the quality of life is above the zero line, the child's life is worth living, albeit barely. If the child is indeed not harmed by being brought into existence, the question arises of whether the prospective parents even wrong the child by conceiving it. It follows from this line of reasoning that preventing the future child's existence cannot be justified by referring to the interests of the future child, since it is in the interest of the child to be born.[96] Nonetheless, some have posed the question of whether the threshold of a life worth living is too low to provide an adequate boundary for distinguishing between wrongful and non-wrongful procreation. For example, Glover wonders whether potential parents should not "be under some moral pressure, at least, to consider whether it is right to bring into the world a child whose life is, by a small margin, just worth living?"[97] In other words, is there an objection against bringing a child into existence whose life is barely worth living and if so, what is this objection?

Some authors have defended the claim that parents wrong the child if it is deliberately conceived, knowing that it would have a life barely worth living. They maintain that if the quality of the child's life falls below a threshold of reasonable well-being,[98] the parents should refrain from conceiving the child. According to Steinbock and McClamrock, for example, prospective parents have a responsibility to do more for their future child than the bare minimum. They argue that good parenthood requires parents to want for their child not just a life worth living, but rather a life *well* worth living, which implies a decent chance at a good life. If the future child cannot be guaranteed a life well worth living, then the principle of parental responsibility entails that the prospective parents better refrain from having children.[99] Archard also sets the threshold for non-wrongful procreation higher. He maintains that parents do wrong if the child's quality of life is above the zero line, but below a certain threshold.[100] He defines this threshold as "a minimally acceptable life as one in which the child has the reasonable prospect of enjoying a good number of rights possessed by all children."[101] Although Archard speaks of birthrights in this context,

96 Roberts, 1998, p. 27, 101; J. Harris, 'Wrongful Birth.' in: D.R. Bromham, M.E. Dalton and J.C. Jackson (eds.), *Philosophical ethics in reproductive medicine*, Manchester University Press, Manchester, 1990, p. 165.

97 Glover, 2006, p. 55.

98 Like the zero line, it is unclear where this threshold exactly lies. According to Glover, "This thought that we owe to our children a decent chance of a good life is intentionally vague. It is a rule-of-thumb test, which leaves a great deal to assessment of particular people and circumstances." Glover, 2006, p. 58.

99 Steinbock and McClamrock, 1994, p. 17.

100 Archard, 2004, p. 405, 415-416.

101 Archard, 2004, p. 406.

a similar concept used by Feinberg, he seems to endorse a different interpretation, setting the bar higher. In his interpretation, birthrights are not only violated by a severe genetic condition that impairs the child's most basic capacities but can also be violated if the child is born into "desperate social and economic circumstances."[102]

Archard as well as Steinbock and McClamrock maintain that it is wrong to reproduce if the child has a life barely worth living, but falls below the reasonable well-being line. They agree, though, that the child in this case is not harmed.[103] Instead, Steinbock and McClamrock believe the child is treated *unfairly*, and because of this the child is wronged. To them, fairness entails respect for the other person's legitimate interests, which differs from the notion of being harmed.

> If you act so as to utterly disregard my legitimate interests for your own (perhaps even minor) benefit, then you've wronged me by treating me unfairly, even if in the end (perhaps by some accident of chance) I end up in a situation preferable to the one I would have otherwise been in. Fairness of treatment is not necessarily determined by the end acceptance or approval of those receiving it with respect to the available alternatives.[104]

In other words, even if life falls below the standard of reasonable well-being line, provided that it is worth living, the child is better off existing.[105] So, reflecting upon Steinbock and McClamrock's and Archard's argument, prospective parents may have a moral obligation to try to give their child a better life than the bare minimum. But even then, failing to do so does not harm the child (provided the child has still a life worth living). As Steinbock and McClamrock point out, even if the legitimate interests of the child are disregarded, the child might still end up in a preferable situation, meaning that the child is better off existing, even if it is treated unfairly. Put differently, in the case of a life worth living, the child may have been wronged because it does not experience reasonable well-being, but it does not have an interest in its own non-existence. For this reason, I conclude that as long as the child does not have a wrongful life, the prevention of the future child's existence cannot be based on the child's interest in non-existence.

---

102 Archard, 2004, p. 406.
103 Archard, 2004, p. 411; Steinbock and McClamrock, 1994, p. 19. See also Wilkinson, 2010, p. 86.
104 Steinbock and McClamrock, 1994, p. 19.
105 See also Archard, 2004, p. 411.

4.5 Conclusion: Wrongful Life in the Regulations on reproduction

In this chapter, I have explored the possibility of an interest in non-existence and the question of when prospective parents' reproductive freedom can be restricted by invoking the interests of the future child. In principle, procreation is not considered problematic in the regulations on reproduction. On the contrary, the prospective parents' procreative freedom requires that the government abstains from interference in their reproductive choices. However, the regulations on reproduction prescribes that some forms of procreation should be prevented to protect the interests of the future child. In these cases, interferences in reproduction are considered justified because of the protection of the child's interests in well-being, identity, and dignity. As a result of these interferences, the future child is prevented from coming into existence (even though in some cases like PGT, an alternative child is born). Assuming that this interference and its result serve the interests of the future child, it follows from the regulatory frameworks that the future child has an interest in its own non-existence.

In this chapter, I intended to show that the assumption of the interest in non-existence as one of the pillars of the 'interests of the future child' construction is problematic. First, this implied interest in non-existence contradicts the conclusions of the German and UK wrongful life lawsuits. Only in the Dutch wrongful life case, is the possibility of an interest in one's own non-existence accepted, albeit indirectly. More importantly, as the discussion of Parfit's non-identity problem has demonstrated, the way in which the 'interests of the future child' are interpreted and operationalised in the regulations on reproduction does not fit with the traditional legal understanding of these concepts.

To say that the child has an interest in its own non-existence, or has been harmed by being brought into existence, the child's life must be of such poor quality that not existing at all would be preferable. In case of a so-called wrongful life or a life not worth living, an interest in non-existence can be assumed. The term 'wrongful life' is a rather abstract notion, serving to conceptualise the situation in which the burdens of life outweigh its good, and many authors refrain from explicating the exact circumstances that would result in a wrongful life and accordingly an interest in one's own non-existence. Despite this, most authors agree that such an interest can only be assumed in the most gruesome cases, which according to most authors are extremely rare. I believe it is highly unlikely that the regulatory frameworks that aim to protect the future child's well-being and prevent it from being harmed, always meet this 'wrongful life' criterion. First, the indication for PGT includes monogenetic conditions that are considered harmful but manifest later in life, and genetic defects that increase the risk of an illness, leaving a chance that the illness will never manifest. It is unlikely that all these conditions will pass Feinberg's hypothetical reincarnation test, namely that the majority of people would rather never have been brought into existence at all than being brought into existence with one of those genetic condition.[106] Second, regulatory frameworks on fertility treatment not only refer to genetic risks, but also to causes for psychosocial harm. Mentioned risk factors, such as the parents' old age or an unstable relationship of the couple, may create less than desirable circumstances for a child to grow up in, but are most likely not so awful that the child would prefer never to have been born at all. The circumstances in these cases reduce the quality of life, but not to such an extent that it is not worth living.[107] Even in the case of irresponsible parenthood and a parent with a history of child abuse, Robertson points out that "[e]ven if she does abuse future children, it is not clear that they will enjoy such a horrible life that they never should have been born at all, and thus are harmed by being born to an abusing mother."[108] But above all, the Dutch professional guidelines explicitly reject the zero line view. According to the guidelines, if prospective parents and medical professionals only aim at achieving a minimum level of well-being for the child (a life just barely worth living), they would set the bar too low.[109] To sum up, these regulatory frameworks apparently allow the prevention of the child's life in cases where the child would not necessarily be better off not existing at all and thus, from the perspective of the wrongful life-debate, would not have an interest in its own non-existence.

The regulatory frameworks that aim to protect the future child's well-being are difficult to justify by appealing to the interests of the future child. As I already discussed in chapter 3, the violation of the child's interests in identity and dignity does not qualify as harm, but constitutes a wrong on a different level.[110] Consequently, it is unlikely that the violation of these interests results in a life not worth living. As Spranger for instance argues, even though reproductive cloning violates the clone's dignity, being born as a clone remains preferable over not existing at all.[111] In addition, the idea that the violation of the child's interest in identity and right to information about its genetic origins do not result in a wrongful life is also illustrated by fertility fraud cases. In case of fertility fraud, the physician has inseminated his patient with his own genetic material instead of a sperm donor's to conceive a child, without the patient knowing or consenting.[112] One example of

106 Feinberg, 1994, p. 22. It is for this reason that Glover proposes a higher standard when asking the question of what we owe to future people. He deems it important to intervene when there is a *serious risk* to a life not worth living. Glover, 2006, p. 63.

107 Cohen, 2011, p. 474.

108 Robertson, 1994, p. 82.

109 NVOG Modelprotocol "Mogelijke morele contra-indicaties bij vruchtbaarheidsbehandelingen", p. 2.

110 See also van Beers, 2009a, p. 130.

111 Spranger, 2010, p 103. See also Glover, 2006, p. 64-65.

112 J.L. Madeira, 'Holding physicians accountable for fertility fraud. From patient experience tolegal reform', *Columbia Journal of Gender and Law* Vol. 39, No. 1, 2020, p. 11-204.

this is the Dutch *Karbaat* case, where at least 49 children turned out to be conceived by Karbaat, the fertility doctor, himself. Moreover, it turned out that Karbaat's clinic mixed donor semen and falsified donor passports, making it impossible for other donor conceived children to find their genetic parents, or used the material of one donor to conceive over 200 children.[113] Because all this was done intentionally, without regard to the wishes of the prospective parents or the interests of the children, it is clear to see that some wrong was done. Nonetheless, it is difficult to pinpoint what the harm is in this case. It is doubtful whether these children would indeed claim that they had rather not been born at all because a different donor was used than that agreed upon, or because donor passports are falsified. Moreover, would having 199 brothers and sisters qualify as harm?[114] According to Madeira, who has investigated various fertility fraud cases, it would be possible for the donor conceived children to (under Indiana law) claim damages based on intentional infliction of emotional distress: "It was foreseeable that these illicit inseminations could cause grievous family discord, subject the children to the risks of consanguineous relationships, and raise concerns of future generations marrying their first cousins."[115] However, without these actions, the child would not have existed at all. Therefore, in order to hold the physician liable based on a tort, these children must claim that they have been harmed by the actions that brought them into existence, which does not seem to coincide with the children's or their parents' feelings.[116] In short, the violation of the future child's interests in dignity or identity does not seem to result in a life not worth living. This means that it is actually in the interest of the future child to come into existence under these circumstances, since its only alternative option is not existing at all.

Some authors have concluded that if the child is not harmed by being brought into existence (and in absence of other significant interests at stake), prospective parents' reproductive autonomy should not be restricted. Consequently, they argue that regulatory frameworks on, for example, sex selection and access to ARTs constitute an unjustified interference with this fundamental right.[117] This perspective sets the bar rather low for our responsibilities and duties towards the future child. It would mean that the only duty we have towards future members of our society is ensuring that the bare minimum of well-being is achieved to make their lives worth living. No matter how miserable their lives may be, as long as it is just preferable over non-existence, no harm and therefore no wrong is done. This approach does not take the future child as a fellow human person seriously. It seems to assume that harm and well-being are the only relevant factors in dealing with

113 van Beers, 2016b, p. 303; M. Guttmann. (2021). *Het zaad van Karbaat.* the Netherlands: 2doc.

114 van Beers, 2016b, p. 304.

115 Madeira, 2020, p. 199.

116 van Beers, 2016b, p. 303-304.

117 See for example, Wilkinson, 2010, p. 249; Robertson, 1994, p. 4, 93.

future people. Moreover, this perception of the human person that solely focuses on tangible interests and harm does not match the normative account of the human person that underlies the regulations on reproduction. This account adopts a higher standard, which includes a reasonable level of well-being and also immaterial interests such as identity and dignity. In order to make sense of this normative account, a different normative framework is needed.[118] Since an interest in non-existence can only be assumed in the most severe cases, invoking the interests of the future child cannot justify all interferences that prevent the future child from coming into existence.

In summation, also the second assumption of the 'interests of the future child' construction is problematic. This assumption fails to meet both criteria of fit and justification. First, tacitly assuming that the future child has an interest in its own non-existence is, in many cases, at odds with how the notions of harm and interest are generally interpreted in the legal context. In cases where the child would still have a live worth living, it cannot be assumed that it would be harmed by being brought into existence or have an interest in its own non-existence. Therefore, in the majority of cases, the assumed interest in non-existence does not fit with the legal interpretation of harm and interests. In addition, because an interest in non-existence can only be assumed in the most extreme cases, the 'interests of the future child' construction fails to justify the regulatory frameworks that prevent the future child's existence in order to secure reasonable well-being or protect the interests in dignity and identity. This construction cannot make sense of the normative account of the human person that incorporates these values. In short, in so far as the child has a life worth living, it cannot be claimed that it has an interest in its own non-existence and for this reason, the regulatory frameworks that prevent the future child's existence cannot be justified by invoking the future child's interests. Importantly, the assumption that the future child has an interest in its own non-existence is untenable in the majority of cases covered by the regulations on reproduction. In a limited number of cases, it would be possible to assume such an interest. In those cases in which the quality of life is below the zero line and the future child would have a life not worth living, it is generally accepted in academic debate that it is in the interest of the future child to have its existence prevented. Accordingly, the 'interests of the future child'-construction would only be tenable in that limited number of cases.

In this chapter and the previous one, I explored two of the four assumptions behind the 'interests of the future child' construction in order to investigate the tenability of this

118 The alternative theoretical framework I propose in chapter 7 includes an alternative normative framework, that in my opinion is better equipped to conceptualise the future child and justify the regulation of reproduction.

construction. This exploration revealed, first, that the interests-construction fails to address all values that are stake, as this construction cannot articulate the collective interests that are involved in the regulation of reproduction. Second, it appears that the prevention of its existence is not in the interests of the future child at all in the majority of cases. As a result, the 'the interests of the future child' construction fails to make sense of various values that underlie the regulations on reproduction and the normative account of the human person that can be distilled from the regulatory frameworks. In conclusion, the tenability of the 'interests of the future child' construction is far more limited than what follows from the regulations on reproduction. In the next chapters, I continue with my assessment of this construction, but I shift the focus. Instead of looking at what is assumed to be the interests of the future child according to the regulations, I explore whether the future child can be a subject in law and a subject of interests in the first place.

5 The Future Child as a Legal Person*

5.1 Introduction

As we saw in the previous chapter, the 'interests of the future child' construction in the regulations on reproduction has received much criticism. Many authors have criticised the assumption that non-existence is in the interests of the future child, and I agree with them that only in the most extreme cases can the future child have an interest in its own non-existence. Accordingly, in most cases covered by the regulations on reproduction it is not possible to assume an interest in non-existence. Because it remains possible in a small number of cases to invoke the interests of the future child to prevent its existence, it is worthwhile to continue the analysis of the interests-construction. In this chapter, I shift the focus of my analysis from the content of the future child's interests to the future child's assumed subjectivity. Not only must we ask whether and, if so, under what circumstances an interest or even a right to one's own non-existence can be assumed, we must also deal with the topic of who the subject of this right is. For this purpose, in this chapter I explore the third assumption underlying the interests-construction, namely, that as a result of the attribution of legally relevant interests, the future child is a legal subject.

But first we must ask the question as to whether the acknowledgement of an interest or a right in non-existence indeed implies that the future child itself has interests or rights. According to Buchanan et al., this is not the case: they maintain that the acknowledgement of prenatal and preconceptual harm – for example, in a wrongful life lawsuit – to an existing child does not mean that we have duties towards a non-existent entity, nor that the child before birth has any rights. In their opinion, the wrongful life claim (and the corresponding assumption that the child would have been better off if it did not exist at all) is based on the violation of the right not to be born into a life not worth living. The assumption of this right and its violation constitute the core of a wrongful life lawsuit. However, according to Buchanan et al. this right comes into existence when the child is born, because only then does a legal subject exist. The creation of the right and its violation happen at the same time, namely the moment the child is born, and consequently, there is no need to attribute interests or rights to the child before its birth: "It is not necessary to attribute to beings that do not yet exist rights not to be brought into existence at some future time with a life not worth living. If the child never is brought into existence, there

* This chapter is an adaption of L. ten Haaf, 'Future Persons and Legal Persons: The Problematic Representation of the Future Child in the Regulation of Reproduction', *Laws*, Vol. 5, No. 1, 2016, doi: 10.3390/laws5010010.

never is a being with the right that would have been violated had it been brought into existence with a life not worth living."[1] In this line of reasoning, it is indeed not necessary to attribute rights or interests to the future child in order to justify a wrongful life claim. However, wrongful life lawsuit significantly differs from the broader regulatory frameworks in an important aspect. The wrongful life claim works retrospectively; once the child is born and harmed by being born, the claim in the lawsuit serves to compensate for the harm. The regulations on reproduction take a forward-looking approach: they aim to prevent the harm from manifesting. Or put more broadly, the regulations aim to prevent the irreversible violation of the future child's core interests. In order to do so, there is a need to anticipate these interests before the child is born. It is for this reason that the interests of the *future child* play an important role in the regulations on reproduction. What is more, some contexts even refer to the future child's rights. For example, the UK and German regulatory frameworks claim that the future child has a right to access information on its genetic origins. In the discussion on compulsory contraception, several proponents of the measure even claim that the future child has a *right* not to be born.[2]

As the future child presumably has legally relevant interests (or even rights in some cases), it is presented as a subject. More specifically, this implies that it has some form of legal subjectivity. This raises the question as to whether law can address and represent this non-existing entity. For the purpose of this study, I consider the possibility that legal subjectivity has various forms. Whereas the following chapter explores an alternative form of legal subjectivity, this chapter discusses the traditional vocabulary for law's subject, which is the legal person. For clarification, I do not understand the legal subject and the legal person as synonyms of each other. Instead, the legal subject can be understood as the overarching term which encompasses both the legal person, which is explored in this chapter, and the subject of legally relevant interests, which is discussed in the following chapter.

In academic literature, two types of legal persons are distinguished: the juridical or artificial person, such as corporations, and the natural person, i.e. the human bearer of legal rights and duties.[3] This chapter focuses on the legal conception of the natural person.

---

1 Buchanan, et al., 2009, p. 236.

2 Editorial, 'Hebben sommige kinderen het recht niet geboren te worden? *Telegraaf* (22 January 2015). Editorial, 'Rotterdamse wethouder: verplichte anticonceptie incompetente ouders', *NOS* (1 October 2016) https://nos.nl/artikel/2135331-rotterdamse-wethouder-verplichte-anticonceptie-incompetente-ouders.html. Whether this should or even can be understood as a *legal* right is further elaborated in chapter 6.

3 H. Kelsen, *Reine Rechtslehre. Einleitung in die Rechtwissenschaftliche Problematik*, Aalen, Scientia Verlag, 1994, p. 52-55; N. Naffine, 'Who are law's persons? From cheshire cats to responsible subjects', *The Modern Law Review*, Vol. 66, No. 3, 2003, p. 348; A. Grear, 'Law's entities: complexity, plasticity and justice', *Jurisprudence*, Vol. 4, No. 1, 2013, p. 78-79; J. Berg, 'Of elephants and embryos: a proposed framework for legal personhood', *Hastings Law Journal*, Vol. 59, 2007, p. 372-373; B.C. van Beers, 'The changing nature of

The legal personality of natural persons, and the capacity to have rights, traditionally starts at birth.[4] This birth threshold is the reason why Buchanan et al. have disputed that the future child can be the subject of rights, including the right not to be born, and why, according to them, the right not to be born into a life not worth living only comes into existence once the child is born and gains legal personality. Nonetheless, Buchanan et al. fail to substantiate this claim through an in-depth legal-philosophical analysis of the nature of legal personhood. Can a certain interpretation of the law's concept of the natural person include the future child?

The legal person can be understood as "he who can act in law"[5] and is the subject of legal rights and duties.[6] It is a complex concept, since most legal systems have no consolidated 'law of the person', i.e. a unified set of rules concerning legal personality and which defines the legal person. On the contrary, Fagundes points out that the legal doctrine of legal personality is fragmented[7] and Naffine argues that law is inconsistent in its definition of the legal person.[8] In other words, different areas of law have different perspectives on legal personality and attribute different features to it.[9] Still, some main perspectives can be discerned. As already briefly addressed above, the legal person encompasses two types: the artificial or juridical person, and the natural person. The natural legal person can be understood as the legal counterpart of the human being. In some discussions, a narrow interpretation of the legal person is endorsed, in which is the legal person is synonym to the artificial person. However, authors like Naffine and Grear endorse a broader interpretation, in which 'legal person' is an overarching term, including both the artificial and the natural person.[10] Because the future child is closely related to the human person, or more precisely, exists in anticipation of a natural legal person, I will focus on natural

law's natural person: the impact of emerging technologies on the legal concept of the person', *German Law Journal*, Vol. 18, No. 3, 2017a, p. 560-561.

4 van Beers, 2009b, p. 231, D. Fagundes, 'Note, What We Talk About When We Talk About Persons: The Language of a Legal Fiction.', *Harvard Law Review*, Vol. 114, No. 6, 2001, p. 1757; Romanis, 2019, p. 94; R. Tur, 'The 'person' in law.' in: A. Peacocke and G. Gillett (eds.), *Persons and personality: a contemporary inquiry*, Basil Blackwell, Oxford, 1987, p. 123; The German legal system has codified this principle. Article 1 of the German Civil Code explicitly states: "Die Rechtsfähigkeit des Menschen beginnt mit der Vollendung der Geburt." Importantly, the born alive threshold has been put under pressure in various ways. See for example, Romanis, 2019; ten Haaf, 2017. Moreover, under German law the embryo is not a full legal subject, but it is considered a constitutional legal subject. See chapter 2.

5 Naffine, 2003, p. 347.

6 The set of rights and duties can differ per individual person.

7 Fagundes, 2001, p. 1746-1747.

8 N. Naffine, *Law's meaning of life. Philosophy, religion, Darwin and the legal person*, Portland, Hart Publishing, 2009, p. 176.

9 Berg, 2007, p. 371.

10 Naffine, 2003; Grear, 2013, p. 78-79. Romanis also speaks of the legal person instead of natural person when discussing the legal status of the gestateling and the foetal operatee: Romanis, 2019.

legal personality in this chapter. Yet, even regarding the natural legal person, different perspectives can be discerned in legal academic debate. In the remainder of this chapter, I explore to what extent the concept of legal personality can be applied to the future child. I do so by systematically analysing three perspectives on law's concept of the natural person. This chapter starts by elaborating the two perspectives that are most dominant in legal-philosophical literature,[11] which are the naturalist approach (section 5.2) and the constructivist approach (section 5.3). Because the analysis shows that both these perspectives struggle to conceive the future child as legal person, I also explore an anticipatory approach (section 5.4). In this exploration, I focus on the question of whether – as the future child must be understood as a construction created to anticipate the interests of the actual child – some form of legal personhood can be construed on the basis of the anticipation of the actual child's legal personality. In the final section, I reflect upon these three approaches to natural legal personality with the objective of critically assessing the tenability of the third assumption made about the future child. This assessment is once again based on Dworkin's constructivism, aiming to answer the question as to whether the future child fits into any of the different perspectives on the legal person. More precisely, in the conclusion I answer the question of whether conceiving the future child, an entity characterised by its non-existence, as a legal person is consistent with the foundational premises of legal personality and thus whether the future child can be addressed as a legal subject with the help of this vocabulary.

5.2 The Naturalist Approach to Legal Personality

The naturalist approach conceives the natural legal person as a representation of the real-life human:[12] an entity with a physical body, who thinks and has emotions and desires. According to this perspective, the human being has specific qualities that separate it from other entities, such as animals, artificial intelligence, or trees, that offer grounds for legal protection. These qualities are reflected in law's concept of the natural person. In other words, in the naturalist approach, the legal person "presuppose[s] a 'natural human being' as the substrate of the 'person' in law and rest[s] on operative suppositions concerning an intrinsic human nature."[13] For this reason, the legal person has distinctive features and not every entity can have legal personality.

Within different areas of law, there are different natural characteristics of the legal person visible. For example, the legal person in family law and biolaw (which the regulations on

11 See for example, van Beers, 2009b; Naffine, 2009; Grear, 2013, p. 80-81.
12 Grear, 2013, p. 81.
13 Grear, 2013, p. 88.

reproduction is part of) are heavily influenced by certain biological facts of life. Therefore, the natural legal person, in particular in these areas, presupposes various biological traits. According to van Beers, the five following biological traits have traditionally been the most prominent:

> (1) All natural persons belong to the human species; (2) The beginning of natural personality coincides with birth; (3) The ending of natural personality coincides with death; (4) Natural persons are born out of a relationship between two persons of the opposite sex; (5) Natural persons are either male or female.[14]

However, as van Beers also writes, this biological interpretation of the legal person is put under pressure: all of these characteristics are being challenged by the advance of biotechnology. For example, the legal acknowledgement of transsexuality, intersexuality, and gender X put the assumption that the legal person is either male or female to question. Reproductive technologies such as surrogacy, MRT and IVG challenge the assumption that the child is born out of a relationship between *two* persons of the *opposite* sex, by facilitating multiplex parenthood and in case of IVG, also same sex parenthood.[15] Van Beers argues that the naturalist approach to legal personhood continues to have merit despite the technological artificialisation of human life. This is illustrated by the numerous references to the biological aspects of life in biomedical law. Nevertheless, there are other natural or intrinsic features reflected in the legal person as well.

Besides its biological nature, the *rational nature* of the human is also represented in the legal person. The rationalistic approach assumes that rationality is the most distinguishing feature of humans and accordingly, the key characteristic for the legal person.[16] In this view, the legal person is capable of forming and expressing a free will, making autonomous decisions and for this reason, can be held accountable for its own actions. This legal person, capable of decision making and responsible for its actions, is present, for example, in criminal law.[17] In order to be held accountable for a criminal act, *mens rea* is required. A crime must not only be committed, but also intended, albeit that there are different modes of culpability.

---

14 van Beers, 2017a, p. 563-564.

15 van Beers, 2017a, p. 564-566.

16 N. Naffine, 'Review Essay: Liberating the Legal Person', *Canadian Journal of Law and Society*, Vol. 26, No. 1, 2011, p. 195. Gray, for example, sees the ratio as the most defining feature of the human being represented in the legal person. J.C. Gray, *The nature and sources of the law*, New york, The Columbia University Press, 1909, p. 27. See also Naffine's elaboration of this perspective on the legal person in Naffine, 2009, p. 59.

17 Naffine, 2009, p. 69.

With regard to the legal person's rationality, the aforementioned inconsistency of law's depiction of the legal person becomes clear. In some cases, a distinction is made between people who are assumed to have full rational capacities and are therefore legally competent on the one hand, and people with reduced rational capacities on the other. The latter category includes minors, who are not allowed to vote, or someone who lacks full rational capacities and is appointed a legal guardian. In these cases, the degree of legal personality that is attributed is adapted to the subject's rational capacities. However, from a purely rationalistic perspective on legal personality, newborns, the mentally ill and coma patients, for example, would not have rights since they cannot exercise their rights,[18] and thus they would lack legal personality.[19] Nevertheless, such individuals remain legally relevant, since they are addressees of the law. In particular, human rights law refers to "everyone" (or "no one"),[20] "all human beings",[21] or "all members of the human family"[22], clearly also addressing those who lack the capability for autonomous decision making. The question that now arises is: which feature is characteristic for the legal person in human rights law and what consequences could this have for attributing legal personality to the future child?

According to the dignitarian perspective, the legal person reflects the human's *metaphysical traits*, namely human dignity.[23] The inherent dignity of every human is a source of legal respect and protection, and for this reason, human dignity would be an inherent characteristic of the legal person. In chapter 3, I already discussed that the concept of human dignity is highly debated, and that its meaning is not clearly and unequivocal defined. Nonetheless, this concept has gained importance in several areas of the law. Van Beers speaks of a juridical renaissance of human dignity as a legal value since World War II.[24] For example, the concept of human dignity can be found in Article 1 of the Universal Declaration of Human Rights. This article states that all human beings are born free and equal in dignity and rights. The preamble of the International Covenant on Civil and Political Rights also stresses that all members of the human family have inherent dignity. This juridical renaissance has become even more visible due to the rise (and the regulation) of human biotechnology.[25] The European Convention on Human Rights and Biomedicine emphasises that human dignity must be safeguarded and that abuse of biomedicine can

18 A. Harel, 'Theories of rights.' in: W.A. Edmundson and M.P. Golding (eds.), *Blackwell guide to the philosophy of law and legal theory*, Blackwell, Cambride, 2005, p. 194.
19 Naffine, 2009, p. 68.
20 For example, the fundamental rights of the European Convention of Human Rights and of the Universal Declaration of Human Rights.
21 Article 1 of the Universal Declaration of Human Rights.
22 Preamble of the Universal Declaration of Human Rights.
23 Naffine, 2009, p. 102.
24 For a more extensive analysis, see van Beers, 2009b, 35-45.
25 van Beers, 2009b, p. 36; Calo, 2012, p. 475.

violate this dignity, which has resulted in the ban on various technologies. Illustrative examples of technologies that are banned on both a national and international level are human cloning[26], sex selection[27], and germline cell therapy[28].

From the brief descriptions of these perspectives, it becomes clear that conceiving the future child as a legal person in the naturalist approach faces an important obstacle. Since the future child does not exist, it does not share the qualities that are deemed inherent to the legal person in this approach. With regard to the biological traits of the natural legal person, the future child lacks all of them since it lacks biological or physical existence in the first place. In addition to that, without existence and a mind of its own, the future child lacks rationality as well. It is also doubtful that the future child itself possess human dignity. Admittedly, the human does not necessarily have to be born in order to have human dignity. Under German law, the foetus is considered to be a subject of human dignity, and some German constitutional scholars maintain that this also applies to the embryo pre nidation and the embryo in vitro.[29] Yet, even under German law, the embryo is only considered to be a constitutional legal person and not a full legal person. Furthermore, Germany should be considered an exception. In the Netherlands and the UK, the possibility of attributing legal personality to the embryo (even by means of the nasciturus fiction which is discussed in section 5.4.1) is explicitly denied. What is more, even if we could speak of the human dignity of the embryo or the unborn child, this does not resolve the situation for the future child. The future child has not been conceived and is merely a hypothetical possibility without a physical existence. Since the future child does not exist, it cannot be part of the human family. Therefore, it seems unlikely that the future child itself has dignity.

In brief, the naturalist approach seems incapable of regarding the non-existent future child itself as a legal person. Nonetheless, as I discussed in the introduction of this research, what the future child and the unborn child have in common that they both are introduced in the legal debate as an anticipation of the child that may be born and thus become a natural person. With regard to the unborn child, the features of the natural legal person are represented in the legal status of *unborn life*. For example, in *Vo v. France*, the European

26 Additional Protocol to the Convention for the Protection of Human Rights and Dignity of the Human Being with regard to the Application of Biology and Medicine, on the Prohibition of Cloning Human Beings.

27 Article 14 of the European Convention on Human Rights and Biomedicine.

28 Article 13 of the European Convention on Human Rights and Biomedicine.

29 See for example, Münch/Kunig, 2012, Art. 2, nr. 49; Stern/Becker, 2016, Art. 2, nr. 57; Sachs, 2014 Art. 1 I GG, nr 62. See also section 2.1.1.1. Some authors maintain that the implanted embryo is entitled to more protection than the embryo in vitro: Maunz/Dürig, 2016, GG Art. 1 Abs. 1, nr 60; Jarass/Pieroth, 2016, Art. 1 Abs. 1, nr 9 and Art 2, Abs. 2, nr. 85.

Court of Human Rights stated that "the potentiality of that being and its capacity to become a person (...) require protection in the name of human dignity ..."[30] The Memorandum to the Dutch Embryo Act states that human dignity must also be respected before the moment of birth. These examples suggest that legal respect can be given by means of anticipating the dignity that the person will have once it exists. This poses the question as to whether legal personhood can be constructed on the basis of the dignity the entity (once born) will possess. Or put more broadly: can we assume legal personality because of the future child's potentiality to possess the qualities that are reflected in the natural person? This question is further explored in section 5.4.

5.3 The Constructivist Approach to Legal Personality

In the constructivist approach[31] the legal person is considered to be a legal construct. In the words of Kelsen – one of the most important proponents of this approach – a legal person is the allocation point of rights and duties or even *is* the bundle of rights and duties.[32] As such, the legal person is merely a fiction:[33] it is an artefact or "an invention"[34] of the law, a "legal metaphor"[35] or a "legal convention."[36] In this approach, humans do not possess legal personality, nor are entitled to it, because the human person has certain distinctive qualities. According to Kelsen a human being is a biological-psychological entity and not a legal concept. The human being in its entirety, with all its physical-biological and mental aspects, is not relevant for the law; only those actions that are addressed by law are important.[37] In other words, the constructivist understanding of the legal person consists of an abstraction of the human, in which biological, rational, or metaphysical qualities are not inherent to the legal person, nor provide themselves a ground for legal respect or legal protection. According to this constructivist interpretation the legal person does not even need a physical body.[38] Instead of reflecting daily life or a biological reality, law 'translates' events of that reality into its own language and as a result it has its own perception of the physical reality, or it 'constructs' its own legal reality. This artificial nature comes to the fore in the temporal boundaries of the legal person. This topic is further elaborated in section 5.4.1, but for now it suffices to say that the beginning

30 ECtHR 8 July 2004 ECLI:CE:ECHR:2004:0708JUD005392400 (*Vo v. France*), par. 84.
31 Constructivist in this context should not be confused with Dworkin's constructivism.
32 Kelsen, 1994, p. 52.
33 van Beers, 2017a, p. 568, 570.
34 Naffine, 2011, p. 194.
35 Fagundes, 2001, p. 1745.
36 van Beers, 2009b, p. 63.
37 Kelsen, 1994, p. 52-53.
38 van Beers, 2009b, p. 396; van Beers, 2017a, p. 574.

and end of legal personality can be artificially altered with the help of legal concepts such as the nasciturus fiction and brain death. These constructs expose the (at least partly) constructivist nature of the legal person: law is not strictly tied to the real human being in its representation, but it makes its own construction of what this entity is in law.

Following this approach, legal personality is not what an entity possesses because it has certain qualities. Instead, the attribution of legal personality depends on a legal construction, i.e. it is a consequence of a legislative decision. In the words of Lawson: "All that is necessary for the existence of the person is that the lawmaker (...) should decide to treat it as a subject of rights or other legal relations."[39] This is illustrated by the legal personality of corporations, international organisations, and nation states. These entities have legal personality not because they meet certain metaphysical requirements, as they are non-corporeal and only exist in the legal reality, rather, they are legal persons because the law attributes legal personhood to them.[40] Since the attribution of legal personality does not depend on inherent traits, it implies that the legal person in this constructivist interpretation has no specific characteristics.[41] Tur points out that this conception of legal personality is "wholly formal"; the legal person is "an empty slot that can be filled by anything that can have rights or duties."[42] It all depends on what law defines as a legal person: "If legal personality is the legal capacity to bear rights and duties, then it is itself an artificial creation of the law, and anything or anyone can be a legal person. It all depends on the particular, concrete rules of particular legal systems."[43]

As a result of this emptiness, anything can be a legal person.[44] To some legal scholars, the emptiness of the constructivist legal person is considered an important benefit for law to address and protect non-human entities.[45] Grear, for example, considers this plasticity a necessary benefit since, in her opinion, it is most responsive towards the complexity of society and the creation of hybrid subjects, and therefore indispensable.[46] New entities, such as trees, animals, future generations, artificial intelligence, unborn and future children, that do not fit in the naturalist perspective of the legal person could be understood

39 F.H. Lawson, 'The creative use of legal concepts', *New York University Law Review*, Vol. 32, 1957, p. 915.
40 In several legal systems, the law explicitly attributes legal personality to these corporations. See for example, the Dutch civil code, Art. 2:3, the Germen civil code title 2, subtitle 1, Section 19, and the Belgian Company code, Section 2, paragraph 2.
41 van Beers, 2009b, 374; Naffine, 2009, 35-36; Naffine, 2003, p. 351; Grear, 2013, p. 82.
42 Tur, 1987, p. 121.
43 Tur, 1987, p. 121.
44 Grear, 2013, p. 85; Naffine, 2003; van Beers, 2017a, p. 574.
45 Berg, 2007, p. 406; Naffine, 2011, p. 201-202.
46 Grear, 2013, p. 86, 100.

as a legal person in a constructivist perspective. In that way, these scholars argue, they could gain more legal protection and their interests could be protected better.[47]

For the same reason, the constructivist approach towards legal personality offers opportunities to conceive the future child as a legal person. After all, if anything can be a legal person, why not also a non-existent entity? As pointed out by van Beers, in this constructivist approach to legal personality, the legal person does not require a body or a physical existence,[48] which is the reason why the future child does not fit the naturalist approach. A constructivist approach could be adopted to evade the birth requirement: following this line of argument, it would not be necessary for the future child to actually be born in order to become a legal person. From a purely legal-technical view, the future child would become a legal person if law attributed legal personality and rights to it. A similar point has been made with regard to the unborn child by Gray: he points out that from a legal perspective *technically* there is no difficulty in attributing rights to an unborn child. A newborn is equally incapable of exercising its rights; it can only exercise its rights through, for example, a legal guardian. Since there is not much difference between the child just before birth and just after birth, "[i]t is just as easy to attribute the will of a guardian, tutor or curator to the one as to the other."[49] In a similar way, this construction could be applied to the future child; technically, the future child could be the allocation point of rights (instead of interests), such as a right not to be born, and by doing so it would be a legal person. Of course, the attribution of rights to an unborn or future child causes other problems, such as conflicts with the rights of the mother in the case of abortion or the impossibility of conducting stem cell research involving the destruction of embryos. However, the question of whether the future child *should* have legal personality, Gray argues, is of a political nature;[50] from a legal perspective (according to the constructivist approach) even a non-existent entity could fill the empty slot.

Nonetheless, the application of a constructivist approach to attribute legal personality to the future child faces a problem. Even as a flexible, plastic legal fiction, the constructivist perspective on legal personality has its limits. As van Beers points out: "legal fictions are the most striking example of law's capacity to bend the truth for its own purposes."[51] In other words, legal fictions serve a purpose or a function.[52] The function or the benefit of

47 Attributing legal personhood in order to protect the interests of an entity is a pivotal point in different discussions, including on the legal status of embryos and stem cell research and the great ape project. See also Berg, 2007, p. 369-370.

48 van Beers, 2009b, p. 396; van Beers, 2017a, p. 574.

49 Gray, 1909, p. 38.

50 Gray, 1909, p. 38.

51 van Beers, 2017a, p. 580.

52 For example, also Fagundes refers to a "functional abstraction". Fagundes, 2001, p. 1761.

having legal personality is securing legal protection. For example, the call for attributing legal personality to animals or future generations springs from the idea that the acknowledgement of their legal rights can protect them from animal abuse or depletion of resources. However, the future child fundamentally differs at this point. Contrary to animals, for example, the future child has no interests of its own that require legal protection. It is not an independent entity that needs protection; instead, the future child exists to anticipate the interests the actual child will have after its birth. This point is illustrated by the chosen formulation of written regulation. For instance, Section 13(5) of the HFE Act speaks of the "child who may be born as a result of the treatment." Moreover, the Dutch medical professional guidelines state that the "well-being of the future child" is determined by the "circumstances the child *is born into*",[53] implying that it is concerned with the harm that the actual, child, once born, might suffer. The interests of the future child are derived from the actual child and this creates an inextricable link between the future child and the actual child, even if the actual child is never born at all. Saying that the future child is a legal person in its own right severs the ties between the future and actual child. For this reason, acknowledging the future child as an independent, legal person, would forfeit the purpose of this legal fiction. Given the fact that the interests of the hypothetical actual child are the future child's *raison d'être*, it may be more fruitful to explore the possibilities of an anticipatory approach. The question then is no longer which approach to legal personality can include the future child as a legal person, but whether the legal personality of the actual child can be extended, i.e. whether its start can be moved to a moment before its conception, so that it includes the future child. In other words, can the fiction of the legal person be understood as an anticipatory fiction?

5.4 Legal Personality as an Anticipation

As I have demonstrated above, both the naturalist approach and the constructivist approach fail to conceive the future child as a legal person. Following the naturalist tradition, the future child lacks the necessary inherent characteristics that are represented in this legal approach to the person. The constructivist approach initially seems promising, but this fiction misses its purpose: it is not the future child's interests that need the protection of legal personality, but the interests the actual child will have once its born. Therefore, it seems more appropriate to explore the possibilities of constructing legal personality based on anticipation. Such an anticipatory approach combines naturalist and constructivist elements. It presupposes a natural counterpart with intrinsic qualities (such

53 NVOG Modelprotocol "Mogelijke morele contra-indicaties bij vruchtbaarheidsbehandelingen", p. 2. Italics added by LtH.

as interests or human dignity) that justify the assumption of legal personality. Still, this legal person is not solely dependent on these natural qualities but is also characterised by constructivist elements that allow the legal person to exist (at least partly) independent of the temporal boundaries of a human being's existence. First, I explore the possibilities of altering the temporal boundaries by invoking a legal construction derived from Roman law and that is already acknowledged in various legal systems: the so-called nasciturus fiction. Second, I explore an alternative theoretical framework on the anticipation of personhood that has been proposed by Karnein.

5.4.1 The Nasciturus Fiction

As discussed in section 5.2, one of the biological traits that is represented in the legal concept of the natural person is the biological birth of the human being. Most legal systems have adopted the birth threshold, stating that legal personality starts once the child is born. Nevertheless, the attachment of the temporal boundaries of legal personality to biological life are not absolute. That is, the beginning of the legal person does not necessarily coincide with biological birth. It is possible to feign an earlier beginning of the legal person with the help of the nasciturus fiction. This fiction entails that the child with which the woman is pregnant is considered to be already born, as this is often in the interests of the unborn child. Since birth marks the beginning of the legal person, the fiction implies that the child is treated as a legal person if its interests require this. Notably, this fiction is not meant to attribute legal personality or legal rights to the embryo itself, but to enable the child, once it is born, to legally respond in retrospect to events that took place before its birth. For example, in Roman law the fiction was operationalised to enable the child to inherit from its father in case the latter died before the child's birth. In modern day use, the fiction is also invoked to enable the child to claim compensation for prenatal harm.[54] The nasciturus fiction can be found in various legal systems in different forms. A direct codification of this fiction can be found in Dutch law in Article 1:2 of the Dutch Civil Code[55] and Article 31(2) of the Swiss Civil Code.[56] In German law, a similar fiction is applied in the context of inheritance law. Article 1923(2) of the German Civil Code states:

54 W.D. Kolkman and F.R. Salomons in: J. de Boer, *Mr. C. Assers Handleiding tot de beoefening van het Nederlands Burgerlijk Recht. 1. Personen- en familierecht. Deel I. De persoon, afstamming en adoptie, gezag en omgang, levensonderhoud, bescherming van meerderjarigen*, 19th ed, Deventer, Wolters Kluwer 2020/36.

55 "A child of which a woman is pregnant, is regarded to have been born already as often as its interests require so. If it is born lifeless, it is deemed to have never existed." Translation by Dutchcivillaw.com.

56 Art 31 Swiss Civil Code: "1 Die Persönlichkeit beginnt mit dem Leben nach der vollendeten Geburt und endet mit dem Tode. 2 Vor der Geburt ist das Kind unter dem Vorbehalt rechtsfähig, dass es lebendig geboren wird." 1 Personality starts with life after birth and ends with death. 2 Before birth the child has legal capacity, provided that it is born alive. Translation by LtH.

"A person who is not yet alive at the time of the devolution of an inheritance, but has already been conceived, is deemed to have been born before the devolution of an inheritance." This fiction allows the unborn child to be an heir.[57] The UK Congenital Disabilities (Civil Liability) Act of 1976 provides for a similar fiction[58] to enable a child to bring an action if it is born disabled due to prenatal harm.[59]

Because of the nasciturus fiction, the beginning of the legal person does not necessarily have to coincide with the child's biological birth. Despite the possibility of feigning an alternative moment of beginning for the legal person, the fiction does not provide a solution for the case of the future child for three reasons. The first of these three reasons is that the fiction normally does not pertain to the future child, but the unborn child. Both the Dutch and the German codification of the fiction require that the child has already been conceived.[60] Moreover, in his discussion on the fiction in common law, Gray states that the child is considered to have been alive from the time it is begotten,[61] thereby making a distinction between the unborn child and the future child. At the same time, the fiction is not always strictly applied to the unborn child only. The German Federal Court of Justice allowed a plaintiff to claim damages for being born with congenital syphilis, resulting from a contaminated blood transfusion that the plaintiff's mother had received a year before the plaintiff's conception. The Court ruled that also the unconceived child could qualify as another person ex Section 823 I of the German Civil Code[62] if it would have been healthy had, the mother not been infected.[63] Another exception to this is the

57 Article 1923(1) German Civil Code: "Only a person who is alive at the time of the devolution of an inheritance may be an heir."

58 According to Tur, the fiction pertains to the moment of causing harm, not the moment of birth and the beginning of legal personhood. The result, nonetheless, is the same as the application of the Dutch article. Tur, 1987, p. 125.

59 MP Mr. Carter claimed during the parliamentary debate that the liability to the child is derived from the liability to its parents. HC Deb (6 February 1976) vol. 904, col. 1592. Even though it concerns derivative liability, some form of personhood must be assumed.

60 The Dutch codification: "het kind waarvan de vrouw zwanger is", and the German codification: "Wer zur Zeit des Erbfalls noch nicht lebte, aber bereits gezeugt war". Italics added by LtH. In Dutch cases concerning the prenatal application of the family supervision order it has been argued that the nasciturus fiction can only be applied after 24 weeks of pregnancy, that is, when the foetus is viable. District Court Dordrecht 7 February 2012 ECLI:NL:RBDOR:2012:BV6246; District Court Zeeland-West-Brabant 22 March 2017 ECLI:NL:RBZWB:2017: 2587. However, this assumption is neither in line with the Dutch legal doctrine concerning the nasciturus fiction, nor does it follow from the article itself. See also ten Haaf, 2017.

61 Gray, 1909, p. 38.

62 This section allows compensation for damages arising out of a tort.

63 BGH 20 December 1952 - II ZR 141/51, BGHZ 8, 243 (*preconceptual harm*). This claim should not be understood as a wrongful life. The harm causing act (the blood transfusion) did not cause the child to come into existence. It only caused the child to come into existence with congenital syphilis. The damage, according to the plaintiff, was not that she was born, but that she was born with this illness.

UK Congenital Disability (Civil Liability) Act 1976.[64] Following Sections 1(2)(a) and 1(4), under this act prenatal harm is not limited to harm caused during the pregnancy. During the parliamentary debate, it was stated that:

> some hesitation at imposing liability for an event occurring before conception, [i]t came to the conclusion that it was right to do so particularly because it is medically difficult to fix a point at which conception occurs, and also because, thanks to modern scientific and technological development, there are occasions when a child may need a remedy for a pre-conceptual event.[65]

However, the possibility of applying the nasciturus fiction to the unconceived child as well is not accepted by everyone. Tur has expressed his reluctance to grant the future child the same position as the unborn child under the Congenital Disability (Civil Liability) Act 1976 in order to protect it from pre-conceptual harm: "But I have more trouble with the idea of that which has not yet been conceived having rights, even if, by virtue of the fiction in the 1976 act, the damage is not assessed until the child is born."[66] Unfortunately, Tur does not explain why he is opposed to the idea.

Even if the fiction were expanded to a moment before conception, there is a second reason why it cannot constitute an anticipatory form of legal personality for the future child whose existence is prevented. This is because the nasciturus fiction works retroactively. That is, it can only be applied after the child is born. Since the fiction works retroactively, the application of the fiction in this specific case would not meet its own criteria. The retroactive nature of the fiction is shown, for example, in the second sentence of the Dutch codification. It stresses that if the child is born dead, it is considered never to have existed at all. In other words, in the case of a stillbirth, the fiction cannot be applied, which implies that in order to be sure that the fiction can be applied, the birth of the child must be awaited. Moreover, it is accepted that the fiction does not aim to attribute legal personality to an embryo, but to enable a child, once born, to respond to matters that occurred during the pregnancy.[67] A similar point was made during the House of Commons debate on the Congenital Disabilities (Civil Liability) Act 1976: "First, there is liability only to the living child. No legal rights are given to the foetus."[68] This is also shown in the chosen wording of

64 Also Feinberg poses an exception, as he argues that the child can also retroactively claim damages for events that took place before its conception. Feinberg, 1994, p. 12.

65 HC Deb (6 February 1976) vol. 904, col. 1593.

66 Tur, 1987, p. 126.

67 van Beers, 2009b, p. 232; K.S.-I. Asser/De Boer, 2020/34; P. Vlaardingerbroek in: S.F.M. Wortmann, *Groene Serie Personen- en familierecht*, ed, Deventer, Wolters Kluwer 2021, aant. 7.

68 HC Deb (6 February 1976) vol. 904, col. 1592. Tur too claims that an action based on the Congenital Disabilities (Civil Liability) Act of 1976 is brought by the child, and not the foetus. Tur, 1987, p. 125. In a

the Act: if a child is *born* disabled, it can claim damages,[69] and born means born alive.[70] In sum, attributing interests to the future child requires a proactive approach in which the child's actual birth is not awaited, while the nasciturus fiction is applied retroactively, and thus at an entirely different moment.

Recent developments in Dutch case law have challenged the idea that the nasciturus fiction can only be applied retroactively, that is, once the child is born. In cases where the pregnant woman's behaviour may cause harm to her unborn child, the nasciturus fiction is invoked to impose a family supervision order on an unborn child.[71] This means that the fiction is applied before the child is born, in a forward-looking manner. This construction bears several problematic aspects.[72] The most important problematic aspect of such a forward-looking application is the risk that the pregnancy results in a stillbirth or miscarriage. In particular, when the unborn child's health interests are at stake, there is an increased risk of a miscarriage. This would undo the first part of the fiction. After all, if the child is not born alive, it has never existed at all, and as a result there is no reason to impose a family supervision order to protect the unborn child in the first place. Although legal doctrine maintains that the nasciturus fiction does not serve to attribute legal personality to an embryo or foetus,[73] elsewhere, I have argued that this proactive application of the nasciturus fiction implies the attribution of legal personality to the viable foetus.[74]

Nonetheless, even if such a forward-looking application were acknowledged, the nasciturus fiction cannot offer legal personality to the non-existent future child for a third and final reason, which pertains to a more fundamental problem. The nasciturus fiction requires

---

similar vein, Gray also maintains that 'the child in the womb' cannot exercise any legal rights. Gray, 1909, p. 38.

69 See for example, Section 1(1) and Section 2 Congenital Disabilities (Civil Liability) Act 1976.

70 Section 4(2)(a). Tur confirms that the child must be born alive in order to be covered by this Act; Tur, 1987, p. 125.

71 See also section 1.2.1. If a family supervision order is issued, the legal authority of the parent(s) is restricted, and a family guardian is appointed to oversee the child's development. The regulation on the family supervision order, Article 1:254 of the Dutch Civil Code, refers to a minor, implying a child already born. Therefore, Article 1:2 is invoked in order to apply this rule to the unborn child as well. According to case law, this construction can only be applied to a viable foetus. District Court Dordrecht 7 February 2012 ECLI:NL:RBDOR:2012:BV6246 (*prenatal family supervision order nonviable foetus*).

72 For a more extensive analysis, see ten Haaf, 2017, p. 1095-1100; L. ten Haaf, 'De ondertoezichtstelling van een nog niet-levensvatbare foetus. Het kan, maar hoe?', *Nederlands Juristenblad*, Vol. 2021, No. 24, 2021, p. 1968-1971.

73 van Beers, 2009b, p. 232; K.S.-I. Asser/De Boer, 2020/34; Tur, 1987, p. 125; Gray, 1909, p. 38.

74 ten Haaf, 2017, p. 1102.

the child to be born,[75] while the future child's interests are often protected by not letting it come into existence. In other words, the 'being born' requirement of the fiction can never be met at all since the legal measures that protect the future child's interests aim to prevent its birth. For these reasons, even with the help of the nasciturus fiction, the beginning of legal personhood cannot be expanded to a moment before conception to include the future child and act on its assumed interest in non-existence.

5.4.2 *The Personhood Dependent Principle*

As explained above, the nasciturus fiction cannot provide the basis for an anticipatory form of legal personality for the future child, due to the fiction's retroactive nature. Nonetheless, the idea that an entity deserves respect due to its potentiality to become a legal person and in anticipation of this legal person is not completely uncommon in law. For example, in the ECtHR case *Vo v. France*, the Court claimed, regarding the embryo, that "the potentiality of that being and its capacity to become a person (...) require protection in the name of human dignity, without making it a 'person' with the 'right to life' for the purposes of Article 2."[76] This notion is further theorised by Karnein, who has developed a moral theory on how to deal with embryonic life called the Personhood Dependent Principle.[77] Although her work mostly focuses on moral personhood, it offers fruitful insights for the anticipation of legal personality as well. According to Karnein, potential, future persons must be treated "in anticipation of the respect due to the later persons."[78] Karnein points out that the stages prior to the attribution of personhood, in this case the stages before birth, matter to the person.[79] After all, events that occur during these stages can affect the actual person. For this reason, once a person exists or is born, obligations towards the entity at a previous stage (such as the embryo) arise retrospectively, for example, not causing prenatal harm. So far, Karnein's theory follows a similar reasoning to the nasciturus fiction. The difference lies in the following step: because we know or may assume that these obligations towards the embryo will retrospectively arise, we should anticipate them now. In other words, the obligations that arise retrospectively are "applied in *a forward-looking manner.*"[80] Karnein's theory may seem puzzling, due to its two time-

75 The versions of the fiction of Feinberg and Gray also require that the child has to be born alive in order to apply the fiction. Feinberg, 1994, p. 12; Gray, 1909, p. 38.

76 ECtHR 8 July 2004 ECLI:CE:ECHR:2004:0708JUD005392400 (*Vo v. France*), par. 84.

77 Karnein, 2012, p. 18.

78 Karnein, 2012, p. 33. "This respect should express itself chiefly by treating embryos with care and by regarding them for 'who' they are genetically encoded to be, that is, without other people interfering with their endowment and certainly without other people taking anything away from them."

79 Karnein, 2012, p. 28.

80 Karnein, 2012, p. 29. Italics added by LtH.

jumps. Still, her theory does explain how interests can transgress the temporal boundaries of the entity's existence and provides a reason to proactively anticipate the interests the actual child has once it has been born.

Karnein limits her research to the status of the embryo and does not include the unconceived, future child. In my opinion, her theory provides a useful starting point for reflection upon the future child because the claim that "previous stages matter" is not necessarily limited to the embryo or foetus. After all, harmful events may occur between conception and birth, but they can also manifest through conception itself. Such harm can only be prevented by anticipating the person that one day may exist when it is still a non-existent future child. Put differently, anticipating the person that one day may exist (in order to prevent all sorts of harm) may also be required in the stage before conception. Consequently, legal protection based upon anticipating later obligations (that arise in retrospect) is not necessarily limited to the embryo but may also apply to the future child. For this reason, I believe Karnein's theory could be helpful to understanding the attribution of interests to both unborn children and non-existent future children. Of course, one could argue that we do not know beforehand which embryo will actually develop into a legal person. As already addressed in the discussion on the forward-looking application of the nasciturus fiction, it is possible that the foetus dies before birth, in particular when the unborn child's health interests are at stake. Karnein responds to this by proposing a precautionary approach. This would require us "to treat all embryos (and Stem cells for that matter) as if they were going to become persons – at least until we have made it the case that they will not, by, for instance, having an abortion or rendering stem cells in a petri dish unable to develop into viable embryos."[81]

While Karnein's theory explains how we can anticipate the (legal) personality of a human being before its birth, this anticipation does not mean that legal personality is expanded and attributed to the unborn child or the future child. Her personhood dependent principle does not prescribe that the unborn child should be treated equally to the legal person.[82] As also expressed in *Vo v. France*, respect for the previous stages of the person does not have to be based on the attribution or extension of personhood itself.[83] Treating the unborn child or the foetus as if it is the person that it will develop into would, according to Karnein, imply that it is impermissible to destroy them.[84] Abortion and stem cell

81 Karnein, 2012, p. 29.

82 Karnein, 2012, p. 33-34.

83 ECtHR 8 July 2004 ECLI:CE:ECHR:2004:0708JUD005392400 (*Vo v. France*), par. 84. "the potentiality of that being and its capacity to become a person (...) require protection in the name of human dignity, *without making it a 'person'*." Italics added by LtH.

84 Karnein, 2012, p. 33.

research would in that case be impermissible. More importantly, treating the unborn child as the person it may develop into would create a self-fulfilling prophecy. The mere potentiality to become a person would constitute an obligation to allow it to become a person. Karnein, therefore, maintains that the possibility of the embryo to develop into a person (and therefore also a legal person) requires us to treat it with respect until we are certain that its potential personhood will not be realised. This requirement does not include an embryo's right to continued existence, because if the unborn child is prevented from coming into existence, no wrong is done.

Karnein's theory of unborn life has potential as a basis for the construction of an anticipatory legal person because it allows a prospective application. Nonetheless, if her theory is applied to the future child whose existence is prevented, we face the same problem as with the nasciturus fiction. In order to anticipate legal personhood, the legal person must come into existence. Without it, there is nothing to anticipate and our obligations towards the previous stages of the person do not arise retrospectively. This point allows Karnein to distinguish between the embryo that is aborted, destroyed, or used for research, and the embryo that is carried to term, that is the unborn child.[85] Only the latter will grow into a person (or, more precisely, there is a clear intention of the parents to let this entity grow into a person. It remains possible that medical complications could alter the actual result). Since the latter embryo will become a person with certain rights and interests, the obligation to anticipate its interests exists. The same goes for future generations: we may not know *which individuals* will be part of future generations but the future generation *as an entity itself* will come into existence, unless the whole human race becomes extinct.[86] Moreover, if the future child comes into existence, it would be possible to anticipate its legal personality and the rights it has once it is born. However, focusing on the future child whose existence is prevented, we stumble upon a complex, paradoxical situation. Since the future child in this case will not come into existence, there will never be a person to anticipate. No individual will ever exist in order to induce the application of retrospective respect for its unborn predecessors, including the future child. In conclusion, Karnein's approach, in which the legal protection of interests is based on anticipation of an actual person, does not offer a solution to the case of the future child whose existence is prevented.

85 Karnein, 2012, p. 34.

86 T. Allen, 'The Philippine children's case: recognizing legal standing for future generations', *Georgetown International law Review*, Vol. 6, 1994, p. 730.

5.5 Conclusion: Representation of the Non-existent

While the 'interests of the future child' construction is based on the assumption that the future child is a legal subject, the future child cannot be understood as a legal subject with the help of law's traditional vocabulary of the (natural) legal person. The future child does not fit in the naturalist approach to legal personality because, due to its non-existence, it lacks the necessary intrinsic qualities. Additionally, a constructivist approach fails to address this inherent connection to the actual child and, as a result, cannot properly conceptualise the future child either. An anticipatory approach towards legal personality combines both naturalist and constructivist elements. It addresses the connection between the future child and the actual child, yet it is not completely bound by natural traits given that the temporal boundaries of legal personhood can be artificially altered. Still, as I discussed in this chapter, an anticipatory approach also does not offer a solution for the conceptualisation of the future child. As the discussion of the nasciturus fiction and the personhood dependent principle demonstrates, the anticipation of legal personality requires that the person in question comes into existence. So, while the anticipatory approach may not serve as a foundation for the future child's natural legal personality, the analysis of this approach still proves to be fruitful, because it brings to light the key difficulty concerning the future child. The greatest obstacle to understanding this entity as a legal person is the fact that it will never exist at all.

The future child's non-existence does not always pose a problem for establishing duties towards the unborn or future child. As Karnein points out, in a forward-looking approach, we cannot always know which potential persons will develop into an actual person. Therefore, a precautionary approach must be adopted until it is certain that a particular embryo will no longer be allowed to develop into a person; up until then, the rights and interests the person will have must be anticipated. This conditional anticipation of personhood is possible because in this case, the status of the embryo and the decision to stop its development into a person are independent from each other. In the case of the future child, however, these two aspects are intertwined. That is, the construction of the future child is created in order to ensure that the actual child does not come into existence. In other words, the future child's entrance into law's *raison d'être* is to be able to justify the intervention that prevent the actual child's conception and birth. Because of this, it is clear from the beginning that the future child does not come into existence.

The paradoxical nature of the future child – it exists in order to have its existence prevented – proves to be the greatest obstacle for the third assumption made about the future child. By invoking the interests of the future child, it is assumed that this entity is a legal subject of some sorts. However, as I have shown in this chapter, the future child cannot be understood as a legal subject with the help of law's traditional vocabulary of natural legal personality. The natural person commences at the moment of biological birth, which, in case of the future child is prevented. Even an anticipatory approach towards legal personality does not suffice, because it requires the anticipated entity to come into existence at some point in time. Therefore, the assumption that the future child is a legal subject with legal personality is untenable because this assumption is at odds with its own premises. Birth, or existence, is a fundamental premise for obtaining legal personality. Consequently, the personification of the future child serves to prevent the actual child from coming into existence and become an actual legal person. In other words, trying to put the future child's legal subjectivity in terms of (natural) personality fails to meet the criteria of fit.

In this chapter, I focused on legal subjectivity by means of legal personality. While the future child cannot be understood as a legal person, its legal subjectivity may be constructed in another way. As Karnein argues, basing the unborn (or in this case, future) child's legal status on the anticipation of legal personality should not be confused with attributing legal personality to that entity. This suggests that apart from the legal person there are other forms of legal subjectivity. For this reason, as explained in the introduction, I do not consider the legal subject and the legal person as synonymous concepts. Instead, the legal person is one of the categories of legal subjectivity. Because, in the majority of cases, the regulatory frameworks seem to prefer to speak of the future child's interests rather than its rights, it appears that the legal subjectivity of the future child can perhaps better be understood as a subject of *legally relevant interests*. More precisely, the 'interests of the future child' construction is built upon a fourth assumption, namely that the future child is a subject of (legally relevant) interests. This raises several questions. First, how does this form of legal subjectivity relate to legal personality? And can the subjectivity indeed be understood as a form of legal personality (in order to substantiate the third assumption in an alternative way)? Second, as the anticipation of the child's interests results in its own non-existence, the question *whose* interests are at stake must be raised. Whether we understand them as either the interests of the non-existent future child itself (contrary to what has been assumed so far), or the interests of a merely potential or hypothetical entity, the same question must be answered. Namely, are such entities capable of having interests in the first place? In order to further critically assess the 'interests of the future child' construction, these questions are taken up in Chapter 6.

6 The Future Child as the Subject of Legal Interests*

6.1 Introduction

As explained in the introduction of this study, the 'interests of the future child' construction rests on four pillars, consisting of four implicit assumptions made about the future child. Two of those assumptions pertain to the nature of the future child's subjectivity. It is assumed that the future child is capable of having (legally relevant) interests, and that the future child is a legal subject. The latter assumption was addressed in the previous chapter, where I concluded that the future child does not fit the traditional vocabulary of law's subject, i.e. the legal person. Nevertheless, there remains the possibility that an alternative form of legal subjectivity is applicable to the future child. In this chapter, I discuss that alternative form, namely the subject of legally relevant interests. In doing so, this chapter conducts a dual assessment of the tenability of both the third and fourth assumptions made about the future child. First, it continues the assessment of the third assumption; it assesses whether the future child can be a legal subject, but this time not as a legal person, but as a subject of legally relevant interests. If a subject of legally relevant interests can indeed by understood as an alternative form of legal subjectivity, the assumption that the future child is a legal subject may be possible. Whether the future child fits this form of legal subjectivity depends on whether the fourth assumption is tenable, namely whether the future child can be a subject of interests. In short, in order to assess the third assumption, I must also scrutinise the fourth assumption.

The possibility of the future child as a subject of interests is not randomly chosen. As discussed in chapter 2, the regulations on reproduction refers more often to the *interests* of the future child than its *rights*. Also in academic debate, the interests-based vocabulary is commonly used. The European Society of Human Reproduction and Embryology (ESHRE) Task Force for example has pointed out that the advances in reproductive biotechnology that made reproduction a matter of intentional choice[1] has given rise to "the idea of respect for the child as a future autonomous person with his or her own

* This chapter is an adaption of my article that was published in 2017 in the German Law Journal: ten Haaf, 2017, p. 1091-1120.

1 Of course, the technology cannot guarantee a child to prospective parents. Yet, it cannot be denied that human reproduction is more and more at our disposal and because of this, there is a strongly felt responsibility towards unborn and future children.

interests."[2] This suggests that the future child generally is not considered to be a legal person, who is the subject of legal rights and duties. However, as already briefly addressed in the previous chapter, in some debates reference is made to the *rights* of the future child. Of particular interest is the *right not to be born*, which is, for example, operationalised in the context of compulsory contraception. It can be argued that framing it as a right not to be born is merely a rhetorical tool to add more weight to the future child's claims, or "a compendious way of referring to the plausible moral requirement that no child be brought into the world unless certain very minimal conditions of well-being are assured…"[3] Bagaric and Allan have addressed the tendency to pose moral claims in terms of rights, arguing that "there seems to be no limit to the types of claims that can be advanced in terms of rights."[4] So it can be questioned whether there is indeed a legal right not to be born, or simply an interest.[5]

In this chapter, I explore the possibilities of understanding the future child as a legal subject in the sense of a subject of legally relevant interests. In order to assess whether the future child can be understood as a subject of legally relevant interests, two questions have to be answered. First, we must establish what the implications of having a legal interest are, as opposed to a right. In order to understand this alternative form of legal subjectivity, the difference between the legal person and the subject of interests, and thus the difference between rights and interests, must be spelled out. This discussion will elucidate the nature of the subject of interests as a legal subject. Whether the future child can be conceptualised as a legal subject in this sense depends on the answer to the second question. This question involves a critical assessment of the fourth assumption of the future child: does the future child whose existence is prevented have the capacity to have interests? For the assessment of the fourth assumption, I investigate whether perceiving the future child as a subject of interests is indeed coherent within the legal-fundamental ideas on the capacity of interests.

The remainder of this chapter aims to address the questions listed above. Section 6.2 attempts to elucidate the subject of interests, and, more specifically, what it means to have legally relevant interests. This question has thus far been barely touched upon in academic debate.[6] In order to come to an answer on this matter, I combine two approaches. To start

2 G. Pennings, G. de Wert, F. Shenfield, J. Cohen, B. Tarlatzis and P. Devroey, 'ESHRE Task Force on Ethics and Law 13: the welfare of the child in medically assisted reproduction', *Human Reproduction*, Vol. 22, No. 10, 2007, p. 2585.

3 Feinberg, 1984, p. 101.

4 Bagaric and Allan, 2006, p. 257.

5 In section 6.3.2., I argue that a prenatal right not to be born (just like the prenatal interest not to be born) is logically inconsistent.

6 An exception is G. Samuel, 'Should Jurists Take Interests More Seriously?', *Law and Method*, Vol. 2017, No. 2, 2017. Also in Dutch legal doctrine, a couple of authors have reflected upon the notion of the interest

with, I discuss academic literature that addresses the relation between rights and interests from a legal-philosophical perspective. This discussion provides important insights in the concepts of rights and interests, but it also has a down side. The legal-philosophical discussion often remains too abstract and does not take into account how the concept of interests actually features in the legal system itself. More particularly, the discussion tends to focus on the relation between rights and interests in general and thereby ignores the distinction that is made within legal doctrine between legally relevant and non-legal interests. Therefore, section 6.2 also discusses legal doctrine to supplement the legal-philosophical debate and gain a more precise understanding of what it means to be the subject of legal interests. After I conclude that the subject of legal interests can indeed be understood as a legal subject, I assess whether the future child can be understood as a subject of interests. To this end, I answer the question what the capacity to have interests requires (section 6.3). I discuss the *interest view*,[7] which assumes conscious awareness or sentience as a necessary and sufficient requirement for having interests. I then apply this view to future entities and explain to what extent it is possible to claim that future entities (such as the future child) are capable of having interests. After this assessment of the fourth and last assumption about the future child, this chapter concludes with reflection upon the tenability of the 'interests of the future child' construction and the inherently paradoxical nature of this construction.

6.2 THE SUBJECT OF INTERESTS

The concept of interests is often used in legal language yet, according to several scholars, the concept remains rather vague.[8] Feinberg, who made an attempt to define the concept, admits that his definition is circular. According to him, having an interest in something implies having a stake in something. "In general, a person has a stake in X (...) when he stands to gain or lose depending on the nature or condition of X."[9] For this reason, Feinberg maintains that an interest is a "distinguishable component of a person's well-being."[10] A similar idea has been expressed by Raz, who defines an interest as "some aspect of one's well-being."[11] Also Kramer relates an interest to its subject's well-being.[12] Others have adopted a wider definition. Samuel defines an interest as a state of affairs that is to the

holder, most notably Wiggers-Rust, 2011.

7 Feinberg, 1974; Steinbock, 2011.

8 H.J. McCloskey, 'Rights', *The Philosophical Quarterly*, Vol. 15, No. 59, 1965, p. 126; Wiggers-Rust, 2011, p. 17.

9 Feinberg, 1984, p. 33-34.

10 Feinberg, 1984, p. 34.

11 Raz, 1988, p. 166.

12 M.H. Kramer, 'Refining the interest theory of rights', *American Journal of Jurisprudence*, Vol. 55, 2010, p. 33.

advantage of a person.[13] In her reflection upon the concept of 'interest' in Dutch law, which translates as 'belang', Wiggers-Rust describes an interest as "something that affects somebody, because it affects his benefit, or his well-being."[14] Also, McCloskey points out that interests are not solely related to well-being: "[I]nterests suggest much more than that which is indicated by the person's welfare. They suggest that which is or ought to be or which would be of *concern* to the person/being."[15] In chapter 3, I already briefly touched upon the relationship between interest, well-being, and harm. Harm was seen as the setback of interests, but only of specific interests, namely those which relate to physical or mental well-being. The regulations on reproduction, however, also attribute other types of interests to the future child. The interests in identity and human dignity do not directly pertain to the individual's well-being and the violation of these interests do not necessarily qualify as harm. On the contrary, it is conceivable, for example, that in some cases, denying someone the right to access to information about his origin story does not have any negative impact on his mental state. It follows from the regulations that people can have a stake in these matters even if there is no measurable physical or mental harm. In line with Samuel, Wiggers-Rust, and McCloskey, I adopt the wider definition of interest, because this is more in line with how the notion is operationalised in the regulations; an interest refers not only to a component of someone's well-being, but also to a component of someone's person. In other words, it is possible to take interest in something, or have a stake in something, that does not necessarily have a tangible or measurable effect, such as one's dignity or identity.

The capability of having interests is deemed relevant for determining one's moral or legal status. According to Steinbock, an entity needs to be capable of having an interest in order to have moral standing.[16] In a similar vein, several legal philosophers have argued that having interests is a necessary requirement for having (legal) rights. In legal doctrine though, having an interest is not always considered to be synonymous with having a right (as will be discussed below). Additionally, not all interests offer legal standing, meaning that not all interests are protected in law. In order to grasp the relation between having an interest and legal status, a distinction must be made between three concepts: rights, legally relevant interests (or legal interests) and non-legal interests.

The distinction between legal and non-legal interests has not been considered in the legal-philosophical literature. Legal doctrine, on the contrary, makes it clear that there is a

13 Samuel, 2017, p. 5.
14 Wiggers-Rust, 2011, p. 18.
15 McCloskey, 1965, p. 126.
16 Steinbock, 2011, p. 2.

difference. This difference between the two notions comes to the fore in the procedural law principle *point d'intérêt, point d'action*. This principle, codified for example in Dutch[17] and French[18] law, and according to Samuel indirectly also acknowledged in UK law,[19] implies that a party has no legal action if he does not have a sufficient interest in the proceedings. Not every interest qualifies as a sufficient interest, which is illustrated by the tragic Dutch case of *Jeffrey*.[20] The case pertains to a young boy, Jeffrey, who, in an unguarded moment after swimming therapy, had gone back to the pool and drowned. Jeffrey's parents demanded the Court to legally declare that the hospital, who was the employer of the therapist, be liable for their son's death. The parents argued that they needed the defendant to be declared responsible as part of their grieving process and to start mourning the loss of their son. The Court stressed that being able to start the grieving process was of immense importance on a personal level. It concluded, however, that the interest in question was a 'purely emotional interest' and did not qualify as a sufficient interest within legal procedure.[21] Put differently, the interest did not qualify as legally relevant. In other words, contrary to other interests, it is not an interest protected by law.[22]

In order to gain a better understanding of the notion of legal interests, it must not only be juxtaposed with non-legal interests, but also with rights. The relationship between (legally relevant) interests and rights has been frequently addressed in legal-philosophical debates. Yet, the exact difference between the two notions is difficult to pinpoint due to the close entanglement of the two concepts. Several legal scholars have addressed the intrinsic connection between rights and interests, particularly in the debate on who may be a subject of rights. For example, civil law scholar Nieuwenhuis points out, a right cannot exist without an interest.[23] Berg maintains that legal personality can only be attributed on the basis of interests, i.e. the attribution of legal personality must serve either the interests of the entity itself or the interests of others.[24] Other philosophers adopt a stricter approach, claiming that only those entities that can have interests themselves are capable of having rights.[25] Feinberg offers two reasons for the close link between rights and interests:[26] first,

17 Art. 3:303 Dutch Civil Code.
18 Art. 31 French Code of Civil Procedure (Code de procédure civile).
19 Samuel, 2017, p. 15.
20 Hoge Raad 9 October 1998 ECLI:NL:PHR:1998:ZC2735 (*Jeffrey*).
21 Hoge Raad 9 October 1998 ECLI:NL:PHR:1998:ZC2735 (*Jeffrey*), R.O. 3.4.3.
22 For another example, see Samuel, 2017, p. 15.
23 J.H. Nieuwenhuis, *Confrontatie en compromis. Recht, retoriek en burgerlijke moraal*, Deventer, Kluwer, 1992, p. 29.
24 Berg, 2007, p. 374, 386.
25 L. Nelson, *A system of ethics*, New Haven, Yale University Press, 1956, p. 136-144; McCloskey, 1965, p. 126; Feinberg, 1974, p. 51, 57; Raz, 1988, p. 176.
26 Feinberg, 1974, p. 51. Feinberg does not maintain that "that for every right there is a particular interest corresponding to it." In other words, an entity can have a right to something without having an interest in

he claims, "a right holder must be capable of being represented and it is impossible to represent a being that has no interests." Second, "a right holder must be capable of being a beneficiary in his own person, and a being without interests is a being that is incapable of being harmed or benefitted, having no good or 'sake' of its own." According to the *interests theory of rights*, the relation between interests and rights is even stronger. The capacity to have interests is not merely a requirement for the capacity to have rights; the function of rights is to protect and further the right holder's interests. Raz, one of the main proponents of the interests theory, says one (X) has a right "if and only if X can have rights, and, other things being equal, an aspect of X's well-being (his interest) is a sufficient reason for holding some other person(s) to be under a duty."[27] For Raz, rights constitute grounds for duties.[28] Therefore, a right is defined by referring to the related duty;[29] a right exists if the right holder's interest is of such significant importance that it generates a legal obligation on others not to violate that interest.

If an interest is a necessary requirement for the existence of a right, the question can be asked as to whether there is a difference between a legal interest and a right. It follows from Raz's and Kramer's theories that having an interest is not synonymous with having a right. Both authors maintain that having an interest is not enough to constitute a right. Kramer points out that in order to speak of a right, there must be a legal basis that bestows such a right on the right holder.[30] He maintains that someone (an interest holder) holds a legal right only if "at least one minimally sufficient set of facts includes the undergoing of detriment by some person Q at the hands of some other person R who bears a duty under contract or norm."[31] According to Raz, an interest can be translated into a right

> only where one's interest is a reason for another to behave in a way which protects or promotes it, and only when this reason has the peremptory character of a duty, and finally, only when the duty for conduct which makes a significant difference for the promotion or protection of that interest does the interest give rise to a right.[32]

---

that same thing. Nonetheless, he does claim that having an interest in something is generally a good reason to claim it has a right, even if having that interest cannot be decisive. But an entity that is not capable of having interests at all cannot have rights. J. Feinberg, 'Is there a right to be born?' in: J. Feinberg (ed.), *Rights, justice, and the bounds of liberty*, Princeton University Press, Princeton, 1980, p. 214.

27 Raz, 1988, p. 166.

28 Raz, 1988, p. 167.

29 See also: M.H. Kramer, 'Rights without trimming.' in: M.H. Kramer, N.E. Simmonds and H. Steiner (eds.), *A debate over rights*, Oxford University Press, Oxford, 1998, p. 13.

30 Kramer, 2010, p. 33. Also McCloskey seems to understand a legal right (as opposed to a moral right) as a claim created by law, or in his words "civil authority." McCloskey, 1965, p. 115-116.

31 Kramer, 2010, p. 36-37.

32 Raz, 1988, p. 183.

In other words, according to them, only those interests that constitute a duty to respect those interests qualify as a legal right. In short, something can be in the subject's interest, even though the subject does not have a right to it.

The theoretical discussion by Raz and Kramer does not offer a complete answer. Neither of the authors distinguish between legally relevant interests and non-legal interests. It is unclear how an interest that does not translate into a right should be understood in their theory. Should those interests be understood as non-legal interests? Are interests that can be translated into rights always legally relevant interests? Or is there a difference between rights and legally relevant interests? To answer these questions, we must look at legal doctrine, in order to understand how the concept of interest is used in law.

In his discussion on (UK) tort law and economic interests, Cane points out that the notion of interest can have various meanings in law. He states that in some contexts, the concept of interest can be "more or less synonymous with the words 'right' or 'claim'."[33] He points out that a 'property interest' implies that the interest holder has some sort of claim or right over a thing, and a 'contractual interest' means that the interest holder has a right by means of contract. However, Cane continues, that interest can also have a "broader sense" in which it refers to a factor that is to the person's advantage.[34] Under such a broader definition, an interest could still be legally acknowledged without automatically turning into a right. Also Wiggers-Rust argues that a legal interest is a much broader category than that of a right, and that these concepts are not interchangeable concepts.[35] Reflecting upon the relationship between right and interest in Dutch law, Wiggers-Rust argues that law (*recht*) is more than a collection of rights, because it also includes interests acknowledged and protected by the law (*rechtsbelang)*.[36] A similar point is made by Nieuwenhuis, who maintains that not everything that is protected by law constitutes a right.[37] This is illustrated by the legislator's choice to use the concept of 'interest' or 'interest holder' instead of 'right' or 'right holder'. The 'interest holder' makes an appearance in several other areas of Dutch law.[38] One of the examples in which Dutch law refers explicitly to interests is in administrative law; the concept "interest holder"[39] is an important notion in this field because only the interest holder can object to decisions made by a public authority. According to legal theorist Bergamin, being an interest holder in administrative law

33 Cane, 1996, p. 4.
34 Cane, 1996, p. 4.
35 Wiggers-Rust, 2011, p. 37-38.
36 Wiggers-Rust, 2011, p. 38.
37 Nieuwenhuis, 1992, p. 134.
38 See for the concept of interests in Dutch administrative and private law in general: Wiggers-Rust, 2011.
39 "Belanghebbende", art. 1:2 Awb. (Dutch General Act Administrative Law).

means that one is a *subject* of administrative law.[40] Only those with a relevant interest can participate in Dutch administrative law and thus become an actor or subject. A similar construction exists in Dutch criminal procedural law: interest holders can file a complaint if the public prosecutor decides not to take a case to court.[41] An interest holder can be the victim of a crime, but it can also be a third party.[42] Through this construction, the subject of an interest can, to a certain extent, participate in a criminal procedure, or, put differently, law opens up to the interest holder. These examples show that the legal subject is not necessarily the holder of rights and duties; the Dutch legal system also responds to interest holders. Following through the distinction between legal interests and non-legal interests, legal interests can give the interest holder some kind legal standing.

The difference between rights and legal interests is also illustrated by cases in which the Court ruled that a party did not have a right to something, but still had an interest and that that interest determined the legal status of the interest holder. One example of particular relevance is the UK case *Wandsworth LBC v. A.* After a parent had been verbally abusive to a staff member of her son's school, she was denied access to the school premises. The Court of Appeal had to decide on the legitimacy of this injunction and commented upon the status of the parent:

> The local authority has an obligation in public law to educate their children... The parent has a correlative interest in seeing the duties of the authority properly performed. That does not give him the right to interfere with how the professional educators undertake their work, but it does give him an interest in being informed about their work, with the possibility of formal representations about it; and generally makes him a more significant figure in the public activities of the school than is a mere visiting tradesman.[43]

In other words, the parent's interest does not translate into a right, but is nonetheless acknowledged by law, as it influences her legal relation with the school. She becomes a more "significant figure" than a random person.

Another example is provided by the Dutch landmark case on wrongful life. In this case, also known as the *Baby Kelly* case, a distinction is made between rights and interests.[44] In this case, the Dutch Supreme Court claimed that although the claimant did not have a

40 R.J.B. Bergamin, *De persoon in het recht*, Nijmegen, Ars Aequi Libri, 2000, p. 44.
41 Art. 12 Sv. (Dutch Criminal procedural code).
42 G.J.M. Corstens, *Het Nederlands strafprocesrecht*, Arnhem, Kluwer, 2005, p. 520-521.
43 [2000] 1 WLR 1246. (Wandsworth London Borough Council v. A.), par. 44.
44 Hoge Raad 18 March 2005 ECLI:NL:HR:2005:AR5213 (*Baby Kelly*).

right to her own non-existence, she did have an *interest* in her own non-existence, which was the legal basis for granting damages. Kelly was born with a severe genetic condition. Had this condition been discovered during the pregnancy with the help of a prenatal test (which the obstetrician considered unnecessary), Kelly's parents would have terminated the pregnancy and Kelly would never have been born at all. Consequently, Kelly claimed that she was harmed by existing as a result of being born with severe disabilities, whereas if the prenatal test had been performed, Kelly would not have been born at all. In considering whether and in what way Kelly was harmed, the Dutch Supreme Court concluded that the hospital had not violated Kelly's rights, because she did not have a 'right to her own abortion' – only the mother can decide whether or not to terminate a pregnancy.[45] Granting the child its own, independent right to non-existence would interfere with the mother's right and possibly result in children suing their own parents for being born in a disadvantaged position. Instead, the Court granted Kelly damages because of the violation of her interests. Based on the fact that the Court not only granted compensation for her disability, but for her whole existence, it is implied that Kelly had an interest (and not a right) in her own non-existence.[46] Because this interest was violated, she was entitled to claim damages. Even though the Court did not address the distinction between a right and an interest in this case, its decision seems to be based on the assumption that a legal interest can exist without being a right.

In brief, the discussion of the interest theory of rights suggests that interests are a requirement for having rights, but that not every interest can be translated into a right. The discussion of legal doctrine illustrates that even though not every interest is translated into a right, they can be acknowledged by law and influence the legal status of the interest holder. Nevertheless, it remains difficult to identify the exact difference between legal interests and rights. According to several legal scholars, the real difference between a legal interest and a right is that although the attribution or acknowledgment of legal interests creates some form of legal standing, it does not offer such a strong claim as having a right.[47] Nieuwenhuis states that a right has a "mysterious preponderance" compared to an interest.[48] According to Bergamin, rights have a symbolic value, due to their great argumentative value because they are a solid element of the law. In a legal dispute, arguments based on rights are usually considered stronger than arguments that do not appeal to rights.[49] It is not only Dutch authors that have noted this difference between

45 Hoge Raad 18 March 2005 ECLI:NL:HR:2005:AR5213 (*Baby Kelly*), par. 4.13 and 4.16.
46 van Beers, 2009b, p. 317.
47 See for example, Wiggers-Rust, 2011, p. 38-39, Cane, 1996, p. 4.
48 Nieuwenhuis, 1992, p. 29.
49 P.W. Brouwer, R.J.B. Bergamin, A.M. Bos, C.L.B. Kocken, E. Poortinga, G.J.M. Veerman and J.J.C.M. Wirken, *Recht, een introductie*, Den Haag, Boom Juridische Uitgevers, 2004, p. 303-304.

rights and interests: also Elliot emphasises the importance of rights when saying, "the pattern of rights determines not what it would be good to do or bad to do but what in the *strongest sense* must be done or must not be done."[50] Dworkin believes too that rights offer a special benefit as he uses the well-known metaphor rights as "trumps":[51] "If someone has a right…this means that it is for some reason wrong for officials to act in violation of that right, even if they (correctly) believe that the community as a whole would be better off if they did."[52] Of course, despite their stronger status, rights are not absolute. This is, for example, illustrated by the European Convention on Human Rights (hereafter ECHR), which shows that breaches of fundamental rights can be considered legitimate. Such a breach needs to meet specific conditions defined in the Convention, which makes it much more difficult to overrule a right. Interests, on the other hand, need to be balanced against each other, but there are usually no requirements given on how this balancing must take place. As a result, interests can more easily be overruled.[53]

It remains difficult to pinpoint the exact difference between a right and a legal interest. The exact nature of the subject of legal interests is difficult to grasp. On the one hand, legislators and courts seem to assume a difference between the two concepts, but do not discuss the nature of this difference, and in particular the relationship between legal interests and rights. In legal philosophical discussions, on the other hand, there is no clear distinction made between legally relevant interests and interests in general. The analysis shows that there are important similarities between the two concepts. Both offer the subject legal standing, and both can be the reason for corresponding legal duties. The *Baby Kelly* case illustrates that Kelly's interest in non-existence gave rise to a claim, namely a claim to compensation. Furthermore, the double responsibility of physicians that is acknowledged in the regulations on reproduction prescribes that physicians have a duty to also consider the future child's legitimate interests. From this it can be concluded that legal interests too can give rise to legal duties. In other words, the presence of a legal duty does not necessarily indicate the existence of a right.[54] Perhaps the difference can be best explained by pointing out that the type of duty an interest generates is slightly different: whereas rights impose a duty to have the interest in question realised (apart from legitimate breaches), a legal interest primarily creates a duty to be considered or to be taken into account. It implies

50 R. Elliot, 'The rights of future people', *Journal of Applied Philosophy*, Vol. 6, No. 2, 1989, p. 159. Italics added by LtH.

51 R. Dworkin, *Taking rights seriously*, Cambridge, Harvard University Press, 1977, p. xi; R. Dworkin, 'Rights as trumps.' in: J. Waldron (ed.), *Theories of rights*, Oxford University Press, Oxford, 1984.

52 Dworkin, 1984, p. 153.

53 Nieuwenhuis, 1992, p. 42.

54 Also Raz admits that even though every right has a corresponding duty, not every legal duty has a corresponding right. Raz, 1988, p. 170. In chapter 7, I explore the possibility of duties based on responsibility instead of an individual's rights or interests.

that the subject exists in law and should be heard. Samuel uses the metaphor of an interest being a "passport to all areas of the law."[55] In conclusion, because the subject of interests should not be understood as synonymous to the legal person, and because having legally relevant interests offers the interest holder legal standing, the subject of legal interests can be understood as a category of legal subjectivity.

This alternative form of legal subjectivity may make it possible to understand the future child as a legal subject. This would render the third assumption about the future child tenable. Furthermore, the subject of legal interests seems a promising construct for the future child because several authors maintain that the subject of interests is a broader category than legal personality. Wiggers-Rust, for example, states that entities that have no legal personality can still have legally relevant interests.[56] Nieuwenhuis argues that future generations can have interests (and that in their case, he thinks it is preferable to use the vocabulary of interests instead of rights).[57] The fact that there is no systematic approach towards the concept of legal interests and its subject may offer this concept the flexibility needed to be applied to entities that do not fit the criteria of legal personality, such as the future child. Nonetheless, in order to assess whether this form of legal subjectivity is applicable to the future child, we must first determine whether the latter can be a subject of interests.

6.3 The Capacity to have Interests

With regard to legal protection of the future child, it is not only important to understand what the subjectivity of interest implies for the future child's legal status; the next question is whether the future child can be the subject of legally relevant interests. In legal doctrine, little has been written about the question of who can have interests. As briefly addressed above, Wiggers-Rust and Nieuwenhuis maintain that entities that do not have legal personality can still be the subject of interests,[58] but they do not go into the question of what the requirements for having interests are. The regulations on reproduction do not go into this matter and simply assume that the future child can have interests without further ado. The problem with this approach is that it fails to address what makes the future child

55 Samuel, 2017, p. 6.
56 Wiggers-Rust, 2011, p. 21, 46.
57 Nieuwenhuis, 1992, p. 134.
58 This is also confirmed in the commentary on the concept of interest holder ("belanghebbende") in Dutch administrative law, where it is stated that the interest holder does not have to be a natural or artificial legal person. J.C.A. de Poorter in: T.C. Borman and J.C.A. de Poorter, *Tekst & Commentaar Algemene Wet Bestuursrecht*, ed, Deventer, Wolters Kluwer 2017, commentary Article 1:2 Awb (General Act Administrative Law).

so unique: the future child is treated as an existent and a non-existent entity at the same time.

The question of which entities can have interests has in fact been addressed by various authors from a legal-philosophical and bioethical angle. Legal philosophers such as Berg, Feinberg, and Dworkin have addressed this question. Dworkin, for example, has posed the question as to whether an embryo or unborn entity can have interests, in order to determine whether invoking the rights or interests of the embryo to make a case against abortion is a valid argument.[59] Feinberg and Berg both maintain that the capacity to have interests is needed to have some form of legal standing.[60] Therefore, in order to assess whether entities such as animals, plants, future generations, embryos, and of course the future child can have legal standing in some form, or whether their interests pose a valid argument for regulation, we must first determine what the capacity to have interests requires. Interestingly, the question of which entities can have interests is not a strictly a legal-philosophical question. An adaption of the idea that only entities that can have interests are entitled to legal standing can also be found in moral philosophy and bioethics. This so-called *interest view*[61] has been adopted by, amongst others, Warren and Steinbock in order to determine which entities should have *moral* standing.[62] Consequently, both of them developed a theory on what the capacity to have interests requires. Similar to Feinberg, Berg, and Dworkin, moral philosophers such as Warren and Steinbock maintain that the capacity to have interests requires some form of conscious or sentient life or awareness.

In this section, I assess the fourth assumption, namely whether the future child can have interests. With this aim in mind, I elaborate on the argument that has been put forward by Berg, Feinberg, and Dworkin, namely that the capacity to have interests requires some form of conscious or sentient existence. In order to critically assess this claim, I will not restrict the discussion to the legal-philosophical context, but also discuss insights from authors who have addressed this question in philosophical or bioethical contexts. These insights are helpful to test the claim that has been put forward by legal philosophers, namely that only beings with conscious awareness are capable of having interests, and to further explore the argument that has been raised in the legal-philosophical debate.

59 Dworkin, 1993, p. 15.

60 Berg, 2007; Feinberg, 1974, p. 51. Berg also argues that legal personality can be construed on the basis the interests of existing natural persons. Berg, 2007, p. 370.

61 Steinbock, 2011, p. 1.

62 M.A. Warren, 'Do potential people have moral rights?', *Canadian Journal of Philosophy*, Vol. 7, No. 2, 1977, p. 283; Steinbock, 2011, p. 1.

6.3.1 *Interests and Existence*

Which entities are capable of having interests and are accordingly entitled to moral or legal standing? This question has been posed with regard to various entities, such as embryo's, foetuses, animals, the environment, and future generations.[63] As described above, an interest implies that one has *a stake in* something that matters to one's well-being or person. Having a stake in something implies that it is of concern to that person, that it matters to him. This has led several authors to conclude that the capacity to have interests requires a kind of conscious or cognitive awareness. Steinbock, for example, maintains that only entities with conscious awareness or sentience can have interests because "without conscious awareness, beings cannot care about anything."[64] Feinberg brings forward a similar argument. According to him, interests spring from desires, wishes, and hopes, and consequently the ability to have interests presupposes "cognitive awareness."[65] Other authors have adopted similar terms. Warren uses *sentience* as the defining criterion: "A being that lacks the capacity to have experiences, and/or to prefer some experiences to others, cannot coherently be said to have moral rights, because it has no interests to be respected."[66] Dworkin uses the term *consciousness*, which he defines as "some mental as well as physical life."[67] While the various authors use different terms, they seem to refer to the same phenomenon.[68] That is, the ability to have interests presupposes awareness to feel pain and pleasure, to have preferences, or to have experiences. This is what Feinberg calls "conative life."[69] As a result of this requirement, not everything can have interests. Mere things, for example, are considered incapable of having interests.[70] Existing people can take interest in a car, a house, or art, but these lifeless things themselves have no interest of their own. It does not matter to these things what is done to them.

Regan is not convinced by the statement that only beings with sentience or conative life can have interests. Regan distinguishes two interpretations of the concept of interests.[71] According to him, the statements that an entity has an interest in something can mean either that this entity is interested in that something, or that this something is in the interest of the entity. The first sense of interest (being interested in something) indeed

63 See for example, Feinberg, 1974 and Berg, 2007.
64 Steinbock, 2011, p. 6.
65 Feinberg, 1974, p. 52.
66 Warren, 1977, p. 283.
67 Dworkin, 1993, p. 16.
68 Steinbock seems to use conscious awareness and sentience interchangeably,
69 Feinberg, 1974, p. 49.
70 Feinberg, 1974, p. 52; Steinbock, 2011, p. 6; Dworkin, 1993, p. 16; McCloskey, 1965, p. 126.
71 T. Regan, 'McCloskey on why animals cannot have rights', *the Philosophical Quarterly*, Vol. 26, No. 104, 1976, p. 253; T. Regan, 'Feinberg on what sort of beings can have rights', *Southern Journal of Philosophy*, Vol. 14, 1976, p. 486-487.

demands the capability to want or desire something.[72] According to Regan, this type of interest indeed requires a form of conative life and cannot apply to mere things. Interest in the second sense, i.e. something being in the entity's interest, implies that it contributes to the entity's good or well-being. This sense is closely related to the definition of interests as described earlier in this chapter. Regan maintains that things can also have interest in the sense that something can be in the interest of a thing, i.e. contributing to its good, because he believes things can have a good of their own. That is, the goodness of a thing does not depend on the interest taken in that thing.

Regan illustrates his point by saying that some cars are better than other cars. According to him, whether a car fulfils its purpose does not depend on whether someone takes an interest in cars:

> Suppose that my Datson is a better car than Randy's Volvo. And suppose that the time comes when neither I nor Randy nor any other human being has an interest in cars. It would still remain true that my car is a better car than Randy's. All that would have changed is the frequency with which we make use of our good (or not so good) cars and the value we attach to having one. What would not have changed is the relative goodness of the cars, qua cars.[73]

In other words, Regan distinguishes between the goodness of something and the value that is attributed to it: whether a car possesses goodness or not does not depend on the value attached to it or whether it fulfils the purpose we attribute to that car. Regan writes: "That a car fulfills our purposes is not what makes it a good car...Rather, a car fulfils our purposes because it is a good car."[74] In my (and other authors') opinion, Regan fails to see the point on what determines the goodness of the car. Such a standard of goodness is perhaps independent of whether people are still interested in cars, but that does not mean their origin is completely independent of human purposes.[75] For example, a good car can be a car that drives fast, that is safe, or that has a low CO2-emission. This depends on what those to whom the car has an instrumental value decide, but it does not depend on the nature of the car itself. Hershenov and Hershenov make a similar point regarding an arrowhead that is used as a paperweight: "Then the wound causing sharpness which was once 'good for the artefact' as an arrowhead and 'in its interest' ceases to be 'good for it' and 'in its interest' as a paperweight for its good and interests are really metaphorical and

72 Regan, 1976, p. 254.
73 Regan, 1976, p. 492.
74 Regan, 1976, p. 492-493.
75 Steinbock, 2011, p. 8

derivative, due to what is in the interest and good for the people making use of it."[76] To the car (and to the arrowhead), it does not matter whether it meets one criterion or another, or any. When we say that it is in the interest of the car to refresh the oil or check the tyre pressure, we indeed say that these things contribute to the car running well. Whether this is a good, however, depends on the criteria for goodness that we have chosen to adopt, which in the end, depends, for example, on the interests of the car owner. The car itself has no stake in working well; it does not benefit from functioning well. In conclusion, as a lifeless thing lacking a consciousness of its own, the car cannot have interests of its own.

Hershenov and Hershenov refute Regan's argument of mere things having interests, but they do not fully agree with the *interest view* as discussed by Feinberg, Steinbock, Warren, and the others. According to Hershenov and Hershenov, living but mindless entities (which are incapable of conative life) are capable of having interests. They maintain that living entities such as plants have a natural function that is independent of human intention or interests, unlike the proper functioning of a car, for example. Therefore, a plant has a good in itself which is realised by its functioning. Because of this, Hershenov and Hershenov maintain that plants, but also other mindless living entities such as an embryo, have an interest "to live on and develop in a healthy fashion by which they will flourish."[77] Steinbock, on the contrary, argues that while non-conscious living beings such as plants may have a *good* of their own that is independent of the purposes imposed by people, they do not have a welfare of their own, meaning that they have a stake in their own well-being. Only if that were the case is it possible to act for the sake of that being. Steinbock writes:

> Whether something has a sake of its own depends on whether it has a stake in its own well-being. In this respect, plants are like bodily parts and mere things. They do not have nervous systems; they are not sentient. They are alive, but they do not experience anything. Without experiences, they cannot have interests – desires, plans, hopes and goals. They cannot take an interest in anything, including their own health, lives and well-being.[78]

In other words, we can say that water or sun light is in the interest of a plant because it contributes to its natural flourishing. However, whether the plant receives water or sun light does not matter to the plant itself. A plant cannot experience anything, nor care

76 D.B. Hershenov and R.J. Hershenov, 'Morally relevant potential', *Journal of Medical Ethics*, Vol. 41, No. 3, 2015, p. 268.

77 Hershenov and Hershenov, 2015, p. 268.

78 Steinbock, 2011, p. 11.

about being watered or having sun light. This does not deny the fact that certain things may have an intrinsic value that ought to be appreciated or respected. I think it is reasonable to say that plants or embryos deserve some respect, because they are part of nature, or in case of the latter, they are a form of human life. Nevertheless, I agree with Steinbock that while this intrinsic value may result in obligations *regarding* these things, it does not imply that we have a duty *to* them. After all, it does not matter to the plant or embryo how it is treated by us. As Steinbock puts it: "It is not *for their* sake that we take steps to preserve them, but for the sake of beings who have interests, such as existing people or animals, or future generations."[79] In conclusion, I believe that the capacity to have interests is not necessary to have some moral status, but sentience or conscious awareness is necessary to be able to have interests.

Obviously, the future child does not meet this requirement: it lacks the capacity to feel or think, to have experiences or form preferences, and in addition it is not even a form of life. Because the future child physically does not exist, it cannot have the necessary capacities. If we follow these criteria strictly, the future child could never be the subject of interests. Such a strict interpretation would also imply that we, as present beings, would not need to consider the interests of future entities. As a result, not only the future child, but also future generations and unborn children would be irrelevant for our normative thinking. However, it seems odd to conclude that alcohol or drug abuse during early stages of pregnancy, which result in severe health problems for the child that is born later, is not problematic since at the moment of the abuse, the foetus from which the child developed had no conscious awareness yet, so no interests were violated. Because our present actions affect the interests of those who exist in the future, it is not controversial to assume that we do have some obligations towards our future descendants. Even if the identity of those who will exist in the future is unknown, it is reasonable to assume that once they exist, they will meet the requirements for having interests. For this reason, knowing that in the future entities that are capable of having interests will exist and will have interests in, for example, a clean environment and a stable economy, or in not being subjected to alcohol abuse during pregnancy, people in the present arguably have at least a moral obligation to take these future interests into account. In other words, the interests of future people can exert a claim upon us even before those future people actually come into existence.[80] In sum, the capacity to have interests requires that the entity in question has conative life or will have it in the future.[81]

79 Steinbock, 2011, p. 7.

80 Feinberg, 1974, p. 62; Steinbock, 2011, p. 31.

81 Steinbock and Feinberg also point out that the interests of people continue to exist even after the entity itself has ceased to exist or has ceased to possess conscious awareness. Steinbock, 2011, 15-31; Feinberg, 1974, p. 57-61.

This discussion on the capacity of having interests illustrates why it is important to see the embryo or foetus on the one hand, and the unborn child on the other as separate entities. The question of whether an embryo itself is capable of having interest is answered negatively by amongst others Berg, Steinbock and Feinberg. As their neural system has not yet developed, embryos are not capable of experiencing something or to have a conscious.[82] Therefore, these entities themselves cannot have interests. They do not have, for example, an interest in their continued existence. Nonetheless, what happens to the embryo may affect the interests of the unborn child. That is, it may affect the interests of a sentient, conscious entity that exists in the future. Of course, it is only possible to speak of the interests of the unborn child if it does actual come into existence and develops the capacity to have interests. There is some discussion on when this happens. Steinbock and Berg, for example, hold it possible that a foetus in a late stadium of the pregnancy has a sufficiently developed neural system to experience pain and to have a rudimentary form of sentience, which could be enough to argue that the foetus itself has interests.[83] Feinberg, on the contrary, denies that a newborn has the capacity to have interests. While admitting that a newborn child is capable of feeling pain, he maintains that "during the first few hours of their lives, at least, they may well lack even the rudimentary intellectual equipment necessary to the possession of interests."[84] In short, it remains open to debate what the exact moment is that a human entity develops sufficient conscious awareness to have interests. Because the human being will have conscious awareness at some point after its birth, it is possible to say that the unborn child and future child can have interests by means of this future conative life.

6.3.2 *Actual and Potential*

As discussed in the previous section, whether an entity, be it an embryo, a future generation, or a future child, will have interests, depends on whether it will come into existence. Not all possible future entities will come into existence. An embryo can be aborted, and the regulations on reproduction contains several frameworks that prevent the future child from being conceived. For this reason, a distinction must be made between actual future people and merely potential future people.[85] Actual future people will come into existence one day, so it follows from this that their interests should be taken into account. Merely potential people, on the contrary, could, hypothetically speaking, have come into existence,

82 Berg, 2007, p. 389; Steinbock, 2011, p. 34-345; Feinberg, 1980, p. 213.
83 Steinbock, 2011, p. 35; Berg, 2007, p. 395.
84 Feinberg, 1974, p. 62.
85 This distinction is made by among others C. Hare, 'Voices from another world: must we respect the interests of people who do not, and will never, exist?', *Ethics*, Vol. 117, 2007, p. 498. Dworkin, 1993, p. 19; Karnein, 2012, p. 28; Warren, 1977, p. 288-289; Feinberg, 1974, p. 63.

but will not because, for instance, their parents did not procreate at the right time, with the right person. Because a merely potential person will never come into existence, it will never have the ability to have interests. Consequently, there will never be future interests of this entity we can anticipate. The distinction between actual and potential people has led Dworkin to conclude that smoking during pregnancy is more harmful than abortion to the child. This may seem counter-intuitive[86] as abortion terminates the foetus's existence, whereas smoking usually 'only' results in damaging health interests. However, in the case of smoking, a child will be born whose interests are violated. In the case of abortion on the contrary, there will be no child and therefore no subject of interests.[87] Hence *from the perspective of the child*, smoking is indeed more harmful, because only in this scenario will the child come into existence with its interests violated. To sum up, only the interests of future entities that will come into existence (or whom we can at least expect will most likely come into existence) need to be considered.

The problem of the future child whose existence is deliberately prevented by the regulations is that it does not really seem to fit this distinction. Clearly, as its existence is prevented, the future child is not an actual future person. At the same time, it is also not merely a potential person. It is not just one of the many options that could have been realised, had its prospective parents procreated at the right time. It is not just a possibility that would have come into existence had another child not been born. The future child is *made* into a merely potential person as a result of the regulations. Without the regulations banning certain technologies or restricting their application, the future child whose existence is now prevented would come into existence. In that case, it would be an actual future person. Yet, because of the regulatory frameworks that claim to serve the future child's interests, the future child becomes a merely potential person. It could be argued that a similar situation occurs in the case of abortion. Before the decision to have abortion is made, the unborn child is an actual future person. Once the decision to abort the child has been made, the child is prevented from coming into existence and transforms into a merely potential being. Still, the future child is somewhat different from the aborted unborn child, as the legal construct that is the future child is solely created to prevent the actual child from coming into existence (assuming that no one gets pregnant solely to be able to abort the child). And that is what makes the future child a paradox. The paradox of the future child is that the future child-construction is created to anticipate the interests of the actual child but at the same time causes the future child to remain a merely potential

86 Steinbock mentions a politician dismissing an anti-smoking campaign that stressed the effect of smoking during pregnancy on the foetus. Allegedly, the politician said "yet the anti-smoking lobby doesn't oppose abortion, which I suppose is also detrimental to foetal health". Steinbock, 2011, p. xiv.

87 Dworkin, 1993, p. 19.

being, incapable of having interests in the first place. Invoking its own interests to have its existence prevented is thus a logical impossibility.

A mere potential entity cannot have interests, because interests (and also rights) are, as Feinberg calls it, *contingent* upon the child's birth.[88] In other words, the rights and interests of unborn children and future people are conditional: they only manifest when the child is born alive and actually has the capacity to have interests. According to Feinberg, there is one exception: he accepts the possibility of a *noncontingent* right not to be born.[89] Put differently, this right or interest does not depend on the child being born. This right has also been mentioned in the Dutch debate on compulsory contraception. Proponents of the compulsory contraception measure argue that in case of irresponsible parenthood, the future child has a right not to be born.[90] If Feinberg is correct, then it would be possible to understand the future child whose existence is prevented as a subject of interests, since the ability to have this specific interest, or right, does not depend on the future child being born. Unfortunately, he does not substantiate his claim elaborately or convincingly. Instead, he simply states that the right not to be born "is based on his future rather than his present interests (he has no actual present interests); but of course it is not contingent on his birth because he has it before birth, from the very moment that satisfaction of his most basic future interests is rendered impossible."[91] In other words, according to this reasoning, the right (and also the interest) not to be born exist regardless of whether its subject exists or not. This raises the question of *whose* interest we are talking about. Feinberg denies that it is the interest of the foetus itself, but rather that it is a future interest. But then it must be the future interest of an entity that is merely potential and which cannot have interests.

In my opinion, Feinberg is incorrect in assuming a noncontingent right to not to be born. Such a right, just like a right or interest to be born, is logically impossible. The impossibility of the latter, an interest to be born, is also acknowledged by Feinberg.[92] First, it makes no sense to speak of the child's interest to be born if that interest only exist after the child is

---

88 Feinberg, 1980, p. 210.

89 Feinberg, 1980, p. 216.

90 Editorial, 'Hebben sommige kinderen het recht niet geboren te worden? *Telegraaf* (22 January 2015). Editorial, 'Rotterdamse wethouder: verplichte anticonceptie incompetente ouders', *NOS* (1 October 2016) https://nos.nl/artikel/2135331-rotterdamse-wethouder-verplichte-anticonceptie-incompetente-ouders.html.

91 Feinberg, 1980, p. 216.

92 Technically, Feinberg does differentiate between interests and rights. He does not claim that because a future or unborn child does not have an interest to be born, it automatically does not have a corresponding right to be born. He maintains "that the fact that a fetus has no actual interest in being born at any time before it is in fact born seems to me to be a very good reason (though not perhaps a conclusive one) for denying that it has an unconditional right to be born". Feinberg, 1980, p. 214-215.

born. So, if there is an interest to be born, it must be in the interest of the foetus. But, Feinberg maintains, a foetus lacks conscious awareness and cannot have any interests, including a right or an interest to be born.[93] What is more, an interest in being born implies the assumption of an interest in the condition that is necessary to have interests in the first place. An interest not to be born is even more puzzling. As follows from the discussion above, if the child is not born, and never develops conative life, it cannot have interests. So, an interest not to be born, implies an interest in a situation that renders it impossible to have interests to begin with. In other words, it is internally contradictory. In addition, since the capacity to have rights demands the ability to have interests, or legal personality (which requires birth), it is similarly impossible to assume a right not to be born. Importantly, this internal contradiction only occurs in cases of a prenatal or preconception interest in non-existence. In wrongful life cases the assumption of an interest not to come into existence is not internally contradictory because the subject of that interest has already come into existence and as a result thereof, it has the capacity to have rights. Whether an interest in non-existence in those cases can be rightfully assumed depends on whether the child would have been better off not existing at all, as discussed in chapter 4. However, if the future child does not exist and never will, it cannot have an interest in not coming into existence. And, as a merely potential person, it cannot have any other interests. This means that the fourth assumption about the future child, and as a result thereof also the third assumption, appear to be untenable: the future child whose existence is prevented cannot be the subject of interests and, consequently, it cannot be understood as a subject of legal interest.

6.4 Conclusion: the Paradox of the Interests of the Future Child

In chapter 5, I concluded that the future child cannot be represented as a legal person. Therefore, I explored in this chapter the possibility of an alternative form of legal subjectivity. As follows from the legal-philosophical discussion of the matter and legal doctrine, the subject of legally relevant interests can indeed be understood as a subject in law. Moreover, this category offers the possibility to include non-human entities, such as future generations and animals, in the legal debate without having to modify or expand the concept of legal personality. At first sight, this alternative form of legal subjectivity

93 Feinberg, 1980, p. 214-215. As discussed earlier, Steinbock and Berg hold it possible that a foetus in the latest stage of pregnancy has the capacity to have interests. So, one could perhaps argue that a fully developed foetus does have an interest in being born. This does not answer the real question at hand, which is whether it is possible to assume that an entity that itself lacks the capacity to have interests, has an interest in getting or developing the capacity to have interests.

seems promising for the third assumption about the future child. Possibly, the future child can indeed be understood as a legal subject in the sense of the subject of legal interests.

Before we can conclude that the future child can indeed be understood as a subject of legal interests, the fourth and last assumption about the future child has to be assessed. That is, can the future child be understood as a subject of interests in the first place? As discussed above, the future child whose existence is prevented, lacks the capacity to have interests. In order to be able to have interests, an entity must be able to have experiences or preferences, to feel pain or pleasure. Only then we can say that it has a good of its own and that what happens to this entity, matters to it. This means that the capacity to have interests requires that an entity must have some kind of sentience, consciousness, or conative awareness. Interests of future entities can also impose duties on those living now, even if the subject of that interest does not exist yet. Notably, it is only possible to assume these future interests if that entity is an actual future person. That is, if that entity will exist in the future and develop a conscious awareness, and thus the ability to have interests. Since the future child's existence is prevented, and, therefore, it will never obtain conscious awareness or conative life, it will never develop the capacity to have interests. A fortiori, conceptualising the future child as a subject of interests is an internally contradictory construction. The interests of the future child are invoked to justify the prevention of the child's existence, which in turn renders it impossible for the future child to have interests. In terms of Dworkin's constructivism, the fourth assumption about the future child fails to meet the dimension of fit. As explained in the introduction, Dworkin's ideal of law as a coherent system of rules and principles also requires that the construction used to conceptualise the future child is coherent with the interpretation of fundamental legal concepts that form the premises of that construction. Treating the future child as a subject of interests is at odds with its own premises, namely, the fundamental legal ideas on what the capacity to have interests requires. The capacity to have interests requires (future) conative life and as a result of attributing interests to the future child, it lacks this capacity.

Answering the question of whether the future child can be a subject of interests has resulted in the conclusion that the fourth assumption of the 'interests of the future child' construction is untenable. Furthermore, this conclusion affects the tenability of the third assumption. Because the future child cannot have interests, it also cannot be attributed the alternative form of legal subjectivity that is discussed in this chapter: the subject of legally relevant interests. Therefore, the third assumption of the construction, that the future child can be represented as a legal subject, becomes questionable, because this entity can neither be understood as a legal person nor as a subject of legally relevant interests. Now that all four assumptions of the future child turn out to be partially or completely untenable, it appears that the 'interests of the future child' construction, which rests on these four pillars, is inadequate to represent the future child and the fundamental values in the regulations on reproduction.

Additionally, the critical assessment of the 'interests of the future child' construction and the assumption that the future child is a subject of interests further unravels the paradoxical nature of the future child as it is represented in the regulations. Through this construction, the future child is treated as a subject of interests. Moreover, these interests are given significance as they form the most important justification for the regulations on reproduction. At the same time, by respecting the future child's assumed interests (i.e. preventing its existence), the necessary condition for its subjectivity is prevented. This conundrum is also pointed out by the Nuffield Council, which is one of the very few occasions that a reference is made to this problem: "The difficulty we have is that of bringing the interests of future people into play in the evaluation of decisions on which their existence, and therefore their capacity to have interests or rights at all, depends."[94] As I argued in this chapter, this difficulty is caused by the internal contradiction of the 'interests of the future child' construction. As a result of invoking the future child's interests in the regulations on reproduction, the future child will never exist. And therefore, it will never have the capacity to have interests. The interests-construction is for this reason highly problematic and untenable. In my opinion, the problem lies in the fact that for the conceptualisation of the future child, a vocabulary is adopted that puts the sole focus on the individual subject. By operationalising the 'interests of the future child' construction, the impression is created that the values at stake only affect or only pertain to the future child or rather the actual child it may develop into. However, as I argued in chapter 3, some of the 'interests' attributed to the future child consist of values that transcend the individual. This suggests that the stakes involved in reproduction surpass the individual child and that what happens to the future child affects humankind as well. In other words, the future child is not only connected to the prevented actual child, but to something larger as well. Chapter 7 explores an alternative theoretical framework in which the relationship between the future child and this broader context is investigated.

94 Nuffield Council on Bioethics, 2018, p. 65-66.

7 The Future Child as the Object of our Responsibility

7.1 Introduction

As discussed in chapter 1, the regulations on reproduction introduces a new entity into the legal debate: the future child. Because the use of reproductive technologies directly affects individual future lives, it is understandable, and perhaps even inevitable, that future people are included in legal decision making. Consequently, in addressing reproductive technologies, the regulator must answer the question of what we owe to future people. Such an answer implies a normative account of what the human person is and what it is entitled to. Only with such an idea of the person, does it become possible to determine the values regarding the human person that are at stake due to the advances in reproductive technologies. From the regulations on reproduction, various aspects of this normative account can be distilled. In chapters 2 and 3 I discussed that in the regulations on reproduction, well-being, personal identity, and dignity are deemed to be important facets of the human person that must be taken into account in regulating reproductive technologies. In order to critically reflect upon these values and to be prepared for the challenges that new advances in the field of reproductive biotechnology will bring we need an adequate theoretical framework for the future child. This framework has to be able to conceptualise the future child and help us understand the nature of this entity and how we can address it. Such a framework is necessary because only then are we able to incorporate this new entity into our normative debates on reproductive technologies and make sense of the values that are at stake. Notably, as I explained in the introduction, in order to be an *adequate* theoretical framework it must meet two criteria derived from Dworkin's constructivism.[1] In order for the conceptualisation of the future child to be the "best interpretation" of this entity it first has to be the best justification for the underlying values. This means it has to be capable of addressing and making sense of the various values that constitute the normative account of the human person underlying the regulations on reproduction. Second, the theoretical framework must fit with its own premises and thus be an internally coherent construction.

As I argued in chapter 1, the future child is currently generally conceptualised as a subject of interests. In the Dutch, German, and UK legal systems, the 'interests of the future child'

1 See section 1.4.1.

construction is used in order to incorporate the future child and relevant values into the normative debate on the regulation of reproductive technologies. This implies that the values that are at stake, i.e. well-being, identity and dignity, can be understood as interests of an individual entity and that this entity can be the subject of interests. In the previous chapters, I argued that this 'interests of the future child' construction is not an adequate way to conceptualise the future child, as the examination of the four assumptions revealed that this construction does not meet the two aforementioned criteria.

First, the conceptualisation of the future child as a subject of interests cannot be understood as the best interpretation of this entity because various values that underlie the regulations on reproduction cannot be understood as in the interest of an individual entity or in the interest of the future child. In chapter 2, I showed that the prevention of the future child's existence is assumed to be in its interest, if its well-being, identity formation, or human dignity would be severely compromised. In particular, the latter, human dignity, includes not only values that are connected to the future child, but to humankind as a whole as well. This means that it includes collective interests and not only individual interests. The 'interests of the future child' construction operationalises vocabulary that puts focus on the individual entity and is therefore not capable of addressing these collective interests. In chapter 4, I showed that the interests-construction also fails to make sense of the other values. The construction is based upon the assumption that the future child has an interest in its own non-existence. Following the philosophical debate on wrongful life and the non-identity problem, elaborated on in chapter 4, such an interest in one's own non-existence can only be assumed when one has a life not worth living – a standard that lies far below the standard that is endorsed in the regulations on reproduction. Accordingly, the future child only has an interest in its own non-existence if it has been harmed by being brought into existence. Such harm only occurs if the child has a life not worth living which would make non-existence preferable and therefore in the future child's interest. In most cases covered by the regulatory frameworks, the quality of the child's life would likely not result in a life not worth living. For example, the frameworks on PGT and access to fertility treatment, for example, claim that it is in the future child's interest to adopt a standard of reasonable well-being rather than a lower standard. Other examples are cases where the 'harm' is less tangible, such as the violation of human dignity or the obstruction of identity formation. In these cases, it is difficult to claim that such a violation renders the child's life not worth living. In sum, the 'interests of the future child' construction fails because, in the majority of cases, it cannot do justice to the underlying values for two reasons. The interests-construction fails to adequately address the collective stakes in the regulation of reproduction. In addition, it invokes the interests of the future child to justify the prevention of the child's conception in cases where the future child's interests do not offer a convincing justification.

Second, the 'interests of the future child' construction is flawed because it is inherently contradictory. It presents the future child as a subject; both as a legal subject and as a subject of (legally relevant) interests. More precisely, the future child is presented as a subject of interests in order to anticipate the actual child that might be born in the future. However, as a result of this anticipation that child will never be born. And if the child will never be born, it cannot be understood as a natural legal person or as a subject of interests. As explained in chapters 5 and 6, these qualities require an entity to be born. In other words, the future child is attributed a quality (either legal subjectivity or the capacity to have interests), but as a result of this attribution, the child will never meet the requirements to have this quality in the first place. The attribution of interests to the future child in order to justify the prevention of its existence renders the future child incapable of having interests in the first place. In other words, conceptualising the future child as legal subject or a subject of interests does not fit with the law's understanding of legal personhood and interests, rendering the interests-construction internally contradictory.

Based on the arguments set out in the previous chapters, the interests-construction is inadequate to conceptualise future people, in particular those whose existence is prevented. Conceptualising the future child as a subject of interests does not offer a useful foundation for a critical discussion of the values and stakes involved in regulating reproductive technologies, because understanding those values as interests of an individual entity has often appeared to be highly problematic. Therefore, if we want to incorporate future people into our normative thinking on reproductive technologies, and critically reflect upon the stakes of these technologies, such as the importance of well-being or the meaning of identity and dignity in this context, we need an alternative theoretical framework that is capable of conceptualising future individual people.

In this chapter, as a more adequate alternative to the dominant interests-construction, I aim to construct a new theoretical framework for the conceptualisation of the future child, and more specifically for the future child whose existence is prevented. This theoretical framework must be able to define the future child in such way that it can explain the relation between this entity and those who exist now, and, more specifically, to account for the duties that we as currently existing people have towards it. It must help us understand what, from a legal-theoretical perspective, the future child is and how we should approach it, in order to have a meaningful discussion on what we owe the future child and why. But in order for such a theoretical framework to offer an adequate conceptualisation, or even the 'best interpretation' of what the future child is, it must meet the requirements of fit and justification. That is, this conceptualisation must fit in the legal system and thus be compatible with other assumptions in law about existence, non-existence, and subjectivity. Moreover, it must be able to conceptualise the future child in such a way that it can make sense of the normative account of the human person which underlies the regulations on reproduction. In other words, the conceptualisation must be able to address and articulate both the subjective and the intersubjective facets of law's interpretation of the human person and the ideas that can be derived from the regulations on reproduction about what we owe to future people. The question of what we owe to future people is undeniably also an ethical question. The theoretical framework must for this reason be able to address this ethical question and make sense of the notions of well-being, identity, and dignity. In sum, it must be able to justify the normative account of the human person that underlies the regulations on reproduction. Importantly, this ethical reflection does not serve to express my own interpretation of the essence of the human person. Instead, I discuss the normative account of the human person that can be distilled from the regulations on reproduction, as discussed in chapters 2 and 3. With the help of a new theoretical framework, it becomes possible to facilitate legal-philosophical and ethical reflection on the normative foundations of the regulations on reproduction. Subsequently, it will also be helpful in addressing future developments in the field of reproductive technologies, like IVG.

For the construction of this alternative theoretical framework, capable of conceptualising the future child, I draw upon the work of the German philosopher Hans Jonas, who developed a theory based on the notion of responsibility. Jonas is one of the first philosophers to systematically address how technological developments, and genetic technology in particular, affect our societal responsibility and normative thinking.[2] His work continues to be relevant within the contemporary debates on bioethics. His ideas have proven to be influential for, amongst others, Habermas[3] and Kass,[4] while others have attempted to debunk Jonas's arguments, like Bostrom[5] and Buchanan et. al.[6] My choice for Jonas's theory as a starting point is based on the fact that it is better equipped to conceptualise future life in the context of regulating reproduction compared to the interests-construction for several reasons. First, it provides a conceptual framework for addressing future life, without having to assume its subjectivity of interests or rights. As discussed in chapters 5 and 6, the future child's assumed subjectivity created an internal

2 Morris states that Jonas's work "stands at the forefront of environmental and ethical thought, although it has sometimes failed to find its acknowledgment there.", T. Morris, *Hans Jonas's ethic of responsibility. From ontology to ecology*, Albany, State University of New York Press, 2013, p. 2. Kampowski calls Jonas "one of the founding fathers of what today is called 'bioethics'". S. Kampowski, *A greater freedom: Biotechnology, love, and human destiny. In dialogue with Hans Jonas and Jürgen Habermas*, Cambridge, The Luttenworth Press, 2014, p. xiii.

3 Habermas, 2003.

4 L. Kass, 'Appreciating *The Phenomonen of Life*', *Hastings Center Report*, Vol. 25, No. 7, 1995; L. Kass, *Life, Liberty and the Defense of Dignity. The Challenge for Bioethics*, San Francisco, Encounter Books, 2002.

5 N. Bostrom, 'In defence of posthuman dignity', *Bioethics*, Vol. 19, No. 3, 2005, p. 210, 211.

6 Buchanan, et al., 2009, p. 197, 198.

contradiction. Jonas too has maintained that due to the fact that future people do not exist (yet), it is impossible for them to have rights now that can constitute a basis for our duties towards them.[7] Second, Jonas's theory provides a normative framework that elucidates what we owe to future people and why, particularly in the technological age where human nature itself has become an object of technology. This normative framework is based on the idea of human beings as free and autonomous ends-in-themselves and shares important similarities with some of the assumptions behind the legal concept of the person in the Dutch, German, and UK legal systems. Accordingly, Jonas's theory is able to provide a more convincing justification of the values underlying the regulations on reproduction than the interests-construction. That is, it can make sense of the normative account of the human person that forms the foundation of the regulations. In short, a conceptualisation of the future child based on Jonas's theory of responsibility is capable of meeting the requirements of fit and justification. Moreover, since the question of what we owe to future people demands an idea of our self-understanding as human beings, the consequences of artificial reproductive technologies and the regulation of reproduction transgress individual interests, as they affect this collective identity. This individual-transcending dimension is neglected in the interests-construction that is characterized by a vocabulary that focuses on the individual subject and appears to obscure the fact that the use of reproductive technologies also affects humankind as a collective. An important benefit of a theory of responsibility is that it offers a more appropriate account of the human person compared to the well-being/harm-vocabulary some authors have adopted to determine what we owe to future children.[8] It also acknowledges that the use of reproductive technologies affects mankind as a whole. It is capable of addressing the stakes that transcend the individual. For these reasons, Jonas's theory of responsibility is a good starting point for a theoretical framework that is able to conceptualise the future child in the context of reproduction.

In order to construct an adequate theoretical framework for the future child, Jonas's theory must be supplemented and thought through further. Because his theory is focused on future humankind as a whole, it does not address the individual future child in the context of reproduction, and more specifically, the future child whose existence is prevented. Therefore, to adapt his theoretical framework to the future child, we need to look at the context in which this entity appears, which is within the regulations on reproduction as discussed in chapter 2. Therefore, for the conceptualisation of the future child, I shall further elaborate both components of Jonas's theoretical framework, namely the conceptual and the normative framework. First, with regard to the conceptual framework, Jonas

7 Jonas, 1984, p. 38-39. This aspect is further elaborated below.
8 See section 4.5.

focuses on our responsibility towards future humankind as a whole. Therefore, I need to explain what this responsibility towards future mankind implies for our responsibility towards future individuals, in order to adapt the conceptual framework to accommodate the future child whose existence is prevented. Second, because Jonas's theory focuses on extreme applications of reproductive technologies and their effects on his normative account of the human person, the normative framework that tells us what we owe to future people must be further thought through as well. Compared to Jonas's predictions on the advances in reproductive technologies, the technological reality has turned out much more complicated. As a result, the regulatory frameworks have to deal with more complexities and nuances. Therefore, I will also supplement the normative framework. The depiction of human persons as autonomous ends in themselves must be further thought through in order to understand how it can include ideas about, for example, narrative identity, the importance of the treatment/enhancement distinction, and standards of well-being.

The remainder of this chapter is structured as follows. Jonas's theoretical framework of responsibility is introduced in section 7.2. More particularly, in this section I discuss two elements of his theory of responsibility which provide the starting points for the construction of my own theory. To begin with, I discuss the concept of responsibility and in particular substantive responsibility, which provides the conceptual framework. On the basis of this conceptual framework, we have obligations towards future people not because they are the subject of interests or rights, but because we are responsible for them. Subsequently, I elaborate on the normative framework. The conceptual framework is in itself not enough to clarify what we owe to future humans. What responsibility towards future life entails is determined by what Jonas calls the "Idea of Man"[9], i.e. a normative depiction of what it means to be human. In section 7.3, I elaborate on these starting points and adapt them into a theoretical framework capable of conceptualising the future child and making sense of the regulatory frameworks on reproduction. I start with explaining how the conceptual framework can be applied to the future child whose existence is prevented. Then, I explore how the depiction of the human being as a free and autonomous end in himself can make sense of the normative account of the human person and the three core values that are distilled from the regulations on reproduction in chapters 2 and 3. In addition to that, I identify different topics within the regulations on reproduction with regard to which the normative account of the human person needs to be fleshed out further.

9 Jonas, 1984, p. 43.

7.2 Jonas's Theory of Responsibility

Jonas's theory of responsibility provides an interesting starting point for the construction of a theoretical framework for the future child, even though his theory is a philosophical rather than a legal theory. Regulating reproduction inherently touches upon ethically sensitive matters, so this area of law needs to integrate insights from ethics and philosophy. In his work, Jonas addresses the same question that underlies this study: how can we incorporate people who do not exist (yet) into our normative discussions, given that they cannot be understood as subjects of rights or interests? Jonas answers this question by proposing an ethical imperative of responsibility. This imperative explains how we, as currently existing people, can approach future people, as well as what duties we have towards future people and why.

In his book, *The Imperative of Responsibility,*[10] Jonas explains why we need to incorporate future people into our normative thinking, particularly when dealing with modern technologies such as reproductive biotechnology. As a result of modern technology, the consequences of human actions have radically expanded in scope, crossing both spatial and temporal boundaries. An example of this is how reproductive biotechnology directly affects the most intimate aspects of the life of someone who has not even been conceived yet and even has the potential to affect future generations. As a result of this expanded scope of human action, existing moral vocabularies fall short in providing normative guidelines for our actions as contemporary ethics is confined to "the immediate setting of action."[11] Jonas therefore argues that we are in need of a new normative vocabulary that is able to address the changed scope of human action and to include future people who are affected by our contemporary decisions. It is not self-evident that future people have rights or interests that we as currently existing people must respect, because future people do not exist yet. From this it follows that, according to Jonas, a normative theory that is able to incorporate future people cannot be based on the reciprocal bond between rights and duties, because, according to him, future people have no rights that impose a duty on those who are alive now:

> For only that *has* a claim that *makes* claims – for which it first of all exists. (…) The nonexistent makes no demands and can therefore not suffer violation of its rights. It may have rights when it exists, but it does not have them by virtue of the mere possibility that it will one day exist. Above all, it has no right to exist at all before it in fact exists. The claim to existence begins only with

10 Jonas, 1984.

11 Jonas, 1984, p. 5.

> existence. But the ethic we seek is concerned with just this not-yet-existent; and its principle of responsibility must be independent of any idea of a right and therefore also of a reciprocity.[12]

To fill this gap, Jonas develops a theoretical framework based on the concept of responsibility.[13]

7.2.1 The Concept of Responsibility

Jonas distinguishes two senses of responsibility. Both senses are constituted by the same requirements. According to Jonas, responsibility can be assumed if three necessary conditions are met. The first of these is causal power. By this Jonas means that one's actions leave a certain impact on the world. Second, these actions must be under the agent's control: the agents must be able to decide or exercise some form of influence over whether or not to perform the action in question. Finally, attributing responsibility requires that the consequences of these actions are, to a certain extent, foreseeable.[14] Applying these requirements to the context of reproductive biotechnology reveals why the responsibility we have towards our future offspring has increased.[15] Our actions directly and intentionally affect future children: after all, the technologies are applied in order to achieve a certain outcome. With regard to the last criterion, foreseeability, one can wonder to what extent the consequences must be foreseeable or determinable in order to assume responsibility. As Jonas points out, one of the characteristics of modern technology, and in particular genetic technologies, is that while it enables us to do things that were impossible before, we cannot predict the outcome of our actions: "Our predictive knowledge falls behind the technical knowledge that nourished our power to act."[16] The fact that we do not know the possible outcomes and risks is also an important reason why, for example, germline modification is prohibited in the United Kingdom and the Netherlands.[17] Also in the German discussion concerning split motherhood, the lack of knowledge about possible psychological harm was one of the reasons to prohibit egg cell donation and surrogacy.[18]

---

12 Jonas, 1984, p. 38-39.

13 Other authors, most notably German philosopher Jürgen Habermas in *The Future of Human Nature*, have been inspired by this theory of responsibility in their discussions on modern reproductive technologies. Habermas in his turn has been discussed by other authors, such as Sandel.

14 Jonas, 1984, p. 90.

15 Amongst others, Sandel and Dworkin have pointed out that biotechnology has altered and increased our responsibility: Dworkin, 1999; Sandel, 2007, p. 87.

16 Jonas, 1984, p. 8.

17 See for example, Department of Health, 2006, p. 16; House of Commons Science and Technology Committee, 2005, p. 39-40; *Kamerstukken II* 2000-2001, 27 423, nr. 3 (*Memorandum Embryo Act*), p. 45-46.

18 BT-Drs. 11/5460, vom 25.10.1989 (*Bill and Memorandum Embryo Protection Act*), p. 7.

Because we simply do not know the possible risks, Jonas pleads for a "recognition of ignorance",[19] which implies focusing on knowing what we do not know. Consequently, not being able to foresee the consequences of our actions does not relieve us from our responsibility as long as we can foresee that we do not know the possible outcome.

7.2.1.1 Formal Responsibility

As explained above, Jonas distinguishes two senses of responsibility, that both have the same requirements (causal power, control, and foreseeability). In the first sense, having responsibility can be understood as being accountable for one's actions.[20] In this sense, the bearer of responsibility must answer for his deeds, for example through punishment or by paying compensation. Jonas calls this form of responsibility "formal responsibility."[21]

Although Jonas focuses on developing an ethical theory, and he does not discuss the applications of his concept of responsibility in law at length, he does point out briefly the connection between formal responsibility and legal liability in the context of both criminal and private law. I will use the concept of (legal) liability for those cases when law has legalised responsibility, that is to say, has acknowledged and attributed legal consequences to it, such as punishment or the obligation to pay compensation.[22] Formal responsibility can be found at the roots of both criminal and private law, but the concept functions in different ways in the different fields of law; what the person is held liable for differs. In private law, the emphasis lies on the consequences for which one is made responsible. One of the functions of liability law is the distribution of risks and the burdens of damage. If an agent can be held responsible for his actions and, accordingly, the consequences of his actions, he must compensate for the damage done. Because the emphasis lies on the consequences of the action, which is the damage done by it, law can be an active mechanism in assigning and distributing liability. A person can be held liable even if he himself did not cause the damage: "Legal responsibility to indemnify can be free of all guilt".[23] For example, a parent can be held liable for the damage caused by his or her child, just as an employer can be held liable for his employee's actions. Yet, Jonas argues that there remains some form of causality here: "The principle of causal attribution is still preserved in the

19 Jonas, 1984, p. 8.
20 Jonas, 1984, p. 90.
21 Jonas, 1984, p. 90.
22 Jonas himself also uses the term legal liability but he does not explicitly describe this term as legalised responsibility. See Jonas, 1984, p. 91. Formal responsibility does not always have to result legal liability, as the law sometimes explicitly excludes liability. For example, under Dutch law, a minor under the age of 14 cannot commit a tort, according to article 6:164 of the Dutch Civil Code. If a 13 year old deliberately threw a stone through his neighbour's window, all three requirements for responsibility are met and in that sense, he is responsible for his actions. From a legal perspective though, he is not liable.
23 Jonas, 1984, p. 91.

relationship, by virtue of which the superior generally represents in his person the performance of his subordinates."[24]

In criminal law, the focus of responsibility does not lie on the consequences of, and harm done, by one's actions, but primarily on the action itself. In criminal law, the conduct itself is deemed morally blameworthy, not (necessarily) because of its consequences. This is demonstrated by the punishability of victimless crimes or the preparation and failed attempt[25] of a criminal act, while in civil law the harm caused is a requirement for liability. Under criminal law "it is the quality rather than the causality of the deed which is the decisive point to answer for."[26]

According to Jonas, formal responsibility (both in the context of criminal and private law) is retroactive. A person is being held responsible for the actions taken. In other words, the responsibility comes into existence or is attributed after the action has taken place. Because the attribution of this type of responsibility is retroactive and depends on the agent's actions, this conception of responsibility does not provide moral guidance in itself. It does not primarily prescribe how we should act with regard to future persons or what we owe future children. As Jonas himself puts it, this notion of responsibility "does not itself set ends or disallow ends but is the mere formal burden on all causal acting among men, namely, that they can be called to account for it."[27] Instead, it raises questions about how we should deal with the increasing responsibility.

7.2.1.2 Substantive Responsibility

Unlike formal responsibility, the second sense of responsibility is able to offer normative guidance for actions that affect (possible) future people. Jonas describes this so-called "substantive responsibility" as responsibility for "particular objects that commits an agent to particular deeds concerning him."[28] In other words, having substantive responsibility for something or someone means that you bear the responsibility to care for it. This sense of responsibility differs from the first one in two ways. First of all, it establishes a relationship between the agent and another object or person, instead of focusing on the relation between the agent and his action, as formal responsibility does. Substantive responsibility creates a connection between the two, making the agent "act on [the object's]

24 Jonas, 1984, p. 91.
25 Jonas acknowledges that the completion of an action is relevant. "And it remains true that the successful deed weighs more heavily than the unsuccessful." Jonas, 1984, p. 91.
26 Jonas, 1984, p. 91.
27 Jonas, 1984, p. 92.
28 Jonas, 1984, p. 90.

behalf."[29] Second, responsibility in this sense is prospective. The responsibility does not arise ex post facto as a result of the agent's actions, but instead prescribes what needs to be done.[30] In other words, it creates obligations. Notably, these obligations are not derived from the corresponding right of the other, but on the simple fact that our actions, over which we can exercise control and the consequences of which we can foresee, affect the other. Or as Jonas puts it: "The well-being, the interest, the fate of others has, by circumstance or agreement, come under my care, which means that my control *over* it involves at the same time my obligation *for* it."[31] For this reason, through the concept of (substantive) responsibility, it is possible to construct obligations towards future people without having to rely on the rights of those future people. We have obligations towards the future child not because of the problematic assumption of the rights of the future child, but because our actions affect the child's existence.

7.2.1.3 Connection between Formal and Substantive Responsibility

Jonas is not the first who has brought up the concept of responsibility in addressing the moral challenges posed by biotechnology. Other authors have pointed out that the introduction of technology has shifted the boundary between chance and choice. Certain matters, such as being able to conceive a child and that child's genetic characteristics, used to belong to the domain of nature. But through technology, prospective parents can exercise control over these matters, becoming responsible for the choices they make. This increase in responsibility has left our vocabulary ill-equipped, resulting in moral challenges of a much more fundamental nature.[32] Jonas's theory of responsibility is of added value, because he distinguishes between formal responsibility, the form of responsibility addressed by for example Sandel and Dworkin, and substantive responsibility. While the former notion helps to identify why our moral vocabulary falls short in articulating the stakes in biotechnology, the latter interpretation of responsibility is capable of providing a theoretical framework for our obligations towards future people and future human life.

In his *Imperative of Responsibility*, Jonas discusses formal and substantive responsibility as separate notions. Formal responsibility is briefly discussed in a legal context as civil and criminal liability. Substantive responsibility is not put in a legal context, but is mostly addressed as an ethical concept, giving rise to moral duties. In order to get a more complete understanding of both senses and the connection between them, I want to take an extra

29 Jonas, 1984, p. 90.
30 Jonas, 1984, p. 92.
31 Jonas, 1984, p. 93.
32 Dworkin, 1999; Habermas, 2003, p. 39; Sandel, 2007, p. 9. See also the introduction of this study.

step, one that Jonas's ethical theory leaves unaddressed and discuss both senses of responsibility in a legal context.

First of all, it must be noted that there are several examples of legalised substantive responsibilities. This means that substantive responsibility can be a ground of legal duties. An example that has already been addressed in this research is the so-called double responsibility of fertility professionals towards both their patient who is undergoing fertility treatment and the child that may result from the fertility treatment, i.e. the future child. This double responsibility places a duty on the medical professional to take care of the well-being of the future child as well, a duty that has been acknowledged in different legal documents. Another example of legal duties arising out of substantive responsibility can be found in article 7:453 of the Dutch Civil Code.[33] This article prescribes that a physician has to act in conformity with the responsibilities laid upon him by professional standards. In the case of reproduction, this includes the physician's double responsibility for the well-being of both the pregnant woman and the child, as stated in the professional guidelines.[34]

In addition, a medical professional can be held *formally* responsible if he does not live up to his substantive responsibilities. In other words, neglecting duties arising out of substantive responsibilities can result in legal liability. This is illustrated by the Dutch wrongful life case.[35] In that case, the Dutch Supreme Court ruled that the physician in question had a responsibility or a duty of care towards the mother and the unborn child to conduct a prenatal test for genetic defects. By violating this responsibility he violated what, according to unwritten law, was proper social conduct, and therefore he had committed a tort towards the unborn child.[36] As a result, he was held liable for the damage suffered by the child. In sum, a person can be held liable, or formally responsible, for his actions if there was an underlying norm or obligation (arising out of substantive responsibility) that has been violated.

Moreover, substantive responsibilities play a role in deciding the scope of legal liability. In order to understand the relationship between formal and substantive responsibility better,

33 Art. 7:453 of the Dutch Civil Code: In providing the medical treatment, the care provider must observe the standards of a prudent care provider and, in doing so, he has to act in conformity with the responsibilities laid upon him by the professional standard for care providers. In Dutch: "De hulpverlener moet bij zijn werkzaamheden de zorg van een goed hulpverlener in acht nemen en handelt daarbij in overeenstemming met de op hem rustende verantwoordelijkheid, voortvloeiende uit de voor hulpverleners geldende professionele standaard." Translation by LtH.

34 NVOG Modelprotocol "Mogelijke morele contra-indicaties bij vruchtbaarheidsbehandelingen".

35 Hoge Raad 18 March 2005 ECLI:NL:HR:2005:AR5213 (*Baby Kelly*).

36 Hoge Raad 18 March 2005 ECLI:NL:HR:2005:AR5213 (*Baby Kelly*), R.O. 4.13.

it is important to realise that legalising formal responsibility, i.e. transforming it into a matter of criminal or civil liability, is a choice for the legislator. This choice can be based on different reasons, for example on socio-economic reasons to spread risk or deter unwanted behaviour, or on moral reasons because it is believed to be just that people should be held accountable for their behaviour. A choice to hold people legally liable for their actions can thus also be based on the intention to acknowledge moral duties arising from substantive responsibilities. Why is it so important to point out this link between substantive responsibility on the one hand and formal responsibility or legal liability on the other? The development of reproductive technologies gives rise to new types of lawsuits. As reproduction increasingly becomes a technological process, it allows for more errors,[37] such as embryo mix-ups, using material from the wrong or a genetically affected donor, or unintended harm through genetic modification. These errors have already resulted in legal claims, such as the Cramblett case,[38] in which the wrong donor was used, and the Dutch Karbaat case,[39] in which the fertility doctor used his own genetic material instead of that of a donor. Judges and legislators must now find a way to deal with these cases, as they struggle to identify the harm done within the existing legal framework. A developed concept of substantive responsibility in the context of reproduction may – in addition to our objective of conceptualising future people in the context of reproduction – be helpful for understanding and articulating the wrong done in these new lawsuits.

7.2.2 *The Object of our Responsibility:* The Idea of Man

Because, as a result of modern technology, our actions affect future people, they become the object of our responsibility. This does not only pertain to future people who come into existence in the near future. Because modern technology is characterised by its far-reaching consequences which transcend spatial and temporal boundaries, Jonas maintains that the "indefinite future… constitutes the relevant horizon of responsibility."[40] Notably, this claim does not in itself indicate what this responsibility entails. It does not tell us how we should act based on our responsibilities towards future people. Jonas answers this question by proposing a new ethical imperative: "Act so that the effects of your actions are compatible with the permanence of genuine human life."[41] This imperative implies that those existing now have a responsibility to ensure that in the future human beings still exist.[42] Moreover, as Jonas speaks of *genuine* human life, we are also responsible for the

37 van Beers, 2016b, p. 303-305.
38 Cramblett v. Midwest Sperm Bank, LLC, 230 F. Supp. 3d 865, 874 (N.D. Ill. 2017).
39 See for an extensive discussion of the Dutch Karbaat case and so-called fertility fraud, Madeira, 2020.
40 Jonas, 1984, p. 9.
41 Jonas, 1984, p. 11.
42 Jonas, 1984, p. 40.

quality of the lives of future people.[43] Ensuring future people enjoy life of a certain quality requires more than ensuring those future people enjoy a certain standard of well-being, or them being content with their lives: "[S]uch agreement or happiness might be the last thing we should wish for a future mankind, namely, if it were purchased with the dignity and vocation of man."[44] So, the attempt to elaborate on the responsibility of contemporary people towards future people must not be guided by the (potential) wishes of the future members of the human race, but by a normative account of what it means to be human. In Jonas's own words:

> ...it means that in the final analysis we consult not our successors' wishes (which can be of our own making) but rather the 'ought' that stands above both of us. To make it impossible for them to be what they ought to be is the true crime, behind which all frustration of their desires, culpable as it may be, takes second place. This means, in turn, that it is less the right of future men (namely, their right to happiness, which, given the uncertain concept of 'happiness', would be a precarious criterion anyway) than their duty over which we have to watch, namely their duty to be truly human: thus over their capacity for this duty – the capacity to even attribute it to themselves at all – which we could possibly rob them of with the alchemy of our 'utopian' technology. To stand guard over this onerous endowment of theirs is our cardinal duty toward the future of humanity as such (its existence presupposed), from which all specified duties toward the well-being of future humans are then derivative.[45]

Instead, according to Jonas the quality of life, or what we owe to future people, is determined by what he calls the Idea of Man.[46] This Idea of Man is Jonas's normative account of humanity, encompassing the characteristics of what makes us 'truly human'. This concept, which in Dutch is known as *mensbeeld* or in German is *Menschenbild*, is difficult to translate in English. Jonas himself describes it as follows: "a concept of the *human being* that informs us what the human *Good* is, what human beings should be, what we are all about, and what is advantageous for us – which at the same time involves what we must *not* be, what diminishes and distorts us."[47] This normative account of human beings is pivotal for a normative framework based on substantive responsibility, because,

43 Jonas, 1984, p. 40.
44 Jonas, 1984, p. 41.
45 Jonas, 1984, p. 41-42.
46 Jonas, 1984, p. 43.
47 H. Jonas, *Mortality and Morality. A search for the good after Auschwitz*, Evanston, Northwestern University Press, 1996, p. 104.

as Jonas points out, it is the object of our responsibility.[48] The Idea of Man sets the parameters for our responsibility towards future people. This normative framework is therefore an essential element in the conceptualisation of the future child. Together with the conceptual framework discussed above, it elucidates how we can incorporate future life into our normative thinking and what we owe to it.

Although it is practically impossible to give a complete and detailed account of the human person, the contours of Jonas's Idea of Man can be discerned throughout his work. For Jonas, all life is an end in itself.[49] Human beings, however, are according to Jonas the only known species capable of assuming responsibility,[50] and for this reason the only beings that are capable of acting morally.[51] This capacity is, according to him, "a distinguishing and decisive feature of human existence."[52] In other words, for Jonas the ability to assume responsibility is regarded as one of those aspects that makes us human, making it part of his Idea of Man. The reason why man is capable of assuming responsibility is man's freedom or autonomy. According to Jonas, it "lies in man's *ontological* capability to choose knowingly and willingly between alternative actions. Responsibility, therefore is complementary to *freedom*."[53] Freedom to choose and responsibility are intrinsically linked: after all, in addition to causal power and foreseeability, control over action is a requirement for responsibility.[54] Once a person is free to choose between alternative actions, he becomes automatically responsible for it.[55]

Freedom and the capacity for responsibility are part of the Idea of Man, and therefore Jonas maintains that the conditions under which future people are brought into existence must be compatible with these characteristics: "we must make sure the *conditions* of their existence do not cause this capacity (which depends upon the freedom of the subject) to disappear."[56] However, modern technologies may form a threat to both human existence and the Idea of Man. As the effects of modern technology transgress spatial and temporal boundaries, modern technology bears the risk of what Jonas calls physical annihilation

48 Jonas, 1984, p. 43. "With this imperative we are, strictly speaking, not responsible to the future human individuals but to the *idea* of Man."
49 Morris, 2013, p. 166.
50 Jonas, 1996, p. 101, 105.
51 Kampowski, 2014, p. 121; Morris, 2013, p. 121, 125.
52 Jonas, 1996, p. 106.
53 Jonas, 1996, p. 101. Jonas calls this an ontological capability because he believes it, the capacity to assume responsibility, is characteristic of the being of man, as an empirical fact. Jonas, 1996, p. 105. See also Morris, 2013, p. 124.
54 See section 7.2.1.
55 Jonas, 1996, p. 101. Jonas: "...with my act as such, I am responsible (and just as responsible if I omit it)..."
56 Jonas, 1996, p. 106.

and existential impoverishment.[57] Jonas does not only fear that technology may result in an ecological catastrophe that would wipe the human species off the face of the earth, but warns us that it is equally destructive for mankind "if the end result is global misery that allows only for an imperative of naked survival devoid of all feeling of ethical responsibility."[58] By this, he means that modern technology may compromise the conditions for the capacity of morality, i.e. responsibility. He lists several specific technologies that, in his eyes, bear the potential to erode or destroy that what makes us human, including the automation of all work and psychological and biological behavioural control. According to Jonas, the most threatening is genetic engineering.[59]

So why is genetic engineering, or put more broadly, control over our offspring's genetic constitution with the help of reproductive technologies, disruptive for the individual's freedom? Underlying this question is the assumption that an original genetic constitution, free from predetermination by others, is essential to understanding ourselves as free human beings.[60] Freedom in this sense must not be understood as absence of genetic determinism: the crux for Jonas does not lie in the fact that the genetically manipulated individual would be incapable of making his own choices regarding his life or that the number of options to choose from would be limited. The problem is that in making these choices the individual will always feel as if he owed something to his creators, preventing the individual from seeing himself as the sole author of his life choices and the originator of his actions and aspirations. Or as Kampowski explains Jonas's ideas: "... the knowledge of owing part of one's very identity to the arbitrary decisions of peers would be a liability in the task of making one's life completely one's own because one could always blame part of who one is without ever being able to make these characteristics really one's own."[61] In other words, freedom may be compromised not because of a reduction of the number of choices, but because authenticity of that choice is compromised.

Because one's self-understanding as authentic, and thus free and autonomous, can be frustrated by a predetermined genetic makeup, Jonas stresses the importance of a natural combination of genetic material.[62] Sexual reproduction, but also artificial reproduction

57 Jonas, 1996, p. 105, 108.
58 Jonas, 1996, p. 108.
59 Jonas, 1996, p. 108.
60 This idea is not only postulated by Jonas, but also by Habermas and Sandel. Habermas, 2003, p. 58; Sandel, 2007, p. 81-82.
61 Jonas, 1996, p. 154.
62 The idea of birth as a new, original beginning is also discussed by Habermas and Sandel. Habermas, for example, inspired by Jonas, maintains that the person himself must be able to trace his own origin back to "a beginning which eludes human disposal". A new birth constitutes such a natural beginning, without

that does not include modifying or extensive selective[63] technologies, produces a *genotype* that is "a novum in itself."[64] Such a genotype is not created or designed by a third party with a specific intention, but a random combination created by nature or fate, and therefore, the child can understand itself as the originator of his actions and aspirations. In addition to this self-understanding as an authentic originator, Jonas also claims that a non-predetermined genotype allows the child to become itself without being guided by the expectations and plans of others.[65] Jonas develops his argument in the context of reproductive cloning. He states that the clone's genotype and phenotype are already known, possibly to the clone himself, but most importantly to its creators. With this knowledge comes "expectations, predictions, hopes and fears, goal settings, comparisons, standards of success and failure, of fulfillment and disappointment."[66] The counterargument that knowledge about the donor prototype is not (fully) applicable to the clone, because the latter is born in a different time and will thus face different circumstances, is dismissed by Jonas. It is not relevant that the knowledge about the clone's genotype is real or accurate. What matters is that its creators *believe* to have such knowledge (after all, they have chosen the clone's genotype is chosen with a specific idea or goal in mind). This assumed knowledge of the original gives rise to expectations and assumptions and is "paralyzing for the spontaneity of becoming himself."[67] One's identity, both as an individual and as a member of mankind, is something that one must discover over the course of one's life, by living it. To this aim, Jonas pleads for a right to ignorance, which he deems a precondition of freedom[68] and authentic action.[69] In order to guarantee our self-understanding as free, authentic, and responsible beings, human beings need to be able to live their lives without being controlled or determined by pre-existing expectations.[70] This requires that not only

---

which the individual "could not perceive himself as the initiator of his actions and aspirations." See Habermas, 2003, p. 58-59.

63 Reproductive cloning, PGD and selecting gamete donors can all be understood as a form of selection, although in case of reproductive cloning the control over the end product is far greater than in the case of selecting a sperm donor with desired traits, in the hope that they will be inherited by the child.

64 Jonas, 1974, p. 159.

65 It may seem that Jonas's argument is slightly different from Habermas's. Whereas Habermas argues that the control over the child's genotype prevents the child from understanding himself as the originator of his actions, Jonas argues that the child is barred from becoming himself. For Jonas, becoming oneself is a necessary condition for one's self-understanding as a free and authentic being.

66 Jonas, 1974, p. 161.

67 Jonas, 1974, p. 161. Later on Jonas elaborates this point, stating that assumed knowledge over one's genetic identity results in assumed knowledge over one's personal identity and that this "spurious manifestness at the beginning destroys that condition of all authentic growth. No matter whether this "knowledge" is true or false…it is pernicious to the task of selfhood: existentially significant is what the cloned individual *thinks* – is compelled to think – of himself, not what he "is" is the substance-sense of being." Jonas, 1974, p. 162.

68 Jonas, 1974, p. 159.

69 Jonas, 1974, p. 163.

70 Of course, one can argue that every parent has certain expectations and hopes for their child, but it is hard to deny that in the case of determining a child's genetic constitution, prospective parents force these

the individual himself is unaware of his genetic constitution, but that his environment is so as well; something that only can be achieved by a natural recombination of genetic material. Otherwise, "he is antecedently robbed of the *freedom* which only under the protection of ignorance can thrive."[71]

In Jonas's view, our genetic constitution forms a key element of what makes us human. Yet, the crux of his argument is not that the human genome itself must be protected. Instead, intentionally determining one's genome implies a problematic attitude towards other human persons in which the other is not respected as an autonomous being. The protection of the human being as free and autonomous requires banning technologies that would approach future people as design objects. Jonas only discusses this argument in the context of reproductive cloning, but it can also be applied to germline modification, an idea which is taken up by Habermas in *The Future of Human Nature*.[72] Habermas refers to Jonas's argument that the problem with genetic modification is not the actual effects on one's phenotypes, which would imply genetic determinism, but the intention with which the genetic modification is executed.[73] As a result of this intention that is incorporated in the child's genetic constitution, the child can no longer understand itself as the originator of its actions.[74]

Jonas himself takes another route in criticizing genetic engineering, one which reveals another element of his Idea of Man. He starts by pointing out the fundamental difference between reproductive cloning and genetic modification: reproductive cloning works with existing, naturally given genes, "rather than the introduction of newly contrived genotypes."[75] Jonas even calls this "the one saving grace of cloning", because it honours "the species that is."[76] Genetic engineering, which he understands as the possibility of removing and adding genes or reshuffling the DNA pattern, is at the moment highly experimental and the results are difficult to predict. Children born as a result of this

---

expectations on the child. See also Habermas, 2003, p. 49-51.

71 Jonas, 1974, p. 162.

72 Habermas, 2003.

73 Habermas, 2003, p. 124n54: "They fail to see that here [reproductive cloning], as in the case of enhancing eugenics, it is primarily the intention governing the eugenic intervention that counts. The person concerned knows that the manipulation has been carried out with the sole intention of acting on the phenotypic molding of a specific genetic program, and this of course on condition that the technologies required for this goal have proved to be successful."

74 Habermas, 2003, p. 59-60, 63. In addition to jeopardizing freedom, Habermas also argues that genetic engineering violates the principle of equality, because the child is no longer treated as an equal, or what he calls a *second person*, but rather as an object of their parents' desires, giving rise to an unequal relationship between the designer and the design object. Habermas, 2003, p. 43, 52.

75 Jonas, 1974, p. 164.

76 Jonas, 1974, p. 165.

technology are not created for their own sake, Jonas argues, but as a utility for the perfection of technology. He fears that this leads to the abandonment of the idea that mankind ought not to be instrumentalised and objectified; that men are not for the use of other men.[77] His critique on genetic modification is grounded in Kant's categorical imperative and the idea that every human being must always be treated as an end in himself. However, his critique, that mankind is used for the perfection of the technology, is only applicable to the use of genetic modification in its developmental stage. Once the technology is fully developed, the future child is no longer born as a utility for perfection. In my opinion, genetic modification can nonetheless be objectionable since the same line of reasoning of the argument against reproductive cloning can be applied. Genetic modification is done with a certain intention, and therefore the creators' hopes, plans, and intentions are forced upon the child. Of course, compared to reproductive cloning, genetic modification facilitates control on a different scale. Germline modification can also be applied to one single gene, while in the case of reproductive cloning, the child's complete genotype is determined. Moreover, genetic modification can also be applied with a therapeutic goal, aiming to remove a genetic defect that may result in a severe illness. In order to determine to what extent germline modification indeed disrespects the future child as an autonomous person, we must understand how these specific applications affect the human person's self-understanding as an equal and autonomous being.

To summarise, in Jonas's Idea of Man, mankind is characterised by its capacity for autonomy, and thus for responsibility. Although Jonas sees these characteristics as inherent to human beings, he also points out that they can be jeopardised by modern technologies. Reproductive technologies may endanger the preconditions of freedom if they strip the individual of the possibility to understand himself as a free and authentic being. Consequently, protecting the human being as a free and autonomous end in himself does not so much require safeguarding a certain number of choices, but rather maintaining certain preconditions for mankind's self-understanding. In addition to this strong focus on freedom and responsibility, Jonas also stresses the idea that human beings must not be instrumentalised. This part of his Idea of Man comes to the fore in his discussion of genetic modification. Jonas fears that the clinical use of genetic modification may not simply result in genetic damage, but in reducing the first generations to test subjects, since there is no other way to discover long term consequences.

What are the implications if reproductive technologies are used that are an affront to this normative account of humanity? In my opinion, this must not be understood as a claim that genetically altered people, clones, or designer babies are not human or that they have

---

77 Jonas, 1974, p. 166.

lost their humanity. Technologies that are an affront to the normative account of the human person, do not take away or mitigate their humanity, but violate it. In a similar vein, it is uncommon to claim that a person who is subjected to torture or inhuman treatment has lost his dignity; instead, we would say that his dignity is violated. Jonas's critique is that the users of these technologies fail in their responsibility towards the resulting child because the mode of conception they used fails to respect the child as a free and autonomous end in itself. In other words, Jonas's Idea of Man is not a tool to distinguish between the human person and other forms of 'no longer human life'. Instead, this conception of the human person tells us what we owe to future people and indicates how we should act in a way that respects them as human persons. In conclusion, Jonas's normative framework together with the conceptual framework, can provide an alternative understanding of the future child within the regulations on reproduction.

7.3 RESPONSIBILITY FOR THE FUTURE CHILD

Jonas's imperative of responsibility offers a basis for the construction of a theoretical framework that can deal with the future child. That is, that can help us understand how we can legally and ethically conceptualise future people and what we owe to them. This theoretical framework, which includes a normative account of the human person, can also address and make sense of the normative foundations of the existing regulations on reproduction. In doing so, it facilitates the possibility of legal-philosophical and ethical reflection upon the regulation of reproductive technologies and the extent to which we are allowed to interfere in the conception of the future child. However, in order to provide a theoretical framework for the unique entity that is the future child, Jonas's theory needs to be elaborated further. As explained above, Jonas focuses on future mankind as a whole as the object of our responsibility, and he discusses our duties towards future people only in the context of extreme cases, such as reproductive cloning and extensive genetic modification. The regulations on reproduction as discussed in chapter 2 are more complex and nuanced than the cases discussed by Jonas. In addition to that, the regulation is geared at preventing certain individual lives, rather than ensuring the future existence of mankind. The confrontation of Jonas's theory of responsibility with the regulations on reproduction raises several questions that need to be addressed in order to construct a theoretical framework that is able to conceptualise the future child. First, in section 7.3.1, I address the conceptual framework, stating that not only future mankind as a whole, but also the future child whose existence is prevented is the object of our responsibility. I elaborate on the relation between individual future people and future mankind and explain why the responsibility for future mankind also implies a responsibility for its individual members. Then, in section 7.3.2, I discuss the normative framework that offers an answer to what our responsibility towards future people entails. In my opinion, Jonas's conception of the human person as a free and autonomous end in himself, i.e. his Idea of Man, can justify the three values that constitute the depiction of the human person in the regulations on reproduction: well-being, identity, and dignity. In section 7.3.2, I discuss how protecting the values of human dignity, well-being, and identity contributes to safeguarding the idea of the human being as a free and autonomous end in itself. This section also identifies the questions that need answering in order to be able to understand what we owe to the future child in the context of specific reproductive technologies. By adapting the conceptual and normative framework, I will be able to construct an alternative theoretical framework: one that is capable of conceptualising the future child in a coherent way, while also making sense of the values and the conception of the human person that underlies the regulations on reproduction. With the help of this theoretical framework, it becomes possible to critically reflect upon these normative/ethical foundations of the regulation of reproductive technologies and to address the regulatory challenges posed by new reproductive technologies.

7.3.1 The Conceptual Framework: the Collective and the Individual

In Jonas's theory of responsibility, future mankind is what we as contemporary people are responsible for. He maintains that we have a duty to ensure that in the future, human beings will exist and to ensure that their humanity will be respected. Although Jonas speaks of future human life as a collective, this conceptual framework can also be applied to the future child in individual cases. In order to adapt this conceptual framework for the future child, two questions must be answered. First, why does a duty to ensure future mankind's existence not contradict the prevention of the future child in some cases? Second, how can we derive responsibilities for an individual entity from our responsibilities towards humankind as a whole? Answering these questions reveals why it is so complicated to understand the future child whose existence is prevented. The crux lies in the asymmetry between existence and non-existence: what we are responsible for regarding the future child depends on whether the child is prevented from coming into existence or not.

At first sight, it may seem that Jonas's theory of responsibility contradicts the idea that the prevention of the future child is justified. After all, one could assume that if we bear the responsibility to ensure that in the future humankind still exists preventing the future child from coming into existence does not contribute to this responsibility, but rather frustrates it. Importantly, the theory of the responsibility to ensure future human life is not at odds with preventing the future child in individual cases. Jonas's theory does not focus on individual persons: the duty to ensure that there is a future mankind "must not be confounded with the conditional duty of each and every man to exist."[78] In other words, Jonas focuses on future mankind as a whole, rather than the individual future members of that group. The reason for this is that Jonas assumes that future people who do not exist (yet) do not have a right to come into existence.[79] After all, as discussed in chapter 6, existence is a prerequisite for having rights or interests. Consequently, the duty to ensure a future humankind cannot be based on a right to come into existence of its members.[80] Rather, Jonas assumes that mankind itself has an inherent value, because human life, and all life, is a good in itself. Because of this, it deserves protection and preservation, giving rise to his imperative to ensure that in the future, mankind still exists, and that the humanity of these future people remains intact.

Jonas's imperative towards future mankind includes a normative idea of what it means to be human, and this element is crucial for understanding how the individual future child whose existence is prevented fits the conceptual framework. The collective notion of humanity that Jonas refers to can be affected by what happens to its individual members. That our responsibility for the future existence of mankind does not imply a duty to bring every individual child into existence does not mean that we do not have to consider individual human beings. In fact, the consequences of our treatment of individual beings are not confined to those individual cases. As different authors already have pointed out, the violation of the normative account of humanity or human dignity on an individual level does not merely affect the individual in question, but others as well.[81] For example, in her reflection on dignity in the context of inhumane treatment, Hale points out that dignity is "janus-faced"[82] – violating someone else's dignity affects one's own humanity. Hale continues, "Respect for the dignity of others is not only respect for the essential humanity of others; it is also respect for one's own dignity and essential humanity."[83] A similar point is made by Dworkin: "You cannot act in a way that denies the intrinsic importance of any human life without an insult to your own dignity."[84] Actions that are an affront to the normative account of the human person are not restricted to an individual level, but bear larger consequences. According to Günther, these consequences reach even

78 Jonas, 1984, p. 37. In addition in this vein is that Jonas's statement that the individual may have a right to suicide under particular circumstances, but mankind as a whole does not have a right to suicide or to terminate its existence. Jonas, 1984, p. 36-37.

79 Jonas, 1984, p. 38-39.

80 Chapter 6 already addressed the impossibility of a right to be born.

81 See also sections 2.4.2.3. and 3.4.

82 Quoting Mountfield and Singh, B. Hale, 'Dignity', *Journal of Social Welfare and Family Law*, Vol. 31, No. 2, 2009, p. 106.

83 Hale, 2009, p. 106.

84 R. Dworkin, *Is democracy possible here? Principles for a new political debate*, Princeton, Princeton University Press, 2006, p. 16.

further than those directly involved. In his comment on the German Embryo Protection Act, he maintains that reproductive technologies that are banned in name of human dignity, would violate both the dignity of the resulting child or other involved parties, and the dignity of the entire human species.[85]

Jonas also discusses the connection between the individual and the collective dimension of human life. Jonas's Idea of Man, or the normative account of the human person, consists of an ideal, something that we should aim to achieve for all human beings. If we allow this ideal to be violated on an individual level, then not only is the humanity of that individual affected, but also the ideal itself is compromised. Even if a few individual human beings are allowed to be treated or conceived in a way that would violate this normative account, "... the very unity of the species would be broken up, and the meaning of the name 'man', no longer unique, would become equivocal."[86] This is because of the interconnectedness of an individual member of the human race and the collective idea of what it means to be human. What we allow to happen on an individual scale tells us something about how human beings in general can be treated. Therefore, violating our responsibility towards one individual can violate the collective idea of mankind as a whole, from which our self-understanding as free and autonomous beings is derived.[87] In conclusion, our responsibility for future mankind also implies a responsibility in individual cases, and our responsibility for individual future people is determined by the collective image of humanity.

This brings us to the key question: how can we conceptualise the future child within the conceptual framework of responsibility? Because of the entanglement between individual human beings and the collective account of humanity, our responsibility for future mankind and its humanity implies a responsibility towards the individual future child. In order to protect the normative account of the human being, we bear the responsibility to ensure that individual future persons can live up to this ideal. In other words, the future child is the object of our responsibility. For this reason, if a child comes into existence under circumstances that are an affront to its humanity, it can complain that we failed in

---

85 Günther, Taupitz and Kaiser, 2014, p. 331. With regard to reproductive cloning, in German: "Der Versuch des Klonens zu Fortpflanzungszwecken verletzt und entsprechend schützt §6 Abs. 1 deshalf die Menschenwürde (Art. 1 Abs. 1 GG) aller Betroffenen, des kopierten Menschen, des geklonten Menschen, der den Klon austragenden Frau wie der Menschheit ingesamt als Gattung." And with regard to human-animal hybrids, p. 340: "Als verletzt werden in Betracht gezogen die Menschenwürde des missbrauchten menschlichen Embryos und (...) die Würde der Menschheit insgesamt (als Gattung).". This view is not accepted by Spickhoff, who rejects the idea that Article 1 GG also protects the dignity of the species because the human species cannot be the subject of fundamental rights. Spickhoff, 2011, §1 BGB nr 13.

86 Jonas, 1974, p. 165.

87 B.C. van Beers, 'Nosce te ipsum. Over *homo sapiens* en *homo juridicus* in een tijdperk van posthumane technologieën.' in: B. van Beers and I. van Domselaar (eds.), *Humo Duplex. De dualiteit van de mens in recht, filosofie en sociologie*, Boom Juridisch, Den Haag, 2017c, p. 327-328; Pessers, 2016, p. 209-210.

our responsibility towards it, and because of that, we wronged the child. Since this individual case is connected with the perspective of humankind as a whole, we failed in our responsibility towards future mankind and the normative account of the human being, as well as in our responsibility towards this future child.

The situation changes if the future child is prevented from coming into existence. This is the core reason why integrating the future child in our normative discussion is such a highly complex matter. The complexity of reproductive issues is caused by the asymmetry between existence and non-existence. What we are responsible for in cases in which the future child does come into existence differs in a way from those cases in which the future child is prevented from coming into existence. If a child will come into existence, it is possible to anticipate the interests and rights it will have once it is born.[88] Moreover, as explained above, if the child is born, it can retroactively complain if we wronged it by not respecting its humanity. However, if the future child does not come into existence, that is, in those cases in which we aim to prevent its existence, we cannot say that our actions honour or violate our responsibility for the future child, because it does not exist and never will. So, who or what is protected if the child is prevented from coming into existence? We cannot say that the child is worse off or better off by not existing at all. Therefore, the regulations that allow for the prevention of the future child's existence is not about whether or not the child is harmed by being brought into existence, or whether it is better off not existing at all. It is rather that we do not want to allow certain practices, because they violate the idea of humanity and contradict our self-understanding as human beings. Indeed, by preventing the future child's existence, we prevent the situation in which someone's self-understanding as a free and autonomous human being is compromised. Yet, the prevention of this situation does not benefit the non-existent entity who might have existed otherwise. This prevention, however, does serve the interests of the collective notion of humanity. Preventing the future child's existence is thus not about protecting the interests of a non-existent subject or protecting it from being harmed; it is about securing our self-understanding as human beings and making sure future human people can be inscribed into this normative account of humanity.

Conceptualising the future child as the object of our responsibility in this way helps to understand why a theoretical framework based on responsibility is more adequate than the 'interests of the future child' construction. A responsibility-based approach is fundamentally different from the interests-construction. First, the responsibility approach does not ignore the consequences involved in regulating reproductive technologies that transcend the individual sphere. A fortiori, our responsibility towards mankind as a whole

88 See also chapter 6.

is the starting point in shaping our duties towards future individuals. Second, the responsibility approach as reconstructed in this chapter can take into account the asymmetry between existence and non-existence, because it does not have to rely on the interests or rights of a non-existent entity. Because it emphasises the entanglement between human life in its individual and collective forms, it does not need to seek a justification in the interests of the future child whose existence is prevented. Instead, the responsibility approach shows that the prevention of the future child, or rather banning certain modes of reproduction aims to protect our humanity. As such, it avoids the internal contradictions inherent to the interests-construction.

Moreover, the responsibility approach offers in my opinion also a better solution to the non-identity problem than the proposed principles discussed in chapter 4. The principles proposed by Parfit and Glover can be understood to a certain extent as utilitarian or consequentialist, because they determine what we owe to the future child (and whether its existence should be prevented) by comparing it to possible alternative situations in which another child is born. As discussed in chapter 4, these principles face an important shortcoming. Parfit's Same Number Quality Claim and Glover's concept of "transpersonal harm"[89] can only be applied to cases in which an equal number of people would exist in all alternative situations. The regulating reproduction, on the contrary, involves many cases in which no substitute child would (necessarily) come into existence if the future child's existence is prevented. One could think of denying prospective parents access to fertility treatment, or the prohibition of a technology like reproductive cloning or genetic manipulation. To address these cases, we need a theoretical framework that explains why the prevention of certain lives is justified or required, even in cases where no alternative child comes into existence. The responsibility approach does not suffer from this shortcoming. This approach is deontological: our duties towards the future child are not dependent on what other possible outcomes could be, but on whether or not the future child's humanity is affected. Therefore, it can analyse each case individually, and can also be applied to cases in which there is no substitute for the future child. After all, it determines our duties towards the future child based on the notion of humanity, not on whether there is a better alternative available.

89 Section 4.3.2.

7.3.2 The Normative Framework: the Notion of the Human in the Regulation of Reproduction

The previous section illustrated that the conceptual and the normative frameworks are connected to each other: the individual future child is also the object of our responsibility, because individual cases may affect and erode the collective self-understanding of mankind. This, however, does not answer what exactly our responsibilities towards the future child entail, that is, what we owe to future people in the context of regulating reproductive technologies. The contents of these duties are determined by a normative account of what it means to be human, i.e. by the normative framework. In his ethics of responsibility, Jonas labelled his interpretation of this normative framework the Idea of Man, in which the human being is perceived as free, autonomous and therefore capable of responsibility, and as an end in himself. Since these are essential characteristics for human beings to understand themselves as 'truly human', it is our responsibility that future people are respected as autonomous ends in themselves.

As the regulation of reproduction is based on an implied idea of what we owe to future people, it implicitly adopts a normative account of the human person. This account needs to be explicated in order to articulate what is at stake in the regulation of reproduction and enable ethical reflection upon how we should deal with future people. As I argued in the previous chapters, the 'interests of the future child' construction falls short in this aspect. Although the interests-construction does include several assumptions about what is important to the future child and which values are in need of protection, it cannot make sense of these values as explained in chapter 3, nor is it sufficiently clear about why certain values are allegedly in the future child's interests. Cohen has pointed out that the 'interests of the future child' construction can serve as a smoke screen.[90] Without a substantive idea of what these interests are and why they are so vital to the human person, that is, what is essential for our humanity, anything can be said to be in the future child's interest. Consequently, the interests of the future child becomes an empty concept, that can be used by anyone to make their case.[91] Therefore, critical reflection upon the regulations on reproduction needs a more fundamental notion of the human person. Such an account of the human person can offer a justification for the values of well-being, identity, and dignity and thus explain why these values are deemed important to the human person. With the

90 Cohen, 2011, p. 426. A similar point is made by the Dutch GCRP: the interests of the future child can be (ab)used as a magic formula that covers up the real motivations and unfounded opinions. Government Committee on the Reassessment of Parenthood (GCRP), 2016, p. 9.

91 Also Jonas notes that when we speak of the interests and needs of future generations, or "our successors' wishes", it is likely contemporary people who determine what these interests are, or in other words, those interests and wishes "can be of our own making." Jonas, 1984, p. 41.

help of such a fundamental account, it becomes possible to critically assess the way these notions are interpreted, determine what we owe to the future child in the context of reproduction and finally, take up the challenges posed to us by the developments of new reproductive technologies.

Jonas's depiction of the human as free, autonomous, and an end in himself provides a useful starting point for a more fundamental notion of the human person that can offer a justification for the values of well-being, identity, and human dignity. The reason why Jonas's Idea of Man provides a useful starting point is because of the similarities with the legal depiction of the human person,[92] beyond the regulatory frameworks on reproduction. Both in the areas of criminal and private law across the three legal systems studied, the legal person is perceived as an autonomous entity who can engage in contracts and be held criminally liable for misconduct. Moreover, human rights treaties emphasise that the human person should be treated as an end in himself.[93] Also, it shows important similarities with the concept of human dignity, which van Beers calls law's normative account of the human being.[94] Therefore, I believe the idea of the human person as an autonomous and free end in itself is able to make sense of the normative account of humanity that forms the foundation of the regulations on reproduction. Put differently, compared to the depiction some authors seem to have adopted in the context of the wrongful life debate that focuses solely on harm and well-being,[95] Jonas's idea of man provides a better justification of this depiction of the human person.

However, Jonas's Idea of Man needs further elaboration in order to be capable of addressing the various complexities that are involved in procreation. Jonas mostly focuses on the extremes, such as reproductive cloning and extensive genetic engineering. Yet, as shown in chapter 2, the regulation of reproductive technologies is much more complex and nuanced, with technologies being applied with less far-reaching effects and with different ends. PGT, for example, does allow a certain control over the future child's genome, but through selection and not modification. MRT does not alter the nuclear DNA, but recombines nuclear DNA and mitochondrial DNA, which makes up only 0,1% of the total DNA and according to some is not responsible for personal characteristics and traits.[96] In addition to that, most technologies are applied with the purpose of creating a healthy

92 See for example, Asser/De Boer, Kolkman & Salomons 1-I 2020/42.

93 Jonas's Idea of Man also shares important similarities with the depiction of the human person in human rights law. For example, the Preamble and Article 1 of the Universal Declaration of Human Rights stresses the inherent dignity, equality, and freedom of the human person.

94 van Beers, 2017b, p. 129.

95 See section 4.5

96 Department of Health, 2014, p. 15.

child, rather than designing the perfect offspring, assuming there is a relevant difference between treatment and enhancement. Moreover, in chapter 2, certain concepts were discussed that Jonas barely touches upon, such as the reasonable standard of well-being, personal identity, and the right to access information about one's own origins. For these reasons, if we want to understand what our responsibility towards the future child entails in the context of reproduction, we must address the questions that are raised by these specific aspects of the regulatory frameworks. Or, put differently, the regulatory frameworks confront us with questions that can only be answered by supplementing Jonas's normative framework. That is, by elaborating what the responsibility for the human person as autonomous and an end in himself requires, with regard to, for instance, PGT, donor anonymity, and gene-editing for medical purposes. The following sections explore what this perception of humanity could mean with regard to the regulatory frameworks that centre around human dignity (section 7.3.2.1), well-being (section 7.3.2.2), and personal identity (section 7.3.2.3). This exploration reveals that there are different aspects or components of autonomy, varying from the metaphysical conditions for one's self-understanding as autonomous and self-authorship, to having different possibilities to choose from. My primary aim here is to point out where Jonas's Idea of Man needs to be supplemented in order to get a more complete idea of the account of humanity underlying the regulations on reproduction, by identifying the questions that need further discussion. Although I offer possible suggestions on how different assumptions can be in line with the perception of the human being as autonomous, it is not my intention to offer a definite answer to these questions. This has to be discussed further in the public debate. As a scholar, I can only identify possible lines of reasoning building on Jonas's normative framework, but the question as to 'what makes us human' is in the end one that must be addressed within the democratic arena.

7.3.2.1 Human Dignity

The concept of human dignity is closely related to Jonas's Idea of Man, as they both involve a notion of what it means to be human. For this reason, it is not surprising that the responsibility approach is better equipped to articulate the stakes in the regulatory frameworks that invoke human dignity than a vocabulary focusing on individual interests. In previous chapters, I already discussed how the interests-construction struggles to articulate the concept of human dignity. Often, the appeal to human dignity is met with the critique that a violation of human dignity, for example through sex selection, does not necessarily result in a life not worth living, and as a result, the future child's interests are not actually harmed.

One of the benefits of the theoretical framework based on responsibility is that it can account for the multifaceted subject of human dignity, whereas the interests-construction cannot. Because the responsibility approach addresses the intertwinement between the individual subject and mankind as a whole, it can support the idea that there can be multiple subjects of human dignity that follows from the different regulatory frameworks that invoke human dignity. As discussed in chapter 2, the regulatory frameworks are not always clear on *whose* human dignity is at stake: is it the dignity of the individual human being who is conceived with the help of reproductive cloning or germline modification, or the dignity of the human species as a whole? The Memorandum to the German Embryo Protection Act, for example, does not refer to the subject of human dignity at all, while the Memorandum to the Dutch Embryo Act seems to refer to different subjects, both mankind as a whole and individual subjects, with regard to different topics.[97] From the perspective of the responsibility approach that assumes the intertwinement of the individual and the collective idea of humanity, it becomes clear that these technologies do not only violate the dignity of the individual resulting from the process, but also the dignity of humanity as a whole. This is also emphasised in German commentaries on the regulation,[98] for example by Günther in his analysis of the German Embryo Protection Act. The bans on reproductive cloning and the creation of chimaeras protect not only the human dignity of the resulting child and other individuals that are involved, such as the persons whose original genetic material is used and the woman who carries the child to term,[99] but also the dignity of the whole of mankind as a species.[100] In other words, allowing these technologies would jeopardise the dignity of both the resulting child and all members of mankind, because they erode the foundation of our self-understanding as free and autonomous beings. Allowing humans, or more specifically, the future child, to be treated as commodities or to be genetically manipulated to fulfil their parents' desires implies a perspective on the human being in general that, under some circumstances, commodification or instrumentalisation of the human person is acceptable. In order to address this collective

97 See also van Beers, 2009a, p. 136.

98 In Article 1 of the German Grundgesetz, for example, both dimensions are represented. This article does not only aim to protect the dignity of the individual, but also the dignity of the human species. Sachs, 2014, Art. 1 I, nr. 52; L. Witteck and C. Eric, 'Straf- und verfassungsrechtliche Gedanken zum Verbot des Klonens von Menschen', *Medizinrecht*, Vol. 6, No. 5, 2003, p. 262; Velte, 2015, p. 69-70. Nonetheless, it is unclear whether Article 1 I GG implies a duty to protect the dignity of humanity or the human species: under German law, human dignity is codified into a fundamental right and critics have argued that 'humanity' itself cannot be the subject of legal rights, including Art. 1 I GG. Dreier, 2014, Art 1 I, nr. 115ff; C. Enders, "Probleme der Gentechnologie in grundrechtsdogmatischer Sicht.' in: R. Mellinghoff and H.-H. Trute (eds.), *Die Leistungsfähigkeit des Rechts. Methodik, Gentechnologie, Internationales Verwaltungsrecht*, R. v. Decker & C.F. Müller, Heidelberg, 1988, p. 197; Spranger, 2010, p. 97-100; R. Müller-Terpitz, *Der Schutz des pränatalen Lebens*, Tübingen, Mohr Siebeck 2007, p. 330-333.

99 With regard to human-animal hybrids, see Günther, Taupitz and Kaiser, 2014, p. 340. in German: "Zudem gerät in Mitleidenschaft die Würde desjenigen Menschen, dessen Erbgut sich in einer Chimäre oder einem Hybridwesen fortpflanzt."

100 Günther, Taupitz and Kaiser, 2014, p. 331, 340.

dimension, an individual-transcending approach is needed, such as a theoretical framework based on responsibility.

In addition to addressing the intertwinement between the collective and the individual, the responsibility approach's normative framework can make sense of various aspects of the normative account of the human person that underlies the regulations on reproduction. In fact, the depiction of the human person as an autonomous end in himself can also fill in in certain gaps in some assumptions that come to the fore in in the regulations on reproduction. Because a theory of responsibility connects the individual dimension to the collective and explicitly explains how the autonomy of the human being can be affected, it can address the way reproductive technologies affect humanity as a whole. A striking illustration of how this normative framework is capable of clarifying the stakes in reproduction can be found in the regulatory frameworks on reproductive cloning. The different regulatory frameworks stress the importance of a non-predetermined or copied genome, referring to the problematic nature of human design by a third party,[101] or the possible violation of "a right to a genetic identity of one's own",[102] which is assumed to be fundamental for the concept of human dignity. Nonetheless, the regulatory frameworks seem to fail to clearly explain the foundation of this assumed importance. A theory of responsibility that mobilises a normative account of the human person is capable of making sense of this assumption. Inspired by Jonas's Idea of Man, we could argue that a non-predetermined genetic makeup is necessary for our self-understanding as autonomous human beings. Consequently, we have a responsibility to ensure that future people do not have a modified or copied genome so that the genetic predetermination does not thwart their self-understanding as autonomous beings. Notably, this line of reasoning is adopted in the Cloning Protocol of the Council of Europe. The explanatory report of the protocol explicitly refers to the collective dimension, connecting a non-predetermined genetic makeup to one's self-understanding as autonomous. It states the predetermination of the genome by third parties is not merely a threat for the individual, but also "a threat to human identity" because a "naturally occurring genetic recombination is likely to create more freedom for the human being than a predetermined genetic makeup."[103] In other words, the responsibility approach can make sense of the assumption that certain

101 See for example, the German Memorandum on reproductive cloning and genetic modification. BT-Drs. 11/5460, vom 25.10.1989 (*Bill and Memorandum Embryo Protection Act*), p. 11. "Die Gefahr des Mißbrauchs — vor allem die Versuchung, die Methode des Gentransfers zu Zwecken der Menschenzüchtung zu verwenden — ist jedenfalls nicht zu übersehen."; "In besonders krasser Weise würde es gegen die Menschenwürde verstoßen, gezielt einem künftigen Menschen seine Erbanlagen zuzuweisen."

102 HL Deb (26 November 2001) vol. 629, col. 52.

103 Council of Europe, Explanatory Report to the Additional Protocol to the Convention for the Protection of Human Rights and Dignity of the Human Being with regard to the Application of Biology and Medicine, on the Prohibition of Cloning Human Beings ETS No.168 (*Cloning Protocol*), paragraph 3.

technologies violate our human dignity because it offers a more elaborate perception of what characteristics define us as human and what it takes to protect those characteristics, than the interests-construction.

While Jonas's Idea of Man is capable of articulating and explaining certain assumptions regarding the use of human dignity in the regulatory frameworks, it is not evident what we owe to future people based on this normative account in the context of other regulatory frameworks referring to human dignity. These regulatory frameworks require an elaboration of the normative account of humanity. One of the concepts that confronts us with the question what our responsibility for the human person as an autonomous end in himself entails, is the distinction between medical treatment and enhancement. Different regulatory frameworks refer to this distinction, implying that the technology must only be used for medical purposes. For example, the regulation of preimplantation genetic diagnosis only allows selection based on medical purposes and explicitly bans non-medical sex selection. In the same vein, proposals in favour of legalising genetic modification state that CRISPR-Cas9 should only be used to prevent genetic illnesses.[104] This raises the question of whether technological interference aiming to prevent genetic diseases should be distinguished from selective reproduction with non-medical purposes, and whether preventing genetic conditions is in line with the perception of the human being as free and autonomous.

Jonas does not explicitly address the question of whether human germline genetic modification or selective reproduction in the context of medical treatment also violates the person's autonomy. Yet various other authors, such as Bostrom and Habermas, offer arguments supporting the idea that the use of reproductive technologies for medical purposes is in line with the understanding of the human being as free and autonomous. Bostrom maintains that genetic engineering can increase choice and consequently autonomy.[105] That is, being free from the limitations imposed by a severe genetic condition may increase the number of possibilities to shape one's life, thereby increasing one's freedom of choice. In other words, being free from genetic defects may increase the future

---

104 Commissie Genetische Modificatie (COGEM) & Gezondheidsraad, 2017. The Nuffield Council questions the efficiency of the medical/non-medical distinction because it is not possible to draw a clear line between what qualifies as treatment and what qualifies as enhancement. They prefer to use the concept of 'welfare' as a criterion to decide on the moral acceptability of genome editing. Welfare could include the absence of heritable diseases. Nuffield Council on Bioethics, 2018, p. 87.

105 Bostrom, 2005, p. 212. A similar argument was made by the Dutch Health Council in favour of MRT and the Dutch Health Council and the Committee for Genetic Modification in favour of germline intervention. Gezondheidsraad, 2001, p. 35-36; Commissie Genetische Modificatie (COGEM) & Gezondheidsraad, 2017, p. 54-55. However, contrary to Bostrom, the Dutch Health Council and COGEM seem to consider only therapeutic genetic interventions acceptable. See also section 3.4.2.

child's *right to an open future.*[106] Another argument as to why genetic engineering with a therapeutic goal does not necessarily frustrate one's autonomy has been raised by Habermas. Contrary to Jonas,[107] Habermas addresses the distinction between treatment and enhancement, arguing that interference with a therapeutic intention differs from interference with design intentions. If genetic engineering is used in order to prevent an illness rather than to attribute specific desired traits to the child, the future child is no longer treated as an object of its parents' desires, but as a *second person.*[108] In those cases, Habermas argues, it is possible to assume the future child's consent. He argues that everyone would want to be free from those severe conditions, so we can assume that the future child who is subjected to technology such as CRISPR-Cas9 would agree to it. For these cases, the prospective parents have the future child's virtual consent, and genetic modification or selection for medical purposes would therefore be in line with the future child's autonomy;[109] not because it increases the number of future possibilities for the child, but because the child is treated as an equal, autonomous partner in the conversation. In summation, both Bostrom and Habermas offer arguments that support the idea that reproductive technologies and genetic interference for medical purposes is in line with respect for the human person's autonomy. Nonetheless, both arguments operationalise a different vision of autonomy. Bostrom seems to understand autonomy as the factual possibility to exercise choice, that is *freedom of choice.* Respect for one's autonomy entails offering someone alternatives to choose from, such as choosing a future rather than having a specific life path forced upon someone by closing off opportunities. Habermas's interpretation of autonomy attaches less weight to whether the child has a more open future but focuses on whether it would consent to the interference in the first place. For this reason, Habermas's argument does not claim that any medical intervention can presuppose the child's consent. "In any case, assumed consensus can *only* be invoked for the goal of avoiding evils which are *unquestionably extreme and likely to be rejected by all.*"[110] Put differently, only in cases of severe illness is it possible to assume the child's consent, respecting the idea of autonomy. Bostrom's argument of the right to an open future would not necessarily be limited to severe illnesses. For example, correcting a minor visual impairment opens the child's future to becoming a pilot. Consequently, any interference or modification that contributes to the child's open future would be in line

---

106 This concept was coined by the philosopher Joel Feinberg. J. Feinberg, *Freedom and Fulfillment. Philosophical Essays*, Princeton, Princeton University Press, 1992, chapter 3.

107 Jonas claims that medical conditions, such as diabetes and schizophrenia, are undesirable and that this is uncontroversial. He does not distinguish between different goals of selective reproduction or genetic engineering. Jonas, 1974, p. 152.

108 By "second person" Habermas means that the other is being treated as an equal partner in the discourse, as opposed to a third person upon whom decisions are imposed without his consent.

109 Habermas, 2003, p. 43, 52.

110 Habermas, 2003, p. 43. Italics added by LtH.

with his concept of autonomy. For this reason, Bostrom maintains that genetic interference should not be restricted to therapeutic purposes but should also be used "to expand [the child's] basic capability set."[111] Habermas's interpretation of autonomy seems to be closer to the notion of autonomy that underlies the regulations on reproduction than Bostrom's. After all, not only do the regulatory frameworks distinguish between therapy and enhancement, reproductive technologies such as PGT and MRT are only allowed in cases of a *severe* illness, not just any illness. Nonetheless, the arguments put forward by these two authors demonstrate that there are different interpretations of the notion of autonomy. So even if it is assumed that genetic intervention with a medical purpose is in line with respect for autonomy, the question remains open as to *why* it is in line with respect for autonomy (i.e., which interpretation of autonomy should be adopted), and related to that, where acceptable medical intervention ends and non-acceptable enhancement starts.

In addition to the notion of autonomy, addressing the distinction between treatment and enhancement sheds light on a second aspect of the normative account of the human person that needs further elaboration. In contrast to the regulatory frameworks on genetic modification, the regulation on PGT focuses not so much on protecting the child's autonomy, but rather on preventing instrumentalisation.[112] As discussed in section 2.4.2.1, in Memoranda and parliamentary discussions it is stated that non-medical selection, such as non-medical sex selection or selection for other personality traits, can be seen as a form of design in which case the child would be used as an object to satisfy its parents' wishes.[113] The ban on instrumentalisation is not only part of the normative account of the human person that underlies the regulations on reproduction, but also of Jonas's Idea of Man. Law's normative account of the human person however, takes a slightly different approach towards what qualifies as instrumentalisation: following the regulatory frameworks, the instrumentalisation in non-medical selective reproduction does not lie in the use of people as test subjects for the technology's improvement, as discussed by Jonas.[114] Instead, it lies in the child becoming a vehicle of its parents' desires, instead of being treated as an

111 Bostrom, 2005, p. 212.

112 A possible reason for this different focus could be the fact that PGD does facilitate some control over the child's genetic blueprint, but it does not allow the same extent of predetermination of the human genome as reproductive cloning or germline modification would. In PGD one can only choose out of a set of embryos with a naturally combined genetic blueprint, while genetic engineering and reproductive cloning enables prospective parents to select and even modify specific traits. In vitro gametogenesis (IVG) enables clinics to create a lot more embryos than that can be created through an IVF procedure. Such a large embryo pool results in more possible options for prospective parents to choose from, and thus in a way offers more control over the child's genetic blueprint.

113 See for example, *Kamerstukken II* 2000-2001, 27 423, nr. 3 (*Memorandum Embryo Act*), p. 41 48; *Kamerstukken II* 2005-2006, 30 300 XVI, nr. 136 (*first explanatory letter PGD*), p. 7, 9; HL Deb (26 November 2001) vol. 629, col. 23, 51; HC Deb (29 November 2001) vol. 375, col. 1196.

114 Jonas, 1974, p. 166.

end in itself. In this perspective, the risk of instrumentalisation still exists if the technology is deemed safe for clinical use. Yet, a closer look at the regulatory frameworks of the three legal systems reveals that the question of what qualifies as (unacceptable) instrumentalisation remains. This question is complicated because the boundary between treatment and enhancement is not always clear;[115] this is illustrated in the discussions on saviour siblings. By selecting based on HLA-type, PGT can be used to select a perfect donor for a sick sibling or relative. This means that the selection does serve a medical purpose, but not for the benefit of the selected child. The question thus arises as to whether the selected child is treated as an instrument or an end in itself. HLA typing is not allowed in Germany,[116] while the Netherlands only allows it as additional selection. The Dutch Memorandum states that if the selection procedure is already necessary to select a healthy embryo in the first place, the child is not solely conceived as a means, that is to say, serving the need of others.[117] The UK regulation allows non-additional tissue typing, arguing that even if the selection process does not primarily benefit the resulting child, that child is still not *merely* used as a means. As Jackson puts it: "In any event, a child born following HLA typing is not used solely as a means, since she is not abandoned after the donation, but rather is overwhelmingly likely to be loved in her own rights as a new and welcome member of the family."[118] All three legal systems subscribe to the idea that the human being must not be used as an instrument for the benefit of others; yet their interpretation of what qualifies as instrumentalisation differs. Given the blurred boundary between therapy and enhancement, the idea of what is (unacceptable) instrumentalisation needs to be further fleshed out.

7.3.2.2 Well-being

Similar to the value of human dignity, the responsibility approach is, compared to the 'interests of the future child' construction, also better equipped to make sense of the value of well-being and can therefore offer a better justification of this aspect of the normative account of the human person. In chapter 2, I elucidated how various regulatory frameworks, in particular those on PGT and access to fertility treatments, explicitly refer to the future child's well-being as an object of responsibility, and maintain that medical professionals should aim to achieve a standard of reasonable well-being, rather than minimal well-being for a life worth living. The Dutch, German, and UK regulations on these topics maintain

115 See also van Beers, 2020, p. 22-23.

116 Using PGD for tissue typing does not fall within the allowed exceptions mentioned in §3a (2). Günther, Taupitz and Kaiser, 2014, p. 292.

117 *Kamerstukken II* 2007-2008, 29 323, nr. 46 (*second explanatory letter PGD*), p. 9. In Dutch: "HLA-typering uitsluitend ten behoeve van een ander kind wijst het kabinet af, omdat het «nieuwe» kind dan alleen ter wereld komt ten behoeve van het andere kind."

118 Jackson, 2016, p. 861.

that the future child's existence should be prevented if a decent chance of reasonable well-being cannot be guaranteed, that is in cases of a high risk of a serious genetic condition. All three legal systems aim to guarantee a standard of well-being that is higher than the bare minimum that makes life worth living, even though, as discussed in chapter 4, this assumption cannot be explained from the perspective of the interests of the future child. Contrary to what the regulatory frameworks assume, the future child does not have an interest in its own non-existence provided its well-being falls above the zero-line and it therefore has a life worth living. This non-identity problem is not addressed in the regulations, which simply assume that medical professionals have a duty to do more than the bare minimum. In addition to that, none of the different regulatory frameworks offer an explanation of why a higher than minimum standard of well-being is chosen. The Dutch professional guidelines simply state that the zero line view, or only aiming to achieve minimum well-being, implies a too-limited view of both parental and professional responsibility.[119] Yet, the adoption of a higher standard of well-being cannot be justified by the 'interests of the future child' construction since it's interests can only justify the prevention of its existence if the child will have 'a life not worth living'. The normative framework of the responsibility approach is able to make sense of a higher standard. In this line of reasoning, securing reasonable well-being is not done in order to prevent the future child from being harmed, but because it is part of our responsibility. This higher standard flows from the perception of the human being as free, autonomous and an ends in themselves. Nevertheless, this does raise the question of why this normative account requires a higher degree of well-being.

While Jonas only briefly touches upon the notion of well-being and does not explicitly connect it to his Idea of Man, he does acknowledge a duty towards future persons to secure a certain degree of well-being.[120] He claims that future people have "a right to accuse us who came before them of being the originators of their misfortune – if we have spoiled for them the world or the human constitution through careless and avoidable deeds."[121] In other words, people existing now do not merely have a duty to ensure a future mankind, but they must also make sure that these future people have the resources and preconditions for a certain quality of life.[122] Unfortunately, Jonas does not elaborate the further details of

119 NVOG Modelprotocol "Mogelijke morele contra-indicaties bij vruchtbaarheidsbehandelingen", p. 2. In Dutch: "De standaard van minimaal welzijn daarentegen gaat uit van een te magere opvatting van ouderlijke en professionele verantwoordelijkheid."

120 Jonas, 1984, p. 40.

121 Jonas, 1984, p. 41.

122 This duty towards the well-being of future persons is derived from their (assumed) existence: given the fact that in the future people will exist, they are entitled to certain living conditions necessary for their quality of life. This second duty is therefore based on different grounds than the first duty that Jonas identifies. The first duty, the duty to guarantee future life, is not based on the interests or rights of future people.

the duty to secure a certain quality of life, including what level of quality future people are entitled to. Given his emphasis on a normative understanding of the human person, I imagine that at least those requirements must be met that allow people to live in a 'truly human' way and live up to the Idea of Man. In the light of reproductive technologies, this means that we must be able to make sense of the need for a reasonable standard of well-being, even though the child is not harmed by being brought into existence.

Within academic literature that addresses the question of what we owe to our offspring, two possible interpretations of the human person and of autonomy can be found that support the regulatory choice for a higher standard of well-being. The first interpretation emphasises the possibility to choose between different alternative possibilities as the relevant element in autonomy. As a human person is a free and autonomous being, it is also entitled to the possibility of exercising this autonomy. A serious genetic condition or a developmental deficit caused by poor parenthood could thwart the child's chances in life. Such conditions could infringe upon the child's *right to an open future*. Feinberg maintains that while a child cannot (fully) exercise autonomous choice yet, it has the right to have "future options kept open until he is a fully formed, self-determining adult capable of deciding among them."[123] These future options could be narrowed down by poor parenting, but also by genetic defects. Adopting a standard of reasonable well-being rather than a standard of minimum well-being could help to ensure that the child does not only have a life worth living, but also sufficient opportunity to make its own choices throughout its life. This argument is closely related to Bostrom's argument that genetic interference for medical purposes (which can also be understood as securing a higher standard of well-being) is in line with the child's dignity. In this interpretation, respect for one's autonomy, and consequently one's dignity, is shown by protecting the child's right to an open future and its freedom of choice by not closing off opportunities and keeping possibilities open.

The second possible interpretation of the human person does not focus on increasing the number of choices for the child, but on whether the child is treated as an equal and autonomous person. This interpretation is given by Steinbock and McClamrock in their notion of parental responsibility.[124] They maintain that prospective parents should not have a child if certain minimum conditions cannot be met.[125] These minimum conditions

123 Feinberg, 1992, p. 77.

124 Steinbock and McClamrock, 1994.This normative concept of parental responsibility is not the same as the legal interpretation of parental responsibility as used in, for example, the HFEA Code of Practice 8th Edition 2009 (last revised 2017), p. 67. The latter implies having legal authority over a child. In the Dutch professional guidelines, the concept of parental responsibility is also mentioned and similarly understood as Steinbock and McClamrock's interpretation.

125 Steinbock and McClamrock, 1994, p. 17.

require more than just a life (barely) worth living. Instead, parents have a responsibility to ensure their child has a "decent chance at a good life."[126] Although they do not precisely indicate what this standard entails, it appears to be rather similar to the standard of reasonable well-being adopted in the regulatory frameworks. If this standard is not met, as Steinbock and McClamrock argue, the child has not been harmed,[127] but it has been treated *unfairly* since its valid interest in a happy life is disregarded. This account of fairness does not depend on whether the outcome of an action or a choice is worse than the counterfactual situation (whereas the concept of harm does). Rather, their notion of fairness depends on *how* someone ought to be treated, regardless of the outcome:

> If you act so as to utterly disregard my legitimate interests for your own (perhaps even minor) benefit, then you've wronged me by treating me unfairly, even if in the end (perhaps by some accident of chance) I end up in a situation preferable to the one I would have otherwise been in. Fairness of treatment is not necessarily determined by the end acceptance or approval of those receiving it with respect to the available alternatives.[128]

By introducing the concept of fairness, Steinbock and McClamrock imply a normative account of the human being. According to this account, the child is not only entitled to be free from harm, but also to be considered as a person or an equal, rather than an object destined to fulfil the wishes of its parents. Put differently, if parents only had the obligation to ensure the future child has a life worth living (and is not harmed by being brought into existence) and nothing else, then the child would simply be at the disposal of its parents' wishes, making it the vehicle of its parents' desires. The child would then be instrumentalised because its own needs and interests are disregarded.

Like Feinberg's right to an open future, the principle of parental responsibility can also justify a higher standard of well-being. Yet both interpretations focus on a different element. Following the right to an open future, not securing a standard of reasonable well-being is morally objectionable because it limits the child's possibilities to exercise its freedom of choice. Following the idea of parental responsibility and treating the child fairly, not securing that standard implies that the child's less tangible interests as a person are not taken into account and that it is treated as an instrument of its parents' wishes. Therefore, this perspective focuses more on the collective, inherent value of the human

126 Steinbock and McClamrock, 1994, p. 17.
127 Steinbock and McClamrock, 1994, p. 19.
128 Steinbock and McClamrock, 1994, p. 19.

being that prohibits objectification and instrumentalisation rather than on the individual's autonomy.

Both interpretations do not necessarily exclude each other. In her discussion on the right to an open future in reproductive issues, Davis combines both perspectives. She states that ignoring the child's right to an open future, for example by forcing it into the parents' perspective of a good life or by limiting its options through genetic or psychosocial conditions, violates the Kantian principle to treat people always as an end in themselves.[129] Davis acknowledges that having a child is, to a certain extent, always instrumental because it is not possible to have the child for its own sake. After all, not having a child does not violate its interests, as there is no right or interest to come into existence. Good parenting, however, exists in finding a balance between the parents' own hopes and wishes for the child, and accepting that the child is her own person, "with her own life to make." Not creating the opportunity for the child to exercise autonomy over its own life is, in Davis's opinion, not just a violation of the child's autonomy, but affects the child on a more fundamental level as it is not treated as an end in itself. "Parental practices which close exits virtually forever are insufficiently attentive to the child as an end in herself. By closing off the child's right to an open future, they define the child as an entity who exists to fulfil parental hopes and dreams, not his own."[130]

Both strains of thought can justify the safeguarding of a higher than minimum standard of well-being and explain why a less than reasonable standard of well-being is at odds with the normative account of the human person. Nonetheless, the different focus points of both interpretations become relevant again when one considers adopting a higher than reasonable standard of well-being. If autonomy is interpreted as freedom of choice and an open future, one could argue that more well-being is favourable when it contributes to a more open future. Reproductive technologies can also be used for the selection of non-medical traits, such as high intelligence, strong physique, resistance, or immunity to other illnesses. Such forms of enhancement are supported by Bostrom, who argues that genetic modification can expand the child's capabilities in a way that it would enjoy even more freedom, as it could choose from even more possibilities.[131] Therefore, putting the focus solely on safeguarding an open future may ignore the distinction between therapy and enhancement that the different legal systems have acknowledged, as non-therapeutical genetic interference through modification or selection should be encouraged if such

129 D.S. Davis, 'Genetic dilemmas and the child's right to an open future', *Rutgers law journal*, Vol. 28, 1997, p. 569.

130 Davis, 1997, p. 570.

131 Bostrom, 2005, p. 212.

interference grants the child more opportunities. This interpretation of autonomy has been criticised by, amongst others, Karnein for being too one-dimensional, for it focuses only on the quantity of choices.[132] As a result, this interpretation ignores the question of whether this child would still consider itself to be the autonomous initiator of the choices it eventually makes. Can the child still regard itself as an autonomous being, or would it have to blame or credit someone else for the characteristics and thus the possibilities it has? These questions constitute the core of the second interpretation of autonomy that, like Jonas's Idea of Man,[133] focuses on the internal condition for the human being's self-understanding as authentic and autonomous. Importantly, this self-understanding as autonomous does not imply that the choice of the child's genetic blueprint should be left to the child itself, since this is simply impossible. Instead, it requires that the child's genome is free from determination by others.[134] A random recombination of genes constitutes a new beginning, "without which he could not perceive himself as the initiator of his actions and aspirations."[135] From this perspective, technological interference can thwart the person's self-understanding as autonomous, meaning it would be a violation of the conception of the human being.[136] The discussion on germline modification and enhancement reveals a tension between autonomy in the sense of having possibilities to choose from, and autonomy in the sense of being the sole chooser and taking responsibility for that choice.

In my opinion, both interpretations represent a vital part of being autonomous. The quantity of options to choose from does not enlarge one's autonomy if that person considers himself merely as an extension of his parents' desires, rather than being able to take authorship of that choice. At the same time, being able to understand oneself as the sole author of one's life offers little solace if there are no actual or few options to choose from, for example due to a life plagued by illness. Therefore, a balance must be struck between both interpretations, that is our self-image as autonomous beings that is primarily derived from the factual possibility of exercising free choice, and this self-understanding derived from the idea that we consider ourselves to be the sole maker of a choice. How this balance must be struck, and what our responsibility for the respective normative accounts

132 Karnein, 2012, p. 148. In a similar vein, Glover maintains that autonomy consists of two values: self-creation and independence. Some parental choices may increase our abilities, resulting in a more open future and offer a greater scope for self-creation, however they reduce our independence, as these choices may make our life paths and identity more dependent on those parental choices. Glover, 2006, p. 71.

133 See section 7.2.2.

134 Habermas, 2003, p. 58-59; Sandel, 2007, p. 81-82.

135 Habermas, 2003, p. 59.

136 Habermas also argues that when selective technologies or genetic engineering is used for the purpose of enhancement it affect the child's self-understanding as a free and autonomous being. Habermas, 2003, p. 51-52.

of the human person requires, is a question that must be addressed in the public debate. When the public debate addresses this balance, it will become possible to offer a solid justification for the standard of reasonable well-being. Moreover, with both perspectives in mind, it also becomes possible to address the interrelated questions to which the notion of reasonable well-being gives rise to such as: What qualifies as treatment and what as enhancement? What qualifies as reasonable well-being? Does the duty to aim for reasonable well-being leave open the option to do more, or not?

7.3.2.3 Personal Identity

The third and last core value I identified in chapter 2 – and that the normative framework of the responsibility approach must be able to address – is the possibility to develop one's personal identity, and the corresponding interest of the child to have access to information about its genetic origins. This value plays an important role in the regulatory frameworks on the disclosure of donor information, which emphasise the importance of the child's biological and genetic history for the development of its personal identity. The Dutch, German, and UK regulatory frameworks banning donor anonymity maintain that knowing its descent may be pivotal for the child's personal narrative. As elaborated in chapter 3, these regulatory frameworks are based on the idea that our identity as individuals depends on the social and genetic relations we have with others. A person's life history is connected to the narratives of other people, in particular to those involved in the conception of that person. They do not only have a genetic bond with the child, but also an existential relationship; without the input of the donor, the child would never exist. For this reason, the role of the donor plays a vital role in the child's origin story. This information is considered to be of such importance for the child's identity that the regulatory frameworks do not simply speak of an interest, but often of a right to information about its descent or put simply, *the right to know*. In previous chapters, I also addressed that the interests-construction struggles to articulate this value. Various authors have pointed out that donor conceived (or adopted) children who do not know their origin story, do not suffer from tangible, psychosocial harm.[137] The harm done touches upon an intangible and difficult to grasp aspect of their person, and because of that, it is unlikely that their quality of life is so severely affected that it would be in their interest not to come into existence.[138] For the responsibility approach, making sense of the value of personal identity may be its biggest challenge. How can these notions of personal identity and intersubjectivity be understood from the perspective of the autonomous human being as

137 See section 3.3.1.

138 Of course, banning anonymous sperm and egg donation does not necessarily prevent the child from coming into existence, but as discussed in the introduction of this study, research has shown that the ban on donor anonymity has affected potential donors' willingness to donate, and thereby changed the stereotype donor.

an end in himself? And does the responsibility to ensure future people's humanity require securing access to information about their origins?

The questions above are not directly addressed by Jonas. While he does briefly touch upon the notion of personal identity, he does so in a different context, namely in his analysis of reproductive cloning. Still, Jonas's analysis may offer an interesting starting point for understanding how the depiction of the human person as an autonomous end in himself can make sense of the notion of personal identity and the right to know. In his essay, 'Biological Engineering – A Preview', Jonas briefly ponders on the notion of personal identity. He states that the answer to the question 'who am I?' must remain unknown to the person himself. One's identity should not be given beforehand, according to Jonas, but a person should discover and develop his identity over the course of his life by living it. As Jonas himself puts it, an individual asking himself 'who am I?', "can find its answer only with the secret there as condition of the search – indeed as a condition of *becoming* what may *then be* the answer."[139] He stresses that the child's identity must not only be a secret to the child itself, so it can develop its own identity, but also to those around him. Reproductive cloning or determining the child's genome through germline intervention violates this principle. Attempts to influence or determine the child's genome are done with a certain intention, namely, to bring about desired characteristics in the child. Therefore, these interferences in the child's genome come with expectations about who the child will be, what its characteristics, appearance, and perhaps even likes and interests are. In other words, according to Jonas, genetic interference not only expresses the intention to influence the child's genetic identity, but also expresses control over its personal identity. Regardless of whether the interference is successful to this extent, it represents an intention to control the child's identity by forcing a narrative upon the child.

For Jonas, controlling the child's personal identity through cloning or genetic modification is problematic because it affects its self-understanding as free and autonomous. Without the imposed personal identity that follows from the intentions and expectations that lie behind the genetic interference, the child is able to develop their own aspirations, hopes, beliefs et cetera, or rather understand those aspirations as its own. However, Jonas reasons, if the child's creators impose their intentions and aspirations on the child through genetic interference, the child may no longer be able understand itself as the authentic originator of its actions.[140] The child is barred from making its life completely its own, because, as Kampowski puts it, "one could always blame or would always have to credit others for

139 Jonas, 1974, p. 162.

140 Jonas, 1974, p. 162. See also Habermas, who mentions this argument in the context of genetic modification.

characteristic marks that form part of who one is without ever being able to make these characteristics really one's own."[141]

The question can be posed as to whether anonymous donor conception, which also leaves its traces on the child's identity formation, must be considered problematic because it frustrates the child self-understanding as autonomous. Parents who opt for anonymous donor conception also attribute themselves control over the child's life history. In this case, however, not by shaping the child's identity through their expectations, but by deleting a part of the child's life history. This implies that the child is denied the opportunity to complete its own origin story. Nonetheless, this control over the child's personal identity and origin story does not, in my opinion, affect the child's autonomy in a similar way as genetic control does. It seems unlikely to me that a child who misses a part of its life history can no longer understand itself as the authentic source of its desires and aspirations, in the same way that a child whose genome is determined by third parties might.

Still, an important parallel can be drawn between obscuring a part of the child's origin story via anonymous donation on the one hand and predetermining the child's genetic make-up and its genetic identity on the other. After all, like its own genealogical history, a child can never choose its own genetic constitution.[142] This point seems to be implicitly acknowledged by Jonas. In his argument against reproductive cloning, Jonas too does not maintain that one must be free to *create* one's identity, but speaks of *finding* one's identity.[143] Therefore, both in the case of predetermining the child's genetic identity and of erasing a part of its life history, the problem is not that the child's autonomy is not respected because a choice is taken away from the child since that choice never existed for the child in the first place. (With regard to donor anonymity, the child is robbed of a different choice, to which I will come back later.) The problem lies in the fact that a third party appropriates the control over a part of the child's identity. As Jonas and Habermas argue, even though the child cannot select its own genetic constitution, that does not imply that others are allowed to make this selection for the child. A similar point can be made regarding the future child's narrative identity. Even though the child cannot be the (sole) author of its own origin story, and for this reason no choice is taken away from the child in this sense, that does not mean that others are entitled to make this choice for the child. The wilful decision of a parent to (partially) write the child's life history, by either removing or rewriting a part of its origin story or by selecting its genetic traits, makes the parent accountable for the child's life history in a way that a parent who refrains from this

141 Kampowski, 2014, p. 154.
142 See also Sandel, 2007, p. 81.
143 Jonas, 1974, p. 161, 162.

meddling is not.[144] With regard to the child's narrative identity, one could argue that the child's parents will always exercise some influence on the child's identity, since the child's narrative is always affected by the identities of those closest to it. However, the fact that our identity depends on the influence of those around us does not imply others can take an active role in determining our identity. By taking up such an active role, the parents claim the role of co-writer of the child's life history, without considering the child's needs or wishes. Once again, it could be said that the child is not treated as a second person, someone who is part of the conversation. Therefore, by opting for an anonymous donor and obscuring the child's life history, the parents take too much control over the child's identity, neglecting their responsibility towards the child.

In addition, the child's autonomy is affected in another way. By opting for an anonymous donor, the child is denied the opportunity to decide for itself how the information about its donor conception and its genetic parent should be part of its identity. As addressed in chapter 3, because the donor's contribution is fundamental to the child's existence, it is a part of its life history that cannot be replaced. It is a part of its origin story in a way that goes further than potential similarities with which the child can identify itself. Donor conceived children also may want to understand the motives of the donor, that is, they want to understand why they were brought into existence. Without this contribution, the child would not have existed at all. This part of the child's narrative cannot be substituted by other legal and social relations. At least, others cannot decide for the child to substitute this part of the child's life history. While the different legal frameworks on donor anonymity maintain that one's genetic origins are central to one's identity, they leave it up to the child to decide whether it wants to know this part of its identity. Nonetheless, this decision cannot be made for the child by another party.

To conclude, both Jonas and the regulatory frameworks on donor anonymity stress the importance of our genetic constitution for our personal identity, but in different ways. The regulations on donor anonymity focuses on our genetic relations as an important factor for our personal identity as an individual. Jonas considers a non-predetermined genetic constitution pivotal for our identity as autonomous human persons. Without supporting the idea of genetic determinism, it appears that our genetic blueprint constitutes an important factor for our self-understanding and who we are, or at least for how we see ourselves. Given the fact that the child's genetic constitution and genetic history can never be at its disposal, it is difficult to understand the nature of the relationship between genetics and identity in terms of autonomy. If the parents take control over aspects of the child's personal identity by either genetic interference or obscuring a part of the information

144 Kampowski, 2014, p. 157; Sandel, 2007, p. 82.

about its descent, they do not take away a choice the child would otherwise have (apart from the chance to decide how the information about its descent fits its narrative). But perhaps exactly because the child has no say in its own genetics, others should refrain from taking control over it, unless they can be certain that they have the child's virtual consent. In sum, respect for the future child as an autonomous person may also include that the child's creators refrain from decisions that cannot be made by the child itself.

7.4 Conclusion

After discussing the question as to why the 'interests of the future child' construction is not adequate, this chapter explored an alternative theory for the conceptualisation of the future child whose existence is prevented. For the construction of this theoretical framework, I used Jonas's theory of responsibility as a starting point. The theoretical framework based on responsibility consists of two components: a conceptual framework and a normative framework. Based on the conceptual framework, the future child, and future human life in general, can be understood as the object of our substantive responsibility. Because our actions directly affect the future child, we bear responsibility for it. However, the duties that arise from this responsibility can only be understood with the help of the normative framework, which offers a normative account of what it means to be human. In this account, the human being is characterised as free, autonomous, and as an end in himself. Therefore, we have a duty towards future people to ensure that they can come into existence under circumstances that allow them to understand themselves as autonomous and as ends in themselves.

The theoretical framework based on responsibility is better suited to provide an account for understanding and conceptualising the future child and the stakes in reproduction than the interests-construction. In previous chapters, I argued that the interests-construction cannot be understood as the best conceptualisation or interpretation of the future child, because it does not meet the criteria of fit and justification. The 'interests of the future child' construction is at odds with various fundamental premises of the notions of legal personhood and legal interests, making the construction inherently contradictory. Additionally, the interests-construction fails to make sense of values that underlie the regulations on reproduction and therefore does not place these values in their 'best light'. The vocabulary operationalised by the 'interests of the future child' construction puts the focus on an individual subject. For this reason, it cannot sufficiently articulate the intersubjective or collective values at stake. In addition, as discussed in chapter 4, formulating these stakes in terms of the 'interests of the child' confronts us with the wrongful life conundrum: preventing the future child's existence in order to prevent the violation of its dignity or its right to information about its origins are supposedly not in the child's interests if it has a life worth living. Therefore, these 'interests of the child' are often discarded as irrelevant because the child is not harmed by these violations or does not have a life not worth living.

The theoretical framework based on responsibility does not face these obstacles. First of all, the responsibility approach meets the dimension of fit, because it is compatible with the fundamental legal premises concerning legal personality and legal interests. Understanding the future child as the object of our responsibility does not involve the problematic attribution of interests or rights to an entity whose existence is prevented as a result of that same attribution. It does not have to invoke the rights or interests of an individual entity in order to establish duties towards future people. Instead, these duties are based on responsibility, which increases as our control and influence over the lives of future people increases. Because of this, the responsibility approach is not subjected to the same critique as the interests-construction I elaborated on in chapters 5 and 6. Subsequently, a theoretical framework based on responsibility also meets the dimension of justification, as it is better equipped to address and do justice to the stakes involved in human reproduction, including notions such as personal identity and human dignity. This is because this theoretical framework adopts a different normative framework than the interests-construction. Following the responsibility approach elaborated on in this chapter, we bear responsibility to respect and secure the humanity of future people. This requires more than harm prevention and focuses on a normative idea of what characteristics make us human. Starting from Jonas's Idea of Man, this normative account depicts the human person as a free and autonomous end in himself. As explained in this chapter, this normative framework can make sense of the various values that underly the regulations on reproduction, namely human dignity, the reasonable standard of well-being, and personal identity. For these reasons, I believe that conceptualising the future child as the object of our responsibility, rather than as a subject of interests or rights, is the best interpretation of this unique entity.

An important benefit of the responsibility approach is its capability to address the complexity of the human being and the intertwinement between individual members of the human family and mankind as a whole. Because of this, it is better equipped to articulate and make sense of those interests and stakes in the technologisation and governance of reproduction that transcends the individual subject. The interests-construction, referring to the interests of the individual future child, obscures the fact that reproductive decisions and technology also have wide-reaching effects. The control we have gained over the conception of new people has not only made us responsible for those individuals, but also for mankind as a whole. As explained above, what we allow to happen on an individual scale indicates an idea of what is allowed to happen to the human person in general. Put differently, individual actions affect the image of humanity as a whole. The understanding of this intertwinement is essential for the conceptualisation of the future child whose existence is prevented: allowing the individual child to be born under circumstances that contradict the normative idea of the human being and hence violate our responsibility towards the future child, affects the normative idea of the human person itself. For this reason, preventing the future child in certain cases is not about preventing an individual human being from being harmed, or sparing it a horrible existence. Rather, it is about preventing certain practices that erode our self-understanding as human beings, meaning both the self-understanding of the child that could have existed and our collective idea of what it means to be human.

In summation, the future child can be conceptualised with the help of the responsibility approach that I developed in this chapter. Based on this approach, future human life is the object of our responsibility. This means that not only is there a duty to ensure that people will still exist in the future, but also that their humanity will be protected as well. This duty may entail that certain modes of reproduction are not allowed as they constitute a violation of future people's humanity, which consequently prevents the resulting child from coming into existence. Therefore, the future child can be understood as the object of our responsibility, and as a part of our responsibility towards future human life. What this approach emphasises in particular, is that the regulation of reproductive technologies and the discussion of what we owe towards future people demands a normative idea of what humanity entails. Of course, this chapter also showed that various aspects of this normative account, and therefore of our duty towards future people, remain a topic for further discussion. The human person is a complex notion, and the discussion of human dignity, identity, and autonomy revealed that there is a myriad of possible interpretations of these concepts. It is perhaps a nearly impossible endeavour to constitute a comprehensive, univocal interpretation of the human person, especially in a pluralist global society. In addition to that, the normative account of the human person is not a static concept and may be reinterpreted over time. Nonetheless, as the regulation of reproduction (and biotechnology in general) touches upon the most intimate aspects of our being, it has become necessary to at least attempt to answer, to the best of our ability, the question: 'what makes us human?'

8 Conclusion – Regulating Non-Existence

8.1 The Interests of the Future Child

The advances in reproductive biotechnology, and the regulation of these developments, have confronted lawyers with a new entity: the future child who may result from the use of this technology. Since this entity is directly affected by these technologies and the existence of the future child has become something that we can exercise control over, it has become necessary and perhaps even inevitable to offer the future child a place in the legal debate. But in order to do so, the future child must first be conceptualised: we need a way to legally capture this entity before we can understand our legal relationship and legal duties towards it.

As I elaborated in chapter 2, regulations on reproduction often speak of 'the interests of the future child'. Three interests in particular are attributed to the future child: the interest in reasonable well-being and being free from harm, the interest in developing its personal identity and access to information about its descent, and finally the interest in respect for its human dignity. Operationalising these interests implies that, in the regulations on reproduction, the future child is conceptualised as a subject of legally relevant interests. Moreover, currently existing people have an obligation to take those interests into account when making reproductive decisions or regulating reproductive technologies. What is important though, is that the interests of the future child are also invoked to justify regulatory decisions that ultimately result in the prevention of the future child's existence. For example, medical professionals have to consider the interests of the future child before they perform fertility treatment; if it is likely that the child will grow up under circumstances that constitute a low standard of well-being, then treatment can be refused on grounds of the interests of the future child, and thus the future child will not be born. Other examples are the ban on reproductive cloning and human germline genetic modification, which prevent the existence of cloned and genetically modified children respectively. In other words, the future child who does not physically exist and never will come into existence is presented as a subject of interests. This leads to the first central question of this research: **is the presentation of the future child whose existence is prevented as a subject of interests an adequate theoretical framework to conceptualise and understand this entity?**

In order to assess whether the 'interests of the future child' construction can be understood as an adequate conceptualisation or interpretation of the future child, I adopted a methodological approach based on Dworkin's constructivism. The construction used to conceptualise the future child can be understood as an interpretation of this entity. In order to be an adequate or even the best interpretation, it must be tested against the dimensions of fit and justification. Testing the construction against the dimension of fit requires not simply assessing whether the 'interests of the future child' construction fits within existing regulations. That would result in circular reasoning, since this construction is distilled from those same regulatory frameworks. Instead, the dimension of fit also requires that the legal construction is coherent with how these the fundamental concepts that form the premises of the interests-construction are interpreted in legal contexts. In other words, I assessed whether the interests-construction is compatible with its own premises, or whether it is internally contradictory. To meet the dimension of justification, the construction has to show the law in "the best light possible".[1] That is, the interests-construction must at least be able to do justice to and articulate the underlying values that constitute the normative account of the human person in the regulations on reproduction. In order to be able to test the 'interests of the future child' construction against the dimensions of fit and justification, I first deconstructed this interpretation of the future child in order to explicate the presuppositions upon which this construction is built. The interests-construction rests upon four implicit assumptions about the future child. First, the core values that the regulations aim to protect can be understood as the interests of an individual subject. Second, the future child has an implicit, assumed interest in its own non-existence. Third, the future child is a legal subject and, fourth, the future child whose existence is prevented is capable of having interests. In chapter 3 through to 6, each of these assumptions was assessed in the light of the dimensions of fit and justification.

8.2 The Four Assumptions of the Interests-Construction

In the first part of this study, I assessed the tenability of the four assumptions and concluded that each of them is partially or completely untenable. With regard to the first assumption – that the interests-construction can do justice to the core values that underly the regulations on reproduction in the jurisdictions examined – the analysis revealed that one of the interests, namely human dignity, encompasses both an individual and a collective dimension. The regulatory frameworks occasionally state that certain modes of reproduction are not only a violation of the individual future child's dignity but are at the same time also an affront to the dignity of humankind. Importantly, both dimensions of human dignity are intertwined: allowing a certain treatment of an individual member of humankind, tells us something about how we see the human species as a whole. Therefore,

1 Dworkin, 1998, p. 243.

the instrumentalisation of the future child, which is considered a violation of its dignity, also implies the violation of human dignity in the collective dimension. However, the fact that reproductive technologies can have far-reaching effects that transcend the individual is obscured by the vocabulary of interests that solely focuses on the interests and dignity of the individual future child. Therefore, the interests-construction is partially untenable because this construction cannot make sense of or do justice to these intersubjective facets of the idea of the human person that underlies the regulations on reproduction.

The second assumption is also partially untenable. By claiming that the regulation, and consequently the prevention of the child's existence serves the interests of the future child, the regulation tacitly implies that the future child has an interest in its own non-existence. Or put differently, that being allowed to come into existence results in harm to the child. Yet, this assumption is at odds with how its premises, namely, the notions of harm and interests, are interpreted in the legal context. Having an interest in one's own non-existence implies that the child is presumably better off not existing at all. This can only be the case if the quality of the child's life is so severely impaired, that one could speak of a wrongful life. The crux of the problem is, however, that such a wrongful life can only be assumed in the most extreme cases. In the majority of cases covered by the regulations, it is unlikely that the expected quality of the prevented life would be so low that the child's life would qualify as a wrongful life. Regulatory frameworks that aim to protect the future child's well-being allow interference if a reasonable standard of well-being cannot be guaranteed, setting the bar higher than solely preventing a wrongful life. In addition, it is unlikely that violating the future child's interests in human dignity and identity results in such a reduction of quality of life that one can speak of a wrongful life. Therefore, in these cases it is not possible to assume that the future child has an interest in its own non-existence which renders the interests-construction untenable in the majority of cases. In these cases, the assumption of an interest in non-existence does not fit with the legal interpretation of harm and interests. What is more, because the interest in non-existence can only be assumed in the most extreme cases, the 'interests of the future child' construction fails to justify the regulatory frameworks that prevent the future child's existence in order to secure a reasonable well-being or protect the interests in dignity and identity. Consequently, this construction cannot do justice to a normative account of the human person that incorporates these three values.

The assessment of the first two assumptions has revealed that vocabulary operationalised within the 'interests of the future child' construction struggles to make sense and do justice to the normative account of the human person and the values it incorporates. But the interests-construction is also problematic on another level. Through the attribution of interests, and more specifically, legally relevant interests, the future child has become an important actor on the legal stage. This brings us to the third assumption underlying the interests-construction, which is that the future child is a legal subject. As I argued in chapter 5, the future child cannot be understood as a legal subject with the help of law's traditional vocabulary: the legal person. First, both the naturalist and the constructivist approaches to (natural) legal personality fail. The naturalist approach presupposes that legal persons have intrinsic qualities, such as biological, rational, or metaphysical features. Since the future child has not been conceived yet and therefore, does not physically exist, it lacks these qualities, namely, biological or rational features, or human dignity. Second, the constructivist approach fails because it severs the inextricable connection between the future child and the actual entity that requires protection: the child once it is born. Finally, an anticipatory approach towards legal personality also fails. The future child's personality cannot be constructed by means of an anticipation of the actual child's personality, since that actual child will not come into existence. In fact, the future child's entrance into law's *raison d'être* is to be able to justify the intervention that prevents the actual child's conception and birth. It appears that the future child's non-existence proves to be the greatest challenge for understanding it as a legal person: as a non-existent entity, it does not fit in any of the three approaches to legal personality.

Yet the future child may be understood as a legal subject with the help of another approach to legal subjectivity. Therefore, the third assumption about the future child may be tenable if legal subjectivity can also be based on the subjectivity of legally relevant interests, and if the future child can be understood as such a subject. In chapter 6, I analysed legal-philosophical and legal-doctrinal literature on the subject of interests in law. Although this topic is not systematically elaborated in either field, it appears that the subject of legally relevant interests does not necessarily have to possess legal personality. However, in order to determine whether the future child can be understood as a legal subject with the help of this alternative vocabulary, the fourth assumption of the future child must be tenable as well; that is, the assumption that the future child whose existence is prevented, is capable of having interests in the first place. Yet, this assumption also appears problematic. The capacity to have interests requires a form of consciousness or conative life, either now or at some point in the future. Without it, an entity cannot have an interest in something. Because the future child is prevented from coming into existence, it will never meet this requirement. Attributing interests to the future child whose existence is prevented is at odds with the legal understanding of having interests, and therefore this assumption does not meet the dimension of fit. Consequently, as the future child cannot have interests, it also cannot be the subject of legally relevant interests. Constructing legal subjectivity with the help of this approach fails, just as legal subjectivity cannot be construed with the help of legal personality. This implies that also the third assumption is untenable. As a result of its own non-existence, the future child cannot be understood as a legal subject.

The assessment of the four assumptions concerning the future child demonstrated that each assumption is partially or completely untenable. Therefore, the presentation of the future child whose existence is prevented as a subject of interests is a highly problematic construction and unfit to adequately conceptualise this entity. In particular, the assessment of the third and fourth assumption revealed the reason why the future child is such a complex entity to grasp. The complexity lies in the paradoxical nature of the entity and the 'interests of the future child' construction. The interests-construction conceptualises the future child as a subject of interests and these interests are considered to be a paramount consideration in the regulations on reproduction. At the same time, respecting the future child's interests can mean that the future child is prevented from coming into existence, and therefore it is prevented from having any interests at all. In chapter 6, I addressed the distinction between actual future people (those who will exist at some point in the future) and merely potential people (those who could have, but never will exist). This distinction touches upon an asymmetry between existence and non-existence: in case of existence, there is a subject, or a subject will exist in the future. For that reason, it becomes possible to attribute interests and rights to it and to say that the child suffers harm or experiences benefits. In the case of non-existence, there is no subject. That is, there is no subject that can be harmed, wronged, or benefitted, or whose interests are respected or violated. The crux of the complexity surrounding the future child lies in the fact that this entity starts as an actual future person that will come into existence if the regulatory frameworks do not allow interference. But because we interfere, the future child is actively transformed into a merely potential being. And while this transformation from actual to merely potential also occurs, for example, in the context of abortion,[2] the future child differs in a fundamental aspect: it is a legal construct that is solely created to prevent the actual child from coming into existence. This is what makes the future child a paradox. The paradox of the future child is that this construct is created to anticipate the interests of the actual child but at the same time causes the future child to remain a merely potential being, incapable of having interests in the first place. Invoking its own interests to have its existence prevented is thus a logical impossibility.

8.3 RESPONSIBILITY FOR THE FUTURE

As the future child's non-existence causes the interests-construction to fail to adequately conceptualise the future child whose existence is prevented, a second question arises. If not as a subject of interests, **how can the future child whose existence is prevented be conceptualised in a more adequate manner?** This question, which is the second central

2 See section 6.3.2.

question of this research, is addressed in the chapter 7. In order to conceptualise the future child in a more adequate manner, I developed an alternative approach for the conceptualisation of the future child. This approach builds on the work of German philosopher Hans Jonas and his notion of responsibility. According to Jonas, as the result of technological developments, the consequences of our actions transgress spatial, but also temporal boundaries, and as a result, future people enter the scope of our ethical thinking. For this reason, Jonas proposes a new ethical imperative: "Act so that the effects of your actions are compatible with the permanence of genuine human life."[3] This imperative implies two (related) things. First, we have a duty to ensure the continuation of human life, so that in the future, human life still exists. Second, we must also guarantee that the humanity of these future people remains intact and that they can live in a genuine human way. According to Jonas, both elements are put at risk by modern technology, such as reproductive biotechnologies. He warns us that modern technology does not only have the potential to destroy human life, but also encompasses the risk of "existential impoverishment",[4] in which human life loses the essential quality that makes us human in the first place: the capacity for responsibility. This capacity for responsibility flows from freedom and autonomy, or the ability to choose knowingly and willingly between alternative actions. However, Jonas fears that in particular genetic interventions erode the capacity for freedom and the human person's self-understanding as an autonomous (and thus responsible) being. Therefore, our duty to ensure human life in the future is also concerned with "the way they exist,"[5] The conditions under which future people come into existence should keep intact their humanity and capacity for freedom. In other words, Jonas operationalises a normative account of the human person that constitutes the core of his theory of responsibility. This normative account of the human person, which Jonas calls 'the Idea of Man', in general perceives the human person as a free and autonomous end in himself. In sum, in Jonas's theory our obligations towards future people are not based on their rights and interests, instead, they are derived from a normative account of what it means to be human.

In chapter 7, I further elaborated on Jonas's ideas to construct a theoretical framework that is capable of conceptualising the future child without facing the problems of the interests-construction. The first step is demonstrating that also the individual future child whose existence is prevented can be understood as the object of our responsibility. Because Jonas focuses on humankind as a whole and maintains that we have a duty to ensure that human life exists in the future, preventing the future child from coming into existence may seem

3 Jonas, 1984, p. 11.
4 Jonas, 1996, p. 108.
5 Jonas, 1996, p. 106.

at odds with this duty. Nonetheless, our responsibility towards future people does not only imply a duty to guarantee the existence of humans in the future, but also a duty to ensure that future human life is 'genuine human life'. This normative account of the human person can be affected by the way we treat individual members of humankind. In both chapter 2 and chapter 7, I elaborated on the intertwinement of the individual dimension and the collective dimension of human life: what we allow to happen to an individual member of the human species says something about how we see humankind in general. This implies that the use of reproductive biotechnology does not only affect those individuals directly involved, but also has consequences that transcend the individual: it affects the collective dimension of human life because it may erode the normative account of the human person and our self-understanding as human beings. Therefore, the responsibility approach can justify the prevention of the future child's existence as certain modes of reproduction violate the normative account of what it means to be human.

The second step of developing an adequate theoretical framework for the future child is explaining how the normative account of the human person can account for the regulations on reproduction and the three values it aims to protect. I argued that while Jonas's Idea of Man (i.e. perceiving the human person as a free and autonomous end in himself) needs to be elaborated further, it can justify the values of human dignity, reasonable well-being, and personal identity. First, the Idea of Man can make sense of both interpretations of human dignity that can be distilled from the current regulations on reproduction and biolaw in general. In the regulations and discussions on reproductive technologies, human dignity is invoked to both support individual freedom of choice and curb individual autonomy. While this may seem contradictory, both interpretations are interrelated: the idea that our dignity lies in our capacity for autonomy is derived from a collective self-image of humankind as autonomous. As individual actions can erode this normative account of the human person, restricting individual freedom of choice can be done in order to protect the human against dehumanisation, i.e. against the erosion of mankind's self-understanding as autonomous ends in themselves. Second, the idea of the human person as an autonomous end in himself can also justify the higher standard of well-being that the regulatory frameworks prescribe. A higher standard of well-being facilitates more possibilities for the child to actually exercise its autonomy. Moreover, it ensures that the child is not merely treated as an instrument of its parents' desires but is taken seriously as another person, with its own (less tangible) needs and interests. Finally, an interesting parallel can be drawn with Jonas's ideas of a personal identity and the concept of narrative identity that underlies the regulations on reproduction. Jonas maintains that a non-predetermined genetic make-up offers the child the possibility to find its own personal identity, rather than having an identity through the expectations of its creators forced upon it. In other words, although the child can never autonomously choose its own personal or genetic identity, this does not mean that third parties can take control over it. In a similar vein, a child is also not able to choose its own narrative identity or origin story. But that does not allow others to obscure information about the child's genetic descent or rewrite its lineage by opting for an anonymous donor.

Therefore, compared to the 'interests of the future child' construction, the responsibility approach that departs from Jonas's theory of responsibility and Idea of Man offers a better conceptualisation of the future child. As the responsibility approach does not have to rely on the attribution of interests and rights to the future child, it avoids the internal contradictions the interests-construction is riddled with. Furthermore, the responsibility approach is not incoherent with the legal interpretation of fundamental notions such as personality, harm, and interests. Therefore, the conceptualisation of the future child fits better with the existing regulations on reproduction and the legal system in general. In addition, whereas the interests-construction often fails to make sense of the values that the regulations aim to protect, our responsibility to ensure future persons can live up to the ideal of the human being as an autonomous end in himself is able to do justice to the values of reasonable well-being, identity, and human dignity. Therefore, I maintain that the responsibility approach offers a more convincing conceptualisation of the future child whose existence is prevented than the interests-construction. Conceptualising the future child as the object of our responsibility is a better interpretation of this entity compared to the current interests-construction.

The main aim of this study is the development of a theoretical framework that is capable of conceptualising the future child whose existence is prevented. Nonetheless, because the responsibility approach does not have to rely on the rights and duties of future people, it can also offer a new perspective on a series of challenges created by reproductive technologies in cases where the future child *does* come into existence. As reproduction has increasingly become a technological process with multiple parties involved, more opportunity for errors arises. Real life examples illustrate the wide variety of possible mistakes made by clinics and medical professionals, such as embryo mix-ups, untraceable donors as the result of poor administration, the use of a donor with the wrong phenotype,[6] or a donor with a genetic condition.[7] These cases have resulted in new types of liability lawsuits. And while in many cases not only the parents, but also the child is affected by the

---

6 See for example Cramblett v. Midwest Sperm Bank, LLC, 230 F. Supp. 3d 865, 874 (N.D. Ill. 2017); A. Phillip, 'White woman accidentally impregnated with black man's sperm loses legal battle', *Washington Post* 5 September 2015.

7 Van der Mee, T. and Wildenborg, F. '… en er zijn nog veel meer 'halfjes'', *AD* 1 October 2016; Manning, S. and Adams, S. 'IVF scare over rogue 'Viking sperm' donor: Danish clinic failed to screen test-tube father of 99 babies for deadly disease… Passed on to British couple's child', *Daily Mail* 5 April 2015.

mistakes made, lawyers often struggle to articulate in what way the child is wronged. The wrong done to the parents can often be qualified as a breach of contract, but the wrong done the child is far more difficult to put in words, since its existence often depends on the actions that are at question. Of particular interest are cases in which a different donor is used than that which was agreed upon by the parents. These include cases in which the children within a family are genetically half-siblings instead of full siblings, or cases of fertility fraud,[8] in which the physician used his own genetic material to conceive a child. While it is clear in these cases that something has gone seriously wrong and that this may also impact the resulting child, claiming that the child's interests have been violated or that it has been harmed seems unconvincing as long as the child does not have a life not worth living. A responsibility approach may prove capable here to address the wrong done. From a responsibility approach, which incorporates a more elaborate idea of what we owe to future people, the wrong can be identified because this approach is capable of articulating aspects of the human person that cannot be conceived in terms of harm. The wrong does not lie in the assumption that because of fertility fraud, the child is forced into an existence that is worse than non-existence. It lies in the fact that the child is not anticipated and taken seriously as a fellow human person: elements that are important for the child's identity as a person are discarded or ignored. From the perspective that emphasises the importance of our genetic origins and genetic relations for our identity, obscuring donor information or using a different donor than that agreed upon is relevant. Creating a narrative or making sense of an origin story characterised by deceit can be just as hard as creating a narrative when the information regarding origin is absent. With the help of the responsibility approach these wrongs can be addressed as the wrongdoer violated his responsibility towards the child.

In addition to conceptualising our responsibilities and duties towards future life (both the life that is prevented and the life that is allowed to come into existence), the responsibility approach possesses another benefit due to the fact that it does not have to rely on individual interests and rights. The shortcomings of a vocabulary of interests and rights in the context of regulating (technologically assisted) reproduction has also been addressed by others. For example, Sandel has argued that the liberal vocabulary of rights and autonomy falls short in articulating the stakes involved in emerging (reproductive) biotechnologies. In my opinion, an important reason for the shortcomings of the liberal vocabulary is that the use of biotechnology, and in particular reproductive technology, by its nature transcends the individual and its interests. Biotechnology challenges natural boundaries and touches upon the nature of the human person itself. Tacit presuppositions about the human that used to be interwoven into our legal and moral thinking can no longer be based on

8 For a more elaborate discussion of this situation see Madeira, 2020.

biological boundaries, as those boundaries become fluid and subjected to our choices due to biotechnological developments. As a result, the question 'what makes us human?' can no longer, without question, be built upon those tacit presumptions, meaning that we are losing a solid point of departure from which to answer that question. At the same time, not taking a stance and allowing every individual to answer this question for himself also implies a certain view of the human person. For this reason, the use of biotechnology does not only affect individual interests, but also collective interests, as it is our humanity that is at stake. While the interests-construction seemed to obscure this collective dimension, the responsibility approach explicitly addresses the intertwinement of the collective and the individual. Consequently, it can address the consequences of reproductive biotechnology that transcend the individual, whereas these consequences for the collective are obscured in the interests-construction.

8.4 The Future of Responsibility

In this study, I have argued that the responsibility approach offers a more adequate theoretical framework for the conceptualisation of the future child compared to the interests-construction that is currently adopted in the regulations on reproduction. An important aspect of the responsibility approach is that it explicates the normative account of the human person. Since regulating human reproduction and reproductive technologies inevitably touches upon our human nature, we are forced to address, to explicate, and to reflect upon our human nature. The regulation of new developments in the field of reproductive biotechnology challenges us to further flesh out law's understanding of the human person. The normative account of the human person I discussed in chapter 7 can, in my opinion, do justice to the various values the regulations on reproduction aim to protect, and therefore allows for a critical reflection on the regulations and the values upon which the regulatory frameworks are based. Nonetheless, this normative account of the human person may in itself give rise to new questions. These questions exist on two levels; first, questions regarding the further elaboration of the normative account and second, questions concerning the correctness of this account itself.

With regard to the first type of question, as new technologies and new applications of existing technologies are introduced, existing boundaries continue to be challenged. For this reason, we remain confronted with the question of what we owe to future people in light of these new possibilities, and how the core notions of well-being, identity, and human dignity should be interpreted. For example, human germline genetic modification has been considered to be an affront to human dignity on both a national and international level. With the introduction of CRISPR-Cas9 human germline genetic modification has become a real possibility and another opportunity to eradicate severe hereditary illnesses. In the debate on CRISPR-Cas9, the UK's Nuffield Council on Bioethics rejected the notion of human dignity as a useful guiding principle for the regulation of germline modification[9] while the Dutch Health Council and COGEM maintained that germline modification for therapeutic purposes was in line with human dignity as they adopted a different interpretation of this notion and ignored the collective dimension.[10] In particular the use of ARTs that results in new genetic relations ask for a further elaboration of the normative account of the human person. These emerging reproductive biotechnologies facilitate new family structures, and as a result of this, our genetic and biological origin stories have become more complex. Consequently, this does not only raise the question as to how the core notions of well-being, dignity, and identity should be interpreted, but also how these three core values relate to each other.

One example is the introduction of mitochondrial replacement therapy. MRT disputes the previously given fact that a child genetically descends from two persons. This technology prevents the transmission of a mitochondrial condition from mother to child, by using the enucleated ovum of a donor. The enucleated egg cell still contains mitochondrial DNA, which makes the resulting child not only genetically related to its (intended) parents, but also approximately 0,1% related to the donor. This gives rise to the question as to whether the notion of narrative identity requires that the so-called mitochondrial donor is considered part of the child's origin story, meaning that the child has a right to access to identifying information about the donor. As explained in chapter 2, the UK legislator, the first to have regulated this technology, maintains that future child's right to know does not pertain to the mitochondrial donor. It reasoned that due to the small genetic contribution, the mitochondrial donor should not be understood as a second mother, nor would the use of a mitochondrial donor result in uncertainty about identity.[11] However, the assumption that only genetic relatedness is relevant for the child's origin story can be questioned. After all, in addition to the (minor) genetic relationship, there also exists an existential relationship. Without the input of the mitochondrial donor, it is likely that the child in question would not have been born at all, since a different recombination of its parents' gametes might have taken place, or the parents might have refrained from conceiving a child, or opted for egg donation to prevent the transmission of a mitochondrial illness. Moreover, the minor genetic relationship through the mitochondrial DNA may prove to be relevant in a different context. Cavaliere and Palacios-González have argued that

9 Nuffield Council on Bioethics, 2018, p. 93-94.

10 Commissie Genetische Modificatie (COGEM) & Gezondheidsraad, 2017, p. 55-56. Both the approach taken by the Nuffield Council and the approach taken by the Dutch Health Council and COGEMN have been criticised by van Beers: van Beers, 2020, p. 28; van Beers, de Kluiver and Maas, 2020, p. 333.

11 Department of Health, 2014, p. 16.

lesbian couples should have access to MRT in order to establish a genetic link between both intended parents and the child.[12] While it is unclear whether there have been any requests for this specific application of MRT, the proposal rests upon the idea that the small genetic bond through the mitochondrial DNA is indeed significant enough to endure the physical and financial investment required. In short, as MRT facilitates the possibility of new types of genetic relationships, it confronts us with the question of how this affects the future child's personal identity and how we should approach this matter in light of constructing a narrative identity.

A final example is offered by the questions raised by in vitro gametogenesis (IVG). In brief, IVG is the creation of egg and sperm cells in a laboratory, through reprogramming skin cells into stem cells (called induced Pluripotent Stem Cells or iPSC), which are in turn programmed to develop into gametes. This technology has the possibility to remove the last frontiers in reproduction. As in theory, both ova and spermatozoa can be created from cells derived from men and women alike, IVG facilitates the possibility of same sex reproduction, allowing same sex-couples to both become genetic parents of the child and forfeiting the need for a donor.[13] In addition, IVG also creates the possibility of multiplex parenthood and even solo parenthood. Importantly, in the case of the latter, while the child has only one genetic parent, it is not (necessarily) an exact clone of its uniparent.[14] Consequently, the question can be posed as to whether the right to two genetic parents that was coined in the cloning debate[15] also applies to the uniparent, since the child's right to a unique identity is not at risk. Do we indeed owe it to the child, in respect of its dignity, to have two genetic parents? And is there also a maximum number of genetic parents? How does the possibility of these novel family structures affect the child's narrative identity if there are no pre-existing stories or narratives that it can relate to? Moreover, as solo procreation is the most extreme form of incest, not only questions relating to the child's dignity and identity, but also to its well-being, surface. Solo procreation raises the risk of genetic conditions caused by recessive genes. At the same time, one of the benefits of IVG over traditional IVF is the number of embryo's that can be created. Since taking a swab of skin cells is far easier and in general less risky than harvesting egg cells through an IVF procedure, hundreds of skin cells can be reprogrammed into ova, which once fertilized result in hundreds of embryos. Each of these embryos can be screened for genetic mutations, and since there are hundreds of possible candidates, the chances of having one

12 Cavaliere and Palacios-González, 2018, p. 835-842.

13 A male couple would of course still need a surrogate.

14 Term coined by Greely. H.T. Greely, *The End of Sex and the Future of Human Reproduction*, Cambridge, Harvard University Press, 2016, p. 136.

15 See for example HL Deb (26 November 2001) vol. 629, col. 52. Earl Howe spoke of a "right to have a genetic father and mother."

healthy embryo available increases significantly. As IVG removes the biological boundaries of reproduction, we are forced to debate which legal boundaries we want to put in place in order to protect the self-images of the human person as an autonomous end in himself. In sum, as new technological developments are introduced, questions can be posed regarding the further elaboration of the normative account of the human person. This includes questions concerning the interpretation of the three values of well-being, dignity, and identity, but also concerning the relation between these three values.

The second type of questions is more fundamental. In addition to questioning how the depiction of the human person as an autonomous end in himself should be interpreted in light of new biotechnological developments, the normative account of the human person may also itself be a topic of debate. As explained, according to the responsibility approach, our obligations towards future people are derived from a normative account of what it means to be human. I argued that the explication of such a normative account is necessary for the regulation of (reproductive) biotechnologies. After all, as a result of biotechnology, biological assumptions that are interwoven into the legal depiction of the human person are no longer given facts. Instead, various aspects of our being have become subjected to technological manipulation. This has forced us to address the question of whether we want to uphold certain biological features in law as part of a human essence that needs to be protected, or whether our human nature is characterised by the use of technology. In other words, what is at stake is nothing less than the question 'what makes us human?'

Yet, answering that question is a complex matter. In my opinion, Jasanoff, Hurlbut and Saha are correct to argue that the regulation of germline modification (and other reproductive technologies in general) should not be left to the scientific community alone but should be addressed through democratic deliberation and public debate. They deem this necessary to avoid these technologies being approached as a risk-calculation, and ignoring larger relevant ethical, legal, and societal questions.[16] Nonetheless, that democratic process faces two challenges in particular. First, those who are affected by the technological interventions the most do not exist yet and therefore cannot speak for themselves. They can only take part in the discussion through representation. In other words, not only must those who exist now make decisions on our humanity, regulating reproduction also involves imagining what future we want for our society and thinking about how democratic notions such as equality should be interpreted in an intergenerational context. In addition, deciding upon a sensitive and difficult topic as the normative account

16 J.B. Hurlbut, K. Saha and S. Jasanoff, 'CRISPR Democracy: Gene Editing and the Need for Inclusive Deliberation', *Issues in Science and Technologie*, Vol. 32, No. 1 (fall 2015), 2015; Jasanoff, Hurlbut and Saha, 2015. See also van Beers, 2017b, p. 125-126.

of the human person proves to be particularly complex in today's postmodern society. As this research has demonstrated, important individual aspects of the human person, such as human dignity, identity and autonomy, are themselves subject to multiple interpretations that may conflict with each other. In a pluralist society, it is perhaps impossible to develop a comprehensive, univocal vision of the human person that is accepted by all. For this reason, the depiction of the human person as an autonomous end in himself, which calls for respect for his well-being, human dignity and personal identity, can be disputed as the best or most desirable interpretation of the human person.

Nonetheless, while the essence of our human nature may be topic for debate, I maintain that the depiction of the human person as reconstructed throughout this research, namely as an autonomous end in itself, offers the most convincing justification of the *current* regulations on reproduction. This interpretation of the human person fits and is capable of doing justice to the various regulatory frameworks that concern the future child. That is, the perception of the human person as an autonomous end in himself can make sense of the pursuit to secure a standard of reasonable well-being, of the multifaceted way the notion of human dignity is interpreted, and of various aspects that are deemed important for personal identity. Moreover, this perception is able to articulate the intertwined relationship between the individual human and humankind as a whole, and therefore able to address the collective interests that are involved in the regulation of reproduction. In sum, even though our humanity may remain topic of public debate, I believe that the depiction of the human person as an autonomous end in himself is the best translation of the normative account of the human person that underlies the current regulations on reproduction. Nonetheless, this depiction of the human person is not set in stone and may change over time as the regulations on reproduction and biolegal frameworks evolve.

More importantly, even if this reconstruction of the underlying concept of the human is open for discussion, the principal contribution of this study is a new theoretical framework for conceptualising the future child which facilitates this discussion. Unborn and future children are increasingly important actors on the legal stage. As Jonas already pointed out, the fact that the consequences of our actions and decisions transcend temporal boundaries and affect those who do not exist yet demands that future people are included in the scope of our ethical thinking. And, as demonstrated in this study, also our legal thinking. In this research, I have argued that future people, and more specifically the future child whose existence is prevented, cannot be approached in a similar manner as existing people, namely as legal persons or as subjects of interests. As a remedy for this problem, I proposed an alternative theoretical framework for addressing future people based on Jonas's theory of responsibility, consisting of a normative framework, i.e. the normative account of the human person, and a conceptual framework. So even if there is discussion on whether the human person should be understood as a free and autonomous end in himself, meaning that there is a discussion to be had on what we exactly owe to future people, the conceptual framework still offers a fruitful way to approach future people by allowing this question to be raised in the first place. That is, instead of treating it as a subject of interests, understanding the future child as the object of our responsibility is a more adequate way to conceptualise this unique entity. The conceptual framework based on responsibility is not subjected to internal contradictions that are inherent to the 'interests of the future child' construction. As a result, the future child can still be the object of our responsibility – and consequently, because of this responsibility we can have duties towards the future child – even if its existence is prevented. So, while the exact content of those duties may be a subject for further debate, conceptualising the future child as the subject of our responsibility offers a coherent ground for those duties, and thereby a more fruitful way to understand our legal relation to this entity.

Not only does a conceptual framework based on responsibility offer a more adequate conceptualisation of the future child, this approach also makes us aware that explicating the idea of what makes us human is a challenge we cannot avoid. Such an account is indispensable for critically reflecting upon existing and new developments in the field of (reproductive) biotechnology. After all, as a result of advances in this field, human nature itself has become the object of technology. Just as the biological and genetic features of the human being are no longer a static fact, but are increasingly challenged and dissolved by technological intervention, so has the notion of the human person that has remained an implicit foundation of our legal thinking become a subject for discussion and revaluation. Of course, addressing the question of our humanity is a complex and perhaps never-ending discussion, particularly in a pluralist society. Nonetheless, precisely because regulating reproductive technologies touches upon the intimate aspects of our humanity, and every regulatory choice in this field implies an idea of what it means to be human, we cannot avoid addressing this fundamental question. Therefore, instead of evading this question due to its complexity, we must take up the challenge to further think through what it means to be human in light of emerging reproductive technologies. By explicating our self-understanding and the depiction of the human person that can be distilled from the regulations on (reproductive) biotechnology, we will not only be able to critically reflect upon the ethical and legal-philosophical foundations of the existing regulatory frameworks, but also be better equipped to take up the new challenges that future technologies will confront us with. By facing the challenge of addressing that question, in combination with the conceptual framework that sees the future child as the object of our responsibility, it becomes possible to debate in a meaningful way what we owe to the future child.

In summation, because the attempt to anticipate the future child in the regulations on reproduction often results in the child's non-existence, this entity cannot be understood as a subject of interests. Instead, I have argued in this study that understanding the future child as the subject of our responsibility offers a more adequate approach to this entity. In order to understand what duties flow from this responsibility and what we owe to the future child, it is necessary to further explicate and develop an idea of what it means to be human. It may be very difficult, if not impossible, to articulate a comprehensive and univocal idea of what makes us human. Nonetheless, as the introduction of (reproductive) biotechnologies questions our existing boundaries and touches upon the most intimate sphere of our existence, we can no longer avoid this challenge. My proposal to conceptualise the future child as the object of our responsibility offers a convincing theoretical framework that allows us to raise this question in the first place and facilitate this inevitable discussion.

Summary

Advances in reproductive biotechnology facilitate increasing control over who is born and under what circumstances. As a result of these developments, we are increasingly confronted with the question: what do we owe to future people who are born with the help of these technologies? In the regulation of reproduction, this question has become a recurring theme. In an attempt to do justice to the future people that result from reproductive technologies, a new entity has appeared in the regulations on reproduction: the future child. This is the child that has not been born or even conceived yet – but might be at some point in the future. In order to be able to address and include this new entity in discussions on the regulations on reproduction, it must be conceptualised. That is, we need a theoretical framework that helps us understand what this entity is and how we can address it. In the regulations on reproduction, the future child is often conceptualised as a subject of rights or interests. At various points in, amongst others, the Dutch, UK, and German legal systems, the regulatory frameworks maintain that the interests of the future child must be taken into account. More particularly, the interests of the future child constitute a key concept for the justification of various regulatory frameworks on reproductive technologies. For example, regulations on access to fertility treatments, preimplantation genetic diagnosis, donor anonymity, and genetic modification invoke the interests of the future child to justify or impose restrictions on the use of these reproductive technologies. Importantly, as a result of these regulatory frameworks that invoke the interests of the future child, the future child itself is ultimately prevented from coming into existence.

Invoking the interests of the future child to prevent its existence has rendered the future child a paradoxical and complex entity. The future child is characterised by its own physical non-existence. It is the child that has not been conceived yet but may be at some point in the future. Yet, as a result of regulatory frameworks that claim to anticipate the future child's interests, the future child is prevented from coming into existence. In other words, the central topic of this study is the future child who does not exist and, as a result of its presumed interests, never will. It only exists as a legal construct, created in order to prevent its actual existence. This gives rise to the central question of this research: **is the presentation of the future child as a subject of interests an adequate theoretical framework to conceptualise and understand this entity?** Is the future child as a subject of interests so to say the best interpretation of this entity?

This research aims to assess the conceptualisation of the future child in the regulations on reproduction, by scrutinizing the tenability of the 'interests of the future child' construction.

The regulation of reproduction is an ethically sensitive matter, in particular when certain lives are prevented. Moreover, the human person himself, including the most intimate spheres of his existence, has become an object of technology, and the decisions we make now have consequences for future generations. It is therefore not surprising that the regulation of reproductive technologies confronts us with the question as to what we owe to future people. The answer to this question requires a normative account of the human person, a preliminary answer to the question 'What makes us human?', which encompasses several values. In my opinion, the regulations on reproduction imply such a normative account that is articulated through the 'interests of the future child'. However, the question is whether these values, i.e. well-being, identity and dignity, can be adequately articulated with the help of the 'interests of the future child' construction.

For the assessment of the adequacy of the 'interests of the future child' construction, I adopt a methodological approach inspired by Dworkin's constructivism. By operationalising the interests-construction, law seems to interpret the future child as a subject of interests and thus the question can be posed as to whether this interpretation is the 'best interpretation' of this entity. To make this assessment, this conceptualisation of the future child must be tested against two dimensions which Dworkin calls the dimensions of fit and justification. Applied to the object of this research, the construction used to conceptualise the future child must first, be coherent with the interpretation of fundamental legal concepts that form the premises of that construction. Second, the construction must also be able to account for and do justice to the values that the regulations on reproduction aims to protect. In order to determine whether the interests-construction meets (or fail to meet) these two dimensions, I deconstruct the 'interests of the future child' construction into the four assumption upon which it is based and assess the tenability of each assumption. The four assumptions made about the future child are: first, the core values underlying the regulations on reproduction can be understood as interests of an individual subject; second, the future child has an implicitly assumed interest in its own non-existence; third, the future child is a legal subject and, fourth, the future child whose existence is prevented is capable of having interests.

Before scrutinising the four assumptions about the future child, chapter 2 first elucidates how the future child is represented in the regulations on reproduction and explores which interests are attributed to this entity. Since procreation is mostly dealt with in national regulations, it is not possible to give one sole perspective of 'the law'. In order to make more general statements on how the future child is represented in legal contexts, the regulatory frameworks of three Western-European legal systems are examined and compared. The legal analysis explores the Dutch, UK, and German regulations on a variety of topics, including access to fertility treatments, embryo selection, the ban on gamete donor anonymity, and the ban on reproductive cloning and genetic modification. This analysis reveals that all three legal systems show strong similarities in their conceptualisation of the future child. In the three jurisdictions, the future child is conceptualised in basically the same manner, namely as a subject of interests. Moreover, this comparative analysis demonstrates that despite the different bioethical orientations and backgrounds of these legal systems, the contents of the interests attributed to the future child share important similarities. While there are still small differences, in all three legal systems, three main interests of the future child can be identified. These are the interest to be free from harm or the interest in reasonable well-being, the interest in forming an identity, and the interest in respect for human dignity.

The first interest, which focuses on prevention of harm, can be found in regulatory frameworks on access to fertility treatments and PGT. With regard to fertility treatments, the regulatory frameworks impose a *double responsibility* upon medical professionals, stating that they not only have a responsibility for their patients (the intended parents), but also for the resulting child. This latter duty implies that the medical professional must ensure that the future child will enjoy a reasonable standard of well-being, which means that it does not run a significant risk of suffering severe harm. A similar criterion is operationalised in the regulation on PGT: preimplantation genetic testing for monogenetic disorders and chromosomal abnormalities is allowed if the future child runs a significant risk of incurring a severe genetic condition. What is important for the discussion in chapter 4, is that this standard of well-being is higher than the so-called 'zero line', that is, a life worth living, in which case the benefits of one's life outweighs the disadvantages, even if they only barely do so.

The interest in identity formation comes to the fore in the regulatory frameworks that ban donor anonymity. In all three legal systems, donor conceived children are able to receive identifying information about the donor when they reach a certain age. The reason for the ban on donor anonymity is the idea that knowledge about one's genetic descent is paramount for the child's identity. Not because the child would otherwise suffer psychological harm, but because being able to form your identity is a value in itself. Genetic information is considered to be of such importance for this, that the interest in having access to it is often acknowledged as a right, commonly known as 'the right to know'. The Dutch and German supreme courts acknowledged that one has a right to information about one's genetic descent and considered this right as part of the so-called general personality right. In the UK, a similar case was presented to the court, but no ruling followed as the law amended in the meantime. The UK court did acknowledge that access to genetic information falls within the scope of Article 8 of the European Convention of Human Rights, which encompasses a general personality right. The rights vocabulary was also adopted in the German and UK regulations on donor anonymity. The Dutch Memorandum to the Donor Information Artificial Reproduction Act, however, referred solely to an interest in access to donor information. It follows from the analysis that in general, the regulatory frameworks assume that the future child has an interest in having access to information about its descent, and often this interest is framed as a right to information. Of course, the question remains as to whether the non-existent future child can also be the subject of this right. This question is addressed in chapter 5.

The final interest of the future child is its interest in human dignity. This interest is invoked in reproductive laws to justify the bans on reproductive cloning, genetic modification, and non-medical embryo selection. Interestingly, where the interest of the future child in being free from harm justifies certain modes of PGT (namely selection in case of a severe genetic or chromosomal condition), its human dignity is invoked to prohibit other forms of selection, such as non-medical sex selection. The interpretation of this interest shows the most variation between the three legal systems, in particular regarding issues such as HLA-tissue typing and genetic modification. With regard to the latter, the United Kingdom deems it less likely that the future child's dignity will be violated, particularly when there are health interests at stake, while Germany is more reluctant to allow the use of these technologies for medical purposes. This illustrates that the concept of human dignity can be interpreted in diverging ways, which is further explored in chapter 3.

In chapter 3, I start with assessing the first assumption about the future child that underlies the 'interests of the future child' construction. This assumption entails that the various values at stake in governing reproduction can be understood as interests of an individual entity, namely the future child. In order to assess this assumption, I further reconstruct the values that underly the regulations on reproduction in order to understand which interpretations of harm, identity, and human dignity underly the regulatory frameworks. Even though the three interests of the future child form prominent concepts in the regulations on reproduction, these core concepts are barely elaborated upon within the regulations. With the help of academic literature on this topic, I aim to come to a better understanding of how these legal notions are operationalised in the regulations on reproduction.

I start with the notion of harm. The regulatory frameworks that refer to the child's well-being and the prevention of significant harm do not explain what constitutes harm. It only becomes clear that there is a strong relation between the two concepts. This relation is confirmed in academic debate: both Feinberg and Raz define harm as a negative impact on someone's well-being. Being harmed thus means being made worse off or experiencing a setback of interests. Importantly, both authors maintain that not every setback qualifies as harm, only interests of a tangible or measurable kind. Feinberg stresses that actions are "harmless" if they do not set back interests of a "tangible and material kind."[1] A similar idea can be found in the regulations on reproduction. The regulatory frameworks that aim to protect the future child's well-being focus only on physical or mental well-being, for example a genetic condition or a developmental deficit due to failing or irresponsible parenting. This means that the future child's other two 'interests', identity and dignity, do not fall within the scope of this definition. Put differently, thwarting the child's identity formation or violating its dignity cannot be understood as harm. As discussed in chapter 3, various authors have, for this reason, questioned the relevance of safeguarding the child's identity formation or protecting its dignity.

The regulations on reproduction do not suggest that the violation of the future child's interests in identity and dignity should be understood as harm to the child. Instead, in the regulations these values are presented as independent values. This shows that in the regulations on reproduction, the human person is considered to be more than a being that can experience harm. More precisely, the notions of identity and dignity operationalise an account of the human person that is intersubjective and connected to others. The notion of personal identity is based on the idea of narrative identity. A person's personal identity can be understood as a narrative that helps to make sense of who that person is, what his dreams and motivations are, and how he remains the same person despite going through changes. According to Ricoeur and MacIntyre, such a life history is entangled with the life stories of others. This includes the child's genetic parents because they are not only related to the child but contributed to its existence: without them, the child would not have existed in the first place. The notion of human dignity encompasses a collective, normative image of the human person, from which the idea of the individual person as autonomous is derived. Reproductive practices that are an affront to human dignity, such as reproductive cloning, are therefore not only a violation of the dignity of the resulting child, but also a violation of the dignity of mankind.

Especially this latter aspect calls the tenability of the 'interests of the future child' construction into question. The 'interests of the future child' construction operationalises vocabulary that focuses on the individual subject. The values the regulation protects are, through this construction, presented as interests of an individual entity. However, the values it aims to articulate include not only individual, but also collective values. In particular, human dignity also encompasses a collective dimension which seems to be obscured in the interests-construction. Because of this I conclude that the first pillar of the 'interests of the future child' construction starts to erode: while it can make sense of the

1 Feinberg, 1987, p. 35.

individual aspects of idea of the human person that forms the foundation of the regulatios on reproduction, it cannot articulate the collective interests that transcend the individual future child. With regards to this collective dimension of the human person, the 'interests of the future child' construction fails to meet the criterion of justification: because the interests-construction cannot make sense of the collective values that are involved in the regulations on reproduction, it cannot show the regulation in its best light possible.

In chapter 4, I continue the critical assessment of the 'interests of the future child' construction, by scrutinising the second assumption. The regulatory frameworks that claim to serve the future child's interests result in the prevention of the future child's existence. Although it is barely made explicit, this construction is based upon the assumption that non-existence in these circumstances is actually in the interest of the future child. Chapter 4 explores the idea of an 'interest in one's own non-existence'.

Because the possibility of an interest in one's own non-existence is barely addressed in regulations or legal debate, I draw upon philosophical and bioethical work that has thought through to what extent the legal interpretations of harm and interests can be applied to reproduction and regulating reproductive technologies, and in doing so, has assessed the possibility of this interest. Chapter 4 therefore elaborates on Parfit's theory of the non-identity problem, which argues that in most cases, the child is not harmed by being brought into existence. Only when the quality of its life is so low that the benefits of life no longer outweigh the disadvantages or the harm, can it be argued that one would be better off not existing at all and, hence, has an interest in one's own non-existence. Such a situation is, in the philosophical debate, often addressed as a life not worth living, and in related tort cases as a wrongful life. Yet, in most cases concerning the regulations on reproduction, the child will presumably not have a life not worth living, and therefore, from this perspective, preventing the future child's existence cannot be justified by invoking its interests. In order to explain the intuition that in some cases it is better to prevent a child from being born, Parfit explores an alternative, utilitarian approach. However, since this alternative solution is only applicable to cases in which a child is prevented for the sake of another child, it cannot provide a justification for preventing the future child's existence in the majority of cases for which the regulations on reproduction are applicable.

The discussion of the non-identity problem further brings into question the tenability of the 'interests of the future child' construction. As explained in this chapter, the child only has an interest in its own non-existence if the expected quality of life is so low that the harm outweighs the benefits of life. That is, the standard of well-being falls below a minimum level and therefore, it can be reasonably assumed that one would be better off not existing at all. Only then is the prevention of its existence, and thus also the regulatory frameworks that result in this prevention, in the future child's interest. The regulatory frameworks that focus on the future child's well-being, however, maintain that the double responsibility of medical professionals entails that they should not just secure a minimum level of well-being for the future child, but a reasonable level of well-being. In other words, the regulation sets the bar higher. Therefore, in most cases covered by the regulatory frameworks invoking the future child's interest in well-being, the child's well-being may indeed be jeopardised, but not to such an extent that it has an interest in its own non-existence. Moreover, also in cases in which the child's interests in identity and dignity are protected, it is unlikely that the child has an interest in its own non-existence. As discussed in chapter 3, the violation of the interests in identity and dignity do not qualify as harm but constitute an intangible form of wrongdoing. It is doubtful that violating these interests affect the quality of the child's life in such way that it results in a life not worth living. As Spranger and Glover for example argue, a cloned child would probably not prefer to not exist at all simply because he is cloned.[2] Consequently, in the majority of cases covered by the regulatory frameworks assuming that the future child has an interest in its own non-existence appears to diverge from the way in which harm and interest are usually interpreted in law. In other words, assuming that the prevention of its existence is in the interest of the future child is at odds with the fundamental understanding of the legal notion of interest. Therefore, in the majority of cases, the assumption that the child has an interest in its own non-existence does not meet the criterion of fit, since it contradicts the interpretation of legal notions and therefore its own premises. In conclusion, the second assumption about the future child is only tenable only in a small number of cases. This means that the tenability of the 'interests of the future child' construction is far more limited that what follows from the regulations on reproduction: only in the case of a life not worth living is it in the interest of the future child to have its existence prevented.

For the assessment of the third and the fourth assumptions, chapters 5 and 6 shift the focus from the future child's interests to the future child's assumed (legal) subjectivity. Chapter 5 focuses on the third assumption, namely the assumption that the future child is a legal subject. After all, as the subject of legally relevant interests, the future child has become a subject in law. More importantly, in some discussions, the *rights* of the future child are mentioned, such as the right to know or the right not to be born. Therefore, the first step of assessing whether the future child can be understood as a legal person is exploring the possibilities of law's traditional vocabulary: the natural legal person endowed with rights and duties.

2 Spranger, 2010, p 103; Glover, 2006, p. 64-65.

Through an analysis of legal-philosophical literature, I discuss the three most important approaches to natural legal personality of the natural person: a naturalist approach, a constructivist approach, and an anticipatory approach. First, I discuss the naturalist approach and the way biological, rational, or metaphysical features of the human being are reflected in the characteristics of the legal person. Due to the fact that the future child has no biological or physical presence, but only exists as a legal construct, this interpretation of the legal person cannot represent the future child. Second, I elaborate on the legal person as an empty, legal-technical construct. By some authors, this emptiness is considered a benefit, as it can be attributed to almost any entity to protect its interests. With regard to the future child however, the fiction misses its purpose because it is not the interests of the future child that must be protected but the interests of the actual child that may eventually result from it. In other words, this approach fails to grasp the inherent connection between the two entities. In response to the shortcomings of the first two approaches, chapter 5 finally explores the possibilities of an anticipatory approach. That is, can legal personality be constructed based on the anticipation of the actual child's personality, or put differently, can the actual child's personality be expanded in order to include the future child? Although there are possibilities to base an unborn or future child's legal or moral status on the anticipation of the actual child's personality, this construction offers no solace for the future child whose existence is prevented. Since its existence is prevented, there is no longer an entity with legal personality that can be expanded or anticipated.

In conclusion, the future child cannot be understood as a natural legal subject with the help of any of the three main approaches to legal personality. The main reason for this is the child's non-existence. All three approaches require that the entity exists in some form or at some moment in order to understand it as a legal person. However, the personification of the future child serves to prevent the actual child from coming into existence and from becoming an actual legal person. As a result, the assumption that the future child is a legal subject with legal personality is untenable because this assumption is logically inconsistent: as a result of bestowing legal personality on the future child, it will never exist and therefore never possess the requirement for legal personality. In other words, trying to put the future child's legal subjectivity in terms of (natural) personality fails to meet the criteria of fit. This does not make the third assumption concerning the future child - that it is a legal subject - untenable per se. It may be inherently contradictory to understand the future child as legal person, but the possibility of alternative forms of legal subjectivity remains. In chapter 6, I explore the most likely candidate, namely the future child as a subject of legally relevant interests.

Chapter 6 continues with the assessment of the third assumption that the future child is a legal subject, by exploring the possibility of an alternative form of legal subjectivity. Since the future child is mostly presented as a subject of interests, I investigate in the first part of this chapter, whether the subject of legal interests can be understood as an alternative legal subject compared to the legal person. To this aim, the sixth chapter elaborates the concept of 'legal interest' and the relation between interests and rights. From this discussion it follows that legally relevant interests can offer the subject some form of legal standing, but do not generate a claim as strong as legal rights. In other words, through the attribution of interests, an entity can also become a legal subject.

The question then arises as to whether the future child fits this alternative form of legal subjectivity. In order to answer this question, the second part of chapter 6 assesses the fourth and last assumption about the future child: can the future child whose existence is prevented indeed be a subject of interests? In order to answer this question, I draw upon the work of various legal philosophers and bioethicists who have addressed this question based on the 'interest view'. This theory maintains that the capability to have interests requires that the entity has some form of consciousness, or 'conative life'; in case of future entities, that the entity will become conscious in the future. When this is applied to the future child who will not come into existence, it becomes clear that the future child cannot meet this requirement. Due to the future child's non-existence, it is not only impossible to understand it as a subject of rights, it is also impossible to understand it as a subject of interests. From this, I therefore conclude that also the fourth, and subsequently the third, assumption about the future child are untenable and fail to meet the dimension of fit. Since the capacity to have interests requires existence, the conceptualisation of the future child as a subject of (legal) interests is at odds with its own premise.

The critical assessment of the four assumptions reveals that each of the four assumptions is questionable. The first and second assumptions are untenable in most cases. The third and fourth assumptions, pertaining to the future child's subjectivity, are completely untenable due to its non-existence. Consequently, the 'interests of the future child' construction that rests upon these four pillars becomes problematic. Understanding the future child as a subject of interests, having an interest in its own non-existence, cannot be the best conceptualisation or interpretation of the future child, since its fails to meet the dimensions of fit and justification. The 'interests of the future child' construction cannot justify every aspect of the normative account of the human person that underlies the regulations on reproduction since its individual-oriented vocabulary cannot make sense of the collective interests that are involved. In addition, this construction is riddled with inconsistencies. The assumption that it is in the interest of the future child to have its existence prevented is, in the majority of cases covered by the regulatory frameworks, at odds with how interest and harm are interpreted in the legal context. Because of this, the interests-construction fails to make sense of the standard of reasonable well-being or intangible values such as identity and dignity. Moreover, approaching the future child whose existence is prevented as a legal subject by means of natural legal personality or the subjectivity of legal interests does not fit with the premises of these notions, namely that legal personality or the capacity to have legal interests requires the future child's to be born. As a result, the construction is internally contradictory. In short, invoking the interests of the future child in order to prevent its existence, bars the child from having the capacity to have interests or legal personality at all. All in all, referring to the interests of the future child in order to prevent its existence results in a paradox.

Because the 'interests of the future child' construction fails to conceptualise the future child in an adequate manner, I propose an alternative theoretical framework that is capable of taking up this task in chapter 7. This alternative approach does not focus on the rights and interests of an individual entity, but on the role and responsibility of those who affect the life and existence of this entity. In the seventh chapter, I argue that a theoretical framework based on responsibility offers a better conceptualisation of the future child since it does not contain internal inconsistencies and because this approach can also make sense of the collective values that are at stake in the regulation of reproduction. For the development of this responsibility-based theoretical framework, I draw upon the ethical theory of Hans Jonas. He claims that as a result of modern technology, our actions now have far-reaching consequences, transgressing spatial and temporal boundaries. Because our actions affect the lives of those who will live in the future, we become responsible for future people. This responsibility entails that we have a duty to ensure that in the future human life still exists and that their humanity is respected. This means that not only must the physical existence of future mankind be secured, we must also ensure that the essence of the human person is respected. To this aim, Jonas develops a normative account of what it means to be human, which he calls the Idea of Man. According to this normative account, the human being is a free and autonomous end in himself, and future people must be capable of understanding themselves as such.

Jonas's theory of responsibility offers a fruitful starting point for conceptualising the future child and explaining what we owe to it. Rather than a subject of interests, the future child can be understood as the object of our responsibility. As such, we can still say that we have duties towards the future child without having to base these duties on the interests or rights of the future child. In order to develop a working theoretical framework for the future child whose existence is prevented, Jonas's theory of responsibility must be further elaborated. First, Jonas's theory of responsibility and his Idea of Man focuses on mankind as a whole, which raises the question what this implies for the individual future child.

More particularly, since Jonas maintains that we have a duty that in the future mankind still exists, preventing the future child's existence may seem at odds with this imperative. I argue that the individual being is intrinsically linked to humanity as a collective because what is allowed to be done to the individual says something about what we owe to the human person in general. For this reason, securing and respecting the normative account of the human person may require the prevention of certain modes of reproduction that are an affront to the idea of the human person as a free and autonomous end in himself, and accordingly, it may require the prevention of the future child's existence. Therefore, in addition to mankind as a whole, also the individual future child whose existence is prevented can be understood as the object of our responsibility. Conceptualising the future child this way does not result in internal contradictions; due to the focus on the intertwinement between the individual child and the collective of mankind, the future child is not attributed any qualities that require existence. This conceptualisation does not conflict with law's premises on personhood and the subjectivity of interests as this conceptualisation does not have to rely on those notions.

The second element that requires further elaboration is the normative account of the human being itself. According to Jonas's Idea of Man, the human being is a free and autonomous end in itself, and this notion of the human being is rather similar to the representation of the human person in law. However, the reality of reproductive technologies is far more complex than Jonas could have foreseen. This gives rise to the question of what the protection of the idea of the human being as an autonomous end in himself demands in the context of, for example, PGT, mitochondrial replacement therapy, access to fertility treatments, and donor anonymity. In the last part of chapter 7, I explore how the idea of the human person as a free and autonomous end in himself can make sense of the normative account of the human person that underlies the regulations on reproduction. For this purpose, I explore how the notion of autonomy can be interpreted in light of dignity, identity, and well-being. By doing so, I demonstrate that the theoretical framework based on responsibility is not only a coherent conceptual framework, but also offers a better justification of the values that constitute law's understanding of the human person than the interests-construction. In sum, conceptualising the future child as the object of our responsibility offers, in my opinion, a better interpretation of this unique entity than the 'interests of the future child' construction. The theoretical framework based on responsibility does not suffer from the same points of critique as the interests-construction. By conceiving the future child as the object of our responsibility, the internal contradictions of the interests-construction can be avoided. Moreover, the normative framework of the responsibility approach, which perceives the human person as a free and autonomous end in himself, can make sense of the three core values that constitute the normative account of the human person that underlies the regulations on reproduction.

In order to regulate reproductive technologies in a way that does justice to those who may result from these technologies an idea of how to conceptualise these future people is necessary. Only when we have a notion of how to approach actual and possible future people can we start pondering over the question of what our duties towards future people entail. As shown, the conceptualisation of the future child whose existence is prevented has proven to be a challenge. With this study, I hope to contribute to the discussion on what we owe to future people by offering an adequate theoretical framework for conceptualising this unique entity. As I argued in the chapter 7, this alternative approach is free of internal contradictions and can make sense of the values the regulations on reproduction aim to protect: the standard of reasonable well-being, human dignity, and identity formation.

However, in order to fully articulate our duties towards the future child it is necessary to further flesh out the normative account of humanity that underlies our regulations on reproduction and other laws in the field of biolaw. The need to articulate this notion has become even more urgent due to the development of reproductive technologies and biotechnology in general. As a result of these developments, human nature itself has become the object of these technologies. The nature of the human being is no longer "given once for all"[3] a given, but the human being is now an entity whose building blocks have become something that can be manipulated. With new technologies and new applications of existing technologies being introduced in the foreseeable future, the notion of the human that has remained implicit in law for a long time needs to be explicated further to answer to the challenges created by new reproductive technologies. In other words, regulating reproduction also involves the task of exploring possible answers to the question: what makes us human? In the last chapter, I identified several topics that demand further discussion of law's perception of the human person. These topics could serve as a starting point for public debate. Since reproductive technologies, and therefore also its regulation, affect not only future people, but also our self-understanding as human persons, the normative account of the human person that underlies the regulatory frameworks is a topic for discussion that needs to take place in society itself.

Looking into the question of our humanity is not an easy feat. The discussions on the notion of human dignity, identity, and autonomy have already revealed the myriad interpretations of these concepts. In addition, these concepts are often hard to put in words, making it difficult to describe and assess the consequences of reproductive technologies. Although the question may seem simple, trying to put in words what makes

3 H. Jonas, 'Technology and Responsibility: Reflections on the New Task of Ethics', *Social Research*, Vol. 40, No. 1, 1973, p. 31.

us human is surrounded by unprecedented complexities. In particular, now that technological developments erode the boundaries between the given and the made,[4] it may seem that we are losing our grip on this endeavour. But precisely because the regulation of (reproductive) biotechnology touches upon the intimate aspects of our humanity, and every regulatory choice in this field implies an idea of what it means to be human, we cannot escape articulating such a collective perspective. Nor can we hide behind the 'interests of the future child' in an attempt to present our perspective on humanity as based on individual interests or rights. Therefore, rather than shy away from it, we must take up the challenge to at least further reflect upon the notion of humanity that forms the foundation of the regulations on reproduction and to attempt to articulate in more depth what it means to be human. Through explicating our self-understanding and the depiction of the human person that can be distilled from the regulations on (reproductive) biotechnology, we will not only be able to critically reflect upon the ethical and legal-philosophical foundations of the existing regulatory frameworks, but also be better equipped to take up the new challenges that emerging technologies will confront us with.

4 Habermas, 2003, p. 42.

Bibliography

LITERATURE

E. Aarden, I. van Hoyweghen, R. Vos and K. Horstman, 'Providing preimplantation genetic diagnosis in the United Kingdom, The Netherlands and Germany: a comparative in-depth analysis of health-care acces', *Human Reproduction*, Vol. 24, No. 7, 2009, pp. 1542-1547.

T. Allen, 'The Philippine children's case: recognizing legal standing for future generations', *Georgetown International law Review*, Vol. 6, 1994, pp. 713-741.

R. Andorno, 'Human dignity and human rights as a common ground for a global bioethics', *Journal of Medicine and Philosophy*, Vol. 34, 2009, pp. 223-240.

D. Archard, 'Wrongful life', *Philosophy*, Vol. 79, 2004, pp. 403-420.

M. Bagaric and J. Allan, 'The vacuous concept of dignity', *Journal of Human Rights*, Vol. 5, No. 2, 2006, pp. 257-270.

M.D. Bayles, 'Harm to the unconceived', *Philosophy and public affairs*, Vol. 5, No. 3, 1976, pp. 292-304.

B.C. van Beers, 'De humaniteit van humane biotechnologie. Juridische perspectieven op menselijke waardigheid en medische biotechnologie', in, *Humane Biotechnologie en Recht (Handelingen Nederlandse Juristen-Vereniging 2009-1)*, Kluwer, Deventer, 2009a.

B.C. van Beers, *Persoon en lichaam in het recht. Menselijke waardigheid en zelfbeschikking in het tijdperk van de medische biotechnologie*, Hoofddorp, Boom Juridische Uitgevers, 2009b.

B.C. van Beers, 'Leeftijdsgrenzen en het grenzeloze verlangen naar een kind. De discussie over de oudste moeder van Nederland vanuit rechtsfilosofisch perspectief', *Ars Aequi*, Vol. 2011, No. 7-8, 2011, pp. 574-583.

B.C. van Beers, 'Is Europe "giving in to baby markets"? Reproductive tourism in Europe and the gradual erosion of existing legal limits to reproductive markets', *Medical Law Review*, Vol. 23, No. 1, 2014, pp. 103-134.

B.C. van Beers, 'From winged lions to frozen embryos: the functions of law in the symbolic mediation of biomedical hybrids', in: B. van Klink, B.C. van Beers and L. Poort (eds.), *Symbolic legislation theory and developments in biolaw*, Springer Verlag, Switzerland, 2016a.

B.C. van Beers, 'Van slaapkamer naar vruchtbaarheidskliniek. Deseksualisering van voortplanting en de 'uitbarsting van verantwoordelijkheid'', *Ars Aequi*, Vol. 2016, No. 4, 2016b, pp. 298-306.

B.C. van Beers, 'The changing nature of law's natural person: the impact of emerging technologies on the legal concept of the person', *German Law Journal*, Vol. 18, No. 3, 2017a, pp. 560-594.

B.C. van Beers, 'Imagining future people in biomedical law: From technological utopias to legal dystopias within the regulation of human genetic modification technologies ', in: M. Ambrus, R. Rayfuse and W. Werner (eds.), *Risk and the regulation of uncertainty in international law*, Oxford University Press, Oxford, 2017b.

B.C. van Beers, 'Nosce te ipsum. Over *homo sapiens* en *homo juridicus* in een tijdperk van posthumane technologieën', in: B. van Beers and I. van Domselaar (eds.), *Humo Duplex. De dualiteit van de mens in recht, filosofie en sociologie*, Boom Juridisch, Den Haag, 2017c.

B.C. van Beers, 'Welkom in de CRISPR-dierentuin. Juridische grenzen aan genetische modificatie van het nageslacht in het CRISPR-tijdperk', *Nederlands Juristenblad*, Vol. 2019, No. 24, 2019, pp. 1722-1730.

B.C. van Beers, 'Rewriting the human genome, rewriting human rights law? Human rights, human dignity, and human germline modification in the CRISPR era', *Journal of Law and the Biosciences*, Vol. 7, No. 1, 2020, pp. 1-36.

B.C. van Beers, C. de Kluiver and R. Maas, 'The regulation of human germline genome modification in the Netherlands', in: A. Boggio, C. Romano and J. Almqvist (eds.), *Human Germline Genome Modification and the Right to Science: A Comparative Study of National Laws and Policies*, Cambridge University Press, Cambridge, 2020.

D. Benatar, *Better never to have been. The harm of coming into existence*, Oxford, Clarendon Press, 2006.

D. Benatar, 'Kids? Just say no', 2017, *Aeon* <https://aeon.co/essays/having-children-is-not-life-affirming-its-immoral> last accessed: 1 January 2023.

R. Bennett and J. Harris, 'Are there lives not worth living? When is it morally wrong to reproduce', in: D. Dickenson (ed.), *Ethical issues in maternal-fetal medicine*, Cambridge University Press, Cambridge, 2002.

J. Berg, 'Of elephants and embryos: a proposed framework for legal personhood', *Hastings Law Journal*, Vol. 59, 2007, pp. 369-406.

R.J.B. Bergamin, *De persoon in het recht*, Nijmegen, Ars Aequi Libri, 2000.

D. Beyleveld and R. Brownsword, *Human Dignity in Bioethics and Biolaw*, Oxford, Oxford Scholarship online, 2012.

J. de Boer, *Mr. C. Assers Handleiding tot de beoefening van het Nederlands Burgerlijk Recht. 1. Personen- en familierecht. Deel I. De persoon, afstamming en adoptie, gezag en omgang, levensonderhoud, bescherming van meerderjarigen*, 19th ed, Deventer, Wolters Kluwer 2020.

T.C. Borman and J.C.A. de Poorter, *Tekst & Commentaar Algemene Wet Bestuursrecht*, ed, Deventer, Wolters Kluwer 2017.

L. Bosch, 'Welk beleid kan het belang van het kind dragen? Het nieuwe wetsvoorstel draagmoederschap nader bekeken.', *Podium voor Bio-ethiek*, Vol. 27, No. 2, 2020, pp. 7-11.

N. Bostrom, 'In defence of posthuman dignity', *Bioethics*, Vol. 19, No. 3, 2005, pp. 202-214.

R. Brandt, 'Mitochondrial donation and 'the right to know'', *Journal of Medical Ethics*, Vol. 42, 2016, pp. 678-684.

M. Brazier, A. Campbell and S. Golombok, *Surrogacy. Review for health ministers of current arrangements for payments and regulation. (Brazier report)*, 1998.

A.L. Bredenoord, W. Dondorp, G. Pennings and G. de Wert, 'Ethics of modifying the mitochondrial genome', *Journal of Medical Ethics*, Vol. 37, No. 2, 2011, pp. 97-100.

D.W. Brock, 'The non-identity problem and genetic harms - the case of wrongful handicaps', *Bioethics*, Vol. 9, 1995, pp. 269-275.

P.W. Brouwer, R.J.B. Bergamin, A.M. Bos, C.L.B. Kocken, E. Poortinga, G.J.M. Veerman and J.J.C.M. Wirken, *Recht, een introductie*, Den Haag, Boom Juridische Uitgevers, 2004.

A. Buchanan, D.W. Brock, N. Daniels and D. Wikler, *From chance to choice*, Cambridge, Cambridge University press, 2009.

J.C. Byk, 'Is human dignity a useless concept? Legal perspective', in: M. Düwell, J. Braarvig, R. Brownsword and D. Mieth (eds.), *The Cambridge handbook of human dignity: interdisciplinary perspectives*, Cambridge University Press, Cambridge, 2014.

N. Cahn, 'Necessary subjecs: the need for a mandatory national donor gamete databank', *DePaul Journal of Health Care Law*, Vol. 12, No. 1, 2009, pp. 203-233.

Z.R. Calo, 'Human dignity and health law: personhood in recent bioethical debates', *Notre Dame Journal of Law Ethics & Public Policy*, Vol. 26, 2012, pp. 473-499.

P. Cane, *Tort law and economic interests*, 2nd, Oxford, Clarendon Press, 1996.

G. Cavaliere and C. Palacios-González, 'Lesbian motherhood and mitochondrial replacement techniques: reproductive freedom and genetic kinship', *Journal of Medical Ethics*, Vol. 44, 2018, pp. 835-842.

I.G. Cohen, 'Regulating reproduction: the problem with best interests', *Minnesota Law Review*, Vol. 96, 2011, pp. 423-519.

I.G. Cohen, 'Beyond best interests ', *Minnesota Law Review*, Vol. 96, 2012, pp. 1187-1274.

Commissie evaluatie regelgeving, *Bereidheid tot donatie van sperma bij opheffing van de anonimiteitwaarborg van de donor*, Den Haag, 1999.

Commissie Genetische Modificatie (COGEM) & Gezondheidsraad, *Ingrijpen in het DNA van de mens. Morele en maatschappelijke implicaties van kiembaanmodificatie*, Bilthoven, 2017.

G.J.M. Corstens, *Het Nederlands strafprocesrecht*, Arnhem, Kluwer, 2005.

K. Daniels, 'Anonymity and openness and the recruitment of gamete donors. Part 2: Oocyte donors', *Human Fertility*, Vol. 10, No. 4, 2007a, pp. 223-231.

K. Daniels, 'Anonymity and openness and the recruitment of gamete donors. Part I: semen donors', *Human Fertility*, Vol. 10, No. 3, 2007b, pp. 151-158.

D.S. Davis, 'Genetic dilemmas and the child's right to an open future', *Rutgers law journal*, Vol. 28, 1997, pp. 549-592.

D. DeGrazia, 'Enhancement technologies and human dignity', *Journal of Medicine and Philosophy*, Vol. 30, 2005, pp. 261-283.

G. Den Hartogh, 'Is human dignity the ground of human rights?', in: M. Düwell, J. Braarvig, R. Brownsword and D. Mieth (eds.), *The Cambridge Handbook of Human Dignity: Interdisciplinary Perspectives*, Cambridge University Press, Cambridge, 2014.

Department of Health, *Review of the Human Fertilisation and Embryology Act. Proposals for revised legislation (including establishment of the Regulatory Authority for Tissue and Embryos)*, 2006.

Department of Health, *Mitochondrial Donation: Government Response to the Consultation on Draft Regulations to Permit the Use of New Treatment Techniques to Prevent the Transmission of a Serious Mitochondrial Disease from Mother to Child*, 2014.

Department of Health and Social Security, *Report of the Committee of Inquiry into Human Fertilisation and Embryology (Warnock Report)*, London, 1984.

J.H.H.M. Dorscheidt, 'Developments in legal and medical practice regarding the unborn child and the need to expand prenatal legal protection', *European Journal of Health Law*, Vol. 17, No. 5, 2010, pp. 433-454.

H. Dreier, *Grundgesetz Kommentar. Band 1, Präambel, Artikel 1-19*, 3rd ed, Tübingen, Mohr Siebeck 2014.

R. Dworkin, *Taking rights seriously*, Cambridge, Harvard University Press, 1977.

R. Dworkin, 'Rights as trumps', in: J. Waldron (ed.), *Theories of rights*, Oxford University Press, Oxford, 1984.

R. Dworkin, *Life's dominion. An argument about abortion, euthanasia, and individual freedom*, New York, Alfred A. Knopf, 1993.

R. Dworkin, *Law's empire*, Oxford, Hart Publishing, 1998.

R. Dworkin, 'Playing God', 1999, *Prospect Magazin* 20 May 1999 <https://www.prospectmagazine.co.uk/magazine/playing-god-genetics-ronald-dworkin> last accessed: 1 January 2023.

R. Dworkin, *Sovereign virtue. The theory and practice of equality*, Cambridge, Harvard University Press, 2000.

R. Dworkin, *Is democracy possible here? Principles for a new political debate*, Princeton, Princeton University Press, 2006.

R. Elliot, 'The rights of future people', *Journal of Applied Philosophy*, Vol. 6, No. 2, 1989, pp. 159-169.

C. Enders, "Probleme der Gentechnologie in grundrechtsdogmatischer Sicht', in: R. Mellinghoff and H.-H. Trute (eds.), *Die Leistungsfähigkeit des Rechts. Methodik,*

Gentechnologie, Internationales Verwaltungsrecht, R. v. Decker & C.F. Müller, Heidelberg, 1988.

Deutscher Ethikrat, *Preimplanation genetic diagnosis. Opinion*, Berlin, 2011.

Deutscher Ethikrat, *Intervening in the Human Germline. Opinion. Executive summary and recommendations.*, Berlin, 2019.

D. Fagundes, 'Note, What We Talk About When We Talk About Persons: The Language of a Legal Fiction.', *Harvard Law Review*, Vol. 114, No. 6, 2001, pp. 1745-1768.

J. Feinberg, 'The rights of animals and unborn generations', in: W.T. Blackstone (ed.), *Philosophy & Environmental Crisis*, The University of Georgia Press, Athens, GA, 1974.

J. Feinberg, 'Is there a right to be born?', in: J. Feinberg (ed.), *Rights, justice, and the bounds of liberty*, Princeton University Press, Princeton, 1980.

J. Feinberg, *Harm to others. The moral limits of the criminal law*, Oxford, Oxford University Press, 1984.

J. Feinberg, *The Moral Limits of the Criminal Law Volume 1: Harm to Others*, Oxford, Oxford University Press, 1987.

J. Feinberg, *Freedom and Fulfillment. Philosophical Essays*, Princeton, Princeton University Press, 1992.

J. Feinberg, 'Wrongful life and the counterfactual element in harming', in: J. Feinberg (ed.), *Freedom and Fulfillment: Philosophical Essays*, Princeton University Press, Princeton, 1994.

R.A. Fenton, 'Catholic doctrine versus women's rights: the new Italian law on assisted reproduction', *Medical Law Review*, Vol. 14, No. 1, 2006, pp. 73-107.

S. Fikkers, 'Urgenda, de zorgplicht en toekomstige generaties', *Nederlands Juristenblad*, Vol. 2015, No. 33, 2015, pp. 2289-2293.

D. Fox, *Birth right and wrongs. How medicine and technology are remaking reproduction and the law*, New York, Oxford University Press, 2019.

M. Freeman, 'Do children have a right not to be born?', in: M. Freeman (ed.), *The moral status of children: essays on the rights of the child*, Martinus Nijhoff Publishers, Den Haag, 1997.

Government Committee on the Reassessment of Parenthood (GCRP), *Child and Parents in the 21st Century*, The Hague, 2016.

Gezondheidsraad, *Celkerntransplantatie bij mutaties in het mitochondriale DNA*, 2001.

H.P. Glenn, 'The aims of comparative law', in: J.M. Smits (ed.), *Elgar Encyclopedia of Comparative Law*, Edward Elgard, Cheltenham, 2006.

J. Glover, *Fertility & the family. The Glover report on reproductive technologies to the European commission*, London, Fourth Estate 1989.

J. Glover, *Choosing children. Genes, disability, and design*, Oxford, Oxford University Press, 2006.

J.C. Gray, *The nature and sources of the law*, New york, The Columbia University Press, 1909.

A. Grear, 'Law's entities: complexity, plasticity and justice', *Jurisprudence*, Vol. 4, No. 1, 2013, pp. 76-101.

H.T. Greely, *The End of Sex and the Future of Human Reproduction*, Cambridge, Harvard University Press, 2016.

H.-L. Günther, J. Taupitz and P. Kaiser, *Embryonenschutzgesetz. Juristischer Kommentar mit medizinisch-naturwissenschaftlichen Grundlagen*, 2, Stuttgart, Kohlhammer, 2014.

L. ten Haaf, 'Een slechte toekomst is geen toekomst', *NJB*, Vol. 2012, No. 17, 2012, pp. 1176-1181.

L. ten Haaf, 'Future Persons and Legal Persons: The Problematic Representation of the Future Child in the Regulation of Reproduction', *Laws*, Vol. 5, 2016, pp. 1-16.

L. ten Haaf, 'Unborn and Future Children as New Legal Subjects: An Evaluation of Two Subject-Oriented Approaches—The Subject of Rights and the Subject of Interests', *German Law Journal*, Vol. 18, No. 5, 2017, pp. 1091-1120.

L. ten Haaf, 'Het recht op donorgegevens bij Mitochondrial Replacement Therapy', *Podium voor Bio-ethiek*, Vol. 27, No. 2, 2020, pp. 12-14.

L. ten Haaf, 'De ondertoezichtstelling van een nog niet-levensvatbare foetus. Het kan, maar hoe?', *Nederlands Juristenblad*, Vol. 2021, No. 24, 2021, pp. 1968-1971.

J. Habermas, *The future of human nature*, Cambridge, Polity Press, 2003.

B. Hale, 'Dignity', *Journal of Social Welfare and Family Law*, Vol. 31, No. 2, 2009, pp. 101-108.

M. Hanser, 'Harming future people', *Philosophy and public affairs*, Vol. 19, 1990, pp. 47-70.

C. Hare, 'Voices from another world: must we respect the interests of people who do not, and will never, exist?', *Ethics*, Vol. 117, 2007, pp. 498-523.

A. Harel, 'Theories of rights', in: W.A. Edmundson and M.P. Golding (eds.), *Blackwell guide to the philosophy of law and legal theory*, Blackwell, Cambride, 2005.

E. Harman, 'Harming as causing harm', in: M.A. Roberts and D.T. Wasserman (eds.), *Harming future fersons. Ethics, genethics and the nonidentity problem*, Springer, Dordrecht, 2009.

J. Harris, 'Wrongful Birth', in: D.R. Bromham, M.E. Dalton and J.C. Jackson (eds.), *Philosophical ethics in reproductive medicine*, Manchester University Press, Manchester, 1990.

J. Harris, 'The welfare of the child', *Health Care Analysis*, Vol. 8, 2000, pp. 27-34.

G. den Hartogh, "In het belang van het kind", in: G. den Hartogh and I. de Beaufort (eds.), *Een hoge prijs voor een kind*, Van Gorcum, Assen, 2006.

D.B. Hershenov and R.J. Hershenov, 'Morally relevant potential', *Journal of Medical Ethics*, Vol. 41, No. 3, 2015, pp. 268-271.

D. Heyd, *Genethics. Moral issues in the creation of people*, Berkeley, University of California Press, 1992.

M. van Hoecke, 'Methodology of Comparative Legal Research', *Law and Method*, Vol. 2015, No. Oct-Dec, 2015, doi: 10.5553/REM/.000010.

House of Commons Science and Technology Committee, *Human Reproductive Technologies and the Law. Fifth Report of Session 2004-2005*, 2005.

Human Fertilisation and Embryology Authority, *Sex Selection: choice and responsibility in human reproduction*, 2003.

Human Fertilisation and Embryology Authority, *Tomorrow's Children. Report of the policy review of welfare of the child assessments in licensed assisted conception clinics.*, 2005.

Human Fertilisation and Embryology Authority, *Mitochondria replacement consultation: Advice to Government*, 2013.

J.B. Hurlbut, K. Saha and S. Jasanoff, 'CRISPR Democracy: Gene Editing and the Need for Inclusive Deliberation', *Issues in Science and Technologie*, Vol. 32, No. 1 (fall 2015), 2015, pp. 25-32

E. Jackson, 'Conception and the irrelevance of the welfare principle', *Modern Law Review*, Vol. 65, No. 2, 2002, pp. 176-203.

E. Jackson, *Medial Law. Text, Cases and Materials*, 4, Oxford, Oxford University Press, 2016.

V. Jadva, T. Freeman, W. Kramer and S. Golombok, 'Experiences of offspring searching for and contacting their donor siblings and donor', *Reproductive Biomedicine Online*, Vol. 20, No. 4, 2010, pp. 523-532.

H.D. Jarass and B. Pieroth, *Grundgesetz für die Bundesrepubliek Deutschland. Kommentar*, 14 ed, München, Verlag C.H. Beck 2016.

S. Jasanoff, J.B. Hurlbut and K. Saha, 'Human genetic engineering demands more than a moratorium', 2015, *The Guardian* 7 April 2015 <https://www.theguardian.com/science/political-science/2015/apr/07/human-genetic-engineering-demands-more-than-a-moratorium> last accessed: 1 January 2023.

J.C. Joerden, 'Menschenwürde als juridischer Begriff', in: J.C. Joerden, E. Hilgendorf and F. Thiele (eds.), *Menschenwürde und Medizin. Ein interdisziplinäres Handbuch*, Duncker & Humblot, Berlin, 2013.

H. Jonas, 'Technology and Responsibility: Reflections on the New Task of Ethics', *Social Research*, Vol. 40, No. 1, 1973, pp. 31-54.

H. Jonas, 'Biological engineering - a preview', in: H. Jonas (ed.), *Philosophical essays. From ancient creed to technological man*, Prentice-Hall, Inc., Englewood Cliffs, New Jersey, 1974.

H. Jonas, *The imperative of responsibility. In search of an ethics for the technological age*, Chicago, The University of Chicago Press, 1984.

H. Jonas, *Mortality and Morality. A search for the good after Auschwitz*, Evanston, Northwestern University Press, 1996.

F.M. Kamm, *Creation and Abortion. A study in moral and legal philosophy*, Oxford, Oxford University Press, 1992.

S. Kampowski, *A greater freedom: Biotechnology, love, and human destiny. In dialogue with Hans Jonas and Jürgen Habermas*, Cambridge, The Luttenworth Press, 2014.

I. Kant, *Grundlegung Zur Metaphysik Der Sitten*, 1785, Reprint: T. Mertens *Fundering voor de metafysica van de zeden*, Amsterdam, Boom, 2008.

A.J. Karnein, *A theory of unborn life. From abortion to genetic manipulation*, New York, Oxford University Press, 2012.

L. Kass, 'Appreciating *The Phenomonen of Life*', *Hastings Center Report*, Vol. 25, No. 7, 1995, pp. 3-12.

L. Kass, *Life, Liberty and the Defense of Dignity. The Challenge for Bioethics*, San Francisco, Encounter Books, 2002.

H. Kelsen, *Reine Rechtslehre. Einleitung in die Rechtwissenschaftliche Problematik*, Aalen, Scientia Verlag, 1994.

T. Khaitan, 'Dignity as an expressive norm: neither vacuous nor a panacea', *Oxford Journal of Legal Studies*, Vol. 32, No. 1, 2012, pp. 1-19.

S.C.J.J. Kortmann, *Geld voor leven: schadevergoeding voor 'niet beoogd' leven.* Address on the occasion of the 80th foundation day of the University of Nijmegen 2003.

S.C.J.J. Kortmann, 'Schadevergoeding voor leven?', *Themis*, Vol. 4, 2004, pp. 205-207.

M.H. Kramer, 'Rights without trimming', in: M.H. Kramer, N.E. Simmonds and H. Steiner (eds.), *A debate over rights*, Oxford University Press, Oxford, 1998.

M.H. Kramer, 'Refining the interest theory of rights', *American Journal of Jurisprudence*, Vol. 55, 2010, pp. 31-39.

F.H. Lawson, 'The creative use of legal concepts', *New York University Law Review*, Vol. 32, 1957, pp. 909-925.

A. MacIntyre, *After Virtue*, 2, Notre Dame, Indiana, University of Notre Dame Press, 1984.

R. Macklin, 'Dignity is a useless concept. It means no more than respect for persons or their autonomy', *BMJ*, Vol. 327, 2003, pp. 1419-1420.

J.L. Madeira, 'Holding physicians accountable for fertility fraud. From patient experience tolegal reform', *Columbia Journal of Gender and Law* Vol. 39, No. 1, 2020, pp. 110-204.

H. Mangoldt, F. Klein and C. Starck, *Kommentar zum Grundgesetz. Band 1: Präambel, Artikel 1 bis 19*, 6th ed, München, Verlag Franz Vahlen 2010.

T. Maunz and G. Dürig, *Grundgesetz-Kommentar. Band 1 Texte Art. 1-5*, 63rd ed, München, Verlag C.H. Beck 2016.

H.J. McCloskey, 'Rights', *The Philosophical Quarterly*, Vol. 15, No. 59, 1965, pp. 115-127.

L. Mela, 'MacIntyre on Personal Identity', *Public Reason*, Vol. 3, No. 1, 2011, pp. 103-113.

I. de Melo-Martín, 'The ethics of anonymous gamete donation: is there a right to know one's genetic origins?', *Hastings Center Report*, Vol. 44, No. 2, 2014, pp. 28-35.

J.S. Mill, *On Liberty*, 1859. Reprint: Mineola, New York, Dover Publications, Inc., 2002.

T. Morris, *Hans Jonas's ethic of responsibility. From ontology to ecology*, Albany, State University of New York Press, 2013.

S. Mukherjee, *The gene. An intimate history*, London, Penguin Random House, 2016.

R. Müller-Terpitz, *Der Schutz des pränatalen Lebens*, Tübingen, Mohr Siebeck 2007.

I. von Münch and P. Kunig, *Grundgesetz Kommentar*, 6th ed, München, Verlag C.H. Beck 2012.

N. Naffine, 'Who are law's persons? From cheshire cats to responsible subjects', *The Modern Law Review*, Vol. 66, No. 3, 2003, pp. 346-367.

N. Naffine, *Law's meaning of life. Philosophy, religion, Darwin and the legal person*, Portland, Hart Publishing, 2009.

N. Naffine, 'Review Essay: Liberating the Legal Person', *Canadian Journal of Law and Society*, Vol. 26, No. 1, 2011, pp. 193-203.

L. Nelson, *A system of ethics*, New Haven, Yale University Press, 1956.

J.H. Nieuwenhuis, *Confrontatie en compromis. Recht, retoriek en burgerlijke moraal*, Deventer, Kluwer, 1992.

Nuffield Council on Bioethics, *Novel techniques for the prevention of mitochondrial DNA disorders: an ethical review*, London, 2012.

Nuffield Council on Bioethics, *Genome Editing and Human Reproduction: social and ethical issues*, London, 2018.

E.J. Oldekamp and M.C. de Vries, 'Nieuwe procreatietechnieken. Achterhaalde juridische kaders?', in, *Nieuwe technieken, nieuwe zorg. (Preadvies Vereniging voor Gezondheidsrecht)*, Sdu, Den Haag, 2018.

D. Parfit, *Reasons and persons*, Oxford, Clarendon Press, 1984.

M. Parker, 'The welfare of the child', *Human Fertility*, Vol. 8, 2005, pp. 13-19.

S.D. Pattinson, *Medical Law and Ethics*, 4, London, Sweet & Maxwell, 2014.

G. Pennings, 'Disclosure of donor conception, age of disclosure and the well-being of donor offspring', *Human Reproduction*, Vol. 32, No. 5, 2017, pp. 969-973.

G. Pennings, G. de Wert, F. Shenfield, J. Cohen, B. Tarlatzis and P. Devroey, 'ESHRE Task Force on Ethics and Law 13: the welfare of the child in medically assisted reproduction', *Human Reproduction*, Vol. 22, No. 10, 2007, pp. 2585-2588.

D. Pessers, *Big Mother. Over de personalisering van de publieke sfeer*, Den Haag, Boom Juridische Uitgevers, 2003a.

D. Pessers, *Verdwaalde seksen. Over sperminators, metroseksuelen en autocopieën*, Nijmegen, Uitgeverij Valkhof Pers, 2003b.

D. Pessers, *Menselijke waardigheid en het persoonsbegrip in het recht*, Utrecht, Lemma BV, 2005.

D. Pessers, 'De terugkeer van de bastaard: een beschouwing over het wetsvoorstel Lesbisch ouderschap van rechtswege.', *Nederlands Juristenblad*, Vol. 88, No. 37, 2013, pp. 2588-2596.

D. Pessers, 'The symbolic meaning of legal subjectivity', in: B. van Klink, B. van Beers and L. Poort (eds.), *Symbolic legislation theory and developments in biolaw*, Springer, Switzerland, 2016.

P.G. Peters, 'Protecting the unconceived: nonexistence, avoidability, and reproductive technology', *Arizona Law Review*, Vol. 31, 1989, pp. 487-548.

S. Pinker, 'The Stupidity of Dignity', 2008, *The New Republic* 28 May 2008 <https://newrepublic.com/article/64674/the-stupidity-dignity> last accessed: 1 January 2023.

S. Pinker, 'The moral imperative for bioethics', 2015, *The Boston Globe* <https://www.bostonglobe.com/opinion/2015/07/31/the-moral-imperative-for-bioethics/JmEkoyzlTAu9oQV76JrK9N/story.html> last accessed: 1 January 2023.

L. Poort, B.C. van Beers and B. van Klink, 'Introduction: symbolic dimensions of biolaw', in: B. van Klink, B.C. van Beers and L. Poort (eds.), *Symbolic legislation theory and developments in biolaw*, Springer Verlag, Switzerland, 2016.

M. Quaas, R. Zuck and T. Clemens, *Medizinrecht*, 3rd ed, München, C.H. Beck 2014.

N.R. Ram, 'Britain's new preimplantation tissue typing policy: an ethical defence', *Journal of Medical Ethics*, Vol. 32, 2006, pp. 278-282.

R. Ratze and B. Luxenburger, *Handbuch Medizinrecht*, 3, Heidelberg, C.F. Müller, 2015.

V. Ravitsky, 'Conceived and deceived: the medical interests of donor-conceived children', *Hastings Center Report*, Vol. 42, No. 1, 2012, pp. 17-22.

J. Raz, *The Authority of law: essays on law and morality*, New York, Oxford University Press, 1979.

J. Raz, *The morality of freedom*, Oxford, Clarendon Press, 1988.

T. Regan, 'Feinberg on what sort of beings can have rights', *Southern Journal of Philosophy*, Vol. 14, 1976, pp. 485-498.

T. Regan, 'McCloskey on why animals cannot have rights', *the Philosophical Quarterly*, Vol. 26, No. 104, 1976, pp. 251-257.

P. Ricoeur, *Time and Narrative volume 3*, Chicago, The University of Chicago Press, 1985.

P. Ricoeur, 'Narrative Identity', *Philosophy Today*, Vol. 35, No. 1, 1991, pp. 73-81.

P. Ricoeur, *Oneself as Another*, Chicago, The University of Chicago Press, 1992.

P. Ricoeur, *The Just*, Chicago, The University of Chicago Press, 2000.

U. Riedel, *„Kind als Schaden". Die höchstrichterliche Rechtsprechung zur Arzthaftung für den Kindesunterhalt bei unerwünschter Geburt eines gesunden, kranken oder behinderten Kindes*, Frankfurt am Main, Mabuse-Verlag GmbH, 2003.

M.A. Roberts, *Child versus childmaker. Future persons and present duties in ethics and the law*, Lanham, Rowman & Littlefield Publishers, Inc., 1998.

J.A. Robertson, *Children of choice. Freedom and the new reproductive technologies*, Princeton, Princeton University Press, 1994.

J.A. Robertson, 'Procreative liberty and harm to offspring in assisted reproduction', *American Journal of Law & Medicine*, Vol. 30, 2004, pp. 7-40.

E.C. Romanis, 'Challenging the 'Born Alive' Threshold: Fetal Surgery, Artificial Wombs, and the English Approach to Legal Personhood', *Medical Law Review*, Vol. 28, No. 1, 2019, pp. 93–123.

H. Rosenau, 'Reproduktives und therapeutisches Klonen', in: K. Amelung, W. Beulke, H. Lilie, H. Rosenau, H. Rüping and G. Wolfslast (eds.), *Strafrecht, Biorecht, Rechtsphilosophie. Festschrift für Hans-Ludwig Schreiber zum 70. Geburtstag am 10. Mai 2003*, C.F. Müller Verlag, Heidelberg, 2003.

M. Sachs, *Grundgesetz Kommentar*, 7nd ed, München, Verlag C.H. Beck 2014.

G. Samuel, 'Should Jurists Take Interests More Seriously?', *Law and Method*, Vol. 2017, No. 2, 2017, doi: 10.5553/REM/.000023.

M.J. Sandel, 'The case against perfection', 2004, *The Atlantic* April 2004 <https://www.theatlantic.com/magazine/archive/2004/04/the-case-against-perfection/302927/> last accessed: 1 January 2023.

M.J. Sandel, 'The ethical implications of human cloning', *Perspectives in Biology and Medicine*, Vol. 48, 2005, pp. 241-247.

M.J. Sandel, *The Case against perfection; ethics in the age of genetic engineering*, Cambridge, Massachusetts, the Belknap Press of Harvard University Press, 2007.

M.J. Sandel, *Justice. What's the right thing to do?*, London, Penguin Books, 2009.

J. Savulescu, 'Procreative Beneficence: why we should select the best children', *Bioethics*, Vol. 15, No. 5/6, 2001, pp. 413-426.

J. Savulescu, 'Is there a right not to be born? Reproductive decision making, options and the right to information', *Journal of Medical Ethics*, Vol. 28, 2002, pp. 65-67.

J. Savulescu, 'New breeds of human: the moral obligation to enhance', *Reproductive BioMedicine Online*, Vol. 10, 2005, pp. 508-529.

J. Savulescu and G. Kahane, 'The moral obligation to create children with the best chance of the best life', *Bioethics*, Vol. 23, No. 5, 2009, pp. 274-290.

S. Schleissing, *Ethik und Recht in der Fortpflanzungsmedizin. Herausforderungen, Diskussionen, Perspektiven* Baden-Baden, Nomos Verlagsgesellschaft, 2014.

A. Schönke and H. Schröder, ed, München, C.H. Beck 2014.

F.C. Schroeder, 'Die Rechtsgüter des Embryonenschutzgesetzes', in: H.-H. Kühne (ed.), *Festschrift für Koichi Miyazawa. Dem Wegbereiter des japanisch-deutschen Strafrechtsdiskurses*, Nomos Verlagsgesellschaft, Baden-Baden, 1995.

R. Scott, 'Reconsidering 'Wrongful Life' in England after Thirty Years: Legislative Mistakes and Unjustifiable Anomalies', *Cambridge Law Journal*, Vol. 72, No. 1, 2013, pp. 115-154.

R. Scott and S. Wilkinson, 'Germline genetic modification and identity: the mitochondrial and nuclear genomes.', *Oxford Journal of Legal Studies*, Vol. 37, No. 4, 2017, pp. 886-915.

S. Sheldon, E. Lee and J. Macvarish, "Supportive Parenting', Responsibility and Regulation: The Welfare Assessment under the Reformed Human Fertilisation and Embryology Act (1990)', *Modern Law Review*, Vol. 78, No. 3, 2015, pp. 461-492.

S. Sheldon and S. Wilkinson, 'Should selecting saviour siblings be banned?', *Journal of Medical Ethics*, Vol. 30, 2004, pp. 533-537.

S.V. Shiffrin, 'Wrongful life, procreative responsibility and the significance of harm', *Legal Theory*, Vol. 5, 1999, pp. 117-148.

A. Smajdor, 'How useful is the concept of the 'harm threshold' in reproductive ethics and law?', *Theoretical Medicine and Bioethics*, Vol. 35, 2014, pp. 321-336.

M.K. Smith, 'The Human Fertilisation and Emrbyology Act 2008: restrictions on the creation of "saviour siblings"and the relevance of the harm principle.', *New Genetics and Society*, Vol. 32, No. 2, 2013, pp. 154-170.

M. Somerville, 'Donor conception and children's rights: 'First, do no harm'', *Canadian Medical Association Journal*, Vol. 183, 2011, p. 280.

H. Somsen, *Regulering van humane genetica in het neo-eugenetische tijdperk*, Nijmegen, Wolf Legal Publishers, 2006.

A. Spickhoff, *Medizinrecht*, 1st ed, München, Verlag C.H. Beck 2011.

T.M. Spranger, *Recht und Bioethik. Verweisungszusammenhänge bei der Normierung der Lebenswissenschaften*, Tübingen, Mohr Siebeck, 2010.

Staatscommissie Herijking Ouderschap, *Kind en ouders in de 21ste eeuw*, Den Haag, 2016.

M. Stauch and K. Wheat, *Text, cases and materials on medical law and ethics*, 5, London, Routledge, 2015.

B. Steinbock, 'The logical case for "wrongful life"', *Hastings Center Report*, Vol. 16, No. 2, 1986, pp. 15-20.

B. Steinbock, 'Wrongful life and procreative decisions', in: M.A. Roberts and D.T. Wasserman (eds.), *Harming future people. Ethics, genetics and the nonidentity problem*, Springer, Dordrecht, 2009.

B. Steinbock, *Life before birth. The moral and legal status of embryos and fetuses*, 2nd, New York, Oxford University Press, 2011.

B. Steinbock and R. McClamrock, 'When is birth unfair to the child? ', *Hastings Center Report*, Vol. 24, No. 6, 1994, pp. 15-21.

K. Stern and F. Becker, *Grundrechte-Kommentar. Die Grundrechte des Grundgesetzes mit ihren europäischen Bezügen*, 2nd ed, Köln, Carl Heymanns Verlag 2016.

A. Supiot, *Homo juridicus. On the anthropological function of the law*, London, Verso, 2007.

D. Teichert, 'Narrative, Identity and Self', *Journal of Conscious Studies*, Vol. 11, No. 10-11, 2004, pp. 175-191.

R. Tur, 'The 'person' in law', in: A. Peacocke and G. Gillett (eds.), *Persons and personality: a contemporary inquiry*, Basil Blackwell, Oxford, 1987.

G. Velte, *Die postmortale Befruchtung im deutschen und spanischen Recht*, Heidelberg, Springer, 2015.

M. Vonk, 'Een huis voor alle kinderen: de juridische verankering van meeroudergezinnen in het afstammingsrecht', *Nederlands Juristenblad*, Vol. 2013, No. 33, 2013, pp. 2244-2249.

S.E.P. Walker, 'Potential persons and the welfare of the (potential) child test', *Medical Law International*, Vol. 14, No. 3, 2014, pp. 157-171.

M.A. Warren, 'Do potential people have moral rights?', *Canadian Journal of Philosophy*, Vol. 7, No. 2, 1977, pp. 275-289.

E. Wicks, *The state and the body. Legal regulation of bodily autonomy*, Portland, Hart Publishing, 2016.

L.F. Wiggers-Rust, *Belang, belanghebbende en relativiteit in bestuursrecht en privaatrecht*, Den Haag, Boom juridische uitgevers, 2011.

S. Wilkinson, *Choosing tomorrow's children. The ethics of selective reproduction*, Oxford, Oxford University Press, 2010.

L. Witteck and C. Eric, 'Straf- und verfassungsrechtliche Gedanken zum Verbot des Klonens von Menschen', *Medizinrecht*, Vol. 6, No. 5, 2003, pp. 258-262.

S.F.M. Wortmann, *Groene Serie Personen- en familierecht*, ed, Deventer, Wolters Kluwer 2021.

CASE LAW

European Court of Human Rights

ECtHR 29 April 2002 ECLI:CE:ECHR:2002:0429JUD000234602 (*Pretty v. the United Kingdom*).
ECtHR 8 July 2004 ECLI:CE:ECHR:2004:0708JUD005392400 (*Vo v. France*).
ECtHR 4 December 2007 ECLI:CE:ECHR:2007:1204JUD004436204 (*Dickson v. the United Kingdom*).
ECtHR 10 April 2007 ECLI:CE:ECHR:2007:0410JUD000633905 (*Evans v. the United Kingdom*).
ECtHR 1 April 2010 ECLI:CE:ECHR:2010:0401JUD005781300 (*S.H. e.a. v. Austria).*
ECtHR 3 November 2011 ECLI:CE:ECHR:2011:1103JUD005781300 (*S.H. e.a. v. Austria*).
ECtHR 28 August 2012, ECLI:CE:ECHR:2012:0828JUD005427010 (*Costa and Pavan v. Italy*).

European Union Court of Justice

Conclusion Stix-Hackl EU CoJ 18 March 2004 ECLI:EU:C:2004:162 (*Omega*).

Germany

BGH 20 December 1952 - II ZR 141/51, BGHZ 8, 243 (*preconceptual harm*).
BGH 18 January 1983 - BGHZ 86, 240 (*Wrongful life*).
BGH 6 July 2010 - 5 StR386/09 (*PGD*).
BGH 28 January 2015 - XII ZR 201/13 (*Disclosure of donor information*).
BVerfGE 25 February 1975 - 39, 1 (*Schwangerschaftsabbruch I*).
BVerfGE 28 May 1993 - 88, 203 (*Schwangerschaftsabbruch II*).

The Netherlands

District Court the Hague 2 June 2021 ECLI:NL:RBDHA:2021:5461 (*Switching Donor 605*).
District Court Gelderland 24 March 2021 ECLI:NL:RBGEL:2021:1388 (*Switching Donor K34*).
District Court Dordrecht 7 February 2012 ECLI:NL:RBDOR:2012:BV6246 (*prenatal family supervision order nonviable foetus*).

Court of Appeal the Hague 9 October 2018 ECLI:NL:GHDHA:2018:2591 (*Urgenda*).
Hoge Raad 15 April 1994 ECLI:NL:HR:1994:ZC1337 (*Valkenhorst*).
Hoge Raad 9 October 1998 ECLI:NL:PHR:1998:ZC2735 (*Jeffrey*).
Hoge Raad 18 March 2005 ECLI:NL:HR:2005:AR5213 (*Baby Kelly*).
Hoge Raad 20 December 2019 ECLI:NL:HR:2019:2006 (*Urgenda*).
Hoge Raad 11 March 2022, ECLI:NL:HR:2022:349.
Hoge Raad 9 December 2022, ECLI:NL:HR:2022:1850 (*Compulsory Contraception*).

The United Kingdom

R (on the application of Rose) v. Secretary of State for Health, [2002] EWHC 1593.
Quintavalle v. Human Fertilisation and Embryology Authority. 2005. UKHL 28.
(*McKay v. Essex Area Health Authority*) [1982] QB 1166.

The United States

Buck v. Bell, 274 U.S. 200 (1927).
Cramblett v. Midwest Sperm Bank, LLC, 230 F. Supp. 3d 865, 874 (N.D. Ill. 2017).

Australia

Victorian Civil and Administrative Tribunal 5 August 2015 - VCAT 1188 (*TRV v. Department of Health and Human Services*).

Glossary and list of abbreviations

Aneuploidy	the presence of an abnormal number of chromosomes in a human cell. In a case of aneuploidy the individual may have extra chromosomes or miss chromosomes, which can result in an illness or miscarriage
ARTs	assisted reproductive technologies
BGB	Bürgerliches Gesetzbuch. The German Civil Code
BGH	Bundesgerichtshof, German Federal Court of Justice
BVerfG	Bundesverfassungsgericht, German Federal Constitutional Court
Chromosome	a threadlike structure found in the nucleus of most living cells, carrying genetic information in the form of genes. A individual usually has 23 chromosome pairs, with one chromosome of each pair inherited from its mother and the other from its father
COGEM	Commissie Genetische Modificatie. Dutch committee on genetic modification
CRC	Convention on the Rights of the Child
CRISPR	Clustered Regularly Interspaced Short Palindromic Repeats. Short segments of repeated codes of DNA
CRISPR-Cas9	A genetic modification technology. The Cas9-proteine is able to cut DNA and the CRISPR-segment identifies the location where the DNA needs to be cut in order to remove or insert a gene
DNA	Deoxyribonucleic acid. A molecule carrying genetic information (genes) for the growth, functioning and reproduction of organisms
ECHR	European Convention of Human Rights
ECtHR	European Court of Human Rights
ESchG	Embryonenschutzgesetz. The German Embryo Protection Act
ESHRE	European Society of Human Reproduction and Embryology
Gametes	spermatozoa (sperm cells) and ova (egg cells). Gametes are haploid, meaning they only contain one set of chromosomes, either from the mother or the father, and fuse with another gamete during fertilisation
GCRP	Government Committee on the Reassessment of Parenthood. In Dutch: Staatscommissie Herijking Ouderschap
Gene	a distinct sequence of nucleotides forming part of a chromosome which contains information necessary for the functioning of cells

Germline modification	the alteration of genetic information by editing, removing, or inserting genes in so-called germ line cells. The modification of these cells can be passed on to offspring
GG	Grundgesetz. The German constitution
HC	House of Commons
HFE Act	Human Fertilisation and Embryology Act
HFEA	Human Fertilisation and Embryology Authority
HL	House of Lords
HLA	Human Leukocyte Antigen. The HLA-type is an important factor to determine whether someone is a suitable donor for another. PGD can be used to select based on HLA type in order to create a saviour child or saviour sibling – a child that is a suitable stem cell donor for example, for an ill sibling or family member
iPSC	induced Pluripotent Stem Cell. A cell that originally was a differentiated cell, but is reprogrammed to be pluripotent stem cell
IVF	In Vitro Fertilisation. A reproduction technique in which an embryo is created outside the female body
IVG	In vitro gametogenesis. A reproduction technique in which differentiated cells such as skin cells are reprogrammed into stem cells, which are then reprogrammed to gametes
mDNA	Mitochondrial DNA. DNA that is located in a cell's mitochondria. Approximately 0,1% of the total DNA consists of mitochondrial DNA. mDNA can only be passed on via the ovum, and thus via the maternal line
Mitochondria	organelles that produce energy for the cell
MRT	Mitochondrial Replacement Therapy. A technology in which the nucleus of an egg cell is transferred to an emptied egg cell from a donor. This technology is developed in order to prevent the transmission of mitochondrial conditions, caused by defects in the mDNA
MST	Maternal Spindle Transfer. A form of MRT
Nidation	the implantation of the embryo in the lining of the uterus. This process takes place approximately 14 days after the conception. After the embryo has nidated, it can no longer develop into twins
NVOG	Nederlandse vereniging voor Obstetrie en Gynaecologie. Dutch professional organisation for obstetrics and gynaecology

PGD	Preimplantation Genetic Diagnosis. In case of PGD, an embryo is screened for an inheritable, monogenetic disorder, i.e. a genetic illness that is caused by mutations in a single gene. PGD is also known as PGT-M, where the M stands for monogenetic
PGS	Preimplantation Genetic Screening. In case of PGS, an embryo is screened for aneuploidy in order to determine whether it has extra chromosomes or is missing chromosomes. PGS is also known as CCS (comprehensive chromosome screening) or PGT-A, where the A stands for aneuploidy
PGT	Preimplantation Genetic Test. PGT is an umbrella term which encompasses various reproductive selection methods, including PGD (or PGT-M) and PGS (or PGT-A). It is a reproductive technology in which several embryos are created in vitro, which are then screened for a specific genetic or chromosomal defects
PNT	Pronuclear Transfer. A form of MRT
SCNT	Somatic Cell Nuclear Transfer. A technology in which the nucleus of a somatic cell is transferred into an enucleated egg cell in order to create an exact copy of the organism from which the somatic cell is derived. A form of reproductive cloning
Stem cells	Undifferentiated cells or cells that can develop in various types of differentiated cells, i.e. cells with a specific function such as blood cells, skin cells etc
WDKB	Wet donorgegevens kunstmatige bevruchting. The Dutch Donor Information Artificial Fertilisation Act
Zygote	a fertilised ovum and a diploid cell that results from the fusion of two gametes

Index

www.ingramcontent.com/pod-product-compliance
Lightning Source LLC
Chambersburg PA
CBHW080938240926
51849CB00004BA/489
* 9 7 8 9 4 6 2 3 6 5 8 2 7 *